INTERNATIONAL BUSINESS

For the Students of MBA, PGDBA, B.Com. and Other Professional Courses

Dr. C.B. GUPTA
M.Com., Ph.D., MIMA
Former Head
Department of Commerce
Shri Ram College of Commerce
University of Delhi

S. Chand And Company Limited
(ISO 9001 Certified Company)

S. Chand And Company Limited

(ISO 9001 Certified Company)

Head Office: D-92, Sector–2, Noida – 201301, U.P. (India), Ph. 91-120-4682700

Registered Office: A-27, 2nd Floor, Mohan Co-operative Industrial Estate, New Delhi – 110 044, Phone: 011-49731800

www.**schandpublishing.com**; e-mail: **info@schandpublishing.com**

Marketing Offices:

Chennai	:	Ph: 23632120; chennai@schandpublishing.com
Guwahati	:	Ph: 2738811, 2735640; guwahati@schandpublishing.com
Hyderabad	:	Ph: 40186018; hyderabad@schandpublishing.com
Jalandhar	:	Ph: 4645630; jalandhar@schandpublishing.com
Kolkata	:	Ph: 23357458, 23353914; kolkata@schandpublishing.com
Lucknow	:	Ph: 4003633; lucknow@schandpublishing.com
Mumbai	:	Ph: 25000297; mumbai@schandpublishing.com
Patna	:	Ph: 2260011; patna@schandpublishing.com

First Edition 2014

Reprints 2018, 2020, 2021

Reprint 2024

ISBN: 978-93-837-4684-2 **Product Code:** H8IBU60BMGT10ENAA14O

PRINTED IN INDIA

By Vikas Publishing House Private Limited, Plot 20/4, Site-IV, Industrial Area Sahibabad, Ghaziabad – 201 010 and Published by S. Chand And Company Limited, A-27, 2nd Floor, Mohan Co-operative Industrial Estate, New Delhi – 110 044.

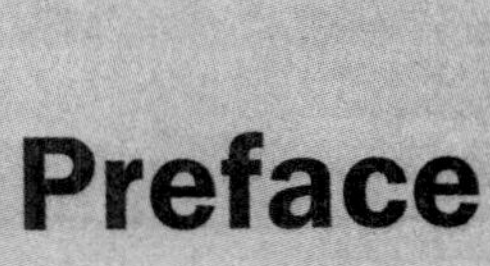

Preface

Economic liberalisation and globalisation have led to increasing academic interest in issues concerning international business. The subject now constitutes an integral part of both undergraduate and postgraduate courses in universities and business schools in India. This book is designed and written to meet the needs of the students of these courses.

Some of the salient features of the book are as follows:

- Full coverage of the prescribed syllabi.
- Chapter outline to give a bird's eyeview of the topics covered in each chapter.
- Tables and diagrams to illustrate the text.
- Examples from India's corporate sector.
- Summary at the end of each chapter for quick revision.
- Test questions for self-examination.
- Lucid style and simple language.

I am grateful to the authors and publishers of standard publications on the subject. Suggestions and comments for improvement of the book are welcome.

Dr. C. B. GUPTA

University of Delhi

B. Com. (Hons.) Course [Semester VI] Syllabus

Paper-Ch 6.1: International Business

Duration: 3 hrs. Maximum Marks:100

Lectures:75

Objective: The objective of the course is to expose students to the concept, importance and dynamics of international business and India's involvement with global business operations. The course also discusses theoretical foundations of international business to extent these are relevant to understand the mechanics of global business operations and development.

No. of Lectures

Unit 1

1. **Introduction to International Business:** Globalisation and its growing importance in world economy; Impact of globalisation; International business contrasted with domestic business complexities of international business; Modes of entry into international business. 6
2. **International Business Environment:** National and foreign environments and their components – economic, cultural and political-legal environments; Global trading environment – recent trends in world trade in goods and services; Trends in India's foreign trade. 8

Unit II

3. **Theories of International Trade:** An overview, Commercial policy instruments – tariff and non-tariff measures; Balance of payment account and its components. 7
4. **International Organisations and Arrangements:** WTO – its objectives, principles, organisational structure and functioning; An overview of other organisations – UNCTAD, World Bank and IMF; Commodity and other trading agreements. 8

Unit III

5. **Regional Economic Cooperation:** Forms of regional groupings; Integration efforts among countries in Europe, North America and Asia. 7
6. **International Financial Environment:** International financial system and institutions; Foreign exchange markets and risk management; Foreign investments-types and flow; Foreign investment in Indian perspective. 9

Unit IV

7. Organisational structure for international business operations; Key issues involved in making international production, finance, marketing and human resource decisions; International business negotiations. 9
8. **Development and Issue in International Business:** Outsourcing and its potentials for India; Strategic alliances, mergers and acquisitions; Role of IT in international business; International business and ecological considerations. 7

Unit V

9. Foreign trade promotion measures and organisations in India; Special Economic Zones (SEZs) and 100% Export-Oriented Units (EOUs); Measures for promoting foreign investments into and from India; Indian joint ventures and acquisitions abroad. 8
10. Financing of foreign trade and payment terms. 6

Guru Gobind Singh Indraprastha University, Delhi

Bachelor of Commerce (Hons.) Syllabus

B. Com. 306 – International Business

L-5 T/P-0 **Credits-5**

Objective: The basis objective of this course is to provide understanding to the students with the global dimensions of management.

Course Contents

Unit I **Lectures: 20**

Overview: International Business Introduction, Concept, Definition, Scope, Trends, Challenges and Opportunities; Nature, Meaning and Importance of International Competitive Advantage, Multidimensional View of Competitiveness Financial Perspectives:

Unit II **Lectures:20**

Theories of International Trade: International Business Theories, Trade Barriers-Tariff and Non-Tariff Barriers.

Unit III

International Bodies: International Monetary Systems and Financial Markets, IMF, World Bank, IBRD, IFC, IDA, Existing International Arrangements; Globalisation and Foreign Investment, Introduction of FDI, National FDI Policy Framework, FPI, Impact of Globalisation.

UNIT IV **Lectures: 15**

Issues in International Business: Otusourcing and its Potentials for India; Strategic Alliances, Mergers and Acquisition; Role of IT in International Business; International Business and Ecological Considerations; Global Human Resource Management – Selection, Development, Performance Appraisal and Compensation, Motivating Employees in the Global Context and Managing Groups across Cultures, Multicultural Management.

University of Lucknow

BBA Syllabus

BBA 604: International Business

(The subject aims to familiarise the students with the concepts of international business, the organisations engaged in global business, Indian export documentation and implications of global trade on India.)

Unit 1: Historic viewpoint of international business, introduction and concepts of the modern international business, domestic and international business. Regional economic blocks NAFTA, SAFTA, ASEAN, SAARC – roles, functions and their effect on emerging global business environment.

Unit II: GAAT and WTO – structure, functions and roles in the current international business scenario, the modern world reasons for venturing into international business. Factors and variables involved in international business. International business strategies and entry modes and techniques. Indian and world MNCs with their merits and demerits.

Unit III: Comparison and contrast between domestic and international marketing, advantages of international marketing various types of international market intermediaries. Comparison and contrast between Domestic and International Human Resource Management, cross-cultural issues. Implications on the host and guest countries, various types of global organisations.

Unit IV: International financial intuitions – Structure, role, functions, World Bank, IMF, UNCTAD, NABARD, ADB, etc. Export documentation and financial support available in India—APEDA, EPZ, SEZs future-trends in international business, concepts of BPO, FDI etc. and their effects on the future of international business. India's attractiveness for FDI vis-à-vis other countries like China, Brazil, Malaysia, etc.

Mumbai University

MBA - Second Year - Third Semester Syllabus

3.01 International Business – University Assessment

Course Content:

1. Overview of the International Business Process
2. PEST Factors Affecting International Business
3. Government Influence on Trade
4. International Trade Theories
5. FDI
6. Country Evaluation and Selection
7. Collaborative Strategies
8. International Marketing
9. International Trade Agreement
10. International Trade Organisations
11. Forex
12. International HR Strategies
13. International Diplomacy

Anna University, Chennai

MBA Syllabus

MBA0932 – International Business Management

Unit	Topics	No. of hours
1	**Introduction:** Nature and Characteristics – Forms – International Trade–Exports and Imports–Organisations Facilitating International Trade–1 WTO, IMF, etc.,	8
2	**Trade Theories:** Mercantilism, Absolute Advantage Theory, Comparative Cost Theory – Heckseher – Ohlin Theory – Product Life Cycle Theory – The New Trait Theory – Porter's Diamond	8
3	**International Business Environment:** Globalisation of Business Economic, Political, Technological, Cultural and Ecological Environment of International Business	8
4	**Multinational Corporations:** Features – Classification – Role of MNCs in Developing Countries – Drawbacks – Conflict – FDI and Portfolio Investment	8
5	**Trade Blocks:** Types of Regional Groupings – Inter-regional Trade among Regional Groups	8
	Total	**40**

Anna University, Coimbatore

Unit – I: Introduction 6

International Business – Definition – Internationalising business – advantages – Factors causing globalisation of business-international business environment – Country attractiveness – Political, economic and cultural environment – Protection vs liberalisation of global business environment.

Unit – II: International Trade and Investment 11

Promotion of global business – The role of GATT/WTO – Multilateral trade negotiation and agreements – VIII & IX, Round discussions and agreements – Challenges for global business – Global trade and investment – Theories on international trade and theories of international investment – Need for global competitiveness – Regional trade block – Types – Advantages and disadvantages – RTBs across the globe – Brief history.

UNIT – III: International Strategic Management 11

Strategic compulsions – Standardisation vs differentiation – Strategic options – Global portfolio management – Global entry strategy – Different forms of international business – Advantages – Organisation issues of international business – Organisational structures – Controlling of international business – Approaches to control – Performance of global business-Performance evaluation system.

Unit – IV: Production, Marketing, Financial and Human Resource Management of Global Business 11

Global production – Location – Scale of operations – Cost of production – Make or Buy decisions global supply chain issues – Quality considerations – Globalisation of markets, marketing Strategy – Challenges in product development, pricing, production and channel management – Investment decisions – Economic – Political risk – Sources of fund – Exchange – Rate risk and Management – Strategic orientation – Selection of expatriare managers-Training and development – Compensation.

Unit – V: Conflict Management and Ethics in International Business Management 6

Disadvantages of international business – Conflict in international business –Sources and type of conflict – Conflict resolutions – Negotiation – The role of international agencies – Ethical issues in international business – Ethical decision-making.

VTU, Belgaum

MBA Syllabus

International Business

International business Environment

Sub-Code	**: 05MBA IB361**	**IA Marks**	**: 50**
No. of Lecture Hrs/ Week	**: 04**	**Exam Hours**	**: 3 Hours**
Total No. of Lecture Hrs	**: 56**	**Exam Marks**	**: 100**

MODULE 1 **(07 Hrs)**

An Overview of International Business Environment – Economic Environment – political and Regulatory Environment – Demographic Environment – Social, Cultural and Technological Environment.

MODULE 2 **(07 Hrs)**

International Economic Environment – Regional Integration and Trade Blocks – Types of Integration – Theory of Customs Union, European Union – Regional Groupings – Integration of Developing Countries – SAARC, SAPTA, International Commodity Agreements – Quota Agreements – Cartels – Bilateral & Multi Lateral Contracts – Economic Institutions – International Monetary Funds (IMF) – World Bank, Asian Development Bank, UNCTAD, UNIDO, International Trade Centre, WTO, GATT, GATS, TRIM, TRIPS.

MODULE 3 **(07 Hrs)**

International Trade and Investment Theory – Historical developments of Modern Trade theory – Investment theories – Theory of capital movements – Market imperfections – Internationalisation – Appropriability – Location specific advangage – eclectic.

MODULE 4 **(07 Hrs)**

International Trade and Payments:

Government Influence on Trade: Trade in Merchandise – Trade in Services – Global Sourcing – Degree of Dependence – Balance of Payments – Trade and BOP of India. Cultural Contacts of Global Management – Understanding the Role of Culture – Communicating Across Cultures – Cross Cultural Negotiations and Decision Making.

MODULE 5 **(07 Hrs)**

International Investment: Types and Significance of Foreign Investments—Factors Affecting International Investment – Growth and Dispersion of FDI – Cross Border Mergers and Acquisitions – Foreign Investment in India – The New Policy – EURO/ADR issues – M & A – Indian Companies Going Global.

MODULE 6 **(08 Hrs)**

Multinational Corporation: Definition and Meaning – Importance and Dominance of MNCs – Code of Conduct – MNCs in India – Transfer of Technology – Global Competitiveness – Indicators of Competitiveness Competitive Advantage of Nations – Technology and Global Competitiveness.

International Operations – Global Chain Management – Global Manufacturing Strategies – Factors Affecting International HRM and Staffing Policy – International Negotiations – International Asset Protection – Protection of IPRs.

MODULE 7 **(05 Hrs)**

International Monetary System and Foreign Exchange Marketing: The Pre-Bretton Wood's Period, Break Down of Bretton Wood System and Emergence of EMS, EU and EURO.

MODULE 8 **(08 Hrs)**

Social Responsibilities and Ethics, MNE Social Responsibilities, Efficiencies, Perspectives, Ethics, Technological Perspective, Foreign Corrupt Practices Act, Case.

University of Delhi

M.Com. Syllabus

International Business

Unit – I: Introduction to International Business: Globalisation and its growing importance in world economy; Impact of globalisation; International business contrasted with domestic business – complexities of international business; Modes of entry into international business.

Unit – II: International Business: National and foreign environments and their components – economic cultural and political – legal environments; Global trading environment – recent trends in world trade in goods and services Trends in India's foreign trade.

Unit – III: International Organisations and Arrangements: WTO – its objectives, principles, organisational structure and functioning; An overview of other organisations – UNCTAD, World Bank and IMF; Commodity and other trading agreements.

Unit – IV: Theories of International Trade – an overview; Commercial Policy Instruments – tariff and non-tariff measures; Balance of payment account and its components.

Unit – V: Regional Economic Co-operation: Forums of regional groupings; Integration efforts among countries in Europe, North America and Asia.

Barkatullah University, Bhopal (M.P.)

MBA Syllabus

International Business Environment

COURSE NO CP: 108

Max. Marks (Ext. Exam): 80

Min. Pass Marks: 32

OBJECTIVE: The primary objective of this course is to acquaint the students to emerging global trends in business environment.

COURSE CONTENTS:

UNIT – I: International Business: An Overview – Types of International Business; The External Environment. The Economic and Political Environment, The Human Cultural Environment.

Unit – II Balance of Payments, WTO and Its Importance for Indian Business, International Monetary Fund (IMF), World Bank (IBRD).

Unit – III: Exchange Rate Determination, Fixed and Flexible Exchange Rate, Convertibility of Rupee and Its Implication, Foreign Institutional Investors (FII), Foreign Direct Investment (FDI), Euro-Currency.

Unit – IV: Regional Blocks; Internationalisation of Service Firms, Export Management; Joint Ventures and Global Competitiveness.

Unit – V: Globalisation and Human Resource Development; Globalisation with Social Responsibility.

Scheme of Examination:

Total Marks: (Internal 20, External 80) = 100 marks

Pattern for External Evaluation:

Section A: (Short answers)	4 out of 8	4 × 8 = 32 Marks
Section B: (Essay type & case)	3 out of 5	3 × 16 = 48 Marks

University of Delhi

Master of International Business (MIB) Syllabus

Course 401: International Business Management

- Factors Which Control a Decision to Enter International Operations.
- International Business and Host, and Home Governments Organisational Design and Structure of International Corporations.
- Long Range Planning and Environmental Scanning International Business Enterprises.
- Locus of Decision-Making and Headquarter Subsidiary Relations in International Business Enterprises.
- Functional Aspects of International Business Enterprises
- Management of Personal from Different Social and Cultural Traditions.

University of Delhi

PG Diploma in Global Business Operations Syllabus

2.1 Global Business Environment

This paper aims at familiarising the participants with business environment at the international level including institutions and agreements.

1. **The Phenomenon of Globalisation:** Forces of globalisation; Trade investment and enterprise linkages in the global economy; internationalisation trends; The evolution of international business enterprise; The Multinational Corporations (MNCs); Competitive strategy and International business.
2. **Theories of International Trade:** Microeconomics theory of gains from trade; Open economy macroeconomics; Alternative approaches to the explanation of international production; International trade and competition; Tariffs and commercial policy in international trade; Balance of payment policy and exchanges rate system.
3. **The Environment of Global Business:** The economic, technological, legal, political and cultural environment of international business; The ethical and social responsibility of international business.
4. **Financial Environment of Global Business:** Foreign exchange market mechanism; Euro-currency market; International banks; Non-bank financial service firms; Stock markets; Financial dervatives.
5. **Policy Regimes for Global Business: Global Regimes:** The UN system; Regional and associative regimes: The European Union, NAFTA, APEC, CMEA, Latin American and the Caribbean, Africa and the Middle East, ASEAN; Trade Regimes: GATT and WTO; Monetary Regime: The gold standard. The Bretton Woods institutions: IMF and the World Bank; Proposals for an international investment regime; Policy regimes for monitoring and regulating international services; Environmental regimes.

Contents

UNIT – I

UNIT – III

UNIT – IV

UNIT – V

UNIT – I

1. Introduction to International Business
2. Globalisation
3. International Business Environment
4. Global Trading Environment

CHAPTER 1

Introduction to International Business

LEARNING OBJECTIVES

After studying this chapter, you should understand:

1.1 Meaning of International Business
1.2 Distinction between International Business and Domestic Business
1.3 Reasons for International Business (Why Companies Go Global?)
1.4 Complexities or Problems of International Business
1.5 Modes of Entry into International Business
- Summary
- Test Questions

One of the most dramatic trends in the world during the last few decades has been the rapid and sustained growth of international business. Markets have become truly global for several products and services. Global flows of trade, investment and technology have multiplied over the years. National economies have been tied together due to these flows. As a result international events are now exercising a greater impact on the economy of a country. Global firms now consider the entire world as their production base and as one market. They freely move factors of production across countries.

1.1. Meaning of International Business

International business refers to business across countries. It includes any type of business activity that crosses national boundaries. International business involves transfer of goods, services, capital, knowledge and information across national boundaries with a view to satisfy the needs of individuals, organisations and governments.

(*i*) As in any business, the purpose of international business is to satisfy the needs of the customers who may be individuals, organisations and governments.

(*ii*) International business may be carried on by individuals, organisations and governments. Individuals and organisations carry on international business with the profit motive. Governments engage in international transactions with the service motive.

(*iii*) The scope of international business is very vast. It includes not only exchange of goods and services but also transfer of knowledge, skills, people, technology capital, information and other resources.

(*iv*) International business transactions may be carried out by an enterprise remaining in the home country through imports and exports. This is known as international trade. Alternatively, the enterprise may establish an entity abroad to carry on business. This is called foreign direct investment. Thus, international trade and foreign direct investment are the main forms of international business.

(*v*) Multinational corporations have emerged as the major player in international business.

(*vi*) International business has become massive in scales. It now exercises a significant influence over economic, social and political life throughout the world.

International business is a wider term than international marketing which in turn is a broader term than international trade. International marketing is the process of focussing the company's resources such as people, funds, physical assets on opportunities and threats in global markets. It involves identifying and satisfying the wants of customers around the world. It refers to the marketing of goods and services across national boundaries. On the other hand, international business is a more comprehensive concept implying a truly global outlook. International trade is a narrow term that simply means imports and exports.

International business refers to business activities that take place across the national boundaries. It involves manufacturing and trade beyond the geographical boundaries of one country. It is different from domestic business which involves business transactions within the boundaries of a nation. International business involves not only international movement of goods and services, it also includes movement of capital, personnel, technology and intellectual property across national boundaries.

International business is a wider term than international trade. In addition to exports and imports it comprises international trade in services, foreign investments, overseas production of goods and services.

The basic reason behind international business is geographical specialisation. Every country specialises in the production of those goods and services which it can produce at lower costs. It buys other goods and services through trade with other countries which they can produce at lower costs. Different countries have different natural resources. Moreover, labour productivity and costs of production differ from country to country due to various socio-economic, geographical and political reasons.

Similarly, a business firm may import what is available at lower prices in other countries. It may export those items which can fetch better prices in other countries than at home.

1.2. Distinction between Domestic Business and International Business

International business differs from domestic business in several ways. Some of these differences are given below:

1. **Nationality of Parties:** In domestic business, both the buyers and sellers are from the same country. It is, therefore, easy for them to understand each other and enter into business transactions. But in international business, buyers and sellers belong to different countries. It is relatively more difficult for them to interact with each other and enter

into business deals due to differences in their languages, attitudes, social customs and business practices.

2. **Mobility of Productive Factors:** Factors of production such as labour and capital are generally less mobile between countries than within a country. There are legal restrictions on their movement across nations. Differences in socio-cultural environment, economic conditions and geographical factors also restrict their movement from country to country. For example, labour finds it difficult to adjust to alien culture and climate.

3. **Heterogeneity of Customers:** Buyers from different countries differ in their tastes, preferences, communication patterns, beliefs and purchase behaviours. For example, people in India use right hand driven cars while those in America use left hand driven cars Similarly, people in the United States change their consumer durables very frequently, those in India do not replace them until the product is worn out. Such differences make it difficult to design products and evolve marketing strategies that are appropriate for customers in international markets.

4. **Political Systems:** Political environment (e.g., party system, type of government, political ideology) differs from country to country and keeps on changing. A businessman is familiar with the political conditions of his country. He can easily predict its impact on business operations. But it is quite difficult to understand and monitor the political environments of other countries. Therefore, special strategies are needed to deal with diverse political risks in international business.

5. **Business Laws and Policies:** Each country evolves its own business laws and regulations. Import quota system, tariff and taxation policies, subsidies and other controls differ from country to country. Business firms setting up plants in foreign countries or interested in exporting their output must understand and follow the laws and policies of other nations.

6. **Business Systems and Practices:** Business systems and practices differ from country to country. Firms interested in international business must adapt their business policies and programmes as per the conditions prevailing in international markets.

7. **Currency Differences:** International business involves the use of foreign currencies. The exchange rate (price of one currency in terms of another currency) keeps on fluctuating. Therefore, while pricing products for international markets foreign exchange risks have to be considered.

8. **Payment Problems:** In international business payments of goods and services have to be made through special means such as letter of credit, documentary bills, etc; Payment is not such a problem in case of domestic business.

Table 1.1: Difference between Domestic Business and International Business

Basis of Difference	Domestic Business	International Business
1. Geographical coverage	Confined to the boundaries of one country	Carried across the boundaries of a country
2. Language use	Local or native language is used	Foreign language is used
3. Nationality of parties	Both the buyer and seller belong to the same country	The buyer and the seller belong to different countries

4. Usual mode of transportation	Roadways and railways	Shipping and airlines
5. Documents and formalities involved	Few documents and formalities and involved	More documents and formalities are involved
6. Currency for payment	Local currency	Foreign currency
7. Government restrictions	Very little restrictions	Restrictions such as tariffs, quotas, etc.

1.3 Reasons for International Business (Why Companies Go Global?)

Business firms go international due to two types of factors – (*i*) pull factors, and (*ii*) push factors. The pull factors refer to the forces that pull business firms to the foreign markets. High growth prospects and better profitability in foreign markets are the pull factors. The push factors refer to the forces that push business firms to the foreign markets. Saturation of domestic markets or too much competition in domestic market are examples of push factors. All these factors are described below.

1. **Higher Profitability:** International business may in some cases be more profitable than domestic business. This may be due to higher prices or lower costs in foreign countries. A product/service may be sold abroad at a higher price than what is available in the domestic market. The more common reason for profit advantage in international business is reduction in cost. For example, a major share of the ready-made garments sold by departmental stores in the United States is manufactured in Asian countries where labour is relatively cheap. Similarly, many European and American firms ship parts and components to countries such as India and Mexico where the labour intensive assembly operations are carried out.

   The Indian subsidiaries of many multinational corporations are contributing a significant portion of the latter's net profits. In some cases the Indian arm is earning huge profits while the parent company abroad is incurring loss. Even when domestic business is more profitable, international operations could increase the total profit of a company. International business can also help in increasing the profitability of domestic business by providing economies of scale.

2. **Better Growth Opportunities:** A major reason which motivates firms to go international is to take advantage of growth opportunities in foreign markets. As income and population in developing countries like India are increasing, more and more multinational corporations from developed countries such as the United States, Germany, Japan are setting up business in the developing nations. Foreign markets also offer tremendous growth opportunities for firms in developing countries. That is why several Indian companies (e.g., Infosys, Wipro, Mahindra & Mahindra, Bharti Airtel, Reliance Industries and so on) have established business units abroad. In fact some Indian pharmaceutical companies such as Ranbaxy have achieved faster growth abroad than in the domestic market. This is so because generics market in the United States is expanding rapidly as more and more products are going off-patent in the United States. About 61 per cent of Tata Group's $ 83 billion revenues comes from overseas operations.

3. **Saturation of Domestic Market**: In some advanced countries, demand for several products stagnates or declines over a period of time. For example, all households in the United States have consumer durables like televisions, refrigerators, cars, etc. In other words, the market potential for these products has been fully tapped. Moreover, population in some developed nations would grow negligibly or may decline. For example, market for several baby products may fall due to decline in birth rate.

   Companies also internationalize when the domestic market is very small. For example, Nestle earns only about two per cent of its sales revenue from Switzerland (its home market) and Philips derives only 8 per cent of its sales from Holland (its home market). Recession in the home market also prompts companies to enter foreign markets. For example, several auto component manufacturing firms in India entered foreign markets due to recession in the domestic automobile industry in the early nineties.

4. **Economies of Scale:** The optimum scale of operations has increased due to technological advances in several industries. In order to attain the optimum size companies have to explore foreign markets, besides the domestic market. Without internalisation, firms in many industries cannot take advantage of economies of scale. For example, multinationals like Samsung, LG, Electrolux and Whirlpool have made huge investments in India, China, Brazil and Mexico. They are customising their products to suit consumers in these developing countries.

5. **Growing Competition:** Rapidly increasing competition has been a major driving force behind international business. Until economic liberalisation in July 1991 the home market in India was largely protected against foreign competition. Therefore, Indian companies had little motivation to seek business opportunities abroad. They did not take foreign market seriously due to the sellers market within the country. Since 1991 competition within the country as well as from foreign firms has increased considerably. As a result, several Indian companies have entered foreign market in a big way. Removal of entry barriers and replacement of Foreign Exchange Regulations Act (FERA) by Foreign Exchange Management Act (FEMA) have led to the entry of foreign multinationals (like Coca Cola, Pepsico, LG Electornics, Samsung, HSBC) in India. In fact the new policy of liberalisation, privatisation and globalisation (LPG) is one of the major causes of internationalisation of Indian industry.

6. **Counter-Competition:** Some companies adopt an offensive competitive strategy for internationalisation. This strategy called *counter-competition* involves penetrating the home market of the potential foreign competitor to reduce its competitive strength and to protect the domestic market share from foreign competition. For example, IBM (a US multinational) moved early and created a strong position for itself in the Japanese market. Similarly, Texas Instruments set up production facilities for semiconductors in Japan to prevent Japanese companies from their own market. Indian companies have rarely used the strategy of counter-competition. But they collaborated with foreign firms to improve their competitiveness in the domestic market.

7. **Monopoly Power:** Firms which enjoy monopoly power or dominant position in terms of patent rights, technology, product differentiation and other services go international to take advantage of their power. Exclusive market information is another driving force behind international business. This includes knowledge about foreign customers and

market places not known to other companies. Such special knowledge may be acquired through international research, special contacts and spotting a business opportunity abroad during foreign travel. Monopoly power provides an initial advantage to the concerned firm. But the firm is likely to face competition in the long run.

8. **Government Policies and Regulations:** Both positive and negative aspects of Government policies and regulations can also lead to internationalisation of business.

1.4 Complexities or Problems of International Business

International business is not an unmixed blessing. It suffers from several problems such as the following:

1. **Political Instability:** The biggest hurdle in the spread of international business in political instability Iran-Iraq war, Indo-Pak war, Arab-Israel conflict, civil war in Sri Lanka, Fiji and Malaysia; military coups in Pakistan and Afghanistan created huge political risks for the growth of international business. Frequent changes in political parties in power and consequent changes in government policies also have adverse impact on international business. Asian crisis and economic crisis in Europe have been a great setback to the spread of international business.
2. **Exchange Rate Fluctuations:** Each country has its own currency. The rate at which one currency is exchanged for another currency is called exchange rate. Imbalances in the balance of payments, political instability and several other factors lead to fluctuations in exchange rate. Such fluctuations create exchange risk and discourage the growth of international business.
3. **Foreign Indebtedness:** The operations of multinational corporations in developing countries create a debt trap for these countries due to their low purchasing power. This has happened in Romania, Poland, Mexico, Brazil, Congo, Indonesia and Kenya.
4. **Entry Regulations:** Governments in domestic countries impose entry restrictions on multinational corporations. For example, a multinational could enter India only with a major Indian shareholding before 1980s. However, most governments have removed many entry restrictions after the establishment of World Trade Organization (WTO).
5. **Tariff and Non-Tariff Barriers:** In order to protect domestic industry, Governments of different countries impose tariffs, quotas and trade barriers. These barriers are imposed depending on political relations among various countries. For example, Pakistan and China have imposed quotas, tariffs and other barriers on imports from India.
6. **Bureaucracy:** Bureaucratic attitudes and practices of government in many countries create considerable delays in granting permission, sanctions and licences to foreign companies. Such practices discourage multinationals. For example, before economic liberalisation in 1991, multinationals who wanted to enter India faced bureaucratic hurdles.
7. **High Cost:** A company which wants to internationalise its operations has to incur high costs and make large investments in market survey, product modification, quality upgradation, managerial training, etc. Such high cost and investment discourage the growth of international business.
8. **Corruption:** High rate of bribes and kickbacks in some countries discourage the foreign companies to enter these countries.

9. **Technological Piracy:** During 1950s and 1960s, copying the original technology, producing imitative products and piracy in other areas of business operations were common in Japan, Korea and India. Foreign companies refrain from internationalising their operations due to fear of piracy.

1.5 Modes of Entry into International Business

1. **Exporting:** This is the traditional and most widely used route to international business. A firm can export directly or through middlemen such as export houses and buying agents.
   Exporting can be in the following forms:
   (*a*) **Direct Exporting:** A company may directly sell its products in a foreign country through its distribution channels or through a company of the host country.
   (*b*) **Indirect Exporting:** In this mode a company exports its products through another domestic company. For example, several publishers in India sell their books to UBS Publishers' Distributors Ltd., New Delhi which in turn exports them to many foreign countries.
   (*c*) **Intracorporate Transfers:** A company in one country may sell its products to its affiliated company in another country. For example, Hindustan Unilever (India) may sell its products to Unilever in the United States.

   A company may adopt exporting strategy either due to opportunities available abroad or because of decline in the demand for its products in the domestic market.

   While exporting, a company should take into consideration the following factors:

   - Government policies concerning exports, imports, foreign exchange, etc.
   - Country image, customer preferences, distribution networks and other marketing factors.
   - Warehousing, transportation, packaging, inventory carrying costs, and other logistics factors.
   - Expert intermediaries and services provided by them.

   Advantages:

   (*i*) Exporting is the simplest and easiest mode of entering foreign markets.
   (*ii*) It requires no or less funds. If a company exports through intermediaries, no investment is needed. Some investment is required when it creates its own distribution network.
   (*iii*) Exporting involves less risk. Once a company's product is accepted in the foreign country's market, it can enter on a full scale later on.

   Limitations:

   (*i*) Cost of products increases and they become less competitive due to packaging, transportation, insurance expenses and customs duties and other charges.
   (*ii*) Exporting is not possible when import restrictions exist in a foreign country. Other options have to be adopted in such a case.

(*iii*) Exporting firms are not able to establish close contacts with customers in foreign countries.

Firms usually start their overseas operations with exports and imports. Once they become familiar with foreign markets, they switch over to other forms of international business.

2. **Contract Manufacturing:** Under this strategy, the company enters into a contract with a firm in the foreign market to manufacture or assemble the product as per its specifications. The company, however, retains the responsibility of marketing the product. For example, Reebok, Nike, Levis, and Wrangler get their products and components produced in developing countries. Contract manufacturing is also called outsourcing.

The **advantages** of contract manufacturing are as follows:

(*a*) The company has not to invest resources in setting up production facilities abroad.

(*b*) The company is free from the risk of investing in foreign markets.

(*c*) The company can start immediately when idle production capacity is available in the foreign country.

(*d*) The product cost in the foreign country may be lower due to lower wages and overheads.

(*e*) Contract manufacturing may enable the company to obtain host country's support.

(*f*) Local producers in foreign countries also gain in terms of better utilisation of capacity, incentives, etc.

The **disadvantages** of contract manufacturing are as under:

(*a*) Potential profits from manufacturing are not available.

(*b*) The company has less control over manufacturing.

(*c*) Local firms might not adhere to production design and quality standards.

(*d*) Local producer in the foreign country loses control over manufacturing process and is not free to sell in open market.

(*e*) There is risk of developing a potential competitor.

(*f*) Contract manufacturing is not suitable in cases involving technical secrets and in high-tech products.

3. **Licensing and Franchising:** Under this form, the local firm (licensee) obtains licence (written permission) from a foreign firm (licensor) to use the latter's patents, trademarks, copyright, technology, know-how or marketing skills in consideration for fee called royalty.

Franchising is a contractual arrangement in which one firm (called franchiser) grants to another firm (called franchisee) the right for use of technology, trademark, brand name and patent in return for the agreed payment for a specific period of time. The franchiser may be a hotel, a restaurant, bank, travel agency or a retailer who has developed a unique technique for creating and marketing of services under its own name and trademark. McDonald, Domino's, Pizza Hut and Wal-Mart are examples of leading franchisers who operate world wide.

Franchising is similar to licensing except two differences. *First*, licensing is used in connection with production and marketing of products, while franchising applies to service business. *Second*, franchising is more stringent than licensing. Franchisers lay down strict rules and regulations which franchisees are required to follow while running their business.

Advantages of licensing and franchising are as follows:

(*i*) It requires virtually no investment and is, therefore, a less expensive mode of entering into international business.

(*ii*) The licensor/franchiser gets a regular fee and is not liable for the losses, if any.

(*iii*) There is lower risk of business takeovers or government interventions because the local person manages the business in the foreign country.

(*iv*) The licensee/franchisee has market knowledge and contacts which can be helpful to licensor/franchiser in his marketing operations.

(*v*) Firms other than the licensee/franchisee in foreign market cannot make use of the copyright, brand names, trademarks and patents of the licensor/franchiser.

Limitations of licensing/franchising are as under:

(*i*) Once the licensee/franchisee becomes skilled in the production and marketing of the product, he may start marketing a similar product under a different brand name. This can create severe competition for the licensor/franchiser.

(*ii*) In case the licensee/franchisee divulges trade secrets in the foreign markets, the licensor/franchiser may suffer heavy loss.

(*iii*) Over time conflicts may develop between the licensor/franchiser and the licensee/franchisee. Such conflicts may result in litigation causing loss to both the parties.

4. **Joint Ventures:** In this method, the company which wants to enter foreign market sets up an enterprise in collaboration with a local firm in the host country. The two firms share the ownership and control of the joint venture. Generally, the multinational provides the capital and technology whereas day-to-day management is left to the local firm. For example, Hero Honda Motors was a joint venture between Hero Cycles of India and Honda Motors of Japan.

A joint venture may be created in any of the three ways:

(*a*) The foreign firm may buy equity in a local company.

(*b*) The local firm may acquire equity in an existing foreign firm.

(*c*) The foreign firm and the local firm may jointly form a new company.

Advantages of a joint venture are as follows:

(*i*) The international firm can expand globally with less investment because the local partner also contributes the equity capital.

(*ii*) The foreign firm benefits from the local partner's knowledge of market, political system, culture, language and business system.

(*iii*) Joint venture helps the international firm to share the risks and costs with the local partner.

(*vi*) Joint ventures are helpful in executing large projects involving huge capital outlays and manpower.

Limitations of joint ventures are as under:

(*i*) The local partner may leak the technology and trade secrets of the foreign firm.

(*ii*) Dual ownership of the joint venture may lead to conflicts between the partners over control of business.

5. **Wholly Owned Subsidiaries:** The foreign firm may establish a wholly owned firm which is registered under the relevant law of the host country. Such an enterprise is known as a greenfield venture. Alternatively the foreign firm may acquire an existing company in the host country.

Advantages of a wholly owned subsidiary are as follows:

(*i*) The parent firm can exercise full control over its business in the host country.

(*ii*) The parent company need not disclose its technology or trade secrets to others.

Limitations of a wholly owned subsidiary are given below:

(*i*) The parent company has to invest 100 per cent equity capital.

(*ii*) The parent company has to bear full risk of loss from failure of its foreign operations.

(*iii*) Some countries do not allow wholly owned foreign firms. Therefore, political risks of a wholly owned subsidiary are high.

Table 1.2: Merits and Demerits of Foreign Market Entry Options

Entry Mode	Merits	Demerits
Exporting	• fairly inexpensive • easy foreign access • no ownership risks	• missed location economies • logistical difficulties (transportation/communication)
Licensing	• fairly inexpensive • useful where trade barriers/ tariffs preclude exporting • leverages location economies without ownership concerns	• risky where intellectual property protection is weak • control ceded to licensee may inhibit coordination • may help create new competitors
Franchising	• low cost, low risk • offers more control than licensing • builds presence fast	• control still an issue • franchisee may not be motivated to adhere to franchisor's standards
Management contracts	• very inexpensive • low-risk revenue	• no long-term presence • may create competitors
Turnkey projects	• an option if direct investment isn't feasible • lowers risk if long-term instability exists	• no long-term presence • may create competitors • vulnerable to political and legislative changes
Contract manufacturing	• little financial risk • reduces manufacturing costs • allows firms to focus on other value-added areas	• less control (may hamper product quality/delivery) • learning is compromised • public image may suffer

Greenfield subsidiaries	• allows high control • offers location economies • can pick own site, workers, technology	• very expensive to set up • time-consuming to set up • requires considerable international expertise • risky due to ownership
Acquired subsidiaries	• allows high control • rapid market entry • offers location economies	• risky due to ownership • cultural differences may be formidable • may be buying problems
Joint ventures	• less financial risk than subsidiaries • Leverages partner's resources, know-how	• risks giving some control or technology to partner • still some ownership risk

Sources: Adapted from R.W., Griffin, and M.W. Pustay, *International Business* (4th Ed.). Upper Saddle Ridge, NJ: Prentice-Hall, 2004

Table 1.3: Factors Affecting Choice of International Entry Mode

Type of Factor	Examples
Firm factors	International experience Core competencies National culture of home country Corporate culture Firm strategy, goals, and motivation
Industry factors	Industry globalization Industry growth rate Technical intensity of industry
Location factors	Extent of scale/location economies Country risk Cultural distance Knowledge of local market Potential of local market
Venture-specific factors	Value of firm assets risked in foreign location Extent to which know-how involved in the venture is informal (tacit) Costs of making/enforcing contracts with local partners Size of planned foreign venture Intent to conduct research and development with local partners

Source: Adapted from A.V. Phatak, *International Management: Concepts and Cases*. Cincinnati, OH: South-Western, (1997).

SUMMARY

Meaning: International business means business in foreign countries.

Differences: Different countries, languages, currencies, modes of transport and government controls.

Reasons: Higher profits, better growth, saturation of domestic demand, economies of scale, increasing competition, counter strategy, monopoly power, government controls.

Complexities: Political instability, exchange rate fluctuation, foreign indebtedness, entry restrictions, trade barriers, bureaucracy, high costs, corruption, technological piracy.

Modes of Entry: Exporting, Licensing, Franchising, Contract Manufacturing, Management Contracts, Turnkey Project, Strategic Alliance, Joint Venture, Merger and Acquisition, Greenfield Strategy.

TEST QUESTIONS

1. Define international business and describe its features.
2. Explain the concept and nature of international business.
3. Distinguish between international business and domestic business.
4. Why companies globalise? Explain with suitable examples.
5. Discuss the complexities and problems involved in international business.
6. Explain the modes of entry into international business, stating the merits and demerits of each mode.
7. "International business is a mixed blessing". In the light of this statement, describe the benefits and problems of international business.
8. Discuss the factors that motivate a firm to enter international business.
9. (*a*) Why do firms go international? Briefly describe the important decisions relating to going international.

   (*b*) Distinguish between Domestic Business and International Business.
10. Identify the entry modes in the following examples:

    (*i*) Tata Motors has purchased all the facilities of Jaguar and Land Rover car brands of UK.

    (*ii*) A British Pharmaceutical Company has granted rights to use its patent to an Indian Company in exchange of royalty payment to it.

    (*iii*) Burger King and Domino's Pizza have entered India without making any investment. However, their business practices are used in totality.

    (*iv*) Disney has allowed with a fee to foreign manufacturers to print Disney's cartoon characters on T- shirts, home furnishing items, jewellery, and the like for the foreign markets.

    (*v*) A manufacturer of Green Mung Dal in India is exporting through a commission agent situated in the UK.
11. Briefly discuss various ways of entering into international markets and their respective merits and limitations. Also explain as to how these alternative entry modes are related to a firm's level of involvement with international markets.
12. How is international business different from domestic business? What are the different modes of international business?
13. Distinguish between licensing and franchising as modes of entry into international business.

CHAPTER

2 Globalisation

LEARNING OBJECTIVES

After studying this chapter, you should understand:

Since the establishment of World Trade Organisation (WTO), globalisation has gained momentum. In fact, globalisation has become an inevitable and irreversible process. Therefore, individual companies and nations must develop appropriate strategies to take advantage of positive consequences of globalisation and to mitigate its negative effects.

2.1 Concept of Globalisation

Globalisation means the process of integration of national economies through cross-border flows of products, services, capital, technology, man power and information. According to the International Monetary Fund (IMF) globalisation is "the growing interdependence of countries worldwide through increasing volume and variety of cross-border transactions in goods and services and of international capital flows, and also through the more rapid and wide-spread diffusion of technology".

Globalisation consists of the following components:

1. **Globalisation of Markets:** Under globalisation, domestic markets of different countries are integrated and merged into a single market. In its true sense, globalisation is a mind-set which considers the entire world as a single market. No distinction is made between the domestic market and foreign market and business firms develop a global outlook. For example, Coca-Cola, Pepsi, McDonald, Sony and many other brands have global acceptance.

Globalisation of markets occurs due to several reasons:

(*i*) When the domestic market is not big enough to absorb the goods produced on mass scale, companies enter foreign markets.

(*ii*) Adverse business environment in the home country pushes companies to globalise their markets.

(*iii*) A company may enter foreign markets to reduce its risk.

(*iv*) Firms enter foreign markets to increase their sales turnover and profits.

(*v*) Companies globalise to meet demand for their products in foreign markets.

(*vi*) Foreign companies enter when domestic firms are unable to meet the needs of local customers.

2. **Globalisation of Production:** Companies locate their manufacturing facilities in different countries to take advantage of national differences in cost, quality and availability of inputs and to reach different markets quickly. For example, Boeing 777 uses 132,500 major components which are manufactured in 545 differnent locations around the globe.

Globalisation of production takes place due to many reasons:

(*i*) Multinational corporations set up plants in other countries to escape restrictions on imports in these countries. For example, Coca-Cola and Pepsi established their bottling plants in India due to import restrictions.

(*ii*) A company establishes manufacturing facilities abroad due to availability of high quality raw materials and components in foreign countries.

(*iii*) Low cost of inputs such as raw material prompts companies to produce abroad.

(*iv*) Companies globalise production due to availability of skilled labour at low cost. For example, India has become the hub of outsourcing because of this factor.

(*v*) Liberal labour laws in other countries also lead to globalisation of production.

(*vi*) Globalisation of production helps to reduce transportation costs and simplifies logistics management.

(*vii*) Establishment of manufacturing facilities abroad helps in exporting to other neighbouring foreign countries. For example, Pearson publishes books in India which are exported to Nepal, Sri Lanka, Pakistan, Bhutan and Bangladesh.

(*viii*) Globalisation of production enables a company to design and manufacture as per the varying preferences of customers in foreign countries.

(*ix*) A company having production facilities abroad can deliver products to foreign markets in the shortest possible time.

3. **Globalisation of Technology:** Information technology (the internet, microprocessors, telecommunications, e-commerce) and transportation technology (commercial jet aircraft, containers, etc.) have reduced the time and cost involved in the process of globalisation. A company with latest technology acquires distinctive competencies and helps it enter foreign markets. It can produce high quality products at low cost. Such a company can enter into technical collaboration with companies in foreign countries.

It may outrightly sell its technology to them or allow them to use its technology on payment of royalty. Multinational corporations from developed nations often globalise technology through joint ventures, acquisitions, mergers, etc. in developing countries.

4. **Globalisation of Investment:** Investment of capital by a global firm anywhere in the world is known as globalisation of investment. This is also called Foreign Direct Investment (FDI) and is motivated by higher profitability. Globalisation of investment can be in various forms such as issue of shares and debentures, global depository receipts, joint ventures and acquisition of foreign companies. For example, Infosys, Reliance and many other Indian companies have issued global depository receipts in USA and Europe. Coca-Cola acquired several bottling plants in India through direct investment.

   Globalisation of investment occurs due to many reasons, such as the following:

   (*i*) Congenial environment for direct investment abroad. For example. Government of India grants automatic approval for FDI up to 100 per cent.

   (*ii*) Domestic firms enter foreign markets through FDI to overcome limitations of exporting and licensing.

   (*iii*) Global companies invest in foreign countries to retain control over their manufacturing and marketing operations in these countries.

   (*iv*) In order to attract foreign capital India allows Foreign Institutional Investors (FIIs) to invest in her capital markets.

   (*v*) Global firms make FDI to overcome export restrictions in host countries.

2.2 Stages of Globalisation

Globalisation is an evolutionary and gradual process. A company passes through different stages of development before it becomes a truly global corporation. O. Wheeler has identified five stages in the development of a firm into global corporation. These stages are as follows:

1. **Domestic Company:** In the first stage a domestic company moves into new markets abroad by linking up with local dealers and distributors in the host country. It does not have a strategy to expand or penetrate into international markets. It only exports.
2. **International Company:** Those domestic companies who decide to exploit opportunities in foreign countries are called international companies. They internationalise their operations by growing beyond their domestic production and or marketing capacities. They extend the domestic business model and practices to the foreign markets. In other words their approach is ethnocentric. Companies follow this approach due to limited resources and to learn gradually from the foreign markets before becoming global firms so as to reduce their risk.
3. **Multinational Company:** At this stage, the international company learns that the strategy of extending the domestic marketing mix to foreign markets will not work. Therefore, it begins to carry out its own manufacturing, marketing and sales in the key foreign markets. For example, when Toyota of Japan found that its Toyopet car was not selling in the United States, it designed new models of car suitable for the US market. Thus, an international company becomes a multinational company when it starts responding

to the specific needs of foreign markets in terms of product, price and promotion. A multinational or a multidomestic company formulates different strategies for different markets. It has a **polycentric orientation** under which its branches or subsidiaries work like a domestic company in each country where they operate.

4. **Global Company:** A multinational company becomes a global company when it adopts a global marketing strategy. It produces in the home country and focuses on marketing its products globally. For example, Dr. Reddy's Laboratories produces drugs in India and markets them globally.
5. **Transnational Company:** In the fifth stage, the company adopts a genuinely global mode of operation. It discards its nationalistic mindset and thinks globally but acts locally. A transnational company invests, produces, markets and operates across the world. It is an integrated organisation which uses global resources for global markets. A true transnational corporation provides good value to customers in all the countries where it does business.

   The assets and key operations (e.g. R&D, HRD, product development) are distributed worldwide. But it adapts its products, marketing strategies and the functional strategies to the needs of each market. It procures world class materials and talent from the best source across the globe. In other words its orientation is geocentric.

Table 2.1 : Stages of Globalisation

Stage and Company	1 Domestic	2 International	3 Multidomestic	4 Global	5 Transnational
Strategy	Domestic	International	Multidomestic	Global	Global
Model	N.A.	Co-ordinated Federation	Decentralized Federation	Centralized Hub	Integrated Network
View of World	Home Country	Extension Markets	National Markets	Global Markets or Resources	Global Markets and Resources
Orientation	Ethnocentric	Ethnocentric	Polycentric	Mixed	Geocentric
Key Assets	Located in home country	Core centralized, others dispersed	Decentralized and self-sufficient	All in home country except marketing or sourcing	Dispersed interdependent and specialized
Role of Country Units	Single country	Adapting and leveraging competencies	Exploiting local opportunities	Marketing or sourcing	Contributions to company worldwide
Knowledge	Home country	Created at centre and transferred	Retained within operating units	Marketing developed jointly and shared	All functions developed jointly and shared.

Source: Warren J. Keegan, *Global Marketing Management,* Prentice Hall of India, New Delhi, 2002, p.52

2.3 Importance of Globalisation

The significance of globalisation in world economy is growing day by day. Globalisation offers the following advantages:

1. **Rapid Industrialisation:** Globalisation helps in free flow of capital and technology from one country to another. It enables the global firms to acquire finance at lower cost of capital. The increased flows of capital from surplus countries to the needy countries leads to increase in global investment. Foreign capital has, for example, increased the pace of economic development in China. Flow of technology from advanced countries helps the developing countries in boosting up their industrialisation.
2. **Balanced Development:** Globalisation leads to spread up of manufacturing facilities in different countries. This in turn leads to the balanced development of all the countries.
3. **Increase in Production:** Rapid industrialisation of world economies leads to increase in output of goods and services. There is increase in per capita consumption in both developed and developing countries.
4. **Higher Standard of Living:** When countries produce goods and services in which they have comparative advantage, productivity increases. Costs of production and prices decline and quality improves. Consumer choice and consumer surplus are enhanced. As a result living standards increase.
5. **Healthy Competition:** Globalisation increases competition among companies. They become more cost and quality conscious to face competition. Global competition keeps a check on prices and the pace of innovation increases. An open world economy spurs innovation through new ideas from aboard. Firms in developing countries get enormous opportunities both in domestic and foreign markets.
6. **Increase in Employment:** Due to globalisation, developing countries can attract more foreign direct investment. Moreover, manufacturing facilities are shifted to low wage developing countries. Therefore, job opportunities increase rapidly in these countries. For example, millions are employed in call centres, foreign multinationals, etc in India.
7. **Common Culture:** Globalisation facilitates cultural exchange between developed and developing countries. For example, Domino Pizza, McDonald Berger, India's masala dosa asd Hyderabadi biryani have become global food items. The term' global village indicates such cultural integration between nations.
8. **Human Development:** Increasing economic development enables governments in developing countries to provide educational, health and other public welfare facilities. There is improvement in the health and skills of people in developing countries.

2.4 Impact of Globalisation

Globalisation is a mixed blessing. Along with its benefits it has disadvantages also. Some adverse effects of globalisation are as follows:

1. **Killing of Domestic Industry:** Globalisation creates opportunities for multinationals of advanced countries to establish manufacturing and marketing facilities in developing

countries. Domestic firms in these countries fail to compete with these multinationals. As a result several domestic companies have to close down. Countries like India and China allow foreign investment even in soft drinks, junk food and such other industries where it is not required. Several Indian, firms have been taken over by foreign companies.

2. **Outdated Technology:** Foreign companies often bring technology that has become obsolete in advanced nations or technology that is not suited to the developing countries. They kill traditional crafts and indigenous industries affecting the lives of people employed in them. Demand for domestic products declines due to superior quality of foreign products.
3. **Exploitation of resources:** Multinationals from advanced countries exploit labour and natural resources of developing countries. They violate labour and environmental standards due to weak laws.
4. **Unemployment:** Killing of domestic business and traditional crafts results in reduction of employment opportunities in developing countries.
5. **Economic Inequalities:** Globalisation widens the gap between rich and poor. Well educated and highly skilled people earn very high incomes while common people fail to earn even minimum.
6. **Threat to National Sovereignty:** Globalisation results in commercial and political colonisation in poor countries. Global corporations exploit the weak bargaining power of governments in these countries. Nexus between multinationals and host Governments is not uncommon. Economic power is shifted from independent countries to supernational organisations such as World Trade Organisation. The sovereignty of democratically elected Governments is undermined because trade policies are often formulated in favour of advanced countries.

Obstacles to Globalisation of Indian Business

1. Restrictive Government policies and bureaucratic procedures.
2. High cost of power and other inputs.
3. Poor infrastructure.
4. Obsolete technology.
5. Resistance to change.
6. Poor quality image of Indian products.
7. Supply constraints.
8. Uneconomic small scale of operations.
9. Lack of experience.
10. Limited R&D and marketing research.
11. Growing competition in foreign markets.
12. Trade barriers by regional economic blocs

Factors Favouring Globalisation of Indian Business

(*i*) Low cost of labour.

(*ii*) Large pool of scientific and technical manpower.

(*iii*) Wide resource and industrial base.

(*iv*) Growing demand.

(*v*) Niche and expanding markets abroad.

(*vi*) Economic liberalisation.

(*vii*) Growing entrepreneurship.

2.5 Essential Conditions for Globalisation

There are several environmental and organisational requirements for the success of globalisation. Some of these are given below:

1. **Economic Liberalisation:** Government rules and regulations (e.g. quotas and tariffs) are the biggest constraint to globalisation. Restrictions on cross-border movement of goods and services, investment, technology etc. and bureaucratic hurdles must be removed to provide adequate freedom to business and industry. In fact, economic liberalisation is the first step towards globalisation.
2. **Sound Infrastructure:** Companies from home country can become global when power, ports, roads and other infrastructural facilities are well developed.
3. **Adequate Resources:** Companies who have access to finance, technology, managerial expertise and R&D facilities can easily enter global markets.
4. **Competitive advantage:** Success in global business requires a competitive advantage. A company can derive competitive advantage from low cost, superior quality, technological superiority, wide distribution network or efficient after-sales service.
5. **Proper Orientation:** A global mindset and appropriate strategies are essential for globalisation.
6. **Government Support:** Government and administrative support speeds up the process of globalisation. Such support can be in various forms like policy and procedural reforms, capital market reforms, R&D support, development of common facilities, etc.

People who have a global mindset are open to actively challenging themselves to operate beyond their comfort zone. A global mindset means learning how to operate in an unfamiliar environment. The global mindset is too complex to define. Its essence lies in a sense of curiosity and openness to learn about cultures and business environments beyond the familiar.

Living and working in a foreign land does not automatically build such a mindset. The biggest challenge is never about the tangible elements like regulations and business processes. It is about getting a global view of people and cultures. That means having to deal with people who are products of different educational and social systems. The biggest lesson in building a global mindset is about getting results while working with people with varying levels of skill. It is about operating effortlessly for long stretches of time in unfamiliar environments.

SUMMARY

Concept: The process of integration of national economies into a global economy through cross-border movement of products, services and factors of production.

Components: Globalisation of markets, production, technology and investment.

Stages: Domestic company, international company, multinational company, global company, transnational company.

Importance: Rapid industrialisation, balanced development, increase in production, higher standard of living, healthy competition, increase in employment, common culture, human development.

Impact: Killing of domestic industry, outdated technology, exploitation of resources, unemployment, economic inequalities, threat to national sovereignty.

Obstacles: Government control, high input costs, poor infrastructure, obsolete technology, resistance to change, poor quality image, supply constraints, small scale, lack of experience, low R&D, competition, trade barriers.

Favourable factors: Low cost labour, large pool of scientific and technical manpower, wide resource base, growing demand, niche markets abroad, economic liberalisation, growing entrepreneurship.

Essential conditions: Economic liberalisation, sound infrastructure, adequate resources, competitive advantage, proper orientation, government support.

TEST QUESTIONS

1. Define the term 'Globalisation'. Describe the stages of globalisation.
2. Explain globalisation of markets, production, technology and investment.
3. Discuss the benefits of globalisation.
4. Explain the impact of globalisation on international business.
5. Discuss the obstacles to and factors favouring the globalisation of Indian business.
6. Explain the essential conditions for globalisation of business.

CHAPTER 3

International Business Environment

LEARNING OBJECTIVES

After studying this chapter, you should understand:

A global firm must formulate appropriate strategies to succeed in highly competitive global markets. Strategy formulation requires a thorough understanding of environment in various countries.

An international business strategy that is successful in one country/market may fail in another country/market due to differences in their environment. Even within a country business environment may differ from one region/state to another. But the differences in business environment between countries are often more substantial than within a country. Therefore, a detailed analysis of business environment of foreign countries is essential for the formulation of international business strategies.

3.1 Concept of Business Environment

International business environment is the aggregate of all the factors, forces, institutions, etc. which influence the functioning and performance of a global firm.

According to Bayord O. Wheeler, business environment refers to "the total of all things external to firms and industries which affect their organisation and operation".

In the words of Arthur M. Weimer, "Business environment encompasses the climate or set of conditions, economic, social, political, or institutional, in which business operations are conducted."

Thus, business environment means all those internal and external factors that have an impact on business.

Business environment is characterised by the following features :

1. **Aggregative:** Business environment is the totality of all the internal and external forces which influence the working and decision-making of an enterprise.
2. **Interrelated:** Different elements of business environment are closely interrelated and interdependent. A change in one element affects the other elements. Economic environment influences the non-economic environment which in turn affects the economic conditions. For example, economic liberalisation in India since 1991 has opened up new opportunities for private sector and foreign entrepreneurs. Similarly, social pressures against pollution led to the enactment of anti-pollution laws. Therefore, managers should not consider environmental factors in isolation from one another. A holistic approach is necessary for proper understanding of business environment.
3. **Dynamic:** Business environment is dynamic in nature as it keeps on changing from time to time.
4. **General and Specific Forces:** Business environment consists of both general and specific forces. General forces such as economic, social, political, legal, natural and technological conditions influence all business enterprises. Specific forces such as investors, customers, competitors, suppliers, etc. affect individual enterprises directly.
5. **Relative:** Business environment is a relative concept. It differs from country to country and even region to region. Capitalist economies like those of USA and UK have a different kind of environment than communist economies. The nature of economic system in a country affects the environment of business.
6. **Inter-temporal:** Business environment is also an inter-temporal concept as it changes over time. For example, business environment in India today is much different from that prevailing before 1991. In the short run business environment may remain static. But in the long run, it does change.
7. **Uncertain:** Business environment is largely uncertain because it is very difficult to forecast the future environment. When the environment is volatile, *i.e.,* changes very fast, uncertainty increases.
8. **Contextual:** Business environment provides the macro framework within which the business firm (a micro unit) operates. The environmental forces are largely those given within which an individual enterprise and its management must function.

3.2 Environment of International Business

A transnational corporation faces three types of external environment:

1. **Domestic Environment:** A company which plans to do business abroad must first consider the home country environment. For example, the government policies and regulations in the home country may restrict domestic firms from doing business in foreign countries.

2. **Foreign Environment:** The environment of other countries in which the firm wants to do business is the foreign environment. For example, foreign environment for Infosys Technologies means the environment of all countries except India where the company operates or wants to operate. Even very powerful multinationals failed when they tried to adopt home country products and business practices in foreign markets. For instance, Proctor and Gamble, Apple Computers, Colgate Palmolive failed in Japan until they modified their products and marketing practices to Japanese culture

3. **Global Environment:** The environmental factors which have a global impact are known as global environment. Principles and agreements of the World Trade Organisation (WTO), other international treaties, conventions and protocols, like in crude oil price are examples of global environment. An Indian company which wants to become global must adopt global standards and practices in accounting, reporting, etc. For example, Infosys, Reliance and other Indian companies adopted the Generally Accepted Accounting Principles (GAAP) of the United States when they made ADR/GDR issues.

4. **Internal Environment:** The internal factors of a company determine its capability to do international business. Vision, mission, commitment and competence of management, organisation structure, decision making system, financial and other resources, etc are the elements of internal environment. International business requires strict adherence to delivery schedules, cost-competitiveness, innovativeness, quick response to customer needs, quality consciousness, etc. The internal environment of a firm has a considerable influence on all these.

The environment of international business is shown in Fig. 3.1.

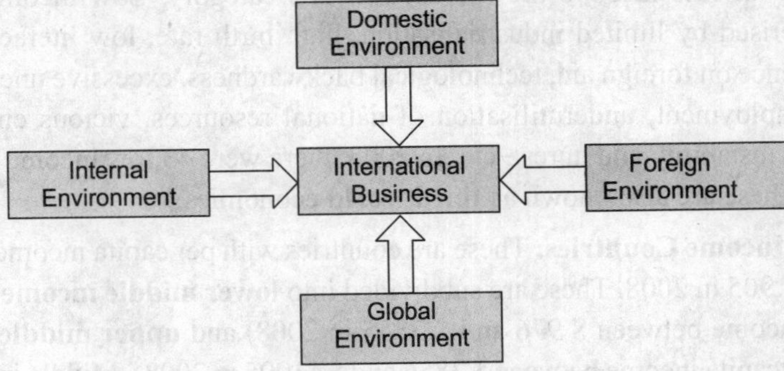

Fig. 3.1 : Environment of International Business

3.3 Economic Environment

Economic environment of different countries exercises the direct and the most influence on international business. The main components of international economic environment are as follows:

- Economic system
- Level and pattern of economic development
- Structure of the economy
- Economic policies
- Economic conditions.

3.3.1 Economic Systems

An economic system consists of institutions set up to satisfy human needs and wants. There are three main types of economic systems – capitalism, communism, and mixed economy.

1. **Capitalism:** Under this system, there is private ownership of production and distribution facilities. Resources are allocated through the market forces of demand and supply. Customers' choice determines what will be produced by whom. USA and UK are the main examples of capitalism.
2. **Communism:** In this system, the state owns all the means of production and distribution. Resource allocation is decided through central planning by the Government. Russia, China, Yugoslavia, Rumania are Communist countries.
3. **Mixed Economy:** There are no examples of pure capitalism or pure communism. All countries have mixed economic systems of varying degrees of market mechanism and centralised planning. India is the best example of a mixed economic system. The major factors of production and distribution are owned and controlled by the Government. Private sector owns and controls the remaining resources.

3.3.2 Level of Economic Development

The level of economic development is different in different countries. On the basis of per capita income, countries are classified as follows:

1. **Low Income Countries:** All countries with per capita Gross National Income (GNI) of $ 975 or less in 2008 are included in this category. Low income countries are characterised by limited industrialisation, high birth rate, low literacy levels, heavy dependence on foreign aid, technological backwardness, excessive unemployment and underemployment, underutilisation of national resources, vicious circle of poverty, political instability and unrest, etc. In 2008, there were 43 low income countries in the world. These are also known as **third world** economies.
2. **Middle Income Countries:** These are countries with per capita income between $ 976 and $ 11,905 in 2008. These are subdivided into **lower middle income** (those with per capita income between $ 976 and $ 3855 in 2008) and **upper middle income** (those with per capita income between $ 3856 and $ 11905 in 2008). Middle income countries are characterised by early stages of industrialisation, expanding consumer markets, increasing urbanisation, rising literacy levels, low cost labour, etc. In 2008, there were 100 middle income countries, including India. These are also known as **second world** economies.
3. **High Income Countries:** These are countries with a per capita income of $ 11906 or more in 2008. These countries are characterised by high level of industrialisation, advanced technology, information age, etc. There are two main categories of high income countries–industrial economies and oil exporting countries. High income countries are also known as **advanced** countries or **first world** countries.

Levels of income do not truly reflect purchasing power or standard of living because the purchasing power of the national currencies differs and there are changes in exchange rates.

Countries are frequently classified as developing and developed countries. Low income and middle income countries are developing countries while high income countries are developed countries. However, all the countries in developing or developed category do not have the same level of economic development. For example, UAE and Kuwait are regarded as developing countries despite high per capita income. Some of the low income countries *e.g.,* Bangladesh, Bhutan, Maldives, Myanmar, Sudan, Zambia, and Yemen are the **least developed countries.** India and China are among the largest economies of the world though their per capita income is low.

The economic power of developing countries is growing rapidly. The GDP and exports of these countries are increasing faster than those of the developed countries. Since economic liberalisation, foreign direct investment (FDI) in developing countries is increasing fast. Firms from developing countries like India are making inroads into markets in USA, Europe and other developed countries.

Levels of per capita income and economic development have significant implications for international business. For example, multinationals such as Hindustan Unilever, Proctor and Gamble, Colgate Palmolive launched low cost products and services to increase their sales turnover in India. In developing countries where income and investment levels are rising steadily and rapidly, there are good business prospects. In developed countries there is considerable replacement demand for consumer durables whereas it is mainly new demand in developing countries.

Within a country, there may be vast differences in the economic conditions between different regions. For example, in India, Gujarat, Maharashtra, Punjab and Haryana are economically much more developed than Bihar, Jharkhand, Meghalaya, and Tripura. Therefore, a country should not be considered a single economic unit for international business.

3.3.3. Structure of the Economy

The relative contributions of primary (mainly agricultural), secondary (industrial) and tertiary (service sectors) linkages between them, and integration of a national economy with the world economy, etc. have major implications for international business. As an economy develops, the share of the service sector increases. International trade in services is increasing faster than that in goods due to the rapid growth of the service sector both in developing and developed countries. India is one of the largest producers of agricultural products and is, therefore, the biggest exporter of rice in the world. Developments in the world economy are influencing India much more since economic liberalisation in 1991.

3.3.4. Economic Policies

Economic policies exercise a significant influence on business. Government policies may offer incentives and subsidies to certain industries which fall within the country's priority sector while–there may be certain restrictions on non-priority industries. Main economic policies are as follows.

1. **Industrial Policy:** This policy defines the scope and role of private, public, joint, cooperative and small sectors in the economy. It has an impact on scale of operations, location of industries, choice of technology, product mix, etc. For example, India's new industrial policy announced in 1991 has opened up new industries for private sector and foreign companies. Banking, insurance, civil aviation, organised retail are examples of such business opportunities. But the new policy has led to cut-throat competition.

2. **Foreign Investment and Technology Policy:** Before 1991 there were restrictions on foreign capital and technology in India. These restrictions affected both Indian and foreign firms. But since 1991 these restrictions have largely been removed. As a result Indian companies are now able to acquire capital and advanced technology from abroad. Foreign companies have made substantial investment in India.
3. **Foreign Trade Policy:** A restrictive import policy protects domestic firms. With liberalisation of imports, competition for Indian firms has increased. Therefore, these firms have become more conscious of cost, quality and after-sales service. Global sourcing for raw materials and other inputs is helping them in becoming competitive.
4. **Foreign Exchange Policy:** Abolition of exchange controls and convertibility of rupee have encouraged cross-border movement of capital.
5. **Monetary Policy:** The policy of the Reserve Bank of India towards cost and availability of credit has a strong impact on savings, investment and consumer spending in India. For example, a reduction in the Cash Reserve Ratio (CRR) and Statutory Liquidity Reserve Ratio (SLR) increases the availability of credit to business and money supply in the economy.
6. **Fiscal Policy:** Government's policy concerning public revenue and expenditure influences the development of various industries and sectors. Reduction in the direct taxes increases the disposable income which in turn can result in increased demand for goods and services.

   Business firms wanting to globalise prefer countries with stable and business friendly economic policies.

3.3.5 Economic Conditions

Rate of economic growth, price level, balance of payments position, trade cycles and other economic conditions in different countries significantly influence international business. Economic crisis in South East Asia and Europe have restricted the growth of global firms in these regions. For example, when steel exports from India to South East Asia declined sharply, Indian steel industry increased exports to the United States and Europe. Increase in growth rate boosts up demand and attracts global firms as has happened in China and India. Similarly, demand prices increase during boom but decline during recession.

Balance of payments position and the current account situation in a country influence its economic policies and business environment. For instance, a sustained current account deficit and adverse balance of payments may prompt the Government to restrict imports and cross-border movement of capital.

Several economic conditions both at home and abroad influence a country's exports and imports. The rate of economic growth, rate of change in price level, rate of growth of world trade, are examples of these economic conditions.

Economic environment exercises a major influence on the product and pricing strategies of business firms. For example, the demand for high priced products is low in low income economies. Therefore, transnational corporations launch low cost models of their products in these economies. For example, several multinationals introduce low priced brands and small size packages in India. Some of them reduced costs of production by producing in developing countries where cost of labour is low. In several developing countries, the demand for many products is restricted due to lack of adequate infrastructural facilities. For example, limited degree of electrification and power supply restricts the demand for electrical appliances. The demand for colour television sets in India began only in the early 1980s when colour telecast was started. Companies in high income countries view low income countries a market for their obsolete products and technologies.

Promotion strategies also need to be modified. In developing countries, most of the consumers need to be educated about many products (*e.g.,* ipad, iphone, tablet, etc.). It is necessary to create primary demand. On the other hand, in developed countries consumers are familiar with these products but most of the demand is replacement demand. Therefore, firms adopt the strategy of planned obsolescence to maintain demand.

Firms of developing countries intending to do business in the developed countries modify their products, packaging and pricing to succeed in highly competitive markets.

3.4 Social Environment

Social environment consists of demographic factors, caste system, family system, migration, ethnic aspects, etc.

1. **Demographic Factors:** Management and market both involve people. Managers get things done through workers and demand depends on people. The main demographic factors and their impact on international business are given below:

   (*i*) Size of Population: The size of population is a major determinant of demand. China and India are huge markets for this reason. Developed countries with large population are also attractive markets. Foreign investment flows into these markets giving rise to severe competition. Markets in developing countries are expanding due to increasing population and a steady rise in income. Supply of labour is also increasing. Several multinationals have invested heavily in developing countries like India to take advantage of huge demand and low cost labour.

   (*ii*) Age Structure: Birth rates are declining in both developed and developing countries. Therefore, the market for baby products is sinking. But with fewer children the child becomes increasingly precious and a larger share of disposable income is spent on him/her. This is happening in China, Italy, Germany and even in India. Young couples with single or no child have more time and income for travel and eating out. Therefore, hotels, airlines and restaurants and amusement parks are benefited. The increasing proportion of the aged in total population is creating new business opportunities for pharmaceutical firms, diagnostic centres and speciality hospitals.

   (*iii*) Gender: With increasing number of women in workforce, demand for ready-to-eat food, home appliances, beauty parlours, etc. is rising.

   (*iv*) Occupation: The occupational and spatial mobility of population has implications for business. Labour problems are reduced with increase in mobility of labour.

   (*v*) Education: As literacy levels are rising, demand for life style products is increasing. Consumers are becoming more quality conscious and expect value for their money.

   (*vi*) Other Trends: Management problems increase when the workforce is diverse in terms of caste, religion, language, etc. Demand patterns become varied and call for differing marketing strategies when the population has varied tastes and preferences.

2. **Migration and Ethnicity:** In developed countries like the USA, the number of migrants from Asia and other regions has increased rapidly. There is heavy concentration of im- migrants in many areas in USA. Southall is the city of Indians, Detroit is called the Arab capital, Miami is becoming Haitian and Jamaican and Silicon Valley is the hub for Asians. Each ethnic group has its own wants and buying habits. Scar Roebuck, Colgate Palmolive and several other companies have modified their marketing strategies to suit the preferences of different ethnic groups.
3. **Family System:** The family system has an impact on international business. Women play a dominant role in the family in Europe and North America. But their role is insignificant in most-of-the Islamic and Asian countries. With the decline of joint family system demand for consumer durables and other products and services is increasing.

3.5 Cultural Environment

Culture is the aggregate of customs, beliefs, values, habits and attitudes that bind people together as a social entity.

According to Mitchell, "culture is a set of learned core values, beliefs, standards, knowledge, morals, laws and behaviours shared by individuals and societies that determines how an individual acts, feels and views oneself and others"[1]. Culture is both material and non-material. **Mateiral culture** consists of man-made things such as telephone, television-automobile, etc. whereas **non-material culture** includes intangible factors such as values, beliefs, ideals, language, knowledge, etc.

Some important **traits or dimensions** of **culture** are as follows:

1. **Low-Context and High-Context Cultures:** A low-context culture is one that emphasises such tangible aspects of a negotiation or business deal as facts, figures and performance. In such cultures, business can be conducted without face-to-face meetings. On the other hand, in a high-context culture personal relationships, respect, religion and trust are given more importance in business dealings.
2. **Masculine and Feminine Cultures:** A masculine culture appreciates aggressiveness and assertiveness while in a feminine culture quality of life and inter-personal relationships are more important than material acquisition. According to Mitchell, "Business people from feminine cultures are often more reserved and less time-driven than those from masculine cultures where achievements are more important than building a long-term relationship."[2]
3. **Monochronic and Polychronic Cultures:** In a monochronic culture, time is considered precious and tasks are done in order of their priority. A polychronic culture gives less importance to time and time is used to achieve diverse goals simultaneously. Developing nations are more polychronic than developed countries.
4. **Universalism vs. Particularism:** Under universalism focus is more on the rules than on relationships and there is close adherence to business contracts. On the contrary, relation-ships and trusts are more important than formal rules under particularism. As people become more known to each other, legal contracts are modified.

1. Charles Mitchell, ***International Business Culture,*** World Press, California, 2000, p.2
2. Charles Mitchell, *op.cit*, p.18.

5. **Individualism vs. Communitarianism:** In individualism, people consider them as individuals whereas in communitarianism they consider themselves as part of a group. Business people from individualism should have patience and should aim at building lasting relationship while dealing with people from communitarianism. On the other hand, people from communitarianism who deal with those from individualism should be prepared to make quick decisions
6. **Neutral vs. Emotional:** In a neutral culture emotions are held in check while emotions are openly expressed in an emotional culture. People from emotional culture doing business in neutral culture should put everything in writing. They should not consider lack of emotion as lack of interest. Similarly, people from neutral culture doing business in emotional culture should respond warmly to the emotions of the other party.
7. **Specific vs. Diffuse:** In a specific culture, people are open and extroverted. They keep work-life and private life separate. On the other hand, people in a diffuse culture are indirect and introverted. They mix work-life and private life. Therefore, people from specific culture doing business in diffuse culture should show patience and should respect the title, age and background of the other person. On the contrary, people from a diffuse culture doing business in specific cultures should get to the point, be efficient and should not use their titles or connections in business deals.
8. **Achievement vs. Ascription:** In achievement cultures, status of a person depends on his performance while in ascription cultures it depends on who or what a person is. Therefore, people from achievement cultures doing business in ascription cultures should ensure that the negotiating team is headed by a senior and formal position holder who can impress the other party. They should also respect the status and influence of the other side. On the contrary, people from ascription cultures doing business in achievement cultures should make use of data, knowledge and technical expertise to impress the other party.

Thus, it is essential that every firm engaged in international business understands the cultures of host countries. Cross-culture literacy is essential. One way to mitigate the dangers of insensitivity to the host country's culture is to employ host country nationals who can help in conducting business to suit the particular culture.

Firms engaged in international business have to face different cultures. They must adapt their business strategies to the requirements of the culture in which they operate. In the absence of proper understanding of the cultural environment, they may suffer cultural shock. Markets which suffer from a cultural lag may not be ready to accept new products. Firms which ignore the customs, traditions, tastes and preferences of their foreign markets suffer heavy losses. For example, Proctor & Gamble, Hindustan Unilever, Nestle, Kellogs and others modified their products to suit tastes and preferences of Indian consumers. According to Ricks, "Cultural differences are the most significant and troublesome variables encountered by the multinational company. The failure of managers to comprehend fully these disparities has led to most international business blunders".[3]

3. David Ricks, ***Blunders in International Business,*** Blackwell, Oxford, 1999, p.4

Religion: Multinationals must be sensitive to the religious beliefs, customs, rituals and festivals of every country in which they operate. For example, in India Hindus regard the cow as sacred and there have been demonstrations against a foreign fast food chain selling beef products. Religion affects customs regarding marriage, naming ceremony of the child, festivals, etc. These have important implications for firms selling clothes, jewellery, etc.

Language: Another problem which global firms have to face is differences in language. For example, the Arabic language is read from right to left whereas Hindi, English, etc are read from left to right. Body language has different meanings in different cultures. A symbol or gesture may denote appreciation in one culture but derogatory in another culture. For instance, a pat on the shoulder represents encouragement in several countries but is offensive in Thailand. Pepsi translated the headline "Pepsi brings you back to life" into Chinese. The translation was interpreted as "Pepsi brings your ancestors back from the grave".

Colours: The same colour has different connotations in different cultures. For example, white dress is the norm at wedding in Christian countries while it is used at mournings/death in India. Green is a favourite colour in Muslim countries but it is a sign of illness in Malaysia.

Etiquette: The way people greet each other differs from culture to culture. Embracing, hugging and kissing is common in some cultures but is highly objectionable in others. Some cultures disapprove shaking hands with people of opposite sex. In some cultures gifts are expected while in others these are considered bribes or insults. Eating habits, dressing styles, need priority vary from one culture to another.

Firms engaged in international business must avoid the **Self Reference Criterion (SRC)** in decision-making. It means an unconscious reference to one's own cultural traits while making decisions. Lee has suggested the following steps to overcome the SRC:[4]

(*i*) Define the problem or goal in terms of home country's cultural traits

(*ii*) Define the problem or goal in terms of the host country's cultural traits.

(*iii*) Isolate the SRC influence in the problem and examine it carefully to see how it complicates the problem.

(*iv*) Redefine the problem without the SRC influence and develop the solution for the foreign market situation.

3.6 Political Environment

Political environment exercises enormous influence on international business. An international business firm must be aware of the political environment of the home country as well as that of the host country. The main components of the political environment are as follows:

1. **Political System:** The type of Government in a country is its political system. Democracy and totalitarianism are two ideologically opposing political systems. **Democracy** is a political system wherein people elect their representatives to run the Government. Global firms need to be careful about two aspects of democratic countries. First, new democracies suffer from political instability due to internal rivalry, corruption, military

4. James A. Lee, "Cultural Analysis in Overseas Operations," ***Harvard Business*** *Review*, March-April 1966, pp. 106-114.

and foreign influence. Bangladesh, Nepal, Maldives, etc. are examples of such countries. Second, in well established democracies such as the United States and India, political power is decentralised. Each state in the country has its own policy towards foreign firms. Therefore, foreign companies must choose the State carefully for locating its operations.

Totatiarianism is a political system wherein an individual or a political group runs the government without the participation of citizens. This system of Government is not ideal for foreign firms.

2. **International Political Relations:** Political relations between countries determine the nature and volume of trade between them. Friendly relations boost bilateral and multilateral trade. For example, both Indians companies and foreign firms in Indian gained due to friendly relations between India and the former USSR. On the other hand, hostilities between countries hurt international business. Arab countries do not like to deal with the business firms of Israel. A third country may also influence trade between two countries. For example, trade between China and Israel suffered when USA threatened to cut economic aid to Israel over its sale of airbone aircraft system to China.
3. **Government Business Relations:** A country may allow entry of foreign firms to increase investment. The Government may itself be in the business. There is thus both cooperation and competition between host country government (*e.g.,* India) and foreign firms. The home country may also encourage domestic firms to invest abroad. For example, the Government of India has helped Indian companies to acquire foreign firms in Europe, USA, Africa, etc.
4. **Political Stability:** International business thrives in stable, dynamic, honest, and efficient political systems. Political instability is a major threat to international business. Social unrest, negative attitudes of people towards foreign firms, hostile policies of the host government, changes in political parties in power all create political instability.

Transnational corporations face **political risks** caused by actions of host governments. Some of these actions are as follows:

(*i*) **Expropriation:** Expropriation means transfer of the assets of a foreign firm to a domestic firm with compensation. It discourages foreign firms to make investment in the host country. It may also induce foreign Government to retaliate. For example, Fidel Castro's Government in Cuba seized the assets of US multinationals with inadequate compensation. As a result the US government imposed trade embargo against Cuba.

(*ii*) **Confiscation:** The seizure of the assets of a foreign firm by the host country Government without any compensation is called confiscation. For example, the Chinese Government confiscated US property in 1949.

(*iii*) **Domestication:** In domestication, the host country Government requires that the ownership and control of foreign firms be gradually transferred to local firms. It is done to reduce the presence of multinationals in non-essential industries such as consumer goods or to protect domestic business from foreign competition. Business of Pepsi and General Motors was domesticated in South Africa. Domestication tends to reduce efficiency in industry.

(*iv*) **Nationalisation:** When the host country Government takes over the ownership of a private firm, it is called nationalisation. For example, Government of India nationalised private sector banks in 1969. The Korean Government nationalised Kia Motors and Burma nationalised entire foreign trade. Nationalisation is considered legitimate when it is done in public interest and with adequate compensation to the private firm.

(*v*) **Operating Risk:** This risk arises when the host Government imposes controls on foreign firms. For example, Government of India asked Coca-Cola and IBM to leave the country in 1977. Bureaucracy in decisions concerning foreign investment and technology, corruption, unreliable judiciary, social boy cott, civil disturbance, terrorism, violence, exchange control, price control, restriction on repatriation of assets or profits, etc. also create operating risk for transnational corporations.

Global firms can take the following **steps to minimise their political risks:**

(*i*) Make an indepth study of the political conditions in the host country before making investment.

(*ii*) Show social concern by employing local people, adhering to product quality, contributing to charities and undertaking social welfare activities that can earn goodwill of the community.

(*iii*) Follow ethical business practices and establish oneself as an exemplary corporate citizen in the host country.

(*iv*) Partner with local firms and use local suppliers.

(*v*) Take insurance cover against extortion, terrorism, confiscation, expropriation, nationalisation, etc.

(*vi*) Engage specialist agencies to monitor political development in the host country and keep close watch to spot potential trouble at the earliest and react quickly to prevent loss.

(*vii*) Assist local companies in technology.

(*viii*) Stimulate local economy by investing in its priority areas and boosting its exports.

(*ix*) Remain politically neutral and do not involve in political affairs of the host country.

(*x*) Indulge in behind-the-scene lobby to influence decisions of the host Government.

3.7 Legal or Regulatory Environment

Regulations concerning business differ widely between countries. For example, certain trade practices and promotional techniques allowed in many countries may be considered unfair and illegal in other countries. In some countries Government exercises strict control over radio, television and print media. Legal or regulatory environment of a country depends on the following:

1. **Legal System:** There are three systems of law—common law, civil law, and theocratic law.

(*a*) **Common Law** is based on tradition, customs, past practices and precedents set by courts. Common law originated in England and is prevalent in England, United States, Canada and other countries which were British colonies. It is flexible but hierarchical because lower courts have to follow the decisions of the higher courts.

(*b*) **Civil Law** is a system of written rules or codes and it originated in ancient Rome. Germany, France, Japan and many other countries have civil law.

In countries having common law contracts are detailed as all contingencies are spelled out. But in civil law countries contracts tend to be brief because civil code consists of details. Therefore, a firm entering into contracts in a host country must understand the country's legal system.

(*c*) **Theocratic Law** is based on religious precepts. Islamic law prevalent in Muslim countries is the best example of theocratic law. It is based on the Koran; the Sunnah (decisions and sayings of the Prophet Muhammad); the writings of Islamic scholars. Islamic law is more a moral code than a commercial law. But it is applied to commercial activities. For example, Islamic law prohibits taking and giving of interest. Therefore, banks operating under this legal system structure fees into their lending.

A transnational corporation has to face laws of the home country, laws of foreign countries and international laws, treaties and conventions.

International Regulations: There are two international laws. The Uniform Law on International Sale of Goods (Uniform Law on the Sales) sets out the obligations of buyers and sellers. The Uniform Law at the Formation of Contract (Uniform Law on Formation) attempts to reconcile the differences of common and civil law on offer and acceptance leading to the formation of an international contract.

In addition, there are several regulations created by WTO and the International Chamber of Commerce.

Settlement of Disputes: Disputes in international trade are settled by the WTO, conciliation, arbitration and through courts. International Council for Commercial Arbitration (ICCA) and the International Centre for Settlement of Investment Disputes help in the settlement of disputes.

Regulations relating to the following are also a part of legal environment for international business:

(*i*) Product standards pertaining to health, quality, safety, etc.

(*ii*) Disclosures about ingredients, potency, shelf life, side effect, etc of products

(*iii*) Laws for environmental protection

(*iv*) Product liability laws

(*v*) Regulations about packing and labelling

(*vi*) Regulations concerning price, advertising, etc.

(*vii*) Regulations about trade practices.

(*viii*) Intellectual property laws—patent, trade mark, copyright, etc.

3.8 Technological Environment

Technology refers to systematic knowledge for the manufacture and distribution of a product, for the rendering of a service and for the application of a process. According to J.K. Galbraith, technology is "a systematic application of scientific or other organised knowledge to particular tasks." Technology includes both machines (hard technology) and ways of thinking (soft technology) used to solve problems and promote progress in society.

Technological progress has been revolutionising business and industry. It facilitates the introduction of new products and services, improves efficiency, and reduces time and cost involved in business activities. Information technology, in particular, has transformed financial and other markets and has speeded up the process of globalisation. Internet, e-mail, video conferencing and e-commerce have facilitiated instant dissemination of information. Advancements in technology have direct and tremendous influence on international business. Modern technology enables large scale production of quality products at low cost. As a result domestic companies enter foreign markets to sell their output. Thus, technology leads to globalisation of business.

According to the Human Development Report of UNDP, the world is evolving into a global village due to shrinking time and space due to technological revolution. Business firms can now transact business at any time in any part of the world without meeting customers and suppliers. They can identify and profile customers and respond to them quickly.

Some of the important issues in technological environment and their implications for international business are given below:

1. **Appropriate Technology:** Technology that suits one country may not be suitable to another country. For example, capital intensive technology of advanced nations may be inappropriate for labour intensive countries like India. Therefore, multinational corporations locate their high technology plants in developed countries and establish their labour intensive facilities in developing countries to take advantage of low cost labour. Multinationals can increase their sales in developing countries through **adaptation of technology.** For example, one multinational found that low income and unreliable power supply hindered the sales of its washing machines in developing countries. It developed a low cost manually operated washing machine for these countries.
2. **Time Lags in Introduction and Absorption of Technology:** There is often a time lag in the adoption and diffusion of technology. The developing countries usually lag behind the developed nations in the adoption of new technology. For example, many developing countries serve as a market for old technology and second hand plant and machinery. In India and several other developing nations colour TV telecast and cable TV began late affecting the business of TV manufacturers and advertising industry. The electronic typewriter restricted the growth of electric typewriter and computer restricted the sales of electronic typewriter. Markets for packaged food widened due to advances in technologies of food processing, packaging and preservation. The pace of globalisation accelerated with drastic reduction in transportation costs due to new and better means of transport. Information technology has increased efficiency of inventory management and distribution systems.
3. **Transfer of Technology:** Dissemination of commercial technology from advanced countries to developing nations fosters international business. Foreign investment, licence agreements and joint ventures are the main channels for transfer of technology. Developing countries often suffer in the flow of technology because they have to pay high cost for inappropriate/outdated technology. They become technologically dependent on advanced nations and their indigenous technology is displaced. Therefore, regulation of technology transfers may be necessary.

3.9 Natural Environment

Natural environment creates both opportunities and constraints for international business. The natural factors and technology are some what interdependent. Application of technology depends on ecology and natural environment can be enhanced or degraded by technology. The natural environment is the source of raw material, energy and other resources. Factor endowment of a country determines the pattern of its foreign trade. International business is necessitated due to specialisation of countries in the production of goods permitted by their natural resources. Weather and climate, topography, water resources, etc. are all important for international business.

SUMMARY

Concept: The sum total of all the factors and forces which influence the functioning and performance of a global firm. A global firm faces domestic, global, foreign and internal environments.

Economic Environment: Economic systems (capitalism, communism, mixed economy), level of economic development (low income, middle income and high income countries), structure of the economy, economic policies (industrial policy, foreign investment and technology policy, foreign trade policy, foreign exchange policy, monetary policy, fiscal policy), economic conditions.

Social Environment: Demographic (size of population, age structure, gender, occupation, education, others), migration, **ethnicity**, family system.

Cultural Environment: Low context and high context, masculine and feminine, monochronic and polychronic, universalism and particularism, individualism and communalism neutral and emotional, specific and diffuse, achievement and aspiration, religion, language, colours, etiquette, self-reliance criterion

Political Environment: Political system (democracy vs. totalitarianism), international political relations, government-business relations-political stability, political risks (expropriation, confiscation, domestication, nationalisation, operating risk)

Legal Environment: Legal system (common law, civil law, theocratic raw), international regulation, settlement of disputes.

Technological Environment: Technological progress, appropriate technology, time lags in technology, transfer of technology.

Natural Environment: Natural resources, climate, natural disasters.

TEST QUESTIONS

1. Define the term 'Business Environment'. Explain the types of environment faced by a transnational corporation.
2. Describe the components of economic environment. How do they influence international business?
3. How does economic environment of a country influence a firm engaged in international business? Explain with suitable examples.
4. "Social forces exercise a dominating influence on international business". Explain.

5. Discuss the role of culture in international business.
6. "Most of the failures in international business arise due to the failure to understand and adapt to cultural differences between countries". Explain. How is cultural understanding helpful for decision making in a global firm?
7. Analyse the components of political environment that are relevant to a global firm
8. "Democracy rather than totalitarianism is conducive to international business". Explain.
9. What are the political risks faced by an international enterprise ? Suggest suitable measures to manage these risks.
10. Describe the major legal systems prevalent in the world. How do differences in the legal system influence the operations of a global firm?
11. How does technology influence globalisation of business?
12. Explain the major technological issues relevant for international business.
13. Discuss the economic policies that influence international business.
14. Write notes on:
    (*a*) Dimensions of Culture
    (*b*) Self-Reliance Criterion (SRC)
    (*c*) Natural Environment
15. (*a*) How does domestic politics impact upon international business decisions?
    (*b*) "Cultural factors are powerful shapers of the business environment and thus the study of cultural environment for the students and managers of international business is a must." Explain.
    (*c*) Why the students, managers and entrepreneurs should study legal environment?
16. (*a*) How important is the legal environment of the host country for the conduct of international business ? Discuss.
    (*b*) What is counter trade? What are the merits and demerits of counter trade?
17. What is culture? What are the main elements of culture in a society? How do these elements influence the conduct of international business?
18. Giving examples, explain the impact of various components of a foreign country's geographical environment on a firm's international marketing strategy.
19. Evaluate the prospect of Indian industry being able to meet the challenge of international competition. Have the difficulties more to do with internal management or with external environment?
20. How would you define competitiveness? Discuss the concept of competitiveness both at the firm and national levels. Suggest measures to build global competitiveness at the firm level.

CHAPTER

4 Global Trading Environment

LEARNING OBJECTIVES

After studying this chapter, you should understand:

4.1 Trade Strategies

Trade strategy refers to a country's approach towards imports and exports. It is a very significant component of global trading environment. Trade strategy has widespread implications. It has an impact on the following:

(*i*) Volume and composition of exports and imports

(*ii*) Pattern of investment

(*iii*) Direction of development

(*iv*) Competition

(*v*) Cost conditions

(*vi*) Entrepreneurship

(*vii*) Consumption patterns

Trade strategies are of two main types:

1. **Inward-oriented Trade Strategy:** The inward-looking trade strategy gives priority to domestic production over foreign trade. It is also known as *import substitution strategy*

because import substitution is its key element. An essential feature of inward-oriented strategy is the protection of domestic industries from foreign competition. Tariffs and non-tariff barriers are used for this purpose. Quantitative methods and administrative restrictions (*e.g.* licensing) are the dominant measures used for protection under the inward-oriented trade strategy.

The inward-looking strategy has an explicit bias against imports. It encourages a high cost and non-competitive economy by protecting the domestic market. As a result exports suffer. In this way the inward-looking strategy is biased against foreign trade.

Several developing countries including India adopted an inward-looking trade strategy in the past. Since economic liberalisation and World Trade Organisation, developing countries across the world have become increasingly outward oriented.

2. **Outward-Oriented Trade Strategy:** An outward-looking trade strategy is an open and neutral strategy. It does not discriminate between purchase of domestic goods and imports. It also does not discriminate between production for the domestic market and exports. It is neither in favour of exports nor against import substitution. It should not be confused with export promotion strategy.

   Outward-looking trade strategy has the following merits:

   (*i*) It expands the scope for international business

   (*ii*) It creates opportunities for global sourcing

   (*iii*) It encourages cost and efficiency consciousness in domestic firms.

   (*iv*) It helps to increase competitiveness

International trade accounts for a major part of international business. The pattern and growth of international trade depends to a great extent on the global trading environment. Such environment influences not only exports and imports but also financial flows and international investment. The global trading environment is very comprehensive. It comprises several factors such as the following:

1. Trade strategies
2. Trade barriers
3. Trade agreements
4. Trading blocks
5. State trading
6. Cartels
7. Multilateral trade negotiations of domestic firms in the international market,

4.2 Free Trade

Free trade means the trade that is free from all artificial barriers such as tariffs, quantitative restrictions, exchange controls, etc.

The main **arguments in favour of free trade** are as follows:

(*i*) Under free trade, each country specialises in the production of those goods in which it has a comparative advantage. Such specialisation leads to the most economic utilisation of world's productive resources.

(*ii*) Free trade leads to intense competition. As a result inefficient producers have to improve their efficiency or quit.

(*iii*) Free trade saves consumers from exploitation by breaking domestic monopolies.

(*iv*) Free trade makes available a larger variety of goods and from the cheapest source.

(*v*) Free trade reduces the scope for corruption which is rampant under protection.

4.3 Protection

Since the creation of GATT and WTO tariffs have been reduced drastically. But non-tariff barriers have proliferated in developed countries. Currency crisis, oil crisis, debt crisis, recession, trade deficits, unemployment and similar problems have led to growing protectionism.

A country imposes trade barriers to achieve the following ***objectives***:

(*i*) To protect domestic industries from foreign competition

(*ii*) To conserve the country's foreign exchange resources

(*iii*) To achieve a favourable balance of payments

(*iv*) To direct the foreign trade in accordance with the country's priorities

(*v*) To encourage indigenous research and development

(*vi*) To mobilise public revenue

(*vii*) To curb conspicuous consumption

(*viii*) To discriminate against unfriendly nations.

4.3.1 Arguments for Protection

1. **Infant Industry:** A new industry requires protection against foreign competition as otherwise it cannot survive and grow. In case an infant industry has to compete with well established and powerful foreign competitors, it will be an unfair competition and will lead to the ruin of the infant industry. Therefore, temporary protection should be given to the infant industry to enable it to overcome its teething troubles. Some economists, however, argue that an infant will always remain an infant in case it is given protection. Moreover, it is very difficult to identify an infant industry that requires protection. There can be better ways than tariff or non-tariff barriers for removing obstacles to the growth of an infant industry.

2. **Employment:** Protection helps to expand employment opportunities by stimulating domestic industry. Restrictions on imports encourage the growth of industries which have to compete with imports. But such restrictions reduce employment and income abroad which may reduce the demand for our exports. Moreover, foreign countries may retaliate by imposing restrictions on our exports.

3. **Balance of Payments:** A country can improve its balance of payments position by restricting imports. Developing countries suffer from shortage of foreign exchange. It is, therefore, necessary to control unnecessary imports.

4. **Key Industries:** A country should develop its own key industries like iron and steel, petrochemicals, machine building, cement, fertilisers, etc. These industries are essential for the development of other industries and for the economy as a whole. In the absence of key industries a country is at the mercy of foreign suppliers. Protection should be given for the survival and growth of key industries.
5. **Diversification:** A strong and reasonably self-reliant economy requires a diversified industrial structure. Otherwise a depression or recession can derail its economy. It also faces risks due to changes in political relations and international economic conditions. Protection becomes necessary to develop a range of industries which provide strength and stability to the country's economy.
6. **Anti-Dumping:** Dumping is very harmful to the domestic industry and can even transmit recession abroad to the home country. Protection is therefore resorted to prevent dumping and thereby protect domestic industries.
7. **Better Terms of Trade:** It is argued that import duties and quota can improve terms of trade. A country may expect to obtain larger quantity of imports for a given amount of exports by imposing tariff. However, terms of trade cannot improve when the foreign supply is elastic. In addition, foreign countries may impose counter tariffs and quotas as a retaliatory measure.
8. **Strategic Trade Policy:** It is argued that protection and government support is necessary for gaining comparative advantage in high-tech industries such as computers, semi-conductors, telecommunications, etc. But such effects may get neutralised because most countries undertake strategic trade policies at the same time. Foreign countries may also retaliate.
9. **National Defence:** A country must develop its own industries for producing defence equipments. Protection may be necessary to develop defence and other industries of strategic importance. India is highly dependent on foreign countries for defence equipments and oil.

4.3.2 Arguments against Protection

Protection is criticised on several grounds:

(*i*) Protection makes domestic producers less quality conscious.

(*ii*) Protection discourages innovation and encourages the survival of inefficient firms.

(*iii*) Protection leads to domestic monopolies.

(*iv*) Protection is harmful for consumers as it increases prices and reduces variety.

(*v*) Protection reduces the volume of international trade.

(*vi*) Protection leads to inefficient utilisation of resources.

(*vii*) Protection encourages corruption.

4.4 Recent Trends in World Trade

Major trends in world trade are described as follows:

1. **Increase in Merchandise Trade:** Global trade is continuously increasing except in 2011. International trade in merchandise has been growing steadily over the years. During the period 2000-2010 the annualised growth rate of merchandise trade has been high. In terms of value the growth of world trade has been quite high since 2003. Rapid increase in global trade is the result of declining barriers and relaxation of monetary and fiscal policies.

Table 4.1 : World Trade in Merchandise

Year	Exports		Imports (USD billion)	
	Value	Growth Rate	Value	Growth Rate
1980	2032		2074	
1990	3479	6.0	3590	6.7
2000	6444	6.8	6642	6.7
2001	6177	– 4.0	6381	– 3.8
2002	6473	4.7	6641	3.7
2003	7527	16.3	7736	16.5
2004	9167	21.8	9447	22.1
2005	10441	13.9	10712	13.4
2006	11983	14.8	1203	13.9
2007				
2008				
2009				
2010				

Source: UNCTAD Handbook of Statistics.

2. **Regional Distribution of Merchandise Trade:** Table 4.2 shows that nearly half of the world trade in merchandise accrues from two countries – Japan and China. Europe dominates international trade with a share of about 43%. Asia occupies the next place with a share of about 27% in exports.

Table 4.2 : Regional Distribution of World Trade in Merchandise, 2005.(USD billion)

Region	Exports		Imports	
	Value	Percentage	Value	Percentage
North America	1478	14.5	2285	21.7
South and Central America	355	3.5	298	2.8
Europe	4372	43.0	4543	43.2
CIS*	340	3.3	216	2.1
Africa	298	2.9	249	2.4
Middle East	538	5.4	322	3.1
Asia	2779	27.4	2599	24.7
Total	**10,159**	**100.0**	**11,511**	**100.0**

*Commonwealth of Independent States

Source: WTO, International Trade Statistics.

Developed countries dominate with a share of about 67% of the world trade. Bulk of the trade takes place among the developed nations. Developing countries export largely to developed countries. However, the share of developing countries in world trade is increasing. Ten per cent of the countries account for about 72% of the world trade. China has emerged as a leading exporter as well as importer.

3. **Composition of Merchandise Trade:** As can be seen from Table 4.3, manufactured goods account for the largest share of world merchandise trade. Exports of pharmaceutical products showed the highest growth rate in all manufactured products. Automotive products had the second highest growth rate. However, price changes affected the growth rate of different items. There was moderate rise in the prices of agricultural and manufactured products. On the other hand, there was rapid increase in the prices of fuel and mining products.

Table 4.3 : Composition of Global Exports in Merchandise

Items	Value (USD billion)	Percentage Share	Annual Growth Rate
Agricultural products	852	8.4	8
Fuel and mining products	1748	17.2	36
Manufactures	7312	72.0	10
Others	247	2.4	9
Total	**10,159**	**100.0**	**13**

Source: WTO International Trade Statistics 2006

4. **Growth of World Trade in Services:** World trade in services has been increasing continuously. However, the growth in services trade has been lower than that of merchandise trade. In services trade too, the developed countries have the largest share. Twenty countries of the world control about 75% share of services trade.

Table 4.4: World Trade in Commercial Services (USD billion)

Year	Exports	Imports
1980	391	436
1990	831	860
2000	1529	1519
2001	1537	1527
2002	1640	1625
2003	1880	1854
2004	2250	2197
2005	2494	2404
2006	2736	2617

Source: UNCTAD Handbook of Statistics

5. **Intra-Regional Trade:** The world trade of the six largest regional trade agreements is given in Table 4.5

Table 4.5: Intra-Regional Trade, 2003 (USD billion)

Regional Trade Agreement	Intra-Trade		Share of Intra Trade in	
	Value	Percentage of World Exports	Exports	Imports
European Union	1795	24.6	61.9	61.7
NAFTA	651	8.9	56.1	36.8
AFTA	105	1.4	23.3	23.3
CEFTA	29	0.4	13.6	11.3
MER COSUR	13	0.2	11.9	19.0
ANDEAN	5	0.1	9.4	17.7

Source: WTO World Trade Statistics 2006.

Trade Winds

International goods trade has increased dramatically in the last 10 years, rising from $6.5 trillion in 2002 to $ 12 trillion in 2006 to reach $ 18 trillion in 2011...

Developed countries remain the main destination of international trade flows

- $10 trillion total imports of developed countries
- $ 9 trillion export value (2011) of developing countries, similar to that of developed countries

Trade flows to and from developing countries largely involve middle income (about half) and high-income countries (about one-third)

WORLD TRADE ($ trillion) Developing Developed

EXPORTS IMPORTS

10 8 6 4 2 0

2002 2006 2011 2002 2006 2011

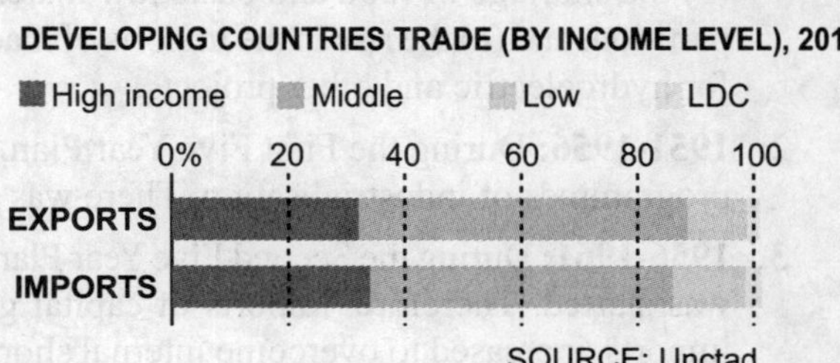

SOURCE; Unctad

Annual Percentage Change in Exports and Imports of Goods 2011-12

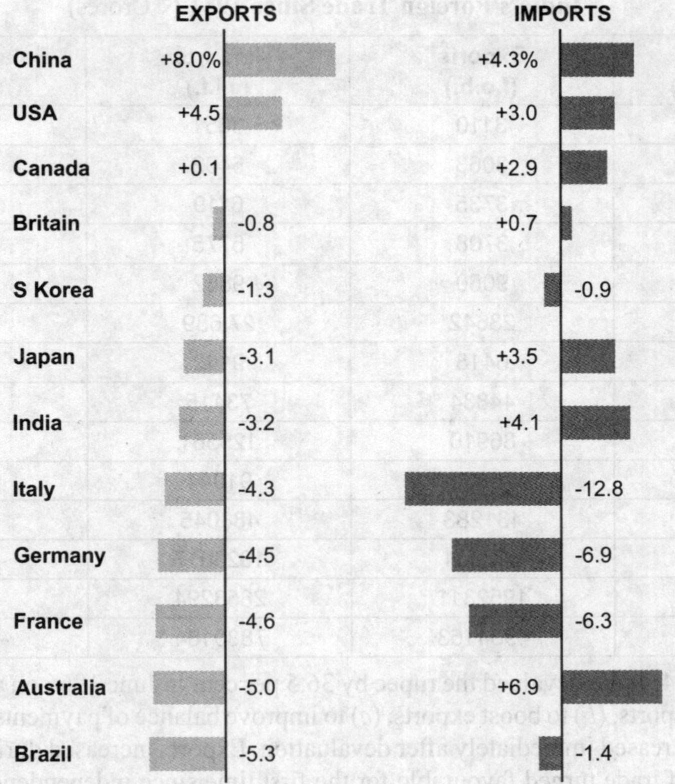

Source: NYT

4.5 Trends in India's Foreign Trade

Before 1947 India was an exporter of foodstuffs and raw materials to England and other industrialised countries and an importer of manufactured goods.

Trends of India's foreign trade since independence may be analysed under the following phases:

1. **1948-1951:** During this period, India's imports exceeded its exports. The rise in imports was mainly due to (*a*) pent-up demand as a result of various restrictions and controls; (*b*) the shortage of food and basic raw materials such as jute and cotton on account of partition; and (*c*) the rise in the imports of machinery and equipment to meet the demand for hydroelectric and other projects.
2. **1951-1956:** During the First Five Year Plan, imports of capital goods increased due to programmes of industrialisation. There was no improvement in exports
3. **1956-1961:** During the Second Five Year Plan, a massive programme of industrialisation was started. Therefore, imports of capital goods rose sharply. In addition, foodgrain imports increased to overcome internal shortages and rising prices. On the other hand, exports declined. There was foreign exchange crisis.
4. **1961-1966:** Imports continued to increase due to rapid industrialisation. More defence goods were imported because of aggression by. China and Pakistan. Extensive failure of crops necessitated large imports of foodgrains.

India's Foreign Trade Since 1951 (₹ Crores)

Year (April-March)	Exports (f.o.b.)	Imports (c.i.f.)	Balance of Trade
1951 – 56	3110	3651	– 541
1956 – 61	3063	5402	– 2339
1961 – 66	3735	6119	– 2384
1966 – 69	3708	5775	– 2067
1969 – 74	9050	9862	– 812
1974 – 79	23642	27,689	– 4047
1979 – 80	6418	9142	– 2724
1980 – 85	44834	73415	– 28581
1985 – 90	86910	125561	– 38651
1990 – 92	76600	91044	14444
1992 – 97	431283	488045	– 56762
1997 – 02	842004	1023817	– 181813
2002 – 07	1952311	2658294	– 705983
2007 – 12	4964153	7880184	–2916031

5. **1966-1974:** India devalued the rupee by 36.5 per cent in June 1966 on account of (*a*) to reduce imports, (*b*) to boost exports, (*c*) to improve balance of payments position. Trade deficit increased immediately after devaluation. Exports increased during 1966-68 and balance of trade turned favourable for the first time since independence. But increase in the prices of petroleum products, fertilisers, non-ferrous metals and newsprint led to a sharp rise in imports and deficit balance of trade in 1973-74.

6. **1974-79:** During the Fifth Plan both imports and exports increased very fast. But import liberalisation led to trade deficit from 1977-78 onwards.
7. **1980-1989:** The import bill shot up due to sharp increase in the prices of petroleum products. Exports too continued to rise but fell much short of exports. The unprecedented trade deficit forced the Government to approach the IMF for a huge loan in November 1981.
8. **1989-1992:** During this period imports reached a record level due to Gulf War but exports did not pick up owing to disintegration of the erstwhile Soviet Union.
9. **1992-97:** During the Eighth Plan exports picked up but there was a jump in imports on account of liberalisation and reduction of customs duties.
10. **1997-02:** As a result of South East Asian crisis, recession in Japan, economic crisis in Russia, India's foreign trade declined. Trade deficit increased sharply.
11. **2002-07:** In the Tenth Plan, there was a jump in exports but imports also rose sharply causing a record level of trade deficit.
12. **2007-13:** There was a sharp increase in imports of petrol and oil. There was some increase in exports, but trade deficit continued to rise.

4.5.1 Composition of India's Foreign Trade

1. **Pattern of imports:** India's imports are classified as follows:

   (i) **Bulk imports:** (*a*) Petroleum, crude oil and petroleum products (*b*) Bulk consumption goods – cereals and pulses, edible oils and sugar, (*c*) other bulk items – fertilisers, non-ferrous metals, paper and paper boards, rubber, pulp and waste paper, metallic ores, iron and steel.

   (ii) **Non-bulk imports:** (*a*) Capital goods – metals, machine tools, electrical and non-electrical machinery, transport equipment and project goods, (*b*) mainly export related items – pearls, precious and semi-precious stones, organic and inorganic chemicals, textile, yarn and fabrics, cashew nuts, (*c*) Others: artificial resins, plastic materials, professional and scientific instruments, coal and coke, chemicals, non-metallic mineral.

There has been a persistently rising trend of imports due to both internal and external factors such as sharp hike in oil prices, drought of 1987, liberalisation policy, rapid industrialisation, etc. However, imports of foodgrains and consumer goods declined owing to self-sufficiency.

Structure of India's Imports (₹ crores)

	1980-81	1990-91	2000-01	2011-12
1. *Bulk Imports*	8739	19464	95095	1029576
(*a*) Petroleum, etc	5267	10816	71497	742764
(*b*) Bulk consumption goods	901	999	6593	55660
(*c*) Other Bulk items	2571	7650	17005	231153
2. *Non-Bulk Imports*	3810	23729	135778	1316396
(*a*) Capital *goods*	1910	10471	40847	476185
(*b*) Mainly export related items	1158	6603	36815	261037
(*b*) Others	742	6655	58116	579175
Total 1+2	12549	43193	230873	2345973

2. **Pattern of Exports:** India's exports are classified as follows:

(*i*) agriculture and allied products.

(*ii*) ores and minerals

(*iii*) manufactured goods

(*iv*) mineral fuels and lubricants

(*v*) others.

Structure of India's Exports (₹corers)

	1970-71	1980-81	2011-12
1. Agriculture and allied products	487	2057	179331
2. Ores and minerals	164	413	39073
3. Manufactured goods	772	3747	895125
4. Mineral fuels and petroleum products	13	28	265819
5. Others	99	465	74933
Total	1535	6710	1459281

It is clear from the above table that there has been a continuous decline in the share of agricultural and allied products in total exports. On the other hand, the share of manufactured goods and non-traditional items has been continuously rising. However, export of iron and steel has not been satisfactory. The exports of rice, fruits and vegetables and processed foods are increasing. Thus, the pattern of India's exports shows that the Indian economy is diversifying.

4.5.2 Direction of India's Foreign Trade

For studying the regional direction of India's foreign trade, the world may be classified into four broad groups – America, Europe, Asia & Oceania and Africa.

Percentage Distribution of India's Exports and Imports

Regions	Exports			Imports		
	1951-52	1960-61	1969-70	1951-52	1960-61	1969-70
1. America	28.2	21.6	19.1	36.3	31.5	34.8
2. Europe	36.8	45.1	42.7	31.5	43.9	37.2
3. Asia and Oceania	27.8	26.0	32.0	22.7	18.6	19.0
4. Africa	7.2	7.3	6.2	9.5	6.0	9.0
Total	100.0	100.0	100.0	100.0	100.0	100.0

The table given above shows that the share of America in India's exports has been declining while that of other regions has been rising. As far as imports are concerned, there is no clear cut trend. The share of OECD countries in both exports and imports has been falling. India's trade with developing countries of Asia, Africa and Latin America and OPEC region has shown an upward trend.

A general feature of India's exports has been the dominance of Asia and Europe, though USA tops the list. Exports to China have increased considerably. Imports have been more widespread than exports, with China accounting for a major share.

Thus, India's foreign trade has become much more diversified. This is a welcome trend in the foreign trade of India.

SUMMARY

Trade Strategies: Inward-oriented, outward-oriented

Free Trade: Advocated on grounds of specialisation, competition, cost reduction, less corruption and consumer welfare.

Protection: Arguments in favour are - infant industry, employment, balance of payments, key industries, diversification, anti-dumping, better terms of trade, strategic trade policy, and national defence. **Arguments against are -** poor quality, higher prices, monopoly, inefficiency, less foreign trade and corruption

Trends in World Trade: (*i*) increase in merchandise trade, (*ii*) regional distribution, (*iii*) composition (*iv*) growth of trade in services, (*v*) intra-regional trade

Trends in India's Foreign Trade: (*i*) composition – bulk and non-bulk imports, (*ii*) pattern – agriculture oriented, (*iii*) direction—mainly to America and Europe

TEST QUESTIONS

1. Explain inward-oriented and outward-oriented strategies of international trade.
2. What is Free Trade? Give arguments in its favour.
3. What are the objectives of protection?
4. Give arguments in favour of and against protection.
5. Explain in brief recent trends in world trade.
6. Describe briefly trends in India's foreign trade.

UNIT – II

5. Theories of International Trade
6. Commercial Policy Instruments—Tariff and Non-Tariff Measures
7. Balance of Payment Account
8. International Organisations and Agreements

CHAPTER

5

Theories of International Trade

LEARNING OBJECTIVES

After studying this chapter, you should understand:

5.1 Mercantilism
5.2 Absolute Cost Advantage Theory
5.3 Comparative Cost Advantage Theory
5.4 Factor Endowment Theory
5.5 Product Life-Cycle Theory
5.6 New Trade Theory
5.7 Theory of National Competitive Advantage

- Summary
- Test Questions

Economists have developed several theories to explain why there should be trade between nations and what goods should a country export or import. During the 16th and 17th centuries, *mercantilism* advocated that a country should encourage exports and discourage imports. In 1776, Adam Smith broke the myth behind mercantilism. He advocated **free trade** among nations for the welfare of all the countries. Smith argued that the invisible hand of the market mechanism rather than Government should decide what a country exports or imports. Other theories expanded on Smith's idea. In the 19th century David Ricardo advanced the **comparative advantage** theory. Heckscher and Ohlin refined Ricardo's theory in the 20th century. The theories of Smith, Ricardo and others identify the specific benefits of international trade. Common sense suggests that a country can benefit by exchanging some of the products for those products that it cannot produce at all. But the theories of Smith and others reveal that a country can gain even by importing products that it can itself produce. The gains arise because international trade allows a country to specialise in the production and exports of products that it can produce most efficiently. For example, India exports rice, Iran exports oil, Brazil exports coffee. Thus, trade theories help to explain the pattern of international trade. According to **factor endowment theory** international trade is necessary because factors of production are available in different proportion in different countries. **New trade theory** suggests that countries specialise in the production and exports of particular products because in certain industries the world market can support only a limited number of firms. The **theory of national competitive advantage** provides an explanation for specialisation of some countries in certain industries.

Theories of international trade also have implications for Government policy. Mercantilism suggests Government internvention in both exports and imports. The theories of Smith, Ricardo and Heckscher-Ohlin advocate free trade. New trade theory and the theory of national competitive advantage justify limited government involvement to support the growth of some exports oriented industries. These various theories are described in this chapter.

5.1 Mercantilism

The first theory of international trade is known as mercantilism. It emerged in England in the 16th century. Mercantilism suggested that the wealth of a nation consisted of gold and silver which were then the currency of trade between countries. With the help of this wealth a country could maintain a large army and wield power on the people. In order to accumulate gold and silver, a country should increase its exports and decrease its imports. A country could accumulate gold and silver by maintaining a surplus in the balance of trade. Government intervention is necessary for this purpose. Exports could be increased through subsidies. Tariff quotas and other controls could be imposed to minimise imports.

In 1752, David Hume, a classical economist, pointed out an inherent inconsistency in mercantilism. According to Hume, if England had a surplus balance of trade, the resulting inflow of gold and silver would increase money supply and inflation in England. On the other hand, the outflow of gold and silver would reduce money supply and prices in France. As a result, France would buy fewer goods from England and England would buy many goods from France. Ultimately, surplus balance of trade of England would disappear. Thus, in the long run the country could sustain surplus in the balance of trade and so accumulate gold and silver as suggested by mercantilism.

Adam Smith and David Ricardo pointed out the basic flaw with mercantilism. It viewed trade as a **zero-sum game** wherein one country's gain is another country's loss. In fact, trade is a **positive-sum game** wherein all countries can gain from trade. However, mercantilism is not dead. Even today many countries adopt the trade strategy of boosting exports and restricting imports. This is called neo-mercantilism.

5.2 Absolute Cost Advantage Theory

Adam Smith opposed mercantilism in his landmark book **'The Wealth of Nations'** in 1776. He argued that certain goods can be produced at a lower cost in one country than in another country. Therefore, a country should specialize in the production of goods for which it has an absolute cost advantage and then trade these goods for goods produced by another country. For example, England could manufacture textiles most efficiently while France could produce wine most efficiently. Therefore, England should concentrate in producing textiles and France in wine. They could exchange their surplus output with each other. By specialising in the production of goods in which each had an absolute advantage, both countries could benefit from trade.

Let us assume a situation that India and Iraq have total resources (labour hours) of 600 and 400 respectively. The number of labour hours required to produce one unit of rice and one unit of oil in both the countries are given in Table 5.1

Table 5.1 : Absolute Cost Advantage

Country	No. of Labour Hours Required Per Unit	
	Rice	Oil
India	10	20
Iraq	20	10

The table shows that India has absolute cost advantage in the production of rice whereas Iraq has absolute cost advantage in the production of oil.

Production Without Specialisation

Let us assume there is no trade between the two countries and both the countries devote their resources equally in the production of these two commodities. The total consumption for them is shown in Table 5.2.

Table 5.2: Consumption Without Trade

Country	Total Production and Consumption	
	Rice	Oil
India	60	30
Iraq	20	40
Total	80	70

Production With Specialisation

Now suppose each country specialises in the production of the commodity in which it has absolute cost advantage. Then the total production and consumption will be as follows:

Table 5.3: Production and Consumption Under Trade

Country	Total Production and Consumption	
	Rice	Oil
India	120	—
Iraq	—	80
Total	120	80

Gains from trade: India has surplus rice while Iraq has surplus oil. Suppose, the exchange rate between rice and oil is 2:1. India will export rice and import oil from Iraq. Similarly, Iraq will export oil to India and import rice from it. Suppose, the two countries agree for an exchange rate of 1:1 and 30 units of each commodity are exchanged' the gains from trade will be as follows:

Table 5.4: Gains from Trade

Country	Consumption Before Trade		Consumption After Trade		Gains From Trade	
	Rice	Oil	Rice	Oil	Rice	Oil
India	60	30	90	30	30	—
Iraq	20	40	30	50	10	10
Total	80	70	120	80	40	10

On account of trade, India gains 30 units of rice and 10 units of oil whereas Iraq gains 10 units of oil. The gains from trade for each country will differ depending upon the international exchange rate agreed between them.

Thus, output and consumption for both countries increase due to specialisation and international trade. In other words, international trade produces gains for all involved.

Limitations: The theory of absolute cost advantage can explain only a small percentage of the world trade between nations. It fails to explain most of the world trade that takes place among developed countries. The absolute cost advantage theory is based on several unrealistic assumptions such as the following:

(*i*) There are two countries.
(*ii*) There are two commodities.
(*iii*) The commodities are homogeneous.
(*iv*) There is only labour cost of production.
(*v*) There is homogeneity of tastes.

Table 5.5: Advantages and Disadvantages of Absolute Cost Advantage Theory

Advantages	Limitations
1. The first theory that suggests international specialisation increases efficiency. 2. The theory indicates what a country should export or import. 3. The first theory that suggests international trade is beneficial for the world as a whole.	1. The theory fails to explain the situation when one country has absolute cost advantage in the production of both the commodities or in neither of them. 2. The theory does not explain why productive capacities of different countries are different. 3. The theory makes extreme predictions about specialisation and direction of trade. 4. The assumption of exchange ratio of 1:1 is not always true.

5.3 Comparative Cost Advantage Theory

The main limitation of absolute cost advantage theory is that it does not explain what happens when one country has an absolute advantage in the production of all goods. David Ricardo removed this limitation in his book. **'Principles of Political Economy'** published in 1817. According to Ricardo's theory of **comparative cost advantage**, it is beneficial for a country to specialise in the production of those goods that it produces most efficiently and to buy the goods that it produces less efficiently from other countries.

Let us assume that the cost of producing one unit of tea and cloth in India and China are as shown in Table 5.6.

Table 5.6: Comparative Costs of Production

Country	Cost Per Unit	
	Tea	Cloth
India	10	15
China	16	20

India has absolute cost advantage in both commodities. A country's comparative cost advantage in the production of a commodity is measured by the relative value of one commodity in terms of the other commodity. In India, cloth costs 1.5 times the cost of tea while in China cloth costs only 1.5 times the cost of tea. Thus, India has a comparative cost advantage in the production of tea while China has comparative cost advantage in the production of cloth. Therefore, it would make sense for India to specialise in the production of tea and to import cloth from China in exchange of surplus tea.

Each country can produce the two commodities in any proportion within the total resources available (India 1200 and China 1600). Assuming the resources are divided equally between two commodities in both the countries, the total production would be as given in Table 5.7.

Table 5.7: Production Without Specialisation

Country	Total Production	
	Tea	Cloth
India	60	40
China	50	40
Total	110	80

Now suppose India specialises in the production of tea and China in the production of cloth. Total production will be as given in Table 5.8.

Table 5.8: Production Under Specialisation

Country	Total Production	
	Tea	Cloth
India	120	—
China	—	80
Total	120	80

Gains from Trade: India will export its surplus tea to China and import cloth from China. For every unit of tea exported India gets about 0.67 units of cloth as the domestic cost ratio between tea and cloth is 10:55. China will offer 0.80 unit of cloth for every unit of tea it imports from India. The international exchange rate will be somewhere in between 0.67 and 0.80. Therefore, both the countries will gain from trade. Let us assume that India exports 27 units of tea in exchange for 20 units of cloth (an exchange ratio of 0.74). The total consumption in both the countries and gains from trade would be as given in Table 5.9.

Table 5.9: Consumption and Gains From Trade

Country	Consumption Before Trade		Consumption After Trade		Gains From Trade	
	Tea	Cloth	Tea	Cloth	Tea	Cloth
India	60	40	66	40	6	—
China	50	40	54	40	4	—
Total	110	80	120	80	10	—

Thus, the comparative cost advantage theory suggests that all countries can gain from international trade. It advocates free trade on the argument that trade is a positive-sum game. Even countries that have no absolute advantage in the production of any commodity benefit in terms of more consumption.

The theory of comparative cost advantage has been criticised for its unrealistic assumptions and oversimplification. It is based on the following **assumptions:**

(*i*) There are only two countries in the world.

(*ii*) There are only two commodities that are produced in the world.

(*iii*) There are no transportation costs.

(*iv*) The two commodities can be exchanged in a one-to-one ratio.

(*v*) The prices of resources are the same in the two countries.

(*vi*) Resources can move freely from the production of one commodity to another.

(*vii*) There are constant returns to scale *i.e.* specialisation has no effect on the amount of resources needed to produce one unit of a commodity.

(*viii*) The stock of resources in each country is fixed.

(*ix*) Free trade has no effect on the efficiency with which resources are used.

(*x*) Trade does not influence income distribution within a country.

5.4 Factor Endowment Theory

The comparative cost advantage theory suggests that comparative advantage arises due to differences between productivity of labour in the two countries. According to Swedish economists Eli Heckscher ("The Effect of Foreign Trade on the Distribution of Income", 1919) and Bertil Ohlin ("Interregional and International Trade" 1933) comparative advantage results from differences in factor endowments. Different countries are endowed with different amounts of land, labour and capital. A country which has abundant amount of capital but less labour has a comparative advantage in the production of that commodity which requires more of capital than labour. Similarly, another country has a comparative advantage in the production of labour intensive product. For example, the USA and Germany export capital intensive products like machinery and engineering items. On the other hand, China and India export labour intensive products like textiles and leather.

The factor endowment theory also suggests that free trade is beneficial. But unlike Ricardo's theory, it argues that differences in factor endowments rather than differences in labour productivity determine the pattern of international trade.

The Leontief Paradox

The factor endowment theory has common sense appeal and it is based on fewer simplifying assumptions than Ricardo's theory. Several empirical studies have been made to test the validity of factor endowment theory. The most famous study was carried out by Wassily Leontief in 1953. Leontief postulated that since the United States had abundance of capital in comparison with other countries, it would be an exporter of capital intensive goods and an importer of labour intensive goods. He, however, found that US exports comprised less capital intensive goods than its imports. His findings are summarised in Table 5.10

Tables 5.10: Capital and Labour Proportions of US Exports and Imports in 1947

	Exports	Imports
Capital in US dollars	25,50,780	30,91,339
Labour in worker-years	182	170
Capital for worker-year ($)	14,105	18,184

The table shows that US imports were more capital intensive than its exports. As the result was contrary to the prediction of the factor endowment theory, it was called ***Leontief Paradox:***

Several hypotheses have been developed to explain the Leontief paradox and to uphold the validity of the factor endowment theory. Some of these explanations are as follows:

(*i*) Leontief used import substitutes. The factor proportion in the manufacturing industries may be different from that found in the USA for same industries.

(*ii*) There is a difference between skilled labour and unskilled labour. The United States had a special advantage in the production and exports of goods that required skilled labour and innovative entrepreneurship e.g. computer software.

(*iii*) Leontief did not consider natural resources. These resources are often used together with capital. Therefore, the countries importing capital intensive goods may be actually importing goods that involved intensive use of natural resources.

(*iv*) The USA could not perhaps import much labour intensive goods due to the existence of trade barriers.

(*v*) Factor endowment theory is based on the assumption that technologies are the same across countries. In reality these are differences in technologies among the countries. Differences in technology may lead to differences in productivity which in turn determine patterns of international trade. For example, Japan's success in exporting automobiles during the 1970's and 1980's was largely due to her higher productivity achieved through innovative manufacturing technology. Empirical studies show that if the impact of technological differences on productivity is controlled, the factor endowment theory seems to be valid.

5.5 The Product Life-cycle Theory

Raymond Vernon developed the product life-cycle theory in 1966. The focus of his theory is on the product rather than the country and its cost advantage. The product life-cycle theory suggests that over a period, a product undergoes different stages along with changes in knowledge, technology, information and costs. These stages in the life-cycle of a product are as follows:

1. **New Product:** Development of a new product requires huge capital investment in research and development and highly skilled labour. Therefore, product innovations mostly occur in advanced countries. During the 20th century, a very large proportion of the world's new products were developed and sold in the US market. The US firms had a strong incentive to develop new products due to the wealth and size of the US market. Moreover, the US firms innovated cost-saving processes on account of high cost of labour. According to Vernon most new products were initially produced in America

because the US firms wanted to locate production facilities close to the market and the decision-making centres because of the risks and uncertainty involved in introducing new products. Their ability to charge relatively high prices for new products also obviated the need to locate in low cost sites in other countries.

Vernon argued that in the early life of a new product, demand in countries other than USA was limited to high income groups. Therefore, other countries imported the new product from the United States to meet the limited initial demand.

2. **Growth Product:** The demand for the new product increases over time in other advanced countries such as Great Britain, France, Germany and Japan. Therefore, it becomes worthwhile for these countries to start producting the new product in their home markets. Moreover, firms from the United States set up production facilities in those advanced countries where demand is growing. The need for highly skilled labour and consequently the cost of production decline as the production technology for the product becomes standardised. Thus, exports of the product from the United States fall.
3. **Mature Product:** The market for the product in the United States and other countries matures and the product gets more standardised. As a result, competition becomes price based and cost becomes the main consideration. The production facilities are shifted to countries with low cost labour. Firms from these countries might now be able to export to the United States.

Thus, production base of the product keeps on changing with change in technology. The competitive advantage of countries also keeps on changing from one stage to another. The pattern of world trade over time undergoes changes. As the production of the product becomes concentrated in low cost countries, the United States switches from being an exporter to an importer.

The pattern of production, consumption, exports and imports in the United States, other advanced countries and developing countries during different stages in the life-cycle of the product are shown in Fig. 5.1.

Evaluation of Product Life-Cycle Theory: The product life-cycle theory has focus on technological progress and costs of the product. It takes into account mobility of capital across countries that was assumed to be immobile under the earlier theories. The theory is able to explain the link between investment and international trade.

The product life-cycle theory seems to explain accurately the patterns of international trade in the past. For example, photocopier was developed in the early 1960s by Xerox in the United States and sold initially in the US market. Initially, Xerox exported photocopiers from the United States to Japan and other advanced countries. With growth in demand for photocopiers, Xerox entered into joint ventures with Fuji in Japan, and Rank in Great Britain. Foreign competitors such as Canon in Japan and Olivetli in Italy entered the market. As a result, exports from the USA declined. Production facilities were shifted to Singapore, Thailand and other developing countries. The United States, Great Britain and Japan became importers of photo copiers. This shifting pattern of international trade in photocopiers is consistent with the predictions of the product life-cycle theory.

The product life-cycle theory is not free from **limitations**. There have been increasing exceptions to its predictions. Several new products are being introduced in Japan, Europe and other regions outside the United States. Laptops, compact disks, digital cameras and other new products were introduced simultaneously in the United States, Japan and other

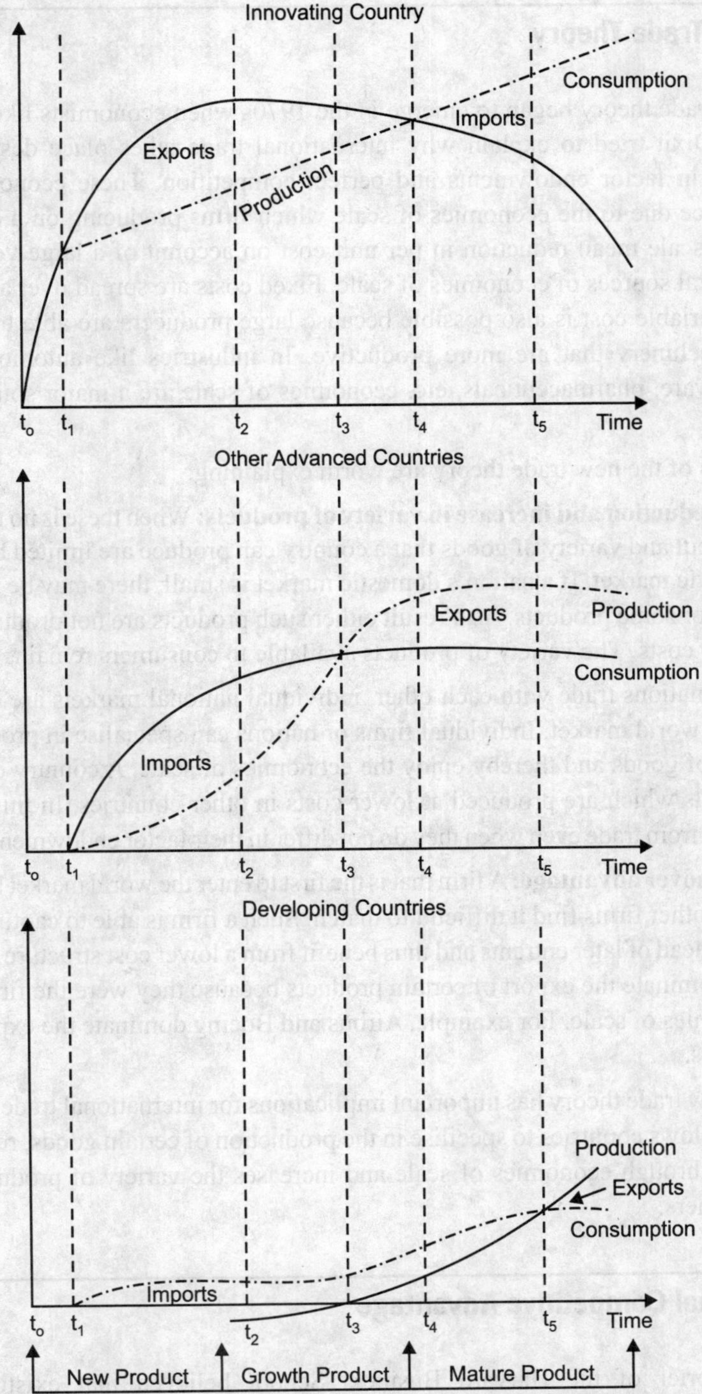

Fig. 5.1 International Product Life Cycle

advanced countries. Thus, Vernon's theory could explain the pattern of international trade during the brief period of US dominance. But its relevance in the modern world appears to be limited. The product life-cycle theory seems to be valid only for technology based products. It does not explain trade in resource based and service based products.

5.6 New Trade Theory

The new trade theory began to emerge in the 1970s when economists like Paul Krugman, Norman and Dixit tried to explain why international trade takes place despite the absence of differences in factor endowments and perfect competition. These economists argue that trade takes place due to the economies of scale which firms producing on a high level enjoy. Economies of scale mean reduction in per unit cost on account of a large volume of output. There are several sources of economies of scale. Fixed costs are spread over a large volume. A reduction in variable cost is also possible because large producers are able to use specialised labour and machinery that are more productive. In industries like automobiles, aerospace computer software, pharmaceuticals, etc. economies of scale are a major source of reduction in per unit cost.

Two points of the new trade theory are worth explaining:

1. **Cost reduction and increase in variety of products:** When these is no trade, the volume of output and variety of goods that a country can produce are limited by the size of the domestic market. If a nation's domestic market is small, there may be no economies of scale for some products. As a result either such products are not produced or produced at high costs. The variety of products available to consumers remains limited.

   When nations trade with each other, individual national markets are combined into a bigger world market. Individual firms or nations can specialise in producing a narrow range of goods and thereby enjoy the economies of scale. A country can import other products which are produced at lower costs in other countries. In this way, countries benefit from trade even when they do not differ in their factor endowments or technology.

2. **First mover advantage:** A firm that is the first to enter the world market has an advantage which other firms find it difficult to match. Such a firm is able to capture economies of scale ahead of later entrants and thus benefit from a lower cost structure. Some countries may dominate the export of certain products because they were the first to capture the economies of scale. For example, Airbus and Boeing dominate the exports of large Jet aircrafts.

   The new trade theory has important implications for international trade. It suggests that trade allows countries to specilise in the production of certain goods, reduces costs and prices through economies of scale and increases the variety of products available to consumers.

5.7 National Competitive Advantage

Michael Porter of the Harvard Business School believed that existing theories of international trade did not explain fully a country's competitiveness. For example, the theory of comparative advantage does not explain why Switzerland is more productive in the production of precision instruments than Great Britain or Germany. He carried out intensive research into 100 industries in 10 countries to determine why some nations succeed and others fail in international competition. He sought answers to questions like: Why does Japan excel in the automobile industry? Why does Switzerland do so well in the production and export of precision instruments and pharmaceuticals? Why does Germany and the United States succeed in the chemical industry? Porter published the results of his research in 1990.

According to Porter four main attributes determine a nation's environment in which domestic firms compete. These attributes determine the country's competitive advantage. These four attributes are as follows:

(*i*) Factor endowments—a country's factors of production such as infrastructure and skilled labour needed to compete in a given industry.

(*ii*) Demand conditions—the nature and volume of domestic demand for the product or service.

(*iii*) Related and supporting industries—the presence of supplier and related industries.

(*iv*) Firm strategy, structure and rivalry—the conditions governing the creation, organisation and management of companies and the nature of rivalry between domestic firms.

Porter has described these four attributes as the **diamond of national advantage.** These attributes are mutually interdependent as the effect of one attribute is dependent on the state of others. For example, favourable demand conditions will give competitive advantage only when the domestic rivalry is adequate. According to Porter chance and government can also influence the national diamond. Chance events like major innovations can modify industry structure. Government policies can alter demand conditions, factor endowments and domestic rivalry.

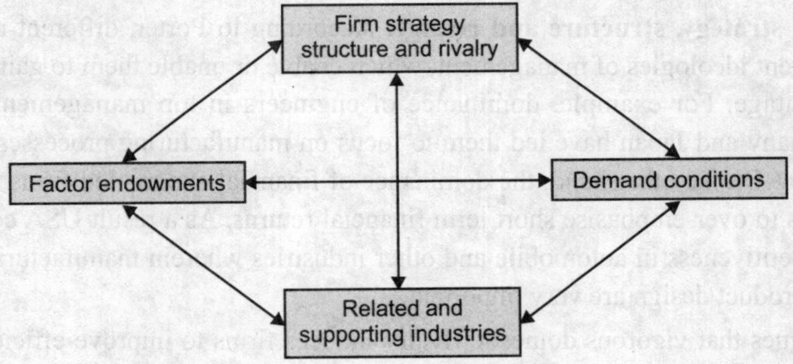

Fig. 5.2 Porter's Diamond of Competitive Advantage

1. **Factor endowments:** Porter identifies two types of factors—basic and advanced. **Basic factors** like natural resources, climate, location and demography are endowed by nature. **Advanced factors** such as infrastructure, skilled labour, research facilities and technical knowhow are developed by individuals, companies and the Government. Basic factors can provide an initial advantage but advanced factors are more important for gaining competitive advantage. Presence of suitable basic factors can be reinforced and extended by suitable investment in advanced factors. On the other hand, absence of basic factors may put pressure for investment in advanced factors to overcome the deficit. For instance, Japan which lacks the basic factors of arable land and mineral deposits has succeeded in manufacturing industries by creating a large pool of engineers.
2. **Demand conditions:** Conditions in the home market provide the necessary environment for the domestic firms to be competitive in world markets. Highly demanding and sophisticated consumers in the home market create pressure on the firms for innovation

and quality. A nation's firms gain competitive advantage through high standards of product quality and innovative products. For example, Japan's sophisticated and knowledgeable buyers of cameras encouraged the camera industry in Japan to improve product quality and to introduce innovative models. Similarly, sophisticated and demanding customers in Scandinavia pushed Nokia of Finland and Ericsson of Sweden to invest in cellular phone technology.

3. **Related and supporting industries:** The presence of internationally competitive suppliers and related industries helps a country's firms to be competitive. Firms operating in a well-knit network of related industries gain advantage through close working relationship, prompt exchange of materials and information and timeliness of product. When related industries invest in advanced factors, the benefits spill over to firms. For instance, Sweden's success in fabricated steel products (ball bearings and cutting tools) was due to its speciality steel industry. Similarly, technological leadership of the semiconductor industry in the United States provided the basis for its success in personal computers. According to Porter, successful industries within a country tend to be grouped into clusters of related industries. One such cluster was in Germany's textile and apparel sector consisting of high quality cotton, wool, synthetic fibres, sewing machine needles and textile machinery. Valuable knowledge flows between firms within a geographic cluster benefiting them all within that sector.
4. **Firm strategy, structure and rivalry:** According to Porter, different nations adopt different ideologies of management, which enable or unable them to gain competitive advantage. For example, dominance of engineers in top management of firms in Germany and Japan have led them to focus on manufacturing processes and product design. On the other hand, the dominance of financial experts led firms in the United States to over-emphasise short term financial returns. As a result USA could not gain competitiveness in automobile and other industries wherein manufacturing processes and product design are very important.

Porter argues that vigorous domestic rivalry induces firms to improve efficiency, quality, service, technology and to reduce costs. All this helps them to become world class competitors.

Evaluation: According to Porter all the four components must be present to boost international competitiveness. Government can influence all the four components either positively or negatively. Policies concerning subsidies, capital markets and education can influence factor endowments. Regulations about product standards and buyer needs affect domestic demand conditions. Government policies and regulations also influence supporting and related industries and firm rivalry.

Porter's theory seems to be applicable to the current trends in international trade. But its validity has not been tested empirically.

Each of the theories given above has an element of truth and can explain the trade pattern in some products. But none of them alone can explain all the reasons for international trade. Collectively, these theories provide valuable insights into the basis for international trade and its pattern.

SUMMARY

Mercantilism: A country should boost exports and restrict imports to accumulate gold and wield power. It is criticised as it views trade as a zero-sum game. Many countries now adopt neo-mercantilism

Absolute Cost Advantage Theory: Adam Smith ("Wealth of Nations", 1776) suggested that a country should specialise in goods which it can produce at less cost and exchange them with other goods. **Advantages:** (*a*) first theory that suggests free trade, (*b*) indicates what a country should export/import, (*c*) suggests trade is beneficial for the world as a whole. **Limitations:** (*a*) fails to explain when a country has absolute cost advantage in both the commodities or in none of them, (*b*) does not explain differences in productive capacities, (*c*) makes extreme predictions, (*d*) assumption of exchange ratio of 1:1 not always true.

Comparative Cost Advantage Theory: David Ricardo ("Principles of Political Economy", 1817) suggested that a country should specialise in goods in which it has a comparative cost advantage. **Advantage:** An improvement over absolute cost advantage theory. **Limitation:** Oversimplified and unrealistic assumptions.

Factor Endowment Theory: Eli Heckscher ("The Effect of Foreign Trade on the Distribution of Income", 1919) and Bertil Ohlin ("Interregional and International Trade," 1933) suggested that free trade is beneficial for all. A country should specialise in a commodity which its factor endowments favour. **Advantages:** (*a*) common sense appeal, (*b*) fewer simplifying assumptions.

Wassily Leontief Paradox (1953): Despite abundance of capital, USA exported less capital goods. Natural resources, trade barriers, technology differences between countries, etc. may be the reasons.

The Product Life-cycle Theory: Raymond Vernon (1966) suggested that over a time period a product undergoes different stages due to changes in knowledge, technology, information and costs. These stages are: new product, growth product, mature product. The production base, competitive advantage of a country and pattern of world trade keep on changing from one stage to another. **Advantages:** (*a*) focus on technological progress and product costs, (*b*) considers mobility of capital, (*c*) more accurate explanation of trade pattern, (*d*) explains link between investment and trade. **Limitations:** (*a*) several exceptions, (*b*) limited relevance in modern world.

New Trade Theory: Paul Krugman, Norman and Dixit (1970s) argue that trade takes place due to economies of scale. Trade leads to **cost reduction and product variety.** A firm enjoying the **first mover advantage** can capture economies of scale earlier than its rivals.

National Competitive Advantage: Michael Porter ("Competitive Advantage of Nations", 1990) has identified four attributes of National Diamond, namely: (*a*) factor endowments, (*b*) demand conditions, (*c*) related and supporting industries, (*d*) firm strategy, structure and rivalry. All the four attributes must be present to boost international competitiveness of a country. Government can have positive or negative influence on these attributes. Empirical validity of Porter's theory is yet to be tested.

TEST QUESTIONS

1. What is mercantilism? State its limitations.
2. Explain the Absolute Cost Advantage Theory of international trade, pointing out its advantages and limitations.
3. Discuss the Comparative Cost Advantage theory of international trade, pointing out its assumptions.
4. How far and in what way the Theory of Comparative Cost Advantage is an improvement over the Absolute Cost Advantage Theory.
5. Describe the sources of cost advantage to a country.
6. Explain the Factor Endowment Theory of International Trade.
7. What is meant by factor endowment? How does it explain international trade?
8. What is Leontief Paradox? Describe its significance.
9. Explain the Product Life-cycle Theory of International Trade. To what extent does it explain the pattern of international trade?
10. Discuss the New Trade Theory. Do you agree with its arguments?
11. Explain Michael Porter's Competitive Advantage of Nations as a theory of international trade.
12. Briefly describe the Product Life-cycle Theory of International Trade. How can you say that its assumptions and predictions are either unclear or do not fit in today's world?
13. Explain National Competitive Advantage Theory of International Trade.
14. How do factor endowments explain international trade patterns?
15. What is the factor proportions theory of international trade? How is it an improvement over the theory of comparative advantage?
16. What are the four elements in the diamond of Porter's theory of national competitive advantage?

CHAPTER 6

Commercial Policy Instruments—Tariff and Non-Tariff Measures

LEARNING OBJECTIVES

After studying this chapter, you should understand:

6.1 Meaning of Commercial Policy
6.2 Need for Commercial Policy
6.3 Commercial Policy of India
6.4 Instruments of Commercial Policy
6.5 Tariff Barriers
6.6 Non-tariff Barriers

- Summary
- Test Questions

6.1 Meaning of commercial Policy

Commercial policy is popularly known as trade policy. It refers to the policy of a country regarding its international trade. The government of each country formulates the commercial policy of the country. Commercial policy does not allow market forces to govern the country's foreign trade. In other words, commercial policy is designed to channelise the country's exports and imports in the desired direction.

The commercial policy of a country has an impact on the volume and composition of its foreign trade. It also influences the country's investment pattern, direction of development and consumption pattern. A country's commercial policy keeps on changing from time to time depending on its objectives and priorities.

Thus, commercial policy signifies Government intervention in foreign trade. It is contrary to the idea of free trade. It is inspired by national interest. It recognises the fact that in reality the world market is not perfect and completely free trade can be harmful to a country's consumers. The theory also points out that a country may become the dominant exporter of a commodity because its firms were the first to produce that commodity. The first mover's ability to benefit from economies of scale creates a barrier to entry of new firms. Thus, the new trade theory has suggested a new source of competitive advantage. Empirical studies seem to support the predictions of the new trade theory.

The new trade theory emphasises the role of luck, entrepreneurship and innovation in providing a firm first mover advantages. It argues that Boeing became the first mover in the manufacture of commercial jet aircraft due to luck and innovation. Dc Harilland and introduced its comet jet airliner two years before Boeing's first jet airliner. But comet was found to be technologically defective. Boeing's technical knownow was innovative. Moreover, US Government paid for the research and development cost of Boeing. The new trade theory suggests judicious use of subsidies for the Government to help the domestic firms become first movers in emerging industries. In this way, new trade theory seems to be in favour of a proactive trade policy.

6.2 Need For Commercial Policy

Every country needs a commercial policy due to the following reasons:

1. **Protection of Domestic Industries:** One of the major objectives of commercial policy is to protect the domestic industry from foreign competition. Such protection is all the more necessary in case of industries which are in the infant stage. For example, many small and medium industrial units have become sick due to the entry of foreign companies and imports of cheap products from China, Korea, etc.
2. **Strategic Consideration:** Government intervention is necessary to help domestic firm to enter foreign markets and get the first mover advantages. The Government should provide subsidies to those domestic firms which have a comparative cost advantage. Foreign companies may create entry barriers to the domestic firms even in the home country. For example, the US government helped the domestic firms when Japanese automobile firms created entry barriers.
3. **Protection of Jobs:** Economic liberalisation in India has led to the closure of several firms, downsizing of others, privatisation of public sector enterprises, and outsourcing of jobs. These have reduced job opportunities for the citizens. Government intervention is necessary to maintain employment opportunities in the country.
4. **National Security:** Strategic industries like defence, aerospace, railways, semiconductors, etc. are essential for the country's security. Government has to control imports and exports in these industries. For example, Government of India has reserved eight strategic industries even under the Industrial Policy of 1991. Excessive dependence on foreign countries for raw material or finished products may be dangerous to the country.
5. **Balanced Development:** Under free trade, a country may specialise only in some industries and totally neglect other industries and sectors. Such lopsided development has several undesirable economic, social and political implications for a country. Commercial policy is needed to ensure balanced development of all sectors of the national economy.
6. **To Check Imports of Harmful Goods:** Free trade may result in import of harmful and inferior products which have adverse impact on the health, safety and welfare of people. Commercial policy can stop such harmful imports.
7. **To Control Foreign Monopoly:** Free trade may encourage emergence of monopolies. Such monopolies hamper the growth of industries and reduce community welfare. For

example, Coca-Cola and Pepsi dominate the soft drinks industry in India. Government intervention is suggested by economists and politicians to check such monopolies.

8. **To Check Dumping:** Countries with better factor endowments may flood the domestic market with low priced goods. Such dumping leads to closing down of local industries. Commercial policy is needed to check the threat of dumping. However, WTO agreements provide safeguards against dumping.
9. **Economic Instability:** Free international trade can lead to economic instability. Trade cycles affect open economies. For example, the Great Depression of 1930s which began in the United States spread to many countries except the erstwhile USSR which was a closed economy.

6.3 Commercial Policy of India

From 1947 to 1991 India followed an inward-looking commercial policy. The policy focussed on import substitution and export promotion. Quantitative restrictions, tariffs, import licensing, local content requirement, phased manufacturing, export obligation and foreign exchange regulations were used to achieve these objectives. Import substitution and protection of domestic industries had several adverse effects such as inefficiency, poor quality levels, high input costs, lack of innovations, etc. As a result exports suffered and trade deficit increased.

In July 1991 commercial policy reforms were announced as an integral part of economic liberalisation. Restrictions on entry of foreign firms, foreign investment and imports were removed. Since then Government of India announces a Five-Year Export-Import policy or foreign trade policy. The preamble to the Foreign Trade Policy 2004-2009 states, "For India to become a major player in world trade, an all-encompassing, comprehensive view needs to be taken for the overall development of the country's foreign trade. While increase in exports is of vital importance, we have also to facilitate those imports which are required to stimulate our economy. Coherence and consistency among trade and other economic policies is important for maximising the contribution of such policies to development. Thus, while incorporating the existing practice of enunciating an annual Exim Policy, it is necessary to go much beyond and take an integrated approach to the development requirements of India's foreign trade. This is the context of new Foreign Trade Policy."

The policy aimed at doubling the country's foreign trade and to generate employment. The Foreign Trade (Development and Regulation) Act 1992 replaced the Imports and Exports (Control) Act 1947. The objective of the Foreign Trade (Development and Regulation) Act is to provide for development and regulations of India's foreign trade by facilitating imports into and augmenting exports from India

Thus, there have been significant changes in India's commercial policy

6.4 Instruments of Commercial Policy

A country's commercial policy contains several measures that are designed to protect domestic industries and the economy from the competition of foreign companies. The protective measures are known as the instruments of commercial policy. They are also called **trade** *barriers* as these restrict free trade between countries. Trade barriers are classified into two broad categories:

1. Tariff barriers, and
2. Non-tariff barriers.

6.5 Tariff Barriers

Tariff means the taxes or duties imposed on imports and exports. Import duties are more common than export duties. In India customs duty is a tariff that is levied on several goods imported into the country. It is imposed on a few items of exports from India.

Types: Tariff can be based on quantity or value of imports. When a specified amount of tariff is charged per unit of the product (*e.g.,* ₹ 100 per tonne of cement) it is called **specific duty.** Tariff levied as a percentage of the product's value (*e.g.,* 10% of the value of cement) is known as **ad *valorem* duty.** A **compound duty** is a tariff that combines both per unit and percentage of value (*e.g.,* ₹ 100 per tonne plus 10 per cent of the value of cement imported).

Objectives: Import duty is levied to achieve the following objectives:

(*i*) to curb import of a commodity

(*ii*) to increase government revenue

(*iii*) to discourage or encourage imports from a particular country.

Importance: Import duties (tariffs) provide gains to the following:

1. As imports become costlier, the domestic industry is protected and its products find a wider market.
2. Government of the imposing country earns revenue.
3. Jobs in the domestic industry are protected.
4. Ancillary industry, servicing firms and market intermediaries are also protected.

Tariffs have **adverse effects** on the following:

(*i*) Consumers have to pay higher price for the product. They have to pay for the inefficiency of the domestic industry.

(*ii*) The industry of the exporting country loses sales and profits.

(*iii*) There is inefficient utilisation of resources due to elimination of competition.

(*iv*) The exporting country may take retaliatory action.

According to Prof. Kindleberger, tariffs are likely to alter trade, prices, output and consumption. They reallocate resources, change factor proportions, redistribute income, change employment, and alter the balance of payments.

Tariff levels in general have declined due to trade negotiations under the World Trade Organisation (WTO).

6.6 Non-Tariff Barriers

Non-tariff barriers are described as new protectionism measures as against tariffs which are considered traditional barriers. Some important non-tariff barriers are described below:

1. **Ban on Imports:** The import of selected items may be prohibited in a country. The purpose may be to protect the domestic industries which have lost international competitiveness or which are politically sensitive.

2. **Import Licensing:** Under this system, those who want to import are required to obtain a licence. In several countries including India import licensing system was used to control the total volume of imports. Exports of certain products may also be regulated through licensing.

3. **Quotas:** Quantitative restrictions in the form of import quotas and export quotas are traditional methods of restricting foreign trade. A quota on the import of a product may be fixed to protect domestic producers or to conserve the country's foreign exchange resources. Similarly, exports of a product may be restricted to protect the interests of domestic consumers. Too much exports of a commodity may create its scarcity and local consumers may have to pay a higher price for it. Sometimes, export and import quotas are fixed due to international commodity agreements.

   Quota is considered worse than tariff. Tariff increases the price of the imported product but import can continue so long as consumers are willing to pay a higher price for foreign goods. Therefore, domestic producers have to maintain prices to increase their sales. But under quota system, the supply of the imported commodity is restricted. As a result there is no pressure on the domestic producers to keep prices at a competitive level. Consumers have to bear the entire burden of higher prices. Secondly, tariff generates revenue for the country while quota generates no such revenue. Only the importers gain by selling the commodity at higher prices. Moreover, implementation of quota system is much more difficult than that of tariff system.

4. **Voluntary Export Restraint:** Quotas may provoke the exporting country to retaliate against the importing country. To avoid this danger, countries resort to voluntary export restraint. It is a bilateral agreement between two governments under which the exporting country voluntarily agrees to restrict exports of the specified commodity to the importing country at the specified level. For example, in 1980s Japan agreed to voluntarily restrict the exports of automobiles to the United States to 1.85 million vehicles per year. A voluntary export restraint is adopted under pressure from the importing country.

   Like a quota, a voluntary export restraint is a quantitative restriction. But voluntary export restraint is better than quota due to two reasons. **First,** it is easier to lift a voluntary export restraint then a quota. **Second**, unlike quota, voluntary export restraint does not spoil political relations between countries as it is the result of a mutual agreement between them.

5. **Exchange Control:** The Government may control the foreign exchange transactions of the country in the following ways:

   (*a*) Exchange Restrictions: Under this form of exchange control, the Government restricts the supply of foreign currency to the importers. All trading in foreign exchange is centralised with the Government or the country's central bank. Exchange of national currency for foreign currencies requires prior permission of the Government. Exchange restrictions can be made in the following two forms:

(*i*) **Blocked Accounts:** The Government keeps the amounts payble to a foreign country's firms in their accounts. The foreign creditor can use the amount only to buy goods from the country blocking the accounts. The amounts cannot be converted into the currencies of the foreigners. Blocked accounts take away the freedom of foreign creditors to use their assets in any other currency for any other purpose. Moreover, blocked accounts reduce international trade because the foreign country would not like to export to the country that blocks funds. Blocking of accounts also leads to black marketing of foreign exchange as the foreigners whose accounts are blocked may sell it to others at lower rates.

(*ii*) **Multiple Exchange Rates:** In order to discourage imports or encourage exports, the Government of a country may fix different exchange rates for transactions in different commodities and also for different currencies. An unfavourable rate of exchange for imports will make imports more costly. When the Government wants to control the direction of the country's trade, it may fix different rates for different currencies. For instance, if the Government of India wants more imports from sterling countries and more exports to dollar countries, it may fix the rupee at ₹ 80 per British pound and ₹ 50 per US dollar while the dollar sterling rate of exchange is 2 US dollars per British pound. The Government may adopt different exchange rates for current account and capital account transactions to prevent flight of capital from the country.

Multiple exchange rates help to improve the country's balance of payments by restricting imports and boosting exports. But the system is complex and confusing because over time the number of exchange rates increase and are purely arbitrary. They create uncertainty and cause inefficient use of domestic resources. The multiple rate system is discriminatory and, therefore, the International Monetary Fund (IMF) disapproves it.

(*b*) **Exchange Intervention:** The Government of a country may buy and sell foreign exchange to influence the exchange rate in the market. Such intervention seeks to keep the exchange rate at the desired level. In a country with deficit balance of payment, the exchange value of the domestic currency falls as its supply exceeds its demand. The Government starts buying the domestic currency to maintain its exchange value. This process is called **Pegging up** but it requires large reserves of foreign currency. On the other hand, a surplus balance of payment may result in rise in the exchange value of domestic currency. In this situation the Government starts selling the domestic currency to prevent increase in its exchange value. This is known as **Pegging down** but it may lend to inflation due to excessive money supply. However, Pegging down is easier than Pegging up because the Government can issue domestic currency without any limit.

(*c*) **Exchange Clearing Arrangement:** Under this system, two countries engaged in trade with each other settle their dues through their respective central banks instead of allowing direct payment between buyers and sellers. Suppose India and the United Kingdom enter into an exchange clearing arrangement. The Reserve Bank of India will open an account in the name of Bank of England. All Indian firms who import goods from the United Kingdom will be required to deposit the amount into Bank of England's account with the Reserve Bank of India. Similarly, all exports by Indian firms to England will be paid from this account. Such bilateral settlement of mutual claims is based on the assumption that the import and export between nations would offset each other.

Unlike exchange restrictions, exchange clearing arrangement does not restrict international trade. As there is no need to find foreign exchange, countries can import even without having foreign exchange reserves. But exchange clearing arrangement suffers from several **limitations. First,** economically strong country may use the system to exploit the weaker country by blocking the latter's funds. **Secondly,** it replaces multilateral trade with bilateral trade. The countries having the bilateral arrangement gain at the cost of other countries which are not parties to such arrangements. **Thirdly,** such arrangements interfere with the working of foreign exchange markets.

6. **Fiscal Barriers:** Fiscal barriers are used to protect the domestic industry from unduly cheap imports. Anti-dumping duties and countervailing duties are the two main fiscal barriers.

   (*a*) **Anti-dumping duties:** These are imposed to counteract dumping by foreign suppliers. Dumping means selling of goods in a foreign market at a price lower than that charged in the domestic market. Firms use dumping either to sell their excess output in a foreign market or to dislodge local competition. When domestic firm fails to compete and closes down, the dumping firm will raise the price to exploit the market. Government imposes anti-dumping duty to save the domestic industry from such attempts.

   (*b*) **Countervailing duties:** These duties are levied when the imported goods are cheaper because the exporting country offers subsidies. The countervailing duty cancels out the impact of subsidy and domestic goods can compete with the imported goods.

7. **Administrative and Technical Regulations:** These include the following measures:

   (*a*) **Administrative regulations:** These regulations are meant to make importing a frustrating experience and thereby restrict imports. Requiring the importers to fill in long and complicated form, delay and red tape in customs clearance, elaborate and expensive import licensing procedure, complicated procedures for obtaining permit, stipulating that samples of the product be submitted along with application for import licence, long delays in the clearance of documents, concentration of all imports at one port to create congestion are examples of administrative measures. These measures and procedures involve delay, cost and uncertainty thereby hampering imports.

   (*b*) **Technical regulations:** These consist of health and safety regulations, sanitary regulations, packing and labelling requirements, industrial standards, etc. These regulations increase the cost to foreign exporters. The condition that the product will be tested and certified only in the importing country is cumbersome and expensive for the exporter. Standards laid down for imported goods protect the citizens of the importing country against substandard and hazardous products. The Government may prescribe unusually high standards to discourage imports.

(*c*) **Local content requirement:** It specifies that the prescribed proportion of the final product will be produced in the importing country. It provides protection to domestic industry and raises the cost to the exporter. It may also be stipulated that the foreign ownership in a domestic firm will not exceed the specified limit (*e.g.*, 49 per cent). This requirement will restrict foreign investment.

(*d*) **Minimum deposit requirement:** Under it, the importer is required to deposit with the government a substantial value of the imports. The deposit may be for the period of import licence and carries no interest.

(*e*) **Reciprocal arrangements:** The Government may stipulate that imports will be paid for by exports rather than in cash. This is called counter-trade arrangement and is adopted mainly in case of high value transactions. Counter-trade may create problem for exporters as they do not get cash for their exports and have to make imports.

8. **State Trading:** In its procurement programme, the Government gives preference to domestic suppliers. The country's law allows the state to accept tenders from domestic firms even when the prices quoted by foreign suppliers are lower. In some nations, the Government invites tenders only from domestic firms.

9. **Export Subsidies:** The purpose of giving export subsidies is to boost the country's exports. These subsidies make it more remunerative for exporters to sell abroad than selling in the domestic market. Various forms of export subsidies are as follows:

   (*a*) cash payment for every unit of export

   (*b*) refund of duties paid on imports

   (*c*) priority in the allotment of scarce raw materials

   (*d*) finance to exporters at lower interest rate

   (*e*) tax concessions for exports

   (*f*) grants for market survey, market research, participation in trade fairs, etc.

   (*g*) domestic procurement at support prices and exporting them at low prices

   (*h*) financing the imports at lower interest rate

   (*i*) grants for research and development.

Export subsidies not only promote exports but also generate employment. These subsidies are most common for agricultural exports. Subsidies are particularly advisable in case of emerging industries because these can help the domestic firms in becoming internationally competitive and in obtaining early mover advantage.

Export subsidies are opposed on the ground that these benefit the importing country at the cost of the exporting country. These subsidies also encourage inefficiency and excess production.

Hold of Non-Tariff Barriers

Among the non-tariff measures (NTMs), technical barriers are the most pervasive, affecting about 20% of product lines and 60% of world trade. Other types of measures are applicable to around 20% of world trade.

Non-Tariff Measures in World Trade (2012)

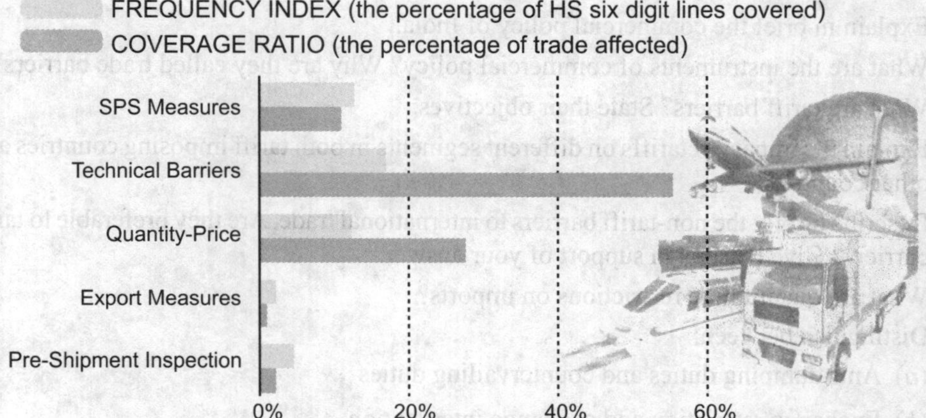

What is interesting is that the use of technical NTMs increases with the level of GDP per capita, while that of non-technical measures decreases. Other measures affect international trade more marginally as their use is specific to serve particular sectors or they are employed by a specific group of countries.

Source: Unctad

SUMMARY

Meaning: Commercial policy or trade policy means Government policy concerning the country's international trade.

Need: (*i*) to protect domestic industries (*ii*) for strategic consideration (*iii*) to protect jobs (*iv*) for national security (*v*) balanced development (*vi*) to check imports of harmful goods (*vii*) to control foreign monopoly (*viii*) to prevent dumping (*ix*) for economic stability.

India's Policy: (1) from 1947 to 1991–inward-looking focus on import substitution and export promotion **(2) 1991 onwards**–free trade with focus on export promotion.

Instruments: (1) Tariffs, (2) Non-tariff barriers

Tariff Barriers: (1) Types–specific, ad valorem, and compound (2) **Objectives**–to check imports and increase government revenue **(3) Impact**–costlier imports, government revenue, domestic jobs, ancillary industry gain. But higher prices for consumers, inefficient resource use, less competition, retaliation by exporting nation. Tariff barriers declining under WTO

Non-Tariff Barriers: (*i*) Ban on import (*ii*) import licensing (*iii*) quotas (*iv*) voluntary export restraint (*v*) exchange control–blocked account, multiple exchange rate, exchange intervention (Pegging up and down), exchange clearing arrangement (*vi*) fiscal barriers–anti-dumping duties, countervailing duties (*vii*) administrative and technical regulations.

administrative, technical, local content requirement, minimum deposit requirement, reciprocal arrangement (*ix*) State trading (*x*) export subsidies.

TEST QUESTIONS

1. What is meant by the term 'commercial policy'? Why does a country need to formulate its own commercial policy?
2. Explain in brief the commercial policy of India.
3. What are the instruments of commercial policy? Why are they called trade barriers"?
4. What are tariff barriers? State their objectives.
5. Explain the impact of tariffs on different segments in both tariff imposing countries and other countries.
6. Describe briefly the non-tariff barriers to international trade. Are they preferable to tariff barriers? Give reasons in support of your answer.
7. What are quantitative restrictions on imports?
8. Distinguish between:
   (*a*) Anti-dumping duties and countervailing duties
   (*b*) Exchange restriction and exchange intervention
9. Write notes on:
   (*a*) Voluntary export restraint
   (*b*) Exchange clearing agreement
   (*c*) Export subsidies
10. Explain the role of administrative and technical regulations as barriers to international trade.
11. Why export subsidies are opposed?
12. Why do countries practise protectionism?
13. "Free market access is blocked by both developed and developing countries in very many ways". Explain the statement.
14. Explain, how counter-trade is different from multilateral trade? What are the different types of counter-trade? What are its merits and demerits?
15. What are the different forms of tariff? How is tariff different from quota ? Explain the impact of tariff.
16. Explain the advantages and disadvantages of tariffs and quotas.
17. Explain the various tariff and non-tariff measures adopted by countries to regulate international trade.
18. (*a*) What are the various non-tariff barriers that are adopted by countries to regulate international trade?
    (*b*) What do you understand by the infant industry argument put forward in favour of government intervention in international trade?

CHAPTER

7 Balance of Payment Account

LEARNING OBJECTIVES

After studying this chapter, you should understand:

7.1 Meaning of Balance of Payment Account

7.2 Difference between Balance of Trade and Balance of Payment

7.3 Components of Balance of Payment Account

7.4 Causes of Disequilibrium in Balance of Payment Account

7.5 Measures to Correct Disequilibrium in Balance of Payment Account

- Summary
- Test Questions

A country's residents enter into transactions with the residents of other countries. These transactions include imports and exports of goods and services, investments made abroad, interest on such investments, etc. These economic transactions influence a country's economy. They have an impact on price level, growth, employment, purchasing power, etc. in the country. These factors in turn influence the Government's monetary and fiscal policies. Every country prepares a summary of all these transactions. Such a summary is known as balance of payments (BOP) account.

7.1 Meaning of Balance of Payment Account

Balance of payment account is a statement that summarises a country's economic transactions with other countries of the world during a specific time period. According to the Reserve Bank of India, BPO is a statistical statement that systematically summarises, for a specific time period, the economic transactions of an economy with the rest of the world.

The IMF publication *Balance of Payments Manual* describes the concept of balance of payments as follows:

The balance of payments is a statistical statement for a given period showing:

1. Transactions in goods and services and income between an economy and the rest of the world.
2. Changes of ownership and other changes in that country's monetary gold, Special

Drawing Rights (SDRs) and claims on and liabilities to the rest of the world.

3. Unequited transfers and counterpart entries that are needed to balance, in the accounting sense, any entries for the foregoing transactions and changes which are not mutually offsetting.

The balance of payments has the following **characteristics:**

1. **Summary:** Balance of payment account is a summary prepared according to the double entry system of accounting. It has two sides — debit and credit, like any other account.
2. **Economic Transactions:** The summary is of economic transactions of a country with the rest of the world. These transactions involve receipts on account of exports of goods and services, and capital received by residents; and payments made for imports of goods and services, capital transferred to non-residents/foreigners; income on investments remitted abroad or received from aboard; and increase or decrease in the international reserves of the country.
3. **Country with Rest of the World:** Balance of payment contains transaction between a country with other countries; Transactions between the residents of the same country are not included in it. However, increase in a country's monetary gold and foreign assets exchanged between residents may be included in the balance of payment account.
4. **A Flow Statement:** Balance of payment account is a compilation of the flow of economic transactions. It is not a statement of the position on a particular date. It is more like a funds flow statement rather than like a balance sheet.
5. **Definite Time Period:** Balance of payment account covers a specific time period, usually one year. However, it may be prepared for shorter time period such as six months, three months or even one month depending upon a country's requirement.
6. **Double Entry System:** Transactions in BOP are recorded as per the double entry system of bookkeeping. Each transaction results in a debit entry and credit entry of equal account. Therefore, balance of payment account must always balance. The total amount of debits must equal the total amount of credits. In some cases, the balancing item **errors** and *omissions* is added to balance the BOP account.

7.2 Difference Between Balance of Trade and Balance of Payment

The balance of trade is a narrow concept. It covers only the transactions arising out of the exports and imports of **visible** items (goods). It does not include the exports and imports of **invisible** items (services) like banking, insurance, transport, tourism, interest, dividends, salaries.

The balance of payments, on the other hand, takes into account the exports and imports of both visible and invisible items (goods and services).

Thus, balance of payments is a much wider term than balance of trade. The balance of payments presents a comprehensive account of economic and financial transactions of a country with the rest of the world.

7.3 Components of balance of Payment Account

The various items recorded in the balance of payment account can be classified under the following heads:

1. Current Account
2. Capital Account
3. Unilateral Payments Account
4. Official Reserves/Assets Account

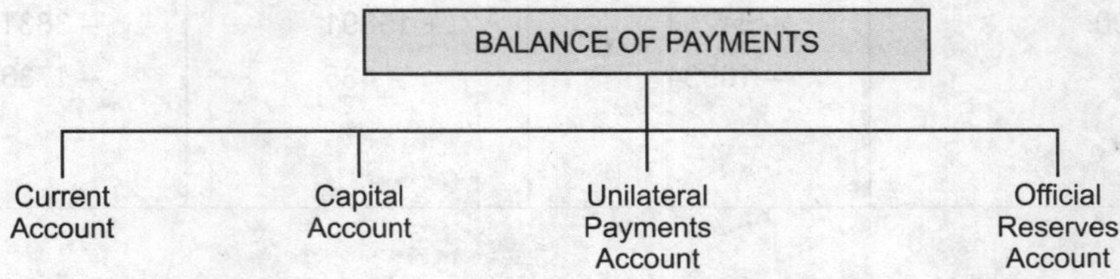

Fig. 7.1. Components of Balance of Payments

Current Account: The current account includes all transactions that increase or decrease the country's national income. It consists of two major groups of items— (*a*) visible or merchandise exports and imports, and (*b*) invisible or service exports and imports. **Merchandise exports** or sale of goods abroad are **credit** entries because these create monetary claims on foreigners. On the other hand, **merchandise imports** or purchase of goods from abroad are **debit** entries because these create money claims of foreigners on the home country.

Invisible exports or sale of services abroad are **credit** entries while invisible imports or purchase of services from aboard are **debit** entries. Invisible exports include sale of services to foreigners. Transportation, insurance, tourism, banking, financial services, salaries, interests and dividends received on loans and investments abroad/are included in invisible exports. Invisible imports include the purchase of services like insurance, tourism, transportation, banking, financial services; and salaries, interests and dividends paid to foreigners.

Various items included in the current account are shown in Table 7.1.

Table 7.1 : Items Under Current Account

Debits	Credits
1. Merchandise Imports (purchase of goods)	1. Merchandise Exports (sale of goods)
2. Invisible Imports (purchase of services)	2. Invisible Exports (sale of services)
(*a*) Transport services	(*a*) Transport services
(*b*) Tourism services	(*b*) Tourism services
(*c*) Insurance services	(*c*) Insurance services
(*d*) Other services	(*d*) Other services
(*e*) Interest and dividend paid on foreign loans and investments	(*e*) Interest and dividend received on loans and investments made abroad
(*f*) Salaries and fees paid to foreigners	(*f*) Salaries and fees received from abroad

Table 7.2 : India's Current Account Since 1951 (₹ crores)

Period	Trade Balance	Not Invisibles	Balance
First Plan (1951–56)	– 542	+ 500	– 42
Second Plan (1956–61)	– 2339	+ 614	– 1725
Third Plan (1961–66)	– 2382	+ 431	– 1951
1966–69	– 2067	+ 52	– 2015
Fourth Plan	– 1564	+ 1664	+ 100
Fifth Plan	– 3179	+ 6221	+ 3082
Sixth Plan	– 30456	+ 19072	– 11384
1985–1990	– 54204	+ 15891	– 38313
1990–91	– 16934	– 435	– 17369
2000–01			
2010–11			

The current account balance indicates the difference between inflows and outflows of the value of the flows of goods, services, income and gifts. When inflows are more than outflows, the current account is said to be positive. A current account surplus means the country has net foreign investment *i.e.,* it is a net lender or investor abroad. Its savings are more than its domestic investment and its total production exceeds its total consumption. On the other hand, when outflows exceed inflows, current account is said to be negative. A deficit current account means the country is a net borrower from abroad, its domestic savings are less than its domestic investment, and the country's expenditure exceeds its production.

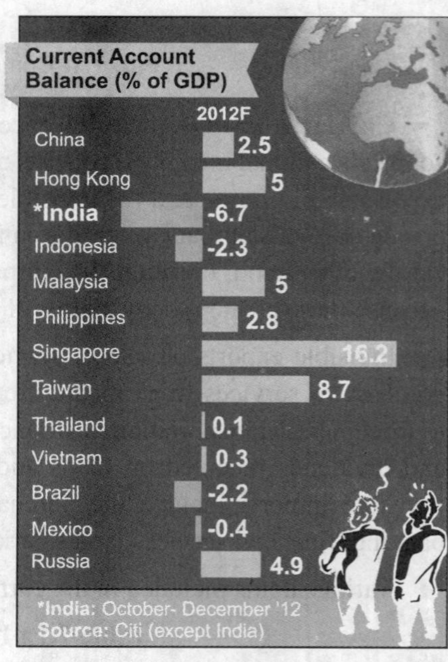

Saving up for a Rainy Day: Current Account Deficit as % of GDP

3.8	4.2	4.3	4.4	3.9	5.4	6.7
Q1 '12	Q2 '12	Q3 '12	Q4 '12	Q1 '13	Q2 '13	Q3 '13

Source: Yes Bank

The large current account deficit essentially underscores that the economy is still in a serious shortage of domestic savings. In that sense we are living beyond our means because much of the rise in CAD is not because investment is surging so that in the future we will be in a stronger position to pay back the current borrowing as growth rises back to the 9% levels.

- **India's current** account deficit is at a record 6.7% of GDP

- **Global portfollo** investors, who are funding the CAD, are fickle, while stable flows like FDIs are slowing
- **The large** CAD points to a shortage of domestic savings
- **Policy makers** blame low savings on people's fetish for assets such as gold
- **Even as** deposit growth is slowing. RBl cut key policy rates to boost growth

2. **Capital Account:** Capital account is divided into three parts—(*a*) private capital, (*b*) banking capital, and (*c*) official capital

   The private account includes short term and long term capital transactions. Short term capital is with a maturity period of one year whereas long term capital has a maturity period of more than one year. Long term capital consists of foreign investments (both direct and indirect), long term loans, foreign currency deposits, etc.

   Banking capital includes movements in the external financial assets and liabilities of commercial banks and cooperative banks which are authorised to deal in foreign exchange.

   Official capital refers to Reserve Bank of India's holdings in foreign currency and Special Drawing Rights with the Government.

   Inflows of capital from abroad are treated as credit items whereas capital inflows from the home country are treated as debit items. For example, if Tata Motors invests ₹ 500 crore in the United Kingdom, it will appear as a debit entry in India's balance of payment and as a credit item in the balance of payment of the United Kingdom.

3. **Unilateral Transfers Account:** Private remittances, government grants, repo ratings, disaster relief and gifts are included in the unilateral transfers account. Unilateral payments made to foreign countries are debits and unilateral payments received from abroad are credits.

4. **Official Reserves Account:** Government's holdings or means of payment held by official agencies that are generally accepted for the settlement of international claims are included in the official reserves account. These are official purchases and sales of foreign currencies and other reserves.

Table 7.4 : Capital Account and Other Non-Current Inflows and Outflows

Capital Account Debits	Capital Account Credits
1. Long-term investments abroad (less redemptions and repayments)	1. Foreign long-term investments in the home country (less redemptions and repayments)
(*a*) Direct investments abroad	(*a*) Direct investments in the home country
(*b*) Investments in foreign securities	(*b*) Foreign investments in domestic securities
(*c*) Other investments abroad	(*c*) Other investments of foreigners in the home country
(*d*) Government loans to foreign countries.	(*d*) Foreign Governments' loans to the home country.

2. Short-term investments abroad.	2. Foreign short-term investments in the home country.
Unilateral Transfers Account	**Unilateral Transfers Account**
1. Private remittances abroad	1. Private remittances received from abroad
2. Pension payments abroad	2. Pension payments received from abroad
3. Government grants abroad	3. Government grants received from abroad
Official Settlements Account	**Official Settlements Account**
1. Official purchases of foreign currencies or other service assets.	1. Official sales of foreign currencies or other reserve assets abroad.

Table 7.5 : India's Balance of Payments

(US $ million)

	1990–91	2000–01	2010–11
Exports	18477	45452	
Imports	27915	57912	
Trade balance	– 9438	– 12460	
Invisibles (net)	– 242	9794	
Non-factor services	980	1692	
Income	– 3752	– 5004	
Private transfers	2069	12854	
Goods and services balance	– 8458	– 10768	
Current account balance	– 9680	– 2666	
External assistance (net)	2264	410	
Commercial borrowing (net)	2254	4303	
Non-resident deposits (net)	1537	2316	
Foreign investment (net)	103	5862	
Other flows (net)	1090	– 4356	
Capital Account total (net)	7188	8535	
Reserve	1278	– 5842	

Source: RBI

7.4 Causes of Disequilibrium in Balance of Payment

The balance of payments of a country is said to be in equilibrium when the demand for and supply of foreign currency are equal. Disequilibrium in balance of payments means either a surplus or deficit in it. When the demand for foreign currency exceeds its supply there will be a **deficit** in the balance of payments. A **surplus** in the balance of payments means the supply of foreign currency exceeds its demand.

Disequilibrium in the balance of payments is caused by the following factors:

1. **Economic Factors:** These include the following:

   (*a*) **Development Disequilibrium:** Developing countries undertake heavy expenditure on the development of industries, power plants, bridges, roads, ports, hospitals, universities, etc. These developmental activities require huge imports of machinery, equipment and other capital goods. In addition, such developmental activities increase income and demand and imports of consumer goods. Large scale imports of capital goods and consumer goods result in deficit in the balance of payments.

   (*b*) **Cyclical Disequilibrium:** Such disequilibrium arises due to fluctuations in imports and exports caused by business cycles. The boom in business activity in a country increases aggregate demand, consumption and prices. The country imports more consumer goods to meet the increase in demand. It also increases imports of capital goods to expand production. On the other hand, depression in a country leads to increase in its exports because production exceeds home demand. Thus, both boom and depression create disequilibrium in the balance of payments.

   (*c*) **Secular Disequilibrium:** Disequilibrium in a country's balance of payments persists for long periods due to secular trends in its economy. In a developed country like the United States, disposable incomes and aggregate demand are generally very high. At the same time, costs of production are high on account of high wage rates. High costs result in higher prices. Therefore, the country imports goods from other countries where quality goods are produced at lower costs. Huge imports creates a deficit in the balance of payments of even a developed country like USA.

   (*d*) **Structural Disequilibrium:** Structural changes in the economy include shift from agriculture to service sector, development of alternative sources of supply development of better substitutes, exhaustion of productive resources, changes in transport routes and costs. These structural changes increase the imports of both capital goods and consumer goods, causing a deficit in the balance of payments.

2. **Political Factors:** Political instability, civil war, riots, terrorism, external war and such other political disturbances create a threat for industry and investment. These factors may lead to large capital outflows and decline in domestic production and exports. Sri Lanka, Pakistan, Bangladesh and Nepal have faced such a situation.

3. **Sociological Factors:** Changes in tastes, preferences, fashions may affect imports and exports which in turn create disequilibrium in the balance of payments.

7.5 Measures to Correct Disequilibrium in Balance of Payments

A country having surplus in its balance of payments may not be worried. But a country facing continuous deficit in its balance of payments takes steps to reduce or eliminate the deficit. The measures taken to correct disequilibrium in balance of payments are divided into two broad categories (Fig. 7.2).

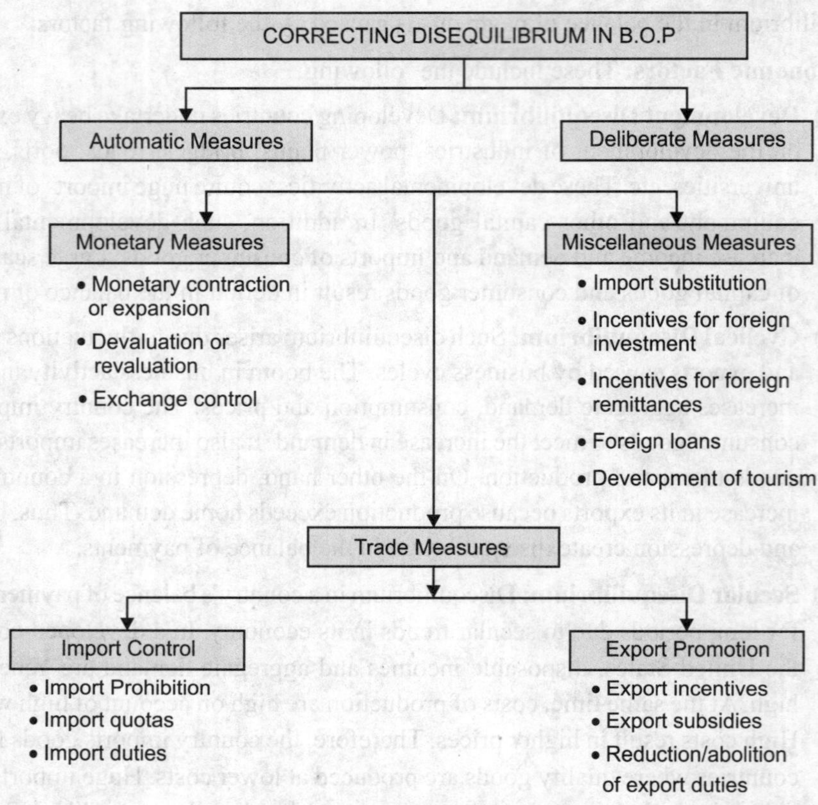

Fig. 7.2. Measures to Correct BOP Disequilibrium

1. **Automatic Correction:** Here the assumption is that if the market forces of demand and supply are allowed to play freely, in course of time, equilibrium in BOP will be automatically achieved. Suppose, India is facing deficit in its balance of payments. The demand for foreign currency exceeds its supply. This will increase the exchange rate and a fall in the external value of rupee. This will make India's exports cheaper and its imports more costly. As a result the increase in the country's exports and decrease in imports will ultimately restore equilibrium in the balance of payments.

2. **Deliberate Measures:** When the disequilibrium is not corrected automatically, deliberate steps are taken. These measures are as follows:

   (*i*) **Monetary Measures:** These are as under:

   (*a*) **Reduction/expansion of money supply:** Deficit in balance of payments can be corrected by reducing money supply in the economy. The country's central bank (*e.g.,* the Reserve Bank of India) reduces money supply through techniques like bank rate, open market operation, Statutory Liquidity Ratio (SLR), Cash Reserve Ratio (CRR), etc. Reduction in money supply leads to a fall in domestic demand and prices. This in turn increases exports and decreases imports thereby reducing the deficit. Similarly, money supply can be expanded to reduce surplus in the balance of payments.

(*b*) **Devaluation:** A country having considerable deficit in its balance of payments may devalue its currency to encourage exports and discourage imports. Devaluation means reduction in the official exchange rate of a currency. For example, Government of India devalued the rupee from ₹ 35 per US $ to ₹ 45 per US $.

(*c*) **Exchange Control:** Under this method the Government or the country's central bank exercises complete control over the foreign exchange reserves and earnings of the country. The exporters are required to surrender foreign exchange for the Reserve Bank of India in exchange in domestic currency (₹). Importers need prior permission of the Reserve Bank of India to use foreign exchange. In this way, the Government controls the imports to reduce deficit in the balance of payments.

(*ii*) **Trade Measures:** These include export promotion measures and import control measures.

(*a*) **Export Promotion:** A country may boost its exports by reducing or abolishing export duties, providing export subsidy; encouraging export promotion and marketing through monetary, fiscal, institutional and physical incentives and facilities. For example, Government of India offers liberal loans and other facilities to export-oriented units. It has set up export processing zones.

(*b*) **Import Control:** Imports are controlled by imposing or increasing import duties, fixing import quotas, import licensing, and prohibiting altogether the imports of certain non-essential items.

(*iii*) **Miscellaneous Measures:** These include raising foreign currency loans, encouraging foreign investment in the home country, developing tourism to attract foreign tourists, and giving incentives to encourage foreign remittances.

SUMMARY

Meaning: BP account is a summary of a country's economic transactions with other countries during a specified time period.

Characteristics: Summary, economic transactions, rest of the world, a flow statement, definite time period, double entry system.

BP vs. B/T: BP is a wider term than B/T which contains imports and exports of goods only.

Components: (*i*) current account, (*ii*) capital account, (*iii*) unilateral payments account, (*iv*) official reserves account

Causes of Disequilibrium: (*i*) Economic factors (development, cyclical, secular, structural), (*ii*) political factors, (*iii*) sociological factors

Measures for Correction: 1. Automatic correction, 2. Deliberate correction (money supply, devaluation, exchange control, export promotion, import control), 3. Miscellancons measures.

TEST QUESTIONS

1. What is meant by 'Balance of Payments'? Differentiate between Balance of Payments and Balance of Trade.
2. Explain the features that characterise balance of payments.
3. What are the components of balance of payments?
4. What is Current Account? Explain the different items in the current account.
5. What is Capital Account? Explain the items included in it.
6. Explain the causes of disequilibrium in the balance of payments.
7. Discuss the measures that are taken to correct disequilibrium in the balance of payments.
8. "Effective management of disequilibrium in the balance of payments is helpful in the growth of international business." Do you agree? Give reasons for your answer.
9. "The balance of payments crisis of 1990 led to economic liberalisation in India." Elucidate.
10. Writes notes on:
    (*a*) Unilateral Transfers Account
    (*b*) Official Reserves Account
    (*c*) Exchange Control
    (*d*) Devaluation
11. Why must a country's BOP always be balanced in an accounting sense?
12. How do we calculate current account balance, capital and finance account balance and statistical discrepancy balance?
13. Explain the position when the current account deficit is lower than the trade deficit. Discuss the absorption approach related to balance of trade adjustment.
14. Explain the elasticity approach to the correction of disequilibrium in the BOP.
15. What is Balance of Payments? What are the major accounts in a country's balance of payments? Examine the trends in India's BOP since 1991.
16. Distinguish between autonomous and accommodating transactions in a country's Balance of Payments.
17. "A fundamental shift in Indian development strategy seems to have occurred following the balance of payments crisis in 1991. The inward character of the earlier development strategy is being altered and markets rather than administrative directives are to play a greater role in the allocation process." Comment on the extent to which the release of market forces has made Indian business and industry more competitive. What are the fresh challenges and problems facing them in the context of liberalisation policies pursued by the Government?

CHAPTER

8 International Organisations and Agreements

LEARNING OBJECTIVES

After studying this chapter, you should understand:

8.1 World Trade Organisation (WTO)

8.2 United Nations Conference on Trade and Development (UNCTAD)

8.3 International Bank for Reconstruction and Development (IBRD or World Bank)

8.4 International Monetary Fund (IMF)

8.5 Commodity agreements

- Summary
- Test Questions

In order to promote and facilitate international business, several international organisations have been established. Arrangements like trade agreements have also been made for the same purpose. Some of these international organisations and arrangements are described in this chapter.

8.1 World Trade Organisation (WTO)

Trade negotiations in 1947 among 23 countries were held to revive economies from recession and to reduce protectionism adopted by the industrialised nations. These negotiations in Geneva led to the establishment of the General Agreement on Tariffs and Trade (GATT). Since the inception of GATT, several negotiations were held. The final Uruguay Round of negotiations held in Morocco in 1994 aimed "to strengthen the world economy and to improve trade, investment, employment and income throughout the world". The World Trade Organisation (WTO) was established on January 1, 1995, in order to implement the Uruguay Round Agreement of GATT.

Table 8.1: Differences Between GATT and WTO

Basis of Difference	GATT	WTO
1. Nature	GATT was an *agreement* with no institutional foundation	WTO is an *institution* with its own secretariat
2. Periodicity	GATT was an ad hoc and *provisional* arrangement	WTO is a *permanent* and full-fledged body

3. Scope	GATT rules Control trade in merchandise	WTO is wider in scope. It covers trade in goods and services, investments, trade related aspects of intellectual property.
4. Parties	GATT had contracting parties	WTO has members
5. Domestic laws	GATT allowed existing domestic legislation even if it violated a GATT agreement	WTO does not allow such legislation
6. Commitment	GATT began as a multilateral instrument applicable to all parties. Later many agreements were added which were applicable to parties selectively.	WTO agreements are almost all multilateral and involve the commitment of all the members.
7. Power	GATT was less powerful. Its dispute settlement. system was slow and less efficient. Its rulings could be easily blocked	WTO is more powerful. Its dispute settlement mechanism is faster and more efficient. It is very difficult to block its rulings
8. Transparency	GATT was less transparent	WTO is based on the principle of transparency. It requires the member countries to disclose their policies and practices. Its regular surveillance encourages transparency

Objectives: The WTO agreements seek to achieve the following objectives:

(*i*) To help trade flow as freely as possible

(*ii*) To achieve trade liberalisation gradually through negotiation

(*iii*) To set up an impartial means of settling disputes.

In other words, WTO aims at expanding international trade and production. These in turn will lead to fuller use of the world's resources, increase in income, full employment and higher standard of living.

Principles: All the WTO agreements are based on a number of simple and fundamental principles. These principles serve as the foundation of the multilateral trading system. These principles are as follows:

1. **Non-Discrimination:** According to this principle, no member country shall discriminate between the members of the WTO in the conduct of international trade. In order to ensure non-discrimination, the member countries agreed to apply the *principle of most favoured nation (MFN)* to all import and export duties. This means concession given to a trading partner (*e.g.*, low rate of customs duty) should be extended to all other member nations. The principle does not imply giving special status to any country.

   Some exceptions are, however, allowed to the principle of non-discrimination. For, example, a country can set up free trade areas or customs union that facilitates trade within the group, discriminating goods from outside. Members can also adopt measures to counter dumping or to check unfair trade. However, such measures cán be applied only against the offending countries.

   The principle of non-discrimination also requires *national treatment*. It means that imported and locally produced goods and services be treated equally after the foreign goods and services have entered the market. The same shall apply to foreign and local trade marks, patents and copyrights. National treatment is applicable only after a product, service or intellectual property item has entered the market. Therefore, charging customs duty on an import does not violate the principle of national interest even if an equivalent duty is not charged on the locally produced product.

2. **Free Trade:** WTO expects its member countries to reduce tariff and non-tariff barriers to encourage free trade. Quantitative restrictions are prohibited. However, developing countries and countries facing difficulties in their balance of payments are allowed to reduce trade barriers gradually.
3. **Predictability:** Under WTO agreements, member countries bind their commitments to open their markets for goods and services. They are not allowed to raise trade barriers arbitrarily. A country can change its commitment but only after negotiating with its trading partners, which could imply compensating them for loss of trade.
4. **Consultation:** WTO seeks to resolve disagreements among member countries through consultation. It provides a forum for continuing consultation among members.
5. **Fair Competition:** WTO is dedicated to open, fair and undistorted competition. Various WTO agreements aim to support fair competition in goods, services and intellectual property. The agreement on government procurement extends rules of competition to purchases by thousands of government entities in several countries.
6. **Development and Reforms:** The purpose of WTO system is to facilatate economic development in the world. It allows developing countries the necessary flexibility and time in implementing the WTO agreements.

Thus, WTO principles are designed to ensure free, fair and transparent trade between the member countries.

Functions: The main functions of the WTO are as follows:

(*i*) Administering and implementing the WTO trade agreements

(*ii*) Acting as a forum for trade negotiations among the member countries

(*iii*) Settling trade disputes between the member countries.

(*iv*) Monitoring national trade policies.

(*v*) Providing technical assistance and training for developing countries

(*vi*) Cooperating with other international organisations like the UNCTAD, IBRD and IMF concerned with global economic policy making.

Organisation Structure

The WTO is run by its member countries. All major decisions are made normally by consensus. WTO has a four-level structure :

1. **Ministerial Conference:** It is the top level decision-making body of the WTO. It consists of representatives of all the member countries. The Ministerial Conference meets at least once every two years to take decisions.
2. **General Council:** This is the second-level body which meets several times a year in the Geneva headquarters. The General Council also works as the Trade Policy Review Body and the Dispute Settlement Body. It consists of all the WTO members. The General Council reports to the Ministerial Council.

The Trade Policy Review Body reviews the trade polices of all member nations. Major trading powers are reviewed every two years and others every four years. The Disputes Settlement Body usually meets twice a month to hear complaints of violations of WTO rules and agreements. It also oversees procedures for settling disputes among member countries. It sets up expert panels to study disputes and decide if the rules are being broken.

3. **Goods Council, Services Council and Intellectual Property Council:** At the third level, these councils deal with trade in goods, services and intellectual property respectively. They are responsible for the working of agreements relating to their respective trade areas.

4. **Subsidiary Bodies:** At the fourth level are specialised committees, working groups and working parties. These deal with individual agreements and other areas such as environment, development, membership applications, regional trade agreements and administrative issues. Various subsidiary bodies keep the General Council informed of their activities regularly.

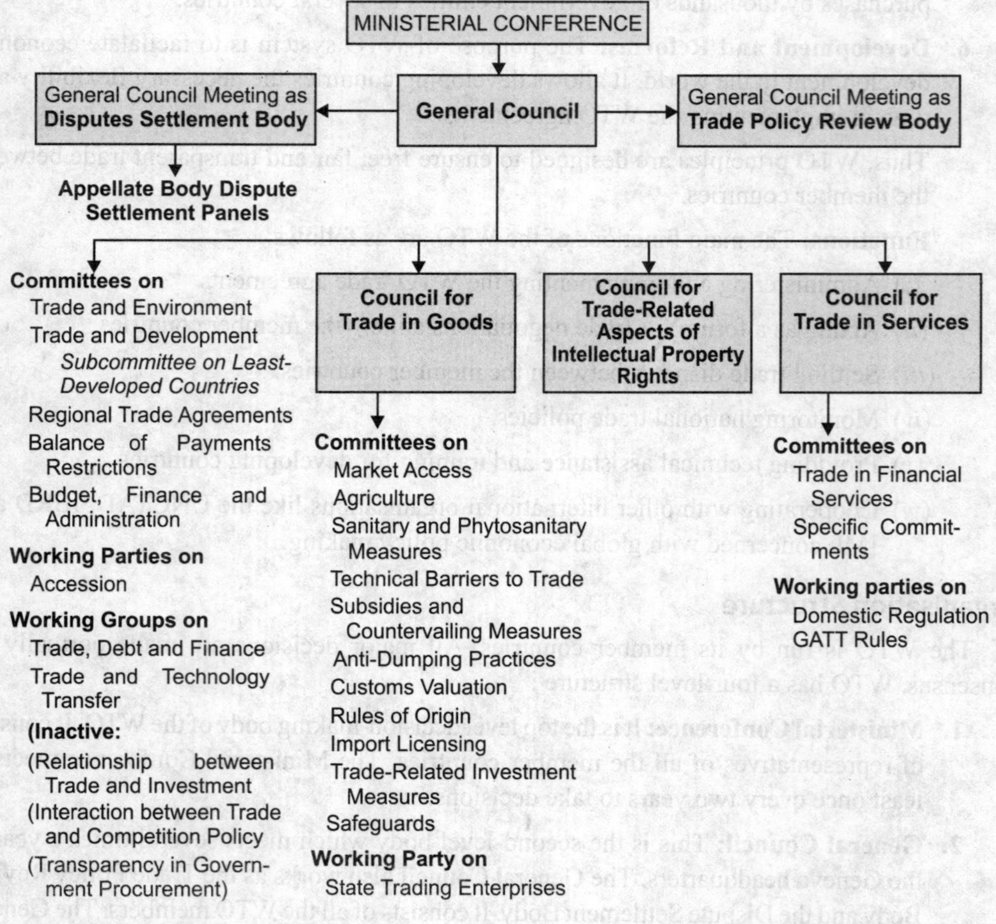

Fig. 8.1. Organisation structure of WTO

Functioning (Working): Member countries of the WTO now account for more than 97 per cent of the international trade. The policies and actions of WTO have very wide economic and social impact on the world. These have a huge scope for orderly development of world trade. WTO has both positive and negative consequences.

Benefits of WTO

1. Reduction in tariff and non-tariff barriers to international trade.
2. The liberalisation of trade increases competition, efficiency in utilisation of resources, productivity and quality.
3. Economic growth of member countries due to liberalisation of trade and investments.
4. Improvement in economic relations between member countries through multilateral discussions.
5. Settlement of trade disputes between nations leads to peace in the world
6. Mechanism for dealing with violation of trade agreements.
7. Free and fair trade helps to raise incomes, consumer choice and standard of living
8. WTO rules and principles make life easier for all.
9. Member Governments are protected from lobbying.
10. Research and dissemination of information about global trade.
11. WTO system encourages good governance.

Criticism of WTO

Arguments against WTO are as follows:

1. Developed countries dominate negotiations and decision making in the WTO.
2. Several developing countries lack the financial resources and knowledge needed for effective participation in WTO discussions and negotiations.
3. Policy liberalisation in WTO are decided without taking into consideration their adverse effects on developing countries.
4. The WTO has failed to impose discipline on the developed nations.
5. Developing countries have been getting a raw deal from the WTO.

Developing countries, in general, feel that WTO is an unfair system because developed countries have been the major beneficiaries. WTO must give more consideration to the problems of developing countries which are unable to participate on an equal footing in WTO negotiations. Developing countries also suffer when developed nations do not implement their commitments. The WTO is undemocratic and dictates policy. Commercial interests take priority over development, environment, health and safety.

8.2 United Nations Conference on Trade and Development (UNCTAD)

The United Nations Conference on Trade and Development (UNCTAD) was established in 1964 as a permanent organ of the United Nations General Assembly.

Objectives: UNCTAD aims at promoting trade and economic development of developing countries. It seeks to integrate developing countries into the world economy. It serves as a focal point for trade and development and the related issues of finance, technology and investment. UNCTAD is also a forum for discussions and deliberations among governments.

Principles: UNCTAD's priorities and action programmes are based on the following principles:

1. Every nation has the sovereign right to dispose of its natural resources for the economic development and well-being of its own people and freely to trade with other nations.
2. Economic and trade relations between countries shall be based on the principles of sovereign equality of states, self-determination of people and non-interference in the internal affairs of other countries.
3. There shall be no discrimination on the basis of differences in socio-economic systems and trading policies and trading methods shall be consistent with this principle.

Functions: The main functions of UNCTAD are as follows:

1. Promoting international trade so as to accelerate economic development.
2. Formulating policies and principles on international trade and related issues.
3. Negotiating multilateral trade agreements.
4. Making proposals for implementation of policies and principles.

UNCTAD undertakes research, policy analysis and data collection for providing inputs for discussions. It provides technical assistance, with special attention to the needs of least developed countries.

Functioning: So a eleven conferences have been held under the anspices of UNCTAD. These have made significant contribution towards/fuller participation of developing countries. and to adapt to changes in the world economy. UNCTAD has played a key role in the emergence of:

(*i*) The Generalised System of Preferences (GSP)
(*ii*) A marine shipping code
(*iii*) Special international programmes to help the least developed nations
(*iv*) International aid targets.

UNCTAD has served as a forum enhancing the interrelationship between trade and development.

8.3 International Bank for Reconstruction and Development (IBRD)

The International Bank for Reconstruction and Development, popularly known as **World Bank,** was established as a result of the Bretton Woods Conference in 1944. Initially, the World Bank concentrated on the reconstruction of the war shattered European economies. Later, the Bank shifted its focus on the development of poor countries.

Objectives: The main objectives of the World Bank, as laid down in its Articles of Agreement, are as follows:

1. To assist in the reconstruction and development of the territories of its member countries by facilitating the investment of capital for productive purposes.
2. To promote foreign private investment by means of guarantees or through participation in loans and other investments made by private investors.
3. When private capital is not available on reasonable terms, to make loans for productive purposes out of its own capital or out of funds raised by it from other sources.
4. To promote the long-range balanced growth of international trade and the maintenance of equilibrium in the balance of payments of members by encouraging international investments for productive purposes.

The focus areas of the World Bank are as under:

(*a*) public health and education

(*b*) reduction in poverty

(*c*) environmental protection

(*d*) development of private business

(*e*) improvement in standards of living

(*f*) strengthening the ability of members to deliver quality services with efficiency and transparency.

Principles: The lending operations of the World Bank are guided by the following principles and policies:

1. Repayment prospects of loans as indicated by the borrowing country's natural resources, its existing productive plant capacity to exploit the resources and operate the plant, and its past debt record.
2. Projects of high priority, and economically and technically sound projects are to be financed. These should be productive such as power, transport and other basic utilities which contribute to economic development.
3. Lending is to be done to meet only the foreign exchange content of a project and the borrowing country should mobilise its domestic resources.
4. The borrowing country is expected to buy machinery, etc. for the project in the cheapest possible market subject to satisfactory performance.
5. The World Bank maintains continuous relations with the borrowing country to monitor the progress of the project. Local private enterprise is to be promoted.

Organisation Structure

The IBRD is managed by a three-tier structure consisting of the following:

1. **Board of Governors:** The Board of Governors is vested with full authority and control over the activities of the IBRD. All member countries are represented in the Board of Governors.
2. **Executive Directors:** A body of 21 Executive Directors supervises the activities of the IBRD. Voting rights of the Governors and the Executive Directors are proportionate to the share capital of the member country which they represent. Executive Directors take

policy decisions and loans and credit proposals within the framework of the Articles of Agreement. They present audited annual accounts, administrative budget and annual report to the Board of Governors.

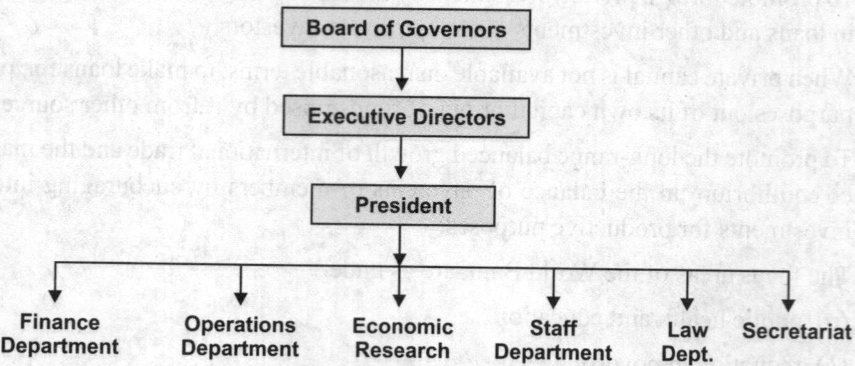

Figure. 8.2. Organisation Structure of the IBRD

Resources

The member countries contribute the capital of the IBRD as follows:

(*a*) 2 per cent of the share capital in the form of gold and US dollars. This portion is freely available for lending.

(*b*) 18 per cent of the share capital in the form of own currency. This portion is available for lending with the consent of the member country whose currency is involved.

(*c*) 80 per cent is kept in reserve to be paid by the member when called. This amount is not available for lending.

The IBRD also borrows in international capital market, from the Central Banks of the member countries and from commercial banks and other financial institutions.

IMF-World Bank Harmony

The IMF and the World Bank work in tandem. World Bank's BOP support is not available without a fund programme, while a fund programme cannot be finalised without the prior negotiation of BOP support from the World Bank and from bilateral donors to fill the programmed resources gap. The bilateral donors do not commit funds until negotiations with the World Bank have been concluded. Whereas the IMF sets the macro-economic guidelines and targets of a programme, the World Bank imposes a list of neo-liberal micro-economic policy reforms on the borrowing country.

How IMF differs from the World Bank?

The table below summarises the basic differences between the two institutions.

Table 8.2: The Distinct Roles of the IMF and the World Bank

International Monetary Fund	The World Bank
• Oversees the international monetary system and promotes international monetary cooperation.	• Seeks to promote economic development and structural reform in developing countries.

• Promotes exchange stability and orderly exchange relations among its members.	• Assists developing countries by providing long-term financing of development projects and programmes.
• Assists members in temporary balance of payments difficulties by providing them with the opportunity to correct maladjustments in their balance of payments.	• Provides special financial assistance to the poorest developing countries through the International Development Association (IDA).
• Supplements the reserves of its members by allocating SDRs if there is a long-term global need.	• Stimulates private enterprise in developing countries through its affiliate, the International Finance Corporation.
• Draws its financial resources principally from the quota subscriptions of its members.	• Acquires most of its financial resources by borrowing on the international bond market.

Lending Activities

The IBRD grants loans to the member countries in the following ways:

(*i*) By granting direct loans out of funds.

(*ii*) By granting direct loans out of funds raised in the market of the member countries.

(*iii*) By guaranteeing loans raised by the member countries from various other sources.

The IBRD offers two types of loan: (*i*)investment loans, and (*ii*) development policy loans. Investment loans are given for creating the physical and social infrastructure necessary for poverty alleviation and sustainable development. Development policy loans are given to support policy and institutional reforms. All loans are governed by the operational policies of the IBRD. These policies aim to ensure that the projects are economically, financially, socially and environmentally sound. The IBRD often joins with governments, multilateral institutions, commercial banks and private sector investors in financing projects.

Technical and Advisory Assistance

IBRD also offers technical and advisory assistance to the member countries. Such assistance comprises:

1. Assessing the economic resources of the member countries and setting up priorities to be followed in developmental programmes.
2. Sending Study missions to member countries for conducting intensive studies of their resources so as to formulate long term development policies.
3. Providing training to the senior officials of developing countries. The IBRD has established the Economic Development Institute for this purpose.

The World Bank serves as a knowledge bank that helps aggregate, distil and disseminate best practices from around the world.

8.4 International Monetary Fund (IMF)

In July 1944, representatives of 44 countries met at Bretton-Woods, New Hampshire, USA. At this conference an agreement was reached to establish two international institutions, namely, IMF and World Bank. The IMF was established on December 27, 1945, but it began its financial operations on March 1, 1947. Initially 29 countries signed its Articles of Agreement.

Since then its membership has increased to 187 countries. Membership of the IMF is open to all countries and it is a prerequisite for membership in the World Bank.

The IMF is the central institution of the international monetary system. Its aim is to prevent crisis in the system by advising and encouraging the member countries to adopt sound economic policies. As a fund, the IMF provides temporary financial assistance to overcome problems in balance of payments.

Objectives: The objectives of the IMF as per its Articles of Agreement are as follows.

1. To promote international monetary cooperation through a permanent institution which provides the machinery for consultation and collaboration on international monetary problems.
2. To facilitate expansion and balanced growth of international trade, and to contribute thereby to the promotion and maintenance of high levels of employment and real income and to the development of productive resources of all members as primary objectives of economic policy.
3. To promote exchange stability, to maintain orderly exchange arrangements among members, and to avoid competitive exchange depreciation.
4. To assist in establishment of a multilateral system of payments in respect of current transactions between members and in the elimination of foreign exchange restrictions which hamper the growth of world trade.
5. To give confidence to members by making the general resources of the Fund temporally available to them under adequate safeguards, thus providing them with opportunity to correct maladjustments in their balance of payments without resorting to measures destructive to national or international prosperity.
6. To make available to member countries the resources so as to help them correct BOP difficulties without harming international prosperity.
7. To shorten the duration and lessen the degree of disequilibrium in the balance of payment of members countries.

The **statutory purposes** of the IMF are: Promoting the balanced expansion of world trade and the stability of exchange rates, the avoidance of competitive currency devaluations, and the orderly correction of a country's balance of payments problems.

Principles: According to its vision the IMF would:

(*i*) strive to promote sustained non-inflationary economic growth that benefits all people of the world;

(*ii*) be the centre of competence for the stability of the international financial system;

(*iii*) focus on its core macroeconomic and financial areas of responsibility, working in a complementary manner with other institutions established to safeguard global public goods; and

(*iv*) be an open institution, learning from experience and dialogue, and adapting continuously to changing circumstances.

Functions

In order to achieve its objectives, IMF performs the following functions:

1. To review and monitor national and global economic and financial developments and to advise member countries on their economic policies.
2. To lend them hard currencies so as to support reform and adjustment policies designed to correct balance of payments problems and to promote sustainable growth.
3. To offer a wide range of technical assistance and training for government and central bank officials in its areas of expertise.
4. To work with its member governments, other international organizations, regulatory bodies, and the private sector for strengthening the international monetary and financial system.
5. To assess, along with IBRD, financial sectors of member countries for identifying actual and potential weaknesses.
6. To prepare country reports in their observance of standards and codes.
7. To conduct research and publish reports.
8. To work with the Bassel Committee on Banking Supervision for improving regulatory standards.

Organisation Structure

The IMF is an autonomous body affiliated to the UNO. Its organisation structure consists of the following:

1. **Board of Governors:** It is the highest policy making authority of the IMF. It consists of one Governor and one Alternate Governor appointed by each member country. A member country appoints its Finance Minister or the Governor of the Central Bank as the Governor. The Board of Governors usually meets once a year at the annual meetings of the IMF.
2. **Executive Board:** The Board of Governors has delegated substantial powers to the Executive Board. These powers include all fund activities including regulatory, supervisory and financial. The Executive Board makes day-to-day decisions. It usually meets three times a week and makes decisions regarding lending, changes in exchange rates and appointment of the Managing Director. The Executive Board consists of 24 executive directors who represent various countries.
3. **Managing Director:** The Executive Board selects the Managing Director who serves as the chairman of the Board and as chief of the IMF staff. The Managing Director conducts the business of the IMF under the direction of the Executive Board. He is appointed for a five-year term which is renewable. The Managing Director is assisted by three Deputy Managing Directors.
4. **International Monetary and Financial Committee:** This committee advises the Board of Governors on supervising the arrangement and on adaptation of the international monetary system.

Fig. 8.3. Organisation Structure of IMF

It meets twice a year to discuss key policy issues relating to the international monetary system.

5. **The Development Committee:** This is a joint committee of the IMF and World Bank. It advises and reports to the Board of Governors on development policy and other matters of concern to developing countries.

Resources and Quotas

The capital of the IMF (General Account) is contributed by the quotas allocated to the member countries on the basis of economic size. Quotas form the basis for voting power and drawing rights of different members. Quotas are reviewed by the IMF at intervals of not more than five years. It necessary, IMF can borrow to supplement the resources made available by quotas. IMF also raises funds by selling its gold reserves to the member countries.

Lending

IMF provides temporary assistance to members to tide over balance of payments deficits. When a member country needs foreign exchange, it tenders its own currency to the IMF and gets the required foreign exchange. IMF lending is conditional as the borrowing country must adopt policies that promise to correct its balance of payments deficit. Moreover, the IMF disburses funds in phases, linked to the borrowing country's meeting its scheduled policy commitments. IMF lending is temporary and in most cases a small portion of a country's external financial requirement is provided.

The member countries can borrow from the IMF according to its tranche policies. The shortfall of member country's currency with IMF over its quota is called Reserve Tranche. The country can draw 25 per cent of its reserve tranche automatically. The remaining balance of quota is called credit-tranche, drawing from which is conditional.

IMF has created several credit facilities to meet specific requirements of the member countries. Low-income countries can borrow at concessional rate under the Poverty Reduction and Growth Facility (PRGF). They can also avail the debt relief under the Heavily Indebted Poor Countries (HIPC) initiative. Non-concessional loans are provided through five main facilities:

Stand-by Arrangements (SBA), Extended Fund Facility (EFF), Supplementary Reserve Facility (SRF), Contingent Credit Lines (CCL) and Compensatory Financing Facility (CFF).

Special Drawing Rights

Shortage of capital is a great hurdle in the progress of developing countries. The need to increase international liquidity *i.e.* resources for the settlement of international debts was strongly felt. IMF introduced the Special Drawing Rights in 1970.

SDRs are entitlements granted to member countries who can draw from the IMF apart from their quotas. When SDRs are allocated the country's special drawing account is credited with the amount allotted. When the country requires foreign exchange it can sell SDRs to another country and get foreign exchange. SDR is merely an asset created out of book entries. It is an independent reserve asset intended to supplement the existing reserve assets. The most important feature of the SDRs is that they are distributed among the member countries in proportion to their quotas. As a result the developed countries possess a dominant share of the SDR holdings. Over the years, SDRs have gained importance both as a reserve asset as well as a means of settlement of international transactions.

Technical Assistance: The IMF provides technical assistance in macroeconomic policy, monetary and foreign exchange policy, fiscal policy and management, external debt, etc. The purpose of such assistance is development of the productive resources of member countries. The IMF provides support for policy design and capacity building. It provides technical assistance in three broad areas:

(*a*) designing and implementing monetary and fiscal policies.

(*b*) drafting and reviewing economic and financial laws, regulations and procedures.

(*c*) institution and capacity building, such as central banks, treasuries, tax and customs department and statistical services.

The IMF also provides training to officials of member countries.

8.5 Commodity Agreements

Developing countries have suffered badly because most of their exports consist of primary products (agricultural items and minerals). These items are characterised by low demand and inelastic supply. Their prices fluctuate widely due to changes in supply and demand. A poor harvest can significantly reduce export revenues and level of employment in the primary sector. Terms of trade have also been against the interest of developing countries. These countries enter into commodity agreements and form cartel in order to protect their interests.

An international commodity agreement is an agreement between governments of leading exporting and importing countries to regulate the terms of trade in a specified commodity. It may serve to stabilise prices by balancing demand and supply in the market. The exporting country is protected against excessive competition and overproduction in the world market. It many also help to assure adequate supply to consumers in the importing country.

The various forms of international commodity agreements are as follows:

1. **Quota Agreements:** The aim of a quota agreement is to prevent a fall in commodity prices by regulating its supply. Under the quota agreement, export quotas are fixed

for each of the exporting countries on the basis of a mutually agreed formula. The participating countries make a commitment to restrict the export to their quotas as decided by the central council. Coffee Agreement among the major producing countries of Latin America and Africa is an example of quota agreement. In the long run, export quotas involve production controls. Otherwise surplus output may induce the countries to cut prices and the quota agreement may ultimately fail.

Quota agreements suffer from the following drawbacks:

(*i*) Control of export and production will adversely affect the growth of the industry. These will be detrimental to the interests of the countries whose interest the agreement seeks to protect.

(*ii*) In the long run, quota agreements may result in the development of substitutes for the products. These will lead to fall in export earnings.

(*iii*) Quotas lead to misallocation of resources in the producing countries. These protect inefficient producers, freeze markets and keep supplies at sub-optimium level.

Quotas are, however, manageable. They require no financing and no continuous operating decisions. Quotas also avoid accumulation of stock. But in actual practice buffer stocks are needed to ensure flexibility of supply in the short term. In addition, quotas may be traded for a price.

2. **Buffer Stock Agreements:** These agreements involve holding and using surplus stocks of a commodity to check wide fluctuations in its price in the international market. An international agency (*e.g.* association of producing countries) with adequate funds absorbs excess supplies of the commodity. Such supply held by the international agency is known as buffer stock. Minimum and maximum prices for the commodity are predetermined. When the price falls below the minimum price due to excess supply, the international agency buys the commodity in large quantities to push the price above the minimum. On the other hand, when price rises above the maximum level on account of short supply, the agency releases the stock to augment supply and reduce the price. Buffer stock agreements have been used in case of tin, cocoa and sugar.

Buffer stock agreements are beneficial to both exporting and importing countries. These agreements reduce the risk and uncertainty caused by prices fluctuations. Such agreements help to maintain export earnings, promote efficiency in production and accelerate economic growth of exporting nations. For the importing countries, buffer stock agreements stabilise commodity prices thereby avoiding inflation.

Buffer stock agreements suffer from the following limitations:

(*i*) It is difficult to decide a target price range that covertly reflects the long term market trend and is acceptable to all countries. Fixing a too high or too low target price range may prove disastrous.

(*ii*) Once fixed, the target price range may require revision from time to time.

(*iii*) The international agency may not have adequate funds to maintain prices within the target range.

(*iv*) Buffer stocks involve high costs of transportation, insurance, labour, etc. Participating countries have to share these costs.

(*v*) Buffer stock agreements can be successful only in case of those commodities which can be stored at a low cost and without risk of deterioration.

3. **Bilateral Agreements:** A major exporter and a major importer may enter into a contract to purchase and sell certain quantities of a commodity at agreed prices. Maximum and minimum prices are specified in such an agreement. If the market price rises above the specified upper limit, the exporting country is obliged to sell the specified quantity of the commodity at the maximum price specified in the agreement. On the other hand, in case the market price falls below the minimum level, the importing country is obliged to purchase the specified quantity at the specified minimum price. The agreement remains inoperative as long as the market price remains within the specified limits.

   A bilateral agreement does not interfere with the allocation of resources, provided it does not cover all the supplies. But it creates a two-price system and requires the exporting country to maintain buffer stock or other domestic control.

4. **Multilateral Agreements:** A multilateral agreement is similar to a bilateral agreement except that the former is made by more than two countries. Major exporting and major importing countries of a particular commodity enter into a multilateral agreement. International Wheat Agreement and International Sugar Agreement are examples of multilateral agreements.

   In comparison with quota agreement and buffer stock agreement, a multilateral agreement causes less distortion in market mechanism and allocation of resources. It does not involve production control and offers security from price fluctuations to both exporting and importing countries.

   Implementation of multilateral agreements involves the following problems:

   (*i*) A multilateral agreement can be effective only when it covers the major proportion of the total international trade in the commodity.

   (*ii*) The range of minimum and maximum prices should not be very wide.

   (*iii*) Unless the target price reflects the long term market price, there may be discrepancies between demand and supply.

   (*iv*) Entry and exit for the participating countries being easy, the agreement offers limited stability in the market.

SUMMARY

WTO: Set up on January 1, 1995, as a successor to GATT. WTO is more permanent, wider in scope, more powerful and more transparent than GATT. It **aims** at boosting world trade. Its basic **principles** are: non-discrimination, free trade, predictability, consultation, fair competition, development and reforms. **Organisation structure:** Ministerial Conference; General Council; councils for goods, services and intellectual property; subsidiary bodies. **Benefits:** reduction in barriers to trade; amicable settlement to trade disputes, economic growth, better governance. **Criticism:** domination by developed countries.

UNCTAD: Set up in 1964 to promote trade and development of developing countries. Its **principles** are sovereign equality, self-determination, non-interference, non-discrimination. Its **functions** are to boost trade, negotiate multilateral agreements, formulate policies, etc.

World Bank: Set up for reconstruction and development, promote FPI, boost international trade. **Principles:** high priority projects, repaying capacity, meeting foreign exchange content, etc. **Organisation structure:** Board of Governors, Executive Director, President, Departments. **Activities:** Lending, technical assistance, research and publications, advisory services.

IMF: Established on Dec. 27, 1945, and began operations on March 1, 1947. **Objectives:** to promote international monetary cooperation, to facilitate balanced growth, to promote stability in exchange rates, to help tide over BP problems. **Principles:** promotion of sustained non-inflationary growth, stabilise international financial system. **Organisation structure:** Board of Governors (interim committee, development committee), Executive Board of Directors, Managing Director, Dy. Managing Directors, IMF Secretariat. **Activities:** Lending, Special Drawing Rights, technical assistance.

TEST QUESTIONS

1. What is World Trade Organisation (WTO)? What are its objectives? State its functions.
2. Explain the principles that govern the working of WTO.
3. Describe the organisation structure of World Trade Organisation.
4. Discuss the benefits of WTO. Why is it criticised?
5. What is UNCTAD? Explain its objectives and functions.
6. What are the principles and role of UNCTAD in international business?
7. Explain the objectives and principles of World Bank.
8. Describe the organisation structure of World Bank.
9. Compare and contrast the roles of the World Bank and the IMF.
10. Describe the lending activities, technical and advisory assistance of the World Bank.
11. Discuss the objectives and principles of the International Monetary Fund (IMF).
12. Describe the organisation structure of the International Monetary Fund (IMF).
13. Explain the lending operations and technical assistance of IMF.
14. Writes notes on:
    (*a*) Special Drawing Rights.
    (*b*) Multilateral trade agreements.
    (*c*) Difference between WTO and GATT.
15. What are commodity agreements? Describe their different types.
16. Explain the weaknesses of the WTO's DSP mechanism.
17. How are disputes settled at WTO? Comment on the challenges the WTO is facing at present.
18. What is WTO? What are its trading principles.
19. What were the key accomplishments of the Bretton-Woods Conference?
20. Comment on the achievements of Uruguay Round negotiations. What are the major challenges facing developing countries in the context of the post-Uruguay/WTO era?

UNIT – III

9. Regional Economic Cooperation
10. International Financial System
11. Foreign Exchange Markets and Exchange Risk Management
12. Foreign Investments

CHAPTER

9 Regional Economic Cooperation

LEARNING OBJECTIVES

After studying this chapter, you should understand:

9.1 Meaning of Regional Economic Cooperation
9.2 Advantages of Regional Economic Cooperation
9.3 Disadvantages of Regional Economic Cooperation
9.4 Forms of Regional Groupings
9.5 The European Union (EU)
9.6 North American Free Trade Agreement (NAFTA)
9.7 Association of South East Asian Nations (ASEAN)
9.8 South Asian Association for Regional Cooperation (SAARC)
9.9 SAARC Preferential Trading Arrangement (SAPTA)
9.10 South Asian Free Trade Area (SAFTA)

- Summary
- Test Questions

An increasing trend in international business is cooperation and integration between countries within regions like Europe, North America, Asia, etc. These regional groupings are known as regional trade blocs or regional trading arrangements. Under such an arrangement countries in a geographic region agree for free flow of goods, services, capital, technology and labour between each other. Members of WTO are required to inform WTO in case they participate in any such arrangement. Since 1991, there has been a rise in these arrangements.

A total of 330 regional trading blocs had been notified to the GATT/WTO until July 2005. Some countries belong to more than one regional trading agreement. More than one-third of world trade now takes place within regional trading blocs.

9.1 Meaning of REgional Economic Cooperation

Regional economic cooperation or integration refers to agreements among countries in a geographic region to reduce, and ultimately remove, tariff and non-tariff barriers to the free flow of goods, services and factors of production between each other.

Regional trading blocs are in operation in several regions such as Europe, North America, Middle East, Africa and Asia. There exist more than one such arrangement with one geographic region. The movement toward regional economic cooperation has been most successful in Europe. The European Union (EU) is an attempt to create a single market and the member countries of the EU launched a common currency, called **Euro.** They are also moving toward a political union.

9.2 Advantages of Regional Economic Cooperation

According to Shiells,[1] regional trading blocs are formed for the following objectives:

1. To obtain economic benefits from achieving a more efficient production structure by exploiting **economies of scale** through spreading fixed costs over larger regional markets, increased economic growth from foreign direct investment, learning from expenence, etc.
2. To pursue non-economic objectives such as strengthening **political ties** and managing migration flows.
3. To ensure increased security of **market access** for smaller countries by forming regional trading blocs with larger countries.
4. To improve members' **bargaining strength** in multilateral trade negotiations or to protest against the slow pace of trade negotiations.
5. To promote regional infant industries which cannot be viable without a protected regional market.
6. To prevent further damage to their trading strength due to further trade diversion from third countries.

Thus, regional economic cooperation is an attempt to achieve gains from free trade and investment. In addition, it is easier to create a free trade and investment regime among a few countries within one geographic region than among a large number of countries from different geographic regions of the world. Countries participating in a regional trading bloc can specialise in the production of goods and services that they can produce most efficiently. Gains from free trade and investment stimulate economic growth in all the member countries. Therefore, it is a win-win situation for all of them.

Regional economic cooperation is beneficial politically also. Economic cooperation fosters political cooperation between the neighbouring countries and reduces the possibility of conflict between them. They can increase their political power in the world by linking their economies. For example, after World War II, the European countries had little hold in world markets and politics. The establishment of the European Community (EC) in 1957 was inspired mainly by the need for a united Europe to deal with the United States and the Soviet Union.

Thus, there are economic as well as political benefits of regional economic cooperation.

1. C. Shiells, " Regional Trading Blocs: Trade Creating or Diverting," *Finance and Development,* 32 (1), 1995

9.3 Disadvantages of Regional Economic Cooperation

Regional economic cooperation may be harmful in the following ways:

1. It may lead to more trade diversion than trade creation. **Trade diversion** takes place when lower cost suppliers outside the regional trading bloc are replaced by higher cost suppliers within the bloc. **Trade creation** takes place when high cost producers (domestic or external) are replaced by lower cost producers (domestic or external). Trade diversion is possible because WTO rules do not cover non-tariff barriers to trade.
2. It is difficult to create and sustain regional trading blocs. A country as a whole may gain but certain groups within it may lose. For example, after the establishment of NAFTA in 1994 textile workers in Canada and the United States lost their jobs as firms in these countries shifted production to Mexico.
3. Regional economic integration may be seen a threat to national sovereignty. Such integration requires the member countries to give up some degree of control over monetary policy, fiscal policy and trade policy. European Union has faced this problem as Great Britain has opted out of euro, the common currency introduced by the European Union.
4. Regional economic grouping can be injurious to a country's economy in the absence of a proper monitoring mechanism. For example, SAPTA is misused for illegitimate entry to India of goods from non-member countries. Similarly, agricultural products of non-member nations enter India freely through Sri Lanka.
5. There can be harmful effects of a regional trading bloc if the firms in a country do not get the same facilities which their counterparts in other member countries enjoy.
6. Tax revenue from tariffs for the importing country is reduced when the exporting country becomes a member of the regional trading bloc.

9.4 Forms of Regional Groupings

The main forms or levels of regional economic integration are as follows:

1. **Free Trade Area:** A free trade area is a grouping of countries which allow free trade between them. All restrictions on trade among the member nations are abolished. But each member country is free to determine its own commercial policy with non-members. When the free trade agreement provides only for concessional tariff among members, it is known as preferential trade agreement. In some cases, a free trade area may cover only selected goods and services. For example, the European Free Trade Agreement (EFTA) does not cover agricultural items and covers only industrial goods.

   A free trade area is the loosest form of economic integration. But it is the most popular form accounting for almost 90 per cent of regional economic groupings. EFTA and North America Free Trade Association (NAFTA) are the prominent examples of free trade areas.
2. **Customs Union:** A customs union is a more advanced form of economic integration than free trade area. There is free trade among the members of the union. All restrictions on

trade among the member countries are removed. In addition, all member nations of the union adopt a uniform commercial policy towards the non-members. All the members of the union may adopt a common tariff structure. An administrative machinery is set to oversee trade relations with non-members. The Southern Africa Customs Union is the most successful and the oldest example of customs union. The European Union also started as a customs union.

3. **Common Market:** A common market allows free trade among its members. The members adopt a uniform commercial policy towards non-members. In addition, there is free movement of factors of production (*e.g.,* labour, capital, technology, etc.) among the members within the region. The European Union worked as a common market for some time before moving to a higher level of integration.
4. **Economic Union:** At this level of economic integration, there is free trade in goods and services, and free movement of factors of production among the members. The members have a uniform commercial policy towards non-members. In addition, the members follow common monetary, taxation and fiscal policies which are harmonised and administered by a supranational institution. There may be a common currency or the currencies of the member countries may be tied together through fixed exchange rates. For example, the European Union has a common currency, **Euro.**
5. **Political Union:** This is the full or ultimate form of economic integration. In this arrangement a central political authority coordinates the economic, social and foreign policy of the member countries. This supranational authority consists of legislative, executive and judicial wings. The European Union is moving towards a political union.

Free Trade Area	Free trade among member nations				
Customs Union	Free trade among member nations	Uniform commercial policy			
Common Market	Free trade among member nations	Uniform commercial policy	Free mobility of factors of production		
Economic Union	Free trade among member nations	Uniform commercial policy	Free mobility of factors of production	Harmonised economic policies	
Political Union	Free trade among number nations	Uniform commercial policy	Free mobility of factors of production	Harmonised economic policies	Supranational body

Fig. 9.1. Levels of Regional Economic Cooperation

9.5 The European Union (EU)

The European Union (EU) is the most successful and the most advanced form of regional economic groupings.

Beginning: The European Economic Community (EEC), also known as the European Common Market (ECM), was formed on January 1, 1958, by virtue of the Treaty of Rome (1957). It originally consisted of six countries, namely, Belgium, France, Germany, Italy, Luxembourg and Netherlands.

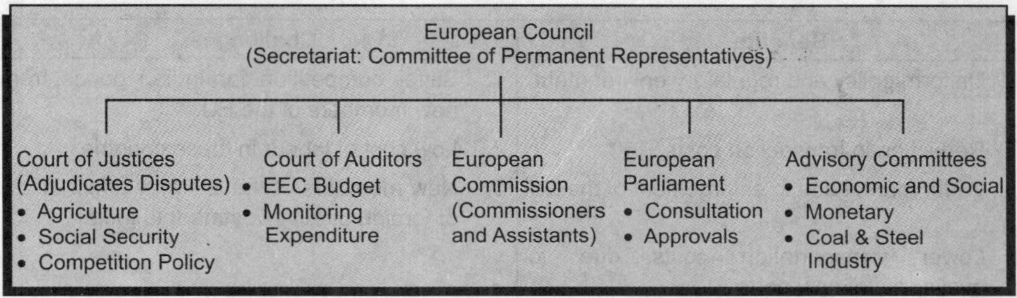

Fig. 9.2. Organisation Structure of the European Economic Community

Under the Treaty of Rome, the member countries agreed to:

(*i*) remove quotas, tariffs and other barriers to intra-community trade.

(*ii*) adopt a common tariff system for their imports from the non-member countries.

(*iii*) allow free movement of factors of production within the community.

(*iv*) harmonise their taxation, monetary and social security policies.

(*v*) develop a common policy on agriculture, transport and competition in industry.

Expansion: The EEC was expanded with the addition of the United Kingdom, Denmark, Ireland, Greece, Spain, Portugal, Austria, Finland and Sweden. The EEC became a customs union by July 1, 1968. In 1979 the European Monetary System was created. In June 1985, a White Paper entitled 'Completing the Internal Market' was adopted by the EC Commission (executive body of EEC). It sought to unify the economies of the member countries into a single market by 1992.

Since January 1, 1993, the European Union is functioning as a single market. Its integration became complete with the evolution of **euro** (in 1999) as a single currency for all EC countries and with the formation of Central Bank for Europe. The **Euro** is issued and administered by an European System of Central Banks (ESCB) which consists of the European Central Bank (ECB) and 12 national central banks. On July 1, 2002, Euro became the sole legal tender in twelve member countries.

The EU expanded further and its membership rose to 27 after the joining of Estonia, Poland, Lithuania, Czech Republic, Slovak Republic, Hungary, Slovenia, Cyprus, Malta, Bulgaria, Romania, and Turkey. Now EU is the largest common market in the world and accounts for a quarter of world trade.

India's Trade with EU: The EU is India's largest trading partner and accounts for about 20 per cent of India's total trade. India's main exports to the EU include textiles, jute, leather and leather goods, polished diamonds, engineering goods, chemicals, etc. India's main imports from the EU include edible oils, dairy products, capital goods, optical instruments, aluminium and copper products, synthetic rubber, etc. The India-EC Joint Commission is the apex form for bialateral economic relations between India and the EU. A continuous dialogue is maintained by India with the EU at both Government and industry levels. However, India is yet to fully exploit the trade potential which the EU offers.

Table 9.1 : The EU—Benefits and Challenges for India.

Benefits	Challenges
1. Uniform policy and regulatory environment	1. Stiffer competition for Indian goods from new members of the EU
2. Reduction in transaction costs	2. Low cost of labour in these countries
3. Wider market due to enlargement of the EU	3. New members of the EU may affect inflow of foreign direct investment to India
4. Lower transportation costs due to availability of new ports	
5. Lower tariffs on exports to the EU countries	
6. Removal of quota restrictions for textiles and clothing	
7. Scope for joint venture with Indian companies	

9.6 North American Free Trade Agreement (NAFTA)

NAFTA was signed between the United States and Canada in 1988. Mexico joined it in 1994. This agreement created the world's largest free trade area with more than 400 million consumers. NAFTA seeks to achieve the following objectives:

(*i*) to facilitate free movement of goods and services between the member countries by eliminating all barriers to trade;

(*ii*) to create fair competition in the free trade area;

(*iii*) to increase investment opportunities in the member countries;

(*iv*) to provide adequate and effective protection of intellectual property rights in each country;

(*v*) to provide a mechanism for amicable settlement of disputes between the members.

A unique feature of NAFTA is that it includes labour standards and environmental standards. NAFTA is a comprehensive agreement as it covers tariff and non-tariff barriers, rules of origin, governmental procurement, health and safety standards, investment, intellectual property and dispute settlement. The principles of national treatment, most favoured nation and transparency guide the operations of NAFTA. Volume of trade among NAFTA countries has more them doubled since 1994. It accounts for more than one-third of total US exports. Canada remains the largest trading partner for USA. India's trade with NAFTA is primarily with USA and Canada and trade with Mexico is negligible. USA is India's largest trading partner but India accounts for only 1 per cent of USA's total foreign trade.

Opinions differ widely over the benefits and harmful effects of NAFTA. Many experts thought USA and Canada would shift production to Mexico where labour costs are considerably lower. Others hoped that job opportunities in USA and Canada would increase due to huge demand for their goods and services in Mexico. There was a fear that Mexican industry would suffer due to stiff competition from US firms. At the same time several people thought that competitiveness of the Mexican industry will increase.

Since the creation of NAFTA foreign investment in Mexico has increased substantially. Companies from non-member nations have made large investment in Mexico to gain a free entry to the huge NAFTA market. Mexico has gained an edge over other developing countries for selling in the USA and Canada. But NAFTA has led to considerable trade diversion.

9.7 Association of South-East Asian Nations (ASEAN)

Five countries, namely, Indonesia, Malaysia, Philippines, Singapore and Thailand, formed the ASEAN in 1967 with a view to accelerate economic growth. Brunei, Dar-us-Salam, Vietnam, Lao PDR, Myanmar and Cambodia joined later. The ASEAN region has a population of about 500 million with a gross domestic product of $ 700 billion and a total trade of $ 1 trillion.

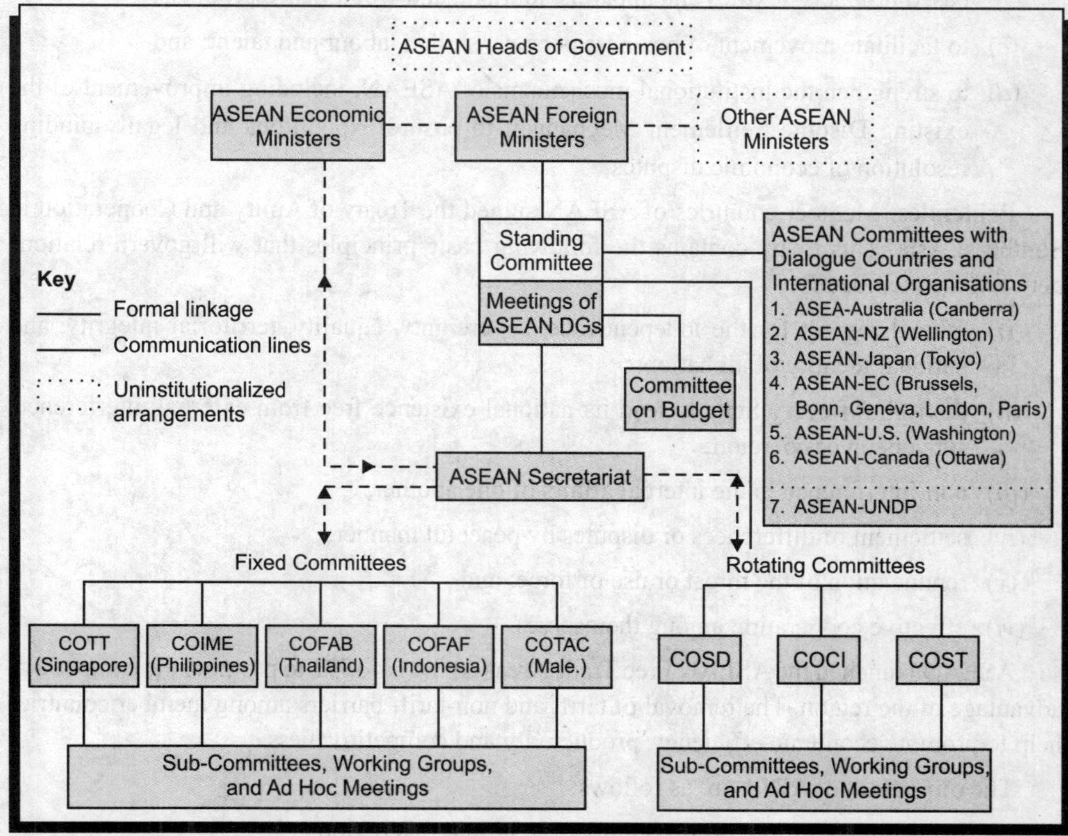

Source : Asean Economic Co-operation, Transition and Transformation, ISEAS, 1997, p.25.

Fig. 9.3. ASEAN Organisation Structure

Objectives: ASEAN aims to:

(*i*) accelerate economic growth, social progress and cultural development in the region; and

(*ii*) promote regional stability and peace through abiding respect for justice and the rule of law in the relationship among member countries and adherence to the United Nations Charter.

The ASEAN Vision 2020 adopted in 1997 has the **ASEAN Economic Community** as its end goal. The purpose is to create a stable, prosperous and highly competitive ASEAN economic region in which there is a free flow of goods, services, investment; equitable economic development, and reduce poverty and socio-economic disparities by the year 2020.

To achieve the goal of ASEAN Economic Community, ASEAN members have agreed to the following:

(*a*) to institute new mechanisms and measures to strengthen the implementation of its existing economic initiatives including the ASEAN Free Trade Area (AFTA), ASEAN Framework Agreement on Services (AFAS) and ASEAN Investment Area (AIA);

(*b*) to accelerate regional integration in the following priority sectors by 2010 : air travel, agro-based products, automotives, e-commerce, electronics, fisheries, healthcare, rubber-based products, textiles and apparels, tourism, and wood-based products;

(*c*) to facilitate movement of business persons, skilled labour and talent; and

(*d*) to strengthen the institutional mechanisms of ASEAN, including improvement of the existing Dispute Settlement Mechanism to ensure expeditious and legally-binding resolution of economic disputes.

Principles: Member countries of ASEAN signed the Treaty of Amity and Cooperation in Southeast Asia. This treaty contains the following basic principles that will govern relations between the members:

(*i*) mutual respect for the independence, sovereignty, equality, territorial integrity, and national identity of all nations;

(*ii*) the right of every State to lead its national existence free from external interference, subversion or coercion;

(*iii*) non-interference in the internal affairs of one another;

(*iv*) settlement of differences or disputes by peaceful manner;

(*v*) renunciation of the threat or use of force; and

(*vi*) effective cooperation among themselves.

ASEAN launched the ASEAN Free Trade Area (AFTA) in 1992 to promote the competitive advantage of the region. The removal of tariff and non-tariff barriers among member countries help to promote economic efficiency, productivity and competitiveness.

The **objectives** of AFTA are as follows:

- to encourage inflow of foreign investment into this region.
- to establish free trade area in the member countries.

- to reduce tariff of the products produced in ASEAN countries. 40% value addition in the ASEAN countries to the product value is treated as manufactured in ASEAN countries.

India is having an adverse balance of trade with the ASEAN region. India's exports to ASEAN countries include petroleum products, oil, gem and jewellery, electronics, cotton yarn, etc. Main imports are coal and coke, gold, vegetable oils, organic chemicals, wood and wood products, non-ferrous metals, etc.

ASEAN is a commendable effort at economic integration is Asia. The rate of economic growth in the ASEAN region has been quite high. India signed a Free Trade Agreement with ASEAN in 2009. In 2002, China and ASEAN signed a major deal to create ASEAN-China free trade zone within ten years.

9.8 South Asian Association For Regional Cooperation (SAARC)

The South Asian Association for Regional Cooperation (SAARC) was established on December 8, 1985, by seven Asian countries, namely, India, Bangladesh, Pakistan, Nepal, Bhutan, Sri Lanka and Maldives. The basic goal of SAARC is to accelerate economic and social development through optimum utilisation of their human and material resources. SAARC provides a forum for the member countries to work together in a spirit of friendship, trust and mutual understanding.

Objectives: The objectives of SAARC are as follows:

1. To promote the welfare of the people of South Asia and to improve their quality of life.
2. To accelerate economic growth, social progress and cultural development in the region and to provide all individuals the opportunity to live in dignity and to realise their full potential.
3. To promote and strengthen collective self-reliance among the countries of South Asia.
4. To contribute to mutual trust, understanding and appreciation of each other's problems.
5. To promote active collaboration and mutual assistance in the economic, social, cultural, technical and scientific fields.
6. To strengthen cooperation with other developing countries.
7. To strengthen cooperation among themselves in international forums on matters of common interests.
8. To cooperate with international and regional organisations with similar aims and purposes.

Principles: The activities of SAARC are guided by the following principles:

(*i*) Cooperation within the framework of the Association shall be based on respect for the principles of sovereign equality, territorial integrity, political independence, non-interference in the internal affairs of other States and mutual benefit.

(*ii*) Such cooperation shall not be a substitute for bilateral cooperation but shall complement it.

(*iii*) Such cooperation shall be consistent with bilateral and multilateral obligations.

(*iv*) Decisions at all levels in SAARC shall be taken on the basis of unanimity.

(*v*) Bilateral and contentious issues are to be excluded from the deliberations of the Association.

The Council
(Represented by the Heads of the Foreign Ministers of the Member Governments)
Highest Policy-Making Body

Council of Ministers
(Represented by the Foreign Ministers of the Member Governments)
Formulates Policies, Reviews the Functioning of SAARC
(Consists of Secretariat, Secretary-General, Directors and General Staff)

Standing Committee
(Represented by Foreign Secretaries of the Member Governments)
Monitors and Coordinates the Programmes

Programming Committee
(Represented by the Senior Officials of the Member Governments)
Scrutinises Budget and Annual Schedule

Technical Committees
(Comprises the Representatives of All Countries)
Formulates, Implements and Monitors Projects

Fig. 9.4. Organisation Structure of SAARC

Regional Integration

Trade within countries in Asia's sub-regions varies enormously and has fallen in recent years while trade between sub-regions is broadly higher and has grown, according to ADB's latest Asian Economic Integration Monitor.

TRADE IN ASIA: 2008-12 Percentage of total sub-regional trade

- Increase from 2000-07 average
- Decrease from 2000-07 average

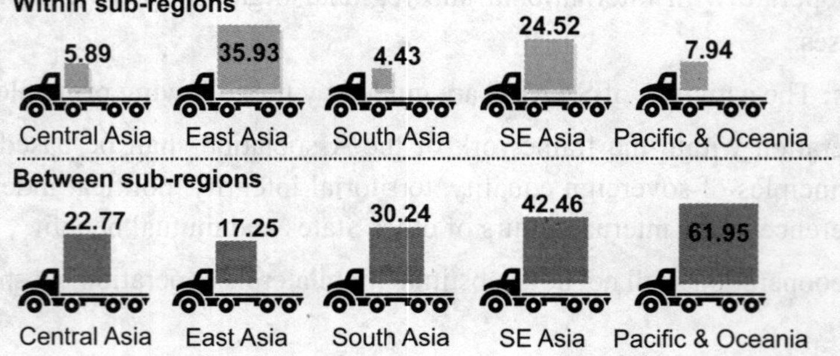

Asia has seen mixed progress in regional integration recently against the backdrop of a shifting economic landscape. Cross-border trade and equity flows have slowed modestly despite improvements in cross-border foreign direct investment, bond purchases and bank credit.

Working: The SARRC countries account for about one-fifth of the world population. All these low income economies and intra-regional trade is at a low level. India is the largest and strongest member of SAARC and other members do not always take it positively. The main areas of cooperation identified in the Integrated Programme of Action (IPA) and pursued through the Technical Committees are as follows:

(*a*) Agriculture and Rural Development.

(*b*) Health and Population Activities.

(*c*) Women, Youth and Children.

(*d*) Environment and Forestry.

(*e*) Science, Technology and Meteorology.

(*f*) Human Resource Development.

(*g*) Transport and Tourism.

(*h*) Radio and Television Broadcasting.

(*i*) Education, and Scientific and Technical Research.

(*j*) Information and Communication Technology.

(*k*) Biotechnology and Energy.

(*l*) Intellectual Property Rights.

9.9 SAARC Preferential Trading arrangement (SAPTA)

At the sixth SAARC summit held in Colombo in December 1991 an idea was mooted to establish a SAARC Preferential Trading Arrangement. The agreement on SAPTA was signed on April 2, 1993, at the seventh SARRC summit in Dhaka. SAPTA became effective from December 7, 1995.

The objectives of SAPTA are to: (*a*) gradually liberalise trade among members of SAARC, (*b*) eliminate trade barriers among member countries, and (*c*) promote and sustain mutual trade and economic cooperation among member countries.

The basic **principles** of SAPTA are as follows:

(*i*) Overall reciprocity and mutuality of advantages so as to benefit equitably all contracting States, taking into account their respective level of economic and industrial development, the pattern of their external trade, and trade and tariff policies and systems;

(*ii*) Negotiation of tariff reform step by step, improved and extended in successive stages through periodic reviews;

(*iii*) Inclusion of all products, manufactures and commodities in their raw, semi-processed and processed forms;

(*iv*) Special and favourable treatment to Least Developed Countries.

The special treatment to Least Developed Countries includes allowing favourable percentage points, application of relaxed rules of origin, favourable terms for technical assistance, duty-free access, deeper tariff preferences, removal of non-tariff barriers, negotiation of long term contracts for sustainable exports, and provision of special facilities for shipping and documentation, training facilities and support to export marketing, etc.

Intra-regional trade accounts for an insignificant share of the total trade of SAARC countries. SAPTA is expected to boost intra-regional trade due to the following reasons:

(*a*) The countries can reduce transport and transit cost due to their geographical proximity.

(*b*) Capital goods produced within the region are more compatible to the factor endowment of member countries than those imported from developed nations.

(*c*) There will be improvement in efficiency because of increased competition among the member countries.

(*d*) Political relations among member states will improve due to stronger economic ties.

(*e*) Regional cooperation may promote regional investment in larger projects.

Brics Low on Biz Trust

Companies in Brazil, Russia, India, China and South Africa still lag in anti-corruption and transparency practices, says a Transparency International report.

20% The proportion of global economic output coming from BRICS

15% Proportion of global trade accounted for by BRICS

India Tops Among Brics Peers

5.4 Average score of Indian companies in the transparency index on a scale of 0-10

- The index is based on unweighted average of results in three categories: reporting on anti-corruption programmes; organisational transparency and country-by-country reporting.
- South Africa is second overall, with an index of 5.1, though it leads India on two factors (see table below).

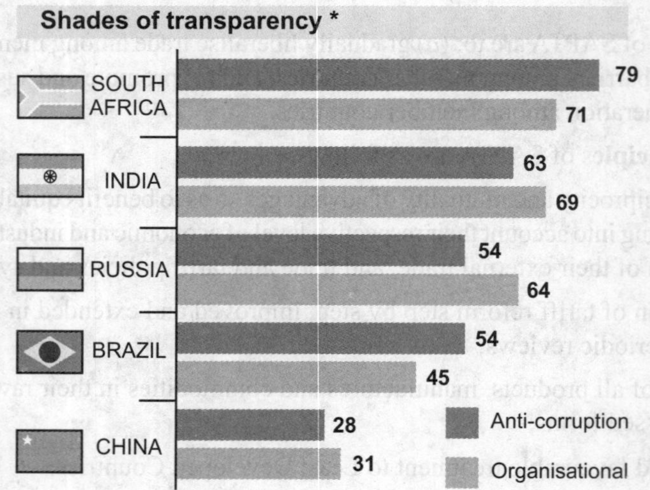

9.10. South Asian Free Trade Area (Safta)

The SARRC Council of Ministers reached an agreement in December 1995 to transform SAPTA into South Asian Free Trade Area (SAFTA). The agreement on SAFTA was signed on January 6, 2004, during the Twelfth SAARC Summit in Islamabad. The SAFTA came into force on January 1, 2006. Negotiations are being held on Rules of Origin, Sensitive Lists of Products, Technical Assistance and Mechanism for Revenue Loss to Least Developed Member States. Customs duties on products from the region will be progressively reduced under the Trade Liberalisation Programme scheduled to be completed by 2016. The Least Developed Member States are expected to benefit from the special and preferential treatment under the agreement.

SUMMARY

Meaning: Economic cooperation and integration among countries within a geographic region.

Benefits: Economies of scale, political ties, market access, improved bargaining power, promotion of infant industries.

Disadvantages: Trade diversion, instability seen as threat to national sovereignty, needs proper monitoring, reduced tax revenue.

Forms: Free trade area, customs union, common market, economic union, political union,

European Union (EU): Works as a single market of fifteen European countries, EURO is its common currency.

NAFTA: A free trade area of North American countries. Includes labour and environmental standards,

ASEAN: An association of eleven countries in South East Asia. Seeks to become an economic community by 2020. It launched free trade area.

SAARC: An association of seven Asian countries including India.

SAPTA: A preferential trading arrangement among members of SAARC.

SAFTA: A free trade area of SAARC countries.

TEST QUESTIONS

1. What do you understand by Regional Economic Cooperation? State its benefits and disadvantages.
2. Explain various types of regional economic groupings with appropriate examples.
3. Describe the nature and working of the European Union (EU).
4. What are the objectives and working of the North American Free Trade Agreement (NAFTA).
5. Discuss the objectives and principles of Association of South-East Asian Nations (ASEAN).

6. Explain the objectives, principles and working of South Asian Association for Regional Cooperation (SAARC).
7. Explain the principles and benefits of SAARC Preferential Trading Arrangement (SAPTA).
8. Write a note on South Asian Free Trade Area (SAFTA).
9. Why do countries opt for Regional Economic Cooperation? Discuss NAFTA.
10. Explain trade creation and trade diversion in an economic integration scheme.
11. What is regional economic integration? Explain the various levels of economic integration.
12. What are the key factors behind the success of East Asian countries? Examine the validity of the East Asian Growth model and examine its applicability to other Asian countries.

CHAPTER 10

International Financial System

LEARNING OBJECTIVES

After studying this chapter, you should understand:

10.1 Exchange Rate Systems
10.2 Exchange Rate Systems under IMF
10.3 Current Exchange Rate Regimes
10.4 Determination of Exchange Rate
10.5 Convertibility of Rupee
10.6 Exchange Control
10.7 Foreign Exchange Management Act
- Summary
- Test Questions

International business involves exchange of currencies between the importing and exporting countries. Each nation has its own currency governed by its monetary policy. The national policies must fit into the international monetary and financial system. A smooth and efficient international financial system is a prerequisite for the growth of international business. Such a system must:

1. ensure easy and quick international payments so as to facilitate trade and capital flows between countries;
2. provide a mechanism for adjusting fluctuations in balance of payments;
3. ensure determination of exchange rate through fair play of market forces; and
4. not interfere with the economic policies of individual nations.

International financial (or monetary) system means the institutional arrangements that govern exchange rates. Foreign exchange markets and government intervention are the two major arrangements. Under the floating exchange rare system market forces of demand and supply govern the exchange rates. Government intervention becomes necessary whenever there is exchange rate crisis, *i.e.,* unprecedented fluctuations in exchange rates over a time period.

10.1 Exchange Rate Systems

There are two major exchange rate systems—fixed exchange rate system and flexible exchange rate system.

1. **Fixed exchange rate system:** Under this system the exchange rate of a currency is determined by the government of the country and is maintained at that predetermined level irrespective of the market forces. Whenever the actual exchange rate differs from this level, the government intervenes.

   Suppose the Government of India determines the exchange rate at Rs. 50 per US dollar, where the demand for rupee is equal to its supply. The domestic cost of production in India increases due to inflation. Imports and the supply of rupee in the foreign exchange market increase leading to fall in the value of rupee to 55 per US dollar. The Reserve Bank of India will sell US dollar from its reserves to absorb the excess supply of rupee. As a result the exchange rate will be restored to Rs. 50.

   On the other hand, when the exchange value of rupee rises above the predetermined level, the Reserve Bank of India will start buying US dollar to restore it to Rs. 50 per US dollar.

   Fixed exchange rate system has the following **advantages:**

   (*i*) Stable exchange rate eliminates uncertainty and risk involved in international payments. It, therefore, helps in orderly development and growth of international trade.

   (*ii*) Exchange rate stability helps to attract foreign capital investment because foreigners prefer to invest in a country with a stable currency.

   (*iii*) Stability of exchange rate helps to prevent outflow of foreign capital.

   (*iv*) Persistent deficit in the balance of payment of a country causes continuous depreciation in the external value of its currency. Fixed exchange rate helps to prevent such depreciation.

   (*v*) A stable exchange rate prevents speculation in the foreign exchange market.

   (*vi*) The successful functioning of regional economic groupings and arrangements requires a stable exchange rate system.

   (*vii*) A stable exchange rate system is essential for the growth of international money and capital markets. Unstable exchange rates create uncertainty and discourage firms and institutions from lending to and borrowing from these markets.

   (*viii*) Stable exchange rate is necessary for orderly development and growth of trade. Both importers and exporters are certain about the amounts they will pay or receive. Stability in exchange rate reduces uncertainty and risk in foreign trade.

   Fixed exchange rate system suffers from the following **disadvantages:**

   (*i*) When the central bank of a country buys foreign currency from the market to reduce the rising external value of domestic currency it causes **inflation.**

(*ii*) The capacity of the central bank to check the rising value of the domestic currency is limited. It may ultimately resort to devaluation and fix a new exchange rate in tune with the current market situation.

(*iii*) The efforts to maintain the fixed exchange rate against a major currency may lead to currency crisis as happened in Argentina, Brazil, Mexico, Russia and South East Asian countries during 1990s. Such crises cause widespread unemployment and other undesirable consequences.

(*iv*) Fixed exchange rate system creates rigidity in the international financial system.

2. **Flexible (free) or floating or fluctuating exchange rate:** Under this system exchange rates are determined by the free play of demand and supply forces in the market. The rates may vary from day to day. A surplus in the country's balance of payments creates an excess demand for its currency and exchange rate tends to rise. On the other hand, a deficit in the balance of payments leads to a fall in the exchange rate. No par value is fixed and the central bank does not intervene in the foreign exchange market. Any disparity in the balance of payments is automatically adjusted through changes in exchange rate. There are no restrictions on buying and selling of foreign currencies in the exchange market.

Flexible exchange rate system offers the following **advantages:**

(*i*) Flexible exchange rate system is simple to operate. The exchange rate moves automatically and freely. Therefore, there is no deficit or surplus of foreign exchange.

(*ii*) The system helps in the promotion of foreign trade as it permits free trade and continuous adjustment of exchange rate.

(*iii*) Flexible exchange rate system helps to increase effectiveness of monetary policy.

(*iv*) Governments have more independence regarding their domestic policies.

(*v*) Expenditure on maintaining official foreign exchange reserves and operation of the fixed exchange rate system is eliminated.

Flexible exchange rate system suffers form the following **disadvantages:**

(*i*) Flexible exchange rate system creates instability, uncertainty and confusion. Frequent changes in exchange rate result in exchange risks impeding international trade and movements of capital.

(*ii*) Market mechanism may fail to determine an appropriate exchange rate. For example, there was a rapid and free fall in the value of Indian Rupee during August-September 2013. The equilibrium exchange rate may fail to indicate correct signals needed to correct the balance of payment position.

(*iii*) Importers and exporters are not certain about the price they will have to pay or receive. This has an adverse impact on foreign trade.

(*iv*) Flexible exchange rate system encourages speculation which has a destablishing effect on the supply of and demand for foreign exchange.

(*v*) This system encourages inflation in the economy. When the currency depreciates due to deficit, imports become costlier leading to a vicious circle of inflation.

Both fixed rate and floating rate systems have merits and demerits. None of them in its pure form is suitable. Most countries have adopted hybrid systems having features of both in different degrees. Economic and political conditions in a country and value judgments influence the choice of the exchange rate system. Many experts argue that flexible exchange rate system is more suitable for globalisation. Convertibility also helps this system.

10.2 Exchange Rate Systems Under IMF

The International Monetary Fund was created soon after World War II with the objective of facilitating smooth working of international trade. It envisaged a fixed exchange rate system for the smooth functioning of international finance. To begin with the IMF scheme made the following provisions:

(*i*) Each member country would declare the external value of its currency in terms of gold and a currency pegged to gold. Most member nations declared values of their currencies in terms of gold and US dollar. This was known as the par value of the currency.

(*ii*) The value of one US dollar was fixed at 35 per ounce of fine gold. The USA made a commitment to convert its dollars into gold at this official price.

(*iii*) The monetary reserves of member countries consisted of gold and US dollars. Thus, US dollar became a reserve asset.

(*iv*) Each member country agreed to maintain the market value of its currency within a margin of 1 per cent of the par value. In case of variation beyond this range the country was expected to devalue its currency to correct the position.

(*v*) Member countries were free to devalue their currencies. But if the devaluation was in excess of 10 per cent, approval of the IMF was necessary. The IMF could approve it or advise a lower rate but had no power to reject the proposal.

(*vi*) Members could obtain short term financial assistance from the IMF to tide over their temporary balance of payments problems. In case of chronic problems they were expected to use permanent solutions like devaluation.

Working of the System

The major industrialised nations other than the USA attempted to minimise changes in exchange rate so as to ensure smooth working of the IMF system. USA played a passive role in foreign exchange markets so as to support other countries' efforts. But like other nations, it endeavoured to maintain a stable price level for tradeable goods. U.S. dollar served as a means of settling international transactions.

This system was distinctly advantageous for the USA because it could get foreign goods and services by merely printing dollars. Dollars provide an additional base for creation of money supply for increase in international trade. But the system depended too much on a single currency.

The IMF system worked smoothly for about two decades. During the late sixties, international liquidity failed to keep pace with increasing volume of international trade. International liquidity was restricted because the supply of gold did not increase. The official price of gold was fixed 35 US dollars per ounce. Most countries found it uneconomical to mine gold due to inflation and increased cost of mining.

Another weakness of the system was undue importance given to a single currency, viz, the US dollar. In order to enable other countries to accumulate reserves, USA had to run deficit in its balance of payments. As every country began accumulating maximum possible dollars ,the value of dollar in the foreign exchange market could not remain stable. Due to sharp fall in the value of dollar, the USA was advised to devalue its currency. Instead, the USA suspended the convertibility of dollar into gold and imposed a surcharge of 10 per cent on its imports. These measures caused a turmoil in the exchange markets and **the system collapsed.**

Ten major industrialised nations (the USA, Britain, Canada, West Germany, France, Italy, Holland, Belgium, Sweden and Japan) met in Washington in December 1971 to solve the dollar crisis. They decided realignment of the currencies. Under the agreement known as **Smithsonian Agreement** the US dollar was devalued by 7.87 per cent. The agrement also allowed exchange rates to fluctuate within 2.25 per cent on either ride. The USA removed the 10 per cent surcharge on its imports but the non-convertibility of dollar into gold continued.

The Smithsonian Agreement failed to solve the crisis and the USA faced unprecedented deficit in its balance of payments. Dollar continued to fall in the exchange market. Several countries tried to save the crisis by purchasing dollar in large quantities. The USA had to devalue dollar again by 10 per cent. Japan, West Germany and UK began to float their currencies and the **Smithsonian Agreement came to an end.**

As dollar continued to fall and the turmoil in the exchange market continued, twenty principal members of the IMF recommended the use of SDR. The official price of gold was abolished in 1975 and **the gold era came to an end**. The countries were now free to buy and sell gold at the prevailing market price. SDR emerged as the international currency but there was no agreement on a new system of exchange rates. The Articles of Association of the IMF was amended. Under the amendment every member country is free to choose its own exchange rate system. But it is expected to ensure stability in the system and orderly conditions in exchange markets. The IMF supervises the exchange rate policies of members to ensure that no member manipulates exchange rates to gain an unfair advantage over other members.

During 1981-1985, the US dollar appreciated by more than 50 per cent due to expansive fiscal policy and tight monetary controls by the US Government. As a result USA lost its export competitiveness. European countries adopted stricter monetary policies to check fall in their currencies but faced poor domestic economic performance. Britain, France, West Germany, Japan and USA (G-5) decided in 1985 to jointly reverse appreciation of the dollar. As a result the dollar fell sharply and G-5 decided in 1987 to stabilise exchange rates at the then existing levels.

10.2 Current Exchange Rate Regimes[1]

On the basis of flexibility, IMF has classified exchange rate policies of its members into eight categories:

1. **Exchange arrangement with no separate legal tender (41 countries):** Under this arrangement the currency of another country circulates as the sole legal tender. For example, US dollar is a legal tender in Ecuador, El Salvador and Panama. Alternatively, the same legal tender is shared by several countries which are members of a monetary or currency union. For example, Euro is the legal tender in 12 European countries. In this system, a country loses control over its monetary policy.

1 IMF Annual Report, 2004

2. **Currency board arrangement (7 countries):** In this type of monetary regime, a country makes a legal commitment to exchange its currency for a specified foreign currency at a fixed exchange rate. In order to fulfil its legal obligation the country issues currency only to the extent of its foreign exchange reserves. This arrangement provides little discretion concerning monetary policy. Bulgaria and Estonia are leading examples of currency board arrangement.
3. **Other conventional fixed peg arrangements (41 countries):** Fixing the value of a currency in terms of another currency is called pegging. The external value of a pegged currency is not dependent upon any independent factor. Rather it changes with changes in the value of the currency to which it is pegged. Pegging can be done in any of the following ways:

   (*a*) Pegging to a major currency, e.g., Chinese Yuan is pegged to US dollar.

   (*b*) Pegging to a basket of currencies. The basket consists of currencies of major trading or financial partners and the weights represent the geographical distribution of trade, services or capital flows.

   (*c*) Pegging to a standardised currency composite such as SDR.

   Under the fixed peg arrangement, the exchange rate is allowed to fluctuate within narrow margin of less than ± 1 per cent. In case no central rate is fixed, the maximum and minimum of the exchange rate may be fixed within a narrow band of less than 2 per cent. The monetary authority uses direct and indirect methods to maintain the fixed parity. Direct intervention involves sale or purchase of foreign currency in the market. Indirect intervention takes the forms of interest rate changes, foreign exchange regulations, moral suction, etc. Monetary authority can perform traditional central banking functions.
4. **Pegged exchange rates with horizontal bonds (4 countries):** This arrangement is similar to the fixed peg with the difference that the fluctuation permitted is beyond ± 1 per cent. The margin between the maximum and minimum value of the exchange rate can exceed 2 per cent. Limited discretion in monetary policy is available depending on the band width. Denmark, Cyprus, Hungary and Tonga have this type of arrangement.
5. **Crawling peg:** Under this system, the currency is adjusted periodically in small amounts at a fixed rate or in response to changes in selective quantitative indicators. The rate of crawl can be set to generate expected inflation-adjusted changes in the exchange rate (backward looking) or set at a pre-announced fixed rate and/or below the projected inflation differential (forward looking). This system imposes constraints on monetary policy like the fixed peg system.
6. **Exchange rates within crawling bands (5 countries):** This arrangement is a combination of horizontal bands and crawling pegs. The currency is maintained within ± 1 per cent around the central rate or between maximum and minimum values exceeding 2 per cent. The central rate or margins are adjusted periodically depending on the band width. There are constraints on monetary policy. Belarus, Honduras, Israel, Romania and Slovenia follow the crawling band system.
7. **Managed floating with no predetermined path for the exchange rate (49 countries):** In this system, the currency is normally floating. But the monetary authority intervenes

when the market fluctuations are violent. There is no specific exchange rate path or target. Balance of payments position, international reserves, parallel market developments are the main indicators. Bangladesh, Thailand, Pakistan, and India are some of the countries which follow managed float.

8. **Independently floating (35 countries):** Under this arrangement the exchange rate is determined by market forces. No country follows this system in its pure form. There is some official intervention to prevent undue fluctuations in the exchange rate. USA, UK, Switzerland and Sri Lanka are some countries which are using independently floating currencies.

10.3 Determination of Exchange Rates

There are two main theories which attempt to explain the determination of exchange rates under the paper currency standard:

1. **Purchasing power parity theory:** Gustav Cassel developed this theory after World War I. According to this theory, in the absence of government control, exchange rate between two currencies is determined by the price levels in the respective countries. In the words of Cassel, " the rate of exchange between two currencies must stand essentially on the quotient of the internal purchasing powers of these currencies".[1]

According to S.E. Thomas, "While the value of the unit of one currency in terms of another currency is determined at any particular time by the market conditions of demand and supply, in the long run, that value is determined by the relative values of the two currencies as indicated by their relative purchasing power over goods and services. In other words, the rate of exchange tends to rest at that point which expresses equality between the respective purchasing powers of the two currencies. This point is called the purchasing power parity."[2]

The purchasing power parity theory suggests that the exchange rate between one currency and another is in equilibrium when their purchasing powers are equivalent. For example, assume that a specific quantity of goods in India costs Rs. 60 and $ 1 in USA. Then the exchange rate will be in equilibrium when the exchange rate is $ 1 = Rs. 60. Whenever deviations occur from this rate, market forces will operate to restore the equilibrium. If the exchange rate deviates to $1 = Rs. 65, dollar holders will convert dollars into rupees to gain Rs. 5 per dollar. As a result, demand for rupee and supply of dollars will increase in the foreign exchange market leading to restoration of equilibrium. Whenever there is a change in purchasing power of currencies, the new equilibrium rate of exchange can be calculated with the help of the formula given below:

$$ER = Er \times \frac{Pd}{Pf}$$

where

ER = Equilibrium exchange rate

Er = Exchange rate in the reference period

Pd = Domestic price index

Pf = Foreign country's price index

1 Cited in M.L. Seth, *Monetary Economics*, Lakshmi Narayan Agarwal, Agra, 1978, p.510

2 *Ibid.*

Merits: The purchasing power parity theory has the following advantages:

(*i*) It indicates the relationship between domestic price levels and exchange rates.

(*ii*) It explains a country's trade status and balance of payments position at a specific point of time.

(*iii*) The theory is applicable to all types of monetary standards.

Demerits: The theory suffers from several drawbacks:

(*i*) The theory is based on the unrealistic assumption, that there are no barriers to international trade.

(*ii*) The theory overlooks the inflow of international capital movements, demand and supply of foreign exchange, transport cost and other factors which influence exchange rate.

(*iii*) The theory suffers from the various limitations of price index number which it uses to measure changes in the equilibrium exchange rate.

(*iv*) The exchange rates calculated on the basis of price indices are unrealistic because the price index includes prices of commodities and services which are no internationally traded.

(*v*) The theory only explains how changes in the purchasing powers of two currencies affect the given exchange rate. It does not explain how that particular exchange rate is determined.

(*vi*) The theory is based on the wrong assumption that the elasticity of demand for exports and imports is equal to unity. This is rarely true.

(*vii*) The theory is against general experience. In a rare case the rate of exchange between two currencies is equivalent to the ratio of their purchasing powers.

(*viii*) The theory fails to explain short term changes in exchange rates.

2. **Balance of payments theory:** Also known as general equilibrium theory and demand and supply theory, it holds that demand and supply in the foreign exchange market determine the exchange rate. The value of a currency appreciates with increase in its demand and depreciates with decrease in its demand. The demand for and supply of a currency depends on the country's balance of payments position. When there is a surplus in the balance of payments, demand for the currency exceeds its supply leading to appreciation in its external value. When there is a deficit, supply exceeds demand causing a fall in the currency's external value.

   Merits: (*i*) The theory takes into account all the items in the balance of payments that determine the exchange rate.

   (*ii*) The theory is in conformity with the general theory of value. Like the price of any other commodity, the exchange rate is determined by the demand and supply forces.

   (*iii*) The theory suggests that adjustments in the exchange rate through devaluation/revaluation can be used to correct disequilibrium in the balance of payments.

   Demerit: The theory fails to consider the influence of rate of exchange on the balance of payments.

10.5 Convertibility of Rupee

Convertibility of a currency means that it can be freely converted into any other currency at rates determined by the market forces of demand and supply and without any interference by the government. There are no quantitative restrictions in the repatriation of the currency. A currency is converted to effect remittances from the country and into the country from abroad. Remittances are classified into two broad categories: (*a*) on current account, and (*b*) on capital account. Remittances on current account represent transactions relating to trade while remittances on capital account relate to investments, loans, etc. In the former no reverse flow of funds is anticipated whereas in case of latter reverse flow in the form of dividend/interest and repatriation of capital is expected. Before 1991 the Rupee was not convertible. From March 1, 1992, the Rupee was made partially convertible. Under this Liberalised Exchange Rate System, 40 per cent of current account transactions were conducted at the rates determined by the Reserve Bank of India and the remaining 60 per cent at market determined rate.

1. **Current account convertibility:** Rupee is now fully convertible on current account. It means the freedom to buy or sell foreign exchange relating to foreign trade, travel, studies, medical treatment, family expenses, etc. The **implications of convertibility** are:
   (*a*) The authorised dealers can release foreign exchange without prior approval of the Reserve Bank of India.
   (*b*) Exporters can easily transact business.
   (*c*) Bureaucratic hurdles involved in obtaining foreign exchange are removed thereby simplifying the job of importers.
   (*d*) More than 100 countries have allowed full convertibility of their currencies on current account.
2. **Capital account convertibility:** It refers to the removal of the restrictions on payments relating to inflows and outflows of capital. In February 1997, the Reserve Bank of India appointed a committee on Capital Account Convertibility (CAC) under the chairmanship of S.S. Tarapore. The committee stipulated the following preconditions for implementation of CAC:
   (*a*) Fiscal consolidation—reduction in gross fiscal deficit to 3.5 per cent of GDP.
   (*b*) Mandated rate of inflation—3 to 5 per cent.
   (*c*) Strengthening of financial system—deregulation of interest rate and reduction in non-performing assets.
   (*d*) Adequacy of reserves.

The committee recommended CAC implementation in three phases—1997-98, 1998-99 and 1999-2000—with careful monitoring. The Asian currency crisis halted India's move towards CAC. But conditions relating to investments abroad and into India are being removed. In March 2006 a committee under the chairmanship of S.S. Tarapore was constituted to set out the Roadmap Towards Fuller Capital Account Convertibility. The committee in its report suggested full CAC by 2011 to be implemented in three phases.

Benefits of CAC

(*i*) CAC makes available a large capital stock to supplement domestic resources and thereby enable the economy to register higher growth, reduce the cost of capital and improve access to international financial markets.

(*ii*) It allows residents to hold an internationally diversified portfolio which reduces the vulnerability of income streams and wealth to domestic stocks, lower funding costs for borrowers, land prospects of higher yields for savers.

(*iii*) Allocative efficiency improves due to financial integration. This can encourage innovation and improve productivity.

(*iv*) It provides impetus for domestic tax regimes, to rationalise land convergence to international tax structures. As a result tax evasion and capital flight on the part of domestic agents are likely to be reduced.

(*v*) It would impose a strong discipline upon the financial system. It would also lead to widening/deepening of markets to enable spreading of risks.

Risks of CAC

(*i*) Credit rating agencies will play a vital role in investors' decisions. The changing views of these agencies may destabilise portfolio flows.

(*ii*) Assets and liabilities of banks are exposed more to price and exchange risks. Fluctuations in exchange rate will affect open foreign currency positions of banks.

(*iii*) Banks may borrow from offshore markets to supplement their domestic deposit base. Volatile interest and exchange rates can be dangerous for weak and fragile banks.

(*iv*) The cost of borrowing for emerging markets may increase due to fluctuations in interest rate. Investing in these markets may become less attractive. There may be currency and maturity mismatches creating huge loss to bank borrowers.

(*v*) The margins for banks may get reduced due to increased competition.

10.6 Exchange Control

Almost every country regulates its foreign exchange resources. The control is exercised usually by the country's Central Bank, *e.g.*, the Reserve Bank of India. The exchange control authority regulates dealings and transactions in foreign exchange. Exporters are required to surrender their foreign exchange earnings to the authority. Similarly, permission of the authority is required to make payments in foreign exchange. Detailed provisions are made to eliminate evasion. The authority allocates foreign exchange according to the national priorities. The authority allows commercial banks, dealers and money changers to handle day-to-day business of buying and selling foreign exchange.

The main objectives of exchange control are as follows:

(*i*) To improve the country's balance of payments position;

(*ii*) To restrict non-essential imports and conspicuous consumption;

(*iii*) To facilitate import of priority items;

(*iv*) To control the outflow of capital;

(*v*) To maintain external value of the domestic currency.

10.7 Foreign Exchange Management Act (FEMA), 1999

The Foreign Exchange Management Act replaced the Foreign Exchange Regulations Act, 1973. FEMA came into effect from January 1, 2000.

Objectives: FEMA aims

(*i*) to facilitate external trade and payments; and

(*ii*) to promote the orderly development and maintenance of foreign exchange market.

Some of the main provisions of FEMA are as follows:

1. **Dealings in foreign exchange:** The Act imposes restrictions on dealings in foreign exchange as well as on receipts from and payments to any person outside India. Without the permission of the Reserve Bank of India and except as provided in the Act no person shall–

   (*a*) deal in any foreign exchange or foreign security with any unauthorised person;

   (*b*) make any payment to or for the credit of any person resident outside India in any manner;

   (*c*) receive any payment by order or on behalf of any unauthorised person resident outside India; and

   (*d*) enter into any financial transaction in India as a consideration for or in association with acquisition or transfer of a right to acquire any asset outside India by any person.

2. **Holding of foreign exchange:** Acquire, hold, own, possess or transfer any foreign exchange, foreign security or any immovable property outside India.

Comparison Between FERA and FEMA

Basis of Comparison	FERA	FEMA
1. Aim	To prevent misuse of foreign exchange	To facilitate external trade
2. Scope	FERA was a larger enactment containing 81 sections	FEMA is a much smaller enactment containing 49 sections
3. Nature	FERA was a prohibitive law	FEMA is a facilitating law
4. Theme	Everything that is specified is under control	Everything other than what is expressly covered is not under control

3. **Current account transactions:** FEMA permits dealings in foreign exchange through authorised persons for current account transactions. However, the Central Government can impose reasonable restrictions in public interest.

4. **Capital account transactions:** Any person may sell or buy foreign exchange to or from an authorised person for a capital account transaction. However, the Reserve Bank of India may prohibit, restrict or regulate the following:

   (*a*) Transfer or issue of any foreign security by a person resident in India;

   (*b*) Transfer or issue of any foreign security by a person resident outside India;

   (*c*) Any borrowing or lending in foreign exchange in whatever form or by whatever name called;

   (*d*) Any borrowing or lending in rupees in whatever form or by whatever name called between a person resident in India and a person resident outside India;

   (*e*) Deposits between persons resident in India and persons resident outside India;

   (*f*) Export, import or holding of currency or currency notes;

   (*g*) Transfer of immovable property outside India, other than a lease not exceeding five years, by a person resident in India;

   (*h*) Acquisition or transfer of immovable property in India, other than a lease not exceeding five years, by a person resident outside India;

   (*i*) Giving of guarantee or surety in respect of any debt, obligation or other liability incurred by a person resident in India or outside India.

   - A person resident in India may hold, own, transfer or invest in foreign currency, foreign security or any immovable property situated outside India if such currency, security or property was acquired, held or owned by such person when he was resident outside India or inherited from a person who was resident outside India.
   - A person resident outside India may hold, own, transfer or invest in Indian currency, security or any immovable property situated in India if such currency, security or property was acquired, held or owned by such person when he was resident in India or inherited from a person who was resident in India.
   - The Reserve Bank of India may prohibit, restrict or regulate establishment in India of a branch, office or other place of business by a person resident outside India for carrying on any activity relating to such branch, office or place of business.
   - The Reserve Bank of India shall not impose any restriction on the drawal of foreign exchange for payments due on account of a amortisation of loans or for depreciation of direct investments in the ordinary course of business.

5. **Export of goods and services:** Every exporter of goods shall—

   (*a*) furnish to the Reserve Bank of India or to such other authority a declaration as specified containing true and correct particulars including the full value or the expected value of goods or services sold outside India; and (*b*) furnish to the Reserve Bank of India such other information as may be required for the purpose of ensuring the realisation of the export proceeds.

For the purpose of ensuring that export value of the goods is received without any delay, the Reserve Bank may direct any exporter to comply with such requirements as it deems fit.

6. **Realisation and repatriation of foreign exchange:** Where any amount of foreign exchange is due or has accrued to any person, he shall take all reasonable steps to realize and repatriate it to India within the time and in the manner prescribed by the Reserve Bank of India. However, several exemptions are granted to this clause.

SUMMARY

Exchange rate systems: 1. Flexible exchange rate system, and 2. Fixed exchange rate system.

Exchange Rate Systems Under IMF: Gold era, Par value system, Triffin Paradox, Smithsonian Agreement, end of gold era

Current exchange rate regimes: No separate legal tender, currency board arrangement, fixed peg arrangement, pegged exchange rates with horizontal bands, exchange rates within crawling bands, managed floating with no predetermined path, independent floats.

Convertibility of Rupee: Free conversion of one currency into another at a rate determined by market forces. 1. Current Account Convertibility. 2. Capital Account Convertibility.

Exchange control: Needed to improve balance of payments, to restrict non-essential imports, to control outflow of capital, to maintain external value of Rupee.

FEMA: Seeks to facilitate foreign trade and foreign exchange market. (*i*) dealings in foreign exchange (*ii*) holding of foreign exchange (*iii*) current account transactions (*iv*) capital account transactions (*v*) export of goods and services (*vi*) realisation and repatriation of foreign exchange.

TEST QUESTIONS

1. What is meant by international financial system? Explain the essentials of a sound international financial system.
2. What is fixed exchange rate system? Describe its advantages and disadvantages.
3. What is flexible (floating) exchange rate system? Discuss its advantages and disadvantages.
4. Explain the exchange rate system under the International Monetary Fund.
5. Discuss the current exchange rate regimes.
6. Explain the Purchasing Power Parity Theory of exchange rate determination, pointing out its merits and demerits.
7. Discuss the Balance of Payments Theory of determining exchange rate, stating its merits and demerits.

8. What is meant by convertibility of Rupee? Discuss the desirability of making Rupee fully convertible on current account.
9. What is Capital Account Convertibility of Rupee? State its benefits and risks.
10. What is exchange control? State its objectives.
11. Explain the objectives and main provisions of the Foreign Exchange Management Act (FEMA).
12. Give a comparison of FERA and FEMA.
13. Write short notes on:
    (*a*) Triffin Paradox
    (*b*) Smithsonian Agreement
    (*c*) Pegged exchange rate
14. How was the fixed exchange rate system established at Bretton Woods different from the Gold Standard? Why did the fixed exchange rate system collapse?
15. Discuss the impact of inflation and interest rate on the exchange rate.
16. What do you mean by floating exchange rate regime? How does the central bank of a country intervene in the foreign exchange market in order to stabilise the exchange rate?

CHAPTER

11 Foreign Exchange Markets and Exchange Risk Management

LEARNING OBJECTIVES

After studying this chapter, you should understand:

11.1 Concept and Features of Foreign Exchange Markets

11.2 Functions of Foreign Exchange Markets

11.3 Dealings or Transactions in Foreign Exchange Markets

11.4 Concepts of Risk and Exposure

11.5 Types of Exchange Risks Exposure

11.6 Methods of Managing Exchange Risks.

- Summary
- Test Questions

Foreign exchange is the process of converting one currency into another currency. It is also the system of transferring money from one country to another. According to Evitt, foreign exchange is "that section of economic science which deals with the means and methods by which rights to wealth in one country's currency are converted into rights to wealth in terms of another country's currency.... It involves the investigation of the method by which the currency of one country is exchanged for that of another, the causes which render such exchanges necessary, the forms which such exchange may take, and the ratios or equivalent values at which such exchanges are effected."[1]

Under the Foreign Exchange Management Act [FERA] 1973, foreign exchange is defined as "foreign currency and includes all deposits, credits and balance payable in any foreign currency and any drafts, traveller's cheques, letters of credit and bills of exchange, expressed or drawn in Indian currency, but payable in any foreign currency".

11.1 Concept and Features of Foreign Exchange Markets

The foreign exchange market is a market in which foreign currencies are bought and sold. In other words, it is a market in which foreign exchange transactions take place.

The salient features of the foreign exchange market are as follows:

1. **Location:** There is no physical place where transactions in foreign exchange take place. It is rather an informal arrangement among the participants who are connected to each

1. Chaeol S. Eun and Bruce G. Restmik, *International Financial Management,* Tata McGraw Hill, New Delhi, 2001; p. 129

other by means of telephone, telex and a satellite communication network (SWIFT). Therefore, foreign exchange market is described as an Over The Counter (OTC) market. In the **wholesale segment** of the market, dealings take place among the banks. In the **retail segment** dealings take place between banks and their customers. The retail segment may be considered as the counters of the foreign exchange market.

2. **Market Size:** Foreign exchange market is the largest financial market in the world. Foreign exchange markets were primarily developed to facilitate settlement of debts airsing out of international trade. But these markets have developed on their own so much so that a turnover of about three days in the foreign exchange market is equivalent to the volume of world trade in goods and services. In April 2004 the average daily turnover in the foreign exchange market was 1.9 trillion US dollars. London, New York. Tokyo, Zurich and Frankfurt are the largest financial markets in the world.
3. **Round-The Clock Market:** Foreign exchange markets work in such a way that where one market closes the other opens so that one or the other market is always operating. Therefore, foreign exchange market is functioning 24 hours of the day. In India, the market is open during regular banking hours. No transactions take place on Saturdays and Sundays.
4. **Participants:** The participants in the foreign exchange market include central bank, commercial banks, exchange brokers, and corporates. The **central bank** may intervene in the market to influence the exchange rate. The central bank may transact in the market on its own for this purpose. It may also buy or sell foreign exchange on behalf of the Government. The Reserve Bank of India intervenes in the foreign exchange market when the exchange rates are moving in a detrimental manner due to speculative forces. **Commercial banks** are the major participants. The buy and sell currencies for their clients. They may also operate on their own to gain from movements in exchange rates. Banks directly deal among themselves for large volume transactions. **Exchange brokers** facilitate deals between banks. They ensure that the most favourable quotation is obtained and at low cost in terms of time and money. Accredited exchange brokers are permitted to contract exchange business on behalf of authorised dealers in foreign exchange subject to the prescribed rules and regulations. **Corporates** consist of business houses, multinational corporations and international investors who operate in the market for their trade and investment needs. They may also buy or sell currencies for trading and speculation but subject to the prescribed rules and regulations.
5. **Currencies Traded:** In most foreign exchange markets, US dollar is used to denominate international transactions. Euro, Yen, and Pound Sterling are other major currencies.
6. **Efficiency:** The foreign exchange market is very efficient due to modern means of communication. The participants keep abreast of current events through services like Dow Jones, Telerate and Reuter. Any significant development any market instantaneously becomes known to other markets and thus has a global impact.

11.2 Functions of Foreign Exchange Market

The main functions of a foreign exchange market are as follows:

1. **Transfer of Purchasing Power:** The primary function of a foreign exchange market is the transfer of purchasing power from one country/currency to another. By performing the international clearing function, foreign exchange markets greatly facilitate international trade and capital movements.
2. **Provision of Credit:** International trade depends largely on credit facilities. Foreign exchange markets help in the growth of foreign trade by performing the credit function. Exporters can get both pre-shipment and post-shipment credit. Importers can also avail of the credit facilities. The Euro-dollar market has emerged as a major international credit market.
3. **Hedging Facilities:** Foreign exchange markets provide hedging facilities which help to cover export risks. With the help of hedging facilities exporters and importers can guard themselves against losses caused by fluctuations in exchange rates.

11.3 Dealings or Transactions in Foreign Exchange Market

Transactions conducted in a foreign exchange market may be classified into the following categories:

1. **Spot Transactions:** These are foreign exchange transactions which require the immediate delivery or exchange of currencies on the spot. In actual practice, the settlement takes place within two days after the date of the contract. For example, if the contract is made on Monday, the delivery must take place by Wednesday. In case Wednesday is a holiday, the delivery will take place on the next day, *i.e.,* Thursday. The date on which the currencies are exchanged is the value date. Both the currencies involved in a transaction are paid on the same day so that there is no loss of interest to the either party.

   When the agreement to buy or sell is executed on the same day, the transaction is known as **cash** or **ready** transaction. It is also known as **value today.** A transaction in which the currencies are to be exchanged the next day of the agreement is called **value tomorrow** or **turn transaction.** When a bank urgently requires foreign exchange it may ask for early settlement. In such a case it may ask for a special quotation for delivery on the same day. The rate of exchange effective for the spot transaction is known as the **spot rate.** The market for spot transactions is called the **spot market.**
2. **Forward Transactions:** The transaction in which the exchange of currencies (delivery) takes place at some specified future date is known as **forward transaction.** A forward transaction can be for delivery one month, two months, three months, etc. after the date of the transaction. The rate of exchange applicable to a forward contract is known as the **forward exchange rate.** The market for forward transactions is called the **forward market.**

   In order to curb speculation in the foreign exchange market, governments of various countries regulate the forward exchange transactions. For instance, commercial banks in India are allowed to offer forward cover only with respect to genuine export and import transactions. Forward exchange transactions are helpful to exporters and importers. They can enter into such transactions to cover risks arising out of fluctuations in exchange rate.

The forward exchange rate may be at par, premium or discount with the spot rate, depending on the demand for and supply of forward exchange.

(*a*) **At Par:** This means the forward exchange rate is quoted equivalent to the spot rate. When the demand for and supply of forward exchange are equivalent, the forward rate will be at par.

(*b*) **At Premium:** The forward rate for a currency, say the dollar, is said to be at a premium when one dollar buys more units of another currency, say rupee, in the forward market than in the spot market. The premium is expressed as a percentage deviation from the spot rate on a per annum basis When the demand for forward exchange exceeds its supply, the forward rate is quoted at a premium.

(*c*) **At Discount:** The forward rate for a currency, say the dollar, is said to be at discount with respect to the spot rate when one dollar buys fewer rupees in the forward market than in the spot market. When the supply of forward exchange exceeds its demand, the forward rate is quoted at discount.

3. **Futures:** A futures contract is similar to a forward contract but there are several differences between the two. A forward contract is customised or tailormade for the client by his/her international bank. But a futures contract has standardised features in terms of size, maturity date, etc. Secondly, a forward contract does not require margin while margins are required in respect of a futures contract. An initial margin must be deposited into a collateral account to create a futures position. Moreover, futures can be traded only on an organised exchange.
   In a futures contract actual delivery does not take place. On the due date, the difference between the spot rate and forward rate agreed under the contract is settled.
4. **Options:** A futures contract protects the buyer from adverse changes in the exchange rate. But it also eliminates the possibility of gain from favourable changes in the exchange rate. For instance, when an Indian exporter makes a forward contract to sell his future dollar receipts at $1 = Rs 60, he is protected against the risk of decrease in the value of dollar to Rs. 58. But at the same time the contract prevents him from gaining from the increase in the value of dollar to Rs 62. Currency options are designed to overcome this limitation of forward contracts.

   An option is a contract that gives its holder the **right** (but not the **obligation**) to sell or buy the specified quantity of an asset at a specified price on a specified date in future. An option to buy is called a **call option,** and an option to sell is called **put option,** Buying or selling the underlying asset via the option is known as exercising the option. The stated price is called the **exercise** or **striking price**. The buyer of an option is called the **long** whereas the seller of an option is called the **short.** The price for the option is called the **premium.**

   Thus, an option combines the advantages of both spot and futures.
5. **Swap Transactions:** Commercial banks who undertake foreign exchange business may enter into swap transactions to adjust their fund position. The term **swap** refers to simultaneous sale of spot currency for the forward purchase of the same currency or the purchase of spot for the forward sale of the same currency. The spot currency is swapped against forward. Therefore, a swap is also known as a **double deal.**

In a swap transaction, the same amount of the same currency is purchased and sold for different maturities. For instance, State Bank of India (SBI) and IDBI make a swap deal under which SBI buys ten million US dollars in spot and sells it forward for two months. A swap deal may also involve two forwards like purchase of three months forward and sale of six months forward.

6. **Arbitrage:** An arbitrage means simultaneous buying and selling of foreign currencies with the intention of making profits from the difference between the exchange rates prevailing at the same time in different foreign exchange markets. For instance, assume that the exchange rate in New York is £ 1 = $ 2.10 while in London it is £1 = $ 2. In this situation, one can earn a profit of $ 100 by buying ten thousand pound sterlings in London and selling the same in New York. This would lead to an increase in demand for pound sterling in London and an increase in supply of pound sterling in New York. Such arbitrage transactions ultimately equalise the exchange rates in the two markets.

   Modern means of communication between financial centres throughout the world are so easy and fast that arbitrage in foreign currencies is possible. Arbitrage operations eliminate differences in exchange rates in different markets. Theoretically speaking, a single world market in foreign exchange is created.

Regulators Widen Global Probe into Forex Market

As part of an international probe into suspected manipulations in foreign exchange markets, a section of traders have come under scanner for possible manoeuvring in rupee trades, which clock an average daily volume of over $50 billion globally.

These groups have been found to be using monikers like "The Cartel", "The Dream Team", "The Bandits' Club" and "The Club" on various online forums, instant messaging platforms such as Whats App and BlackBerry Messenger and are suspected to be engaged in manipulation of numerous foreign exchange rates.

The manipulation is suspected to have spread across the world, including the US, the UK, Switzerland and Europe and Asian nations such as India, Singapore, Hong Kong and Indonesia.

Regulators from across the world, including India, are cooperating with each other in the worldwide probe into forex markets, which, according to some estimates, clock trades worth $5.3 lakh crore a day.

This includes trades worth over $50 billion a day involving Indian rupee, although half of these trades take place outside India and in markets such as London, Singapore, Dubai, Switzerland, the UK, Hong Kong and the US.

Those suspected to be involved in possible manipulations include some forex traders, as also certain Swiss banks and other European financial institutions, while it is unlikely that any Indian bank or financial services firm might be directly involved.

The possible manipulation in rupee trades might have taken place outside India, although the role of certain executives at Indian branches of suspected European banks might not be completely ruled out.

11.4 Concepts of Exchange Risk and Exposure

Currency exchange rate risk is one of the important problems which a firm faces in international business. Exchange risk means the possibility of loss due to fluctuations in the rate of exchange between two or more currencies. It is the net potential loss to a firm with foreign exchange exposure which can arise from changes in exchange rate. A company engaged in export/import is affected by a change in the rate of exchange between the domestic currency and the currency in which the transaction is designated. For example, an Indian company which imports raw material from USA when the $ was quoted at ₹ 58 per dollar will suffer a loss if the dollar appreciates to ₹ 66 per dollar by the time the imports are paid for. Similarly, an Indian company which has a subsidiary in Germany denominates the subsidiary's assets and liabilities in Euro. The overall financial position of the parent company would be affected when the value of Euro in terms of rupees depreciates.

It is possible that an adverse change in exchange rate may turn an otherwise profitable deal into a loss. For example, assume an Indian company makes an export deal with a profit margin of 10 per cent. In the meantime foreign currency in which the deal is denominated depreciates by 15 per cent. The company would suffer a loss of 5 per cent on the deal. When the change in exchange rate is favourable, the company will make a windfall gain. The concept of exchange risk covers both the possibilities.

11.5 Types of Exchange Risks

There are three types of foreign exchange risks or exposures. The term exposure means the degree to which a company is affected by changes in exchange rate.

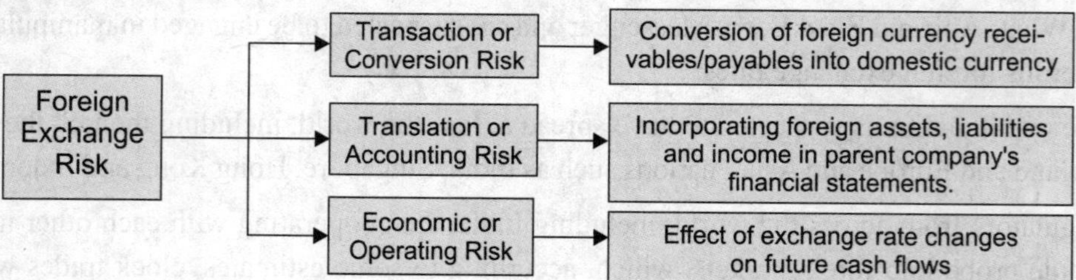

Fig. 11.1 : Types of Foreign Exchange Risks

1. **Transaction or Conversion Exposure:** It means the risk associated with change in the exchange rate between the date of the transaction and the date of its settlement. It is concerned with changes in cash flows arising out of existing contractual obligations. For example, an Indian exporter enters into an export transaction with a Japanese firm at the value of 50,000 Yen. On the date of the transaction the exchange rate is ₹ 40 per Yen. Therefore, the exporter hopes to receive ₹ 20 lacs on the execution of the order. The order is executed after three months when the exchange rate moves to ₹ 35 per Yen. The exporter will receive ₹ 17.50 lacs, therefore, suffering a loss of ₹ 2.50 lacs. Such loss or gain arising out of exchange rate fluctuations when the foreign currency denominated transaction is settled and converted into the domestic currency is known as the transaction exposure or conversion exposure. Such exposure occurs whenever a

company has foreign currency denominated receivables or payables. The receivables or payables are created before the change but settled after the change in exchange rate. The degree of exposure depends on unsettled receivables and payables or non-executed export/import orders.

2. **Translation or Accounting Exposure:** It arises when a company has assets or liabilities denominated in foreign currency and these have to be shown in the financial statements in the domestic currency. For example, an Indian company has a subsidiary in New York. The subsidiary's assets are worth one million US dollars. For the purpose of reporting and consolidation the subsidiary's assets are shown in the parent company's balance sheet in rupees. When the exchange rate changes, loss or gain may arise in foreign exchange translation. Assets and liabilities that are translated at the current exchange rate (after the change) are exposed. Thus, translation exposure is the difference between exposed assets and exposed liabilities. No exposure arises in respect of assets and liabilities valued at historical cost as these are not affected by exchange rate changes.

   Translation exposure is also known as accounting exposure because it relates only to book values, and does not involve cash flows. When the parent company prepares its final accounts the assets and liabilities of its foreign subsidiary are merged with its own to present a consolidated statement to provide an overall picture of the company. The translation loss/gain is shown as a separate component of the equity in the balance sheet. It does not affect the company's current earnings.

3. **Economic or Operating Exposure:** It refers to the effect of unexpected change in exchange rates on the future operating cash flows of the company. The value of a firm is measured by the present value of its expected future cash flows. A change in the exchange rate can alter a company's future revenues and costs and thereby its future cash flows. As a result the actual net present value of the company may differ from the anticipated value. Suppose a multinational corporation has concentrated its production in domestic country but sells its output across the world. When the domestic currency appreciates, its products will become costly in terms of foreign currencies. Its profit margins and its competitiveness are likely to decline. Several Japanese multinationals had to shift their production bases overseas to guard against this risk.

   The economic exposure is insidious. Therefore, it is more difficult to measure and manage. But it has wider and far reaching effects than the accounting exposure. It is easier to measure and provide for accounting exposure. Economic exposure is also known as competitive exposure because it involves the actions of competitors and consumers in addition to those of the company. For example, an Indian company's exports of textiles to USA may decline because the currencies of other countries who export textiles to USA depreciate but Indian rupee does not depreciate. Indian exports become costlier as compared to those of other countries.

11.6 Methods of Managing Exchange Risks

The main objective of exchange risk management is to eliminate or minimise the losses that may arise due to fluctuations in exchange rate. Various methods used for managing exchange risks may be classified into two broad categories as follows:

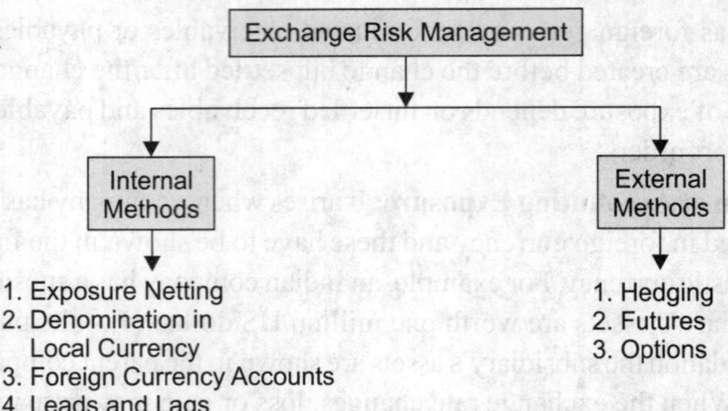

Fig. 11.2 : Methods of Managing Exchange Risks

1. **Exposure Netting:** It means managing the size of receivables and payables in a foreign currency in such a way that they match each other. The loss in payables is offset by gains in receivables and *vice versa*. This is possible when a company has both receivables and payables in the same foreign currency. In a company having receivables and payables in several currencies, exposure netting involves grouping the currencies into two: (*i*) Those whose value is likely to appreciate, and (*ii*) those whose value is likely to depreciate. The exposure due to receivables in a currency which is likely to appreciate may be offset by payables in another currency which is also likely to appreciate. For example, if both US dollars and Euro are expected to appreciate, a company having receivables of 10 million US dollar can manage its exposure by having equivalent amount of payables in Euro. Similarly, a company's receivables in a currency which is likely to depreciate may be offset by its payables in another currency which is also likely to depreciate. Another way of netting is to have equal amounts of receivables in two currencies—one likely to appreciate and the other likely to depreciate.

   Exposure netting is possible in case of multinational companies having a portfolio of currency positions. They have the leverage of designating their receivables and payables in different currencies. For the net position that remains exposed after netting, technique, like forward cover can be adopted.

2. **Denomination in Local Currency:** The exchange risk can be totally avoided by denominating the transaction in local currency. In such a case, the other party to the transaction will bear the exchange risk. For example, when exports from India are invoiced in Indian rupees, the importer is under the obligation to pay a fixed sum of rupees. If the value of rupee appreciates the importer will have to pay more in terms of his own currency and *vice versa*. Similarly, an Indian importer can avoid the exchange risk by denominating the transaction in Indian rupees.

   Denomination of the transaction in local currency puts the other party at a disadvantage. Therefore, the other party would like to safeguard itself. For example, an exporter from USA may quote a higher price (*e.g.,* ₹ 65) than the prevailing exchange rate (*e.g.,* ₹ 60 per $). In this case the Indian importer may not gain by denominating the deal in rupees. Alternatively, the transaction may be invoiced partly in local currency and partly in foreign currency. But such a measure will lead to sharing the gain/loss from exchange rate changes between the two parties.

An importer/exporter can insist on invoicing in his own currency only when his bargaining power is stronger than that of the other party. For example, most of India's foreign trade is denominated in foreign currencies like US dollar, Pound sterling, Deutsche Mark and Japanese Yen. Invoicing in Indian rupees has been possible in trade with countries with which India had bilateral trade agreements.

3. **Foreign Currency Accounts:** A manufacturer-exporter who imports sizeable amount of raw materials/components, or a trader who is engaged in both exports and imports can minimise his exchange risk by maintaining an account abroad through which all transactions are routed. He is exposed to exchange risk only for the net balance because exports can pay for imports. The loss of exchange in converting from foreign currency into domestic currency is also avoided.

   Under the Exchange Earners Foreign Currency (EEFC) Account Scheme in India, the beneficiary of an inward remittance is permitted to retain the full amount of remittance in foreign currency. The balance in this account can be used for imports and other prescribed purposes. The Reserve Bank of India permits exporters with good track record and net exchange earners of ₹ 4 crore and above to maintain foreign currency accounts abroad subject to the specified terms and conditions.

4. **Leads and Lags:** Exporters and importers try to hasten or postpone the time or receipt or payment of foreign currency on the basis of their estimates as to whether the currency will depreciate or appreciate in future. This timing of receipt/payment upon the expectations of change in exchange value is known as 'leads and lags'.

   When the exporter expects depreciation of foreign currency, he would insist for payment earlier than due date. On the other hand, when the currency is expected to appreciate, an importer would make the payment earlier than the due date. In both these cases, the exporter/importer is said to 'lead' the payment.

   When an exporter expects appreciation of foreign currency he would like to delay the payments from the importer. On the other hand, when a depreciation of foreign currency is expected, an importer would like to delay the payment. In both these cases, the exporters importer is said to 'lag' the payment.

   Leads and lags tend to aggravate the forces causing depreciation or appreciation in a currency. According to exchange regulations in India, payments for exports and imports must be completed within six months from the date of shipment. Therefore, exporters and importers can indulge in 'leads and lags' within a period of six months.

5. **Hedging:** It means establishing an offsetting currency position so that loss/gain on the original currency exposure is offset by a corresponding gain/loss on the currency hedge. Hedging may be used in three situations:

   (*a*) **Hedging transaction exposure:** It involves buying or selling foreign exchange for future delivery to match a given foreign currency receipt or payment. This is called contractual or monetary hedging.

   (*b*) **Hedging balance sheet exposure:** It involves making short term forward contracts to offset 'paper' losses or gains on the long term assets and liabilities of foreign subsidiaries.

(*c*) **Hedging economic exposure:** It involves offsetting the effect of exchange rate fluctuation on the overall profitability of the company.

Hedging can be forward contract hedge or money market hedge.

(*i*) **Forward Contract Hedge:** Under a forward exchange contract, a banker and a customer or another banker agree to buy or sell a fixed amount of foreign currency on a specified future date at a predetermined exchange rate. For example, an exporter who has extended three months credit to his customer may agree to sell to his banker the specified amount of foreign currency at the end of three months. In this way the risk arising out of exchange rate change on his export deal is offset by the forward contract.

The forward contract under which the delivery is to take place on a specified future date is known as **'fixed forward contract'.** It is not always possible for an exporter to give delivery of foreign exchange on the specified date as several types of delays and constraints are involved in international trade. In order to overcome this problem, the exporter may seek the choice of delivering foreign exchange during a given time period. The arrangement under which one can sell or buy foreign exchange on any day during a given time period at a predetermined exchange rate is called **"option forward contract".** This period is called 'option period' and the predetermined rate is called 'option forward rate'.

(*ii*) **Money Market Hedge:** In this type of hedging, a firm borrows or lends in the domestic and foreign money markets to guard against transaction exposure. It may borrow to hedge its foreign currency receivables and sell to hedge its foreign currency payables. For example, an Indian firm which has receivables in US dollars may borrow the required amount in dollars for the period of receivables, convert them into rupees and invest them. The dollar amount can be paid off when the receivables are realised.

6. **Currency Futures:** A futures contract is an agreement entered into with the specified futures exchange. It gives the right to buy or sell a standard amount of foreign currency at a specified price on a specified date in future.

The salient features of a futures contract are as follows:

(*a*) **Standard Size:** The size of the transaction is standardised. For example, at Chicago Mercantile Exchange, the standard size of a futures contract is £ 62,500, Euro 10,000, yen 12,500,000 and so on.

(*b*) **Futures Exchanges:** A futures contract can be made only on a recognised futures exchanges such as London International Financial Futures Exchange (LIFFE). There are more than fifty futures exchanges in the world.

(*c*) **Delivery Dates:** Futures contracts fall due on a specified day in specified months during the year. For example, at Chicago Exchange, the delivery date is third Wednesday of March, June, September and December.

(*d*) **Trading through Members:** Buyers and sellers of futures contracts place orders with members of the exchange. The deal by a member or broker is made when someone is willing to buy or sell at the agreed price.

(*e*) **Price Movements:** The price for the futures is quoted as so many units of US dollar per unit of foreign currency. For example, the Euro futures may be bought at a price of $1.10. The exchange may fix the minimum size of price movements, known as tick. The exchange may also fix the maximum inter-day movements of the price. In case price varies beyond the prescribed limit, the exchange may suspend trading until the margin accounts are properly adjusted.

(*f*) **Settlement through Clearing House:** The transaction between two members (buyer and seller) is settled through the clearing house. The buying member accepts delivery and the selling member gives delivery of the foreign exchange. Such arrangement protects members against default.

(*g*) **Margins:** The members are required to keep margins ranging from 2.5 per cent to 10 per cent of the outstanding contracts with the exchange. The margin deposited at the time of making the contract is called **initial margin**. The margin money is adjusted according to changes in the value of futures. In case the margin money falls below the maintenance level, additional margin has to be deposited to bring it to the initial level.

(*h*) **Marking to Market:** It is the process of revaluing the contract on the basis of future contract's ruling price. This is necessary for adjusting the margin money.

(*i*) **Liquidity:** The buyer of the future need not hold it until maturity date. He can sell to another to wind up his position. Similarly, a seller can square his position. Most of the future contracts are squared up through counter deals. This ensures liquidity in the exchange.

There is intense competition in the futures market. Therefore, futures are an effective tool for hedging large exposures. However, a part of the exposure may remain uncovered due to standard size of contract. Moreover, transactions fall due throughout the year whereas future contracts mature only at specified dates in each quarter. Currency futures are, therefore, not a popular tool of hedging exchange risks.

BRICS erects $100bn wall to stem currency slide

Joint Fightback: Emerging economies come together in tough times to form special fund; India to contribute $18bn, China will give largest chunk of $40bn.

St. Petersburg: India is joining hands with four other top developing economies to set up a $100 billion fund that could help it weather currency storms like the one that has blown the rupee away this year.

The biggest of the five BRICS economies, China, will contribute $41 billion, while India, Brazil and Russia will pay in $18 billion and South Africa $5 billion, officials said after the group of leaders met informally on the margins of the G20 summit in St Petersburg, Russia.

The fund, or Contingency Reserve Arrangement (CRA), could become a reality next year, though hurdles remain. It is expected to function as a second layer of cushion after domestic foreign exchanges reserves.

In effect, much like a chit fund or a group insurance scheme in the case of individuals, these economies can lean on each other's reserves through the CRA in proportion to their contribution and use any borrowing from the International Monetary Fund (IMF) only as a last resort. The IMF imposes stringent, politically challenging conditions that these economies want to avoid.

India has reserves of $278 billion, enough for about seven months imports. It has been dipping into its reserves to defend the rupee, which has fallen by about 20% this year. Central banks sell dollars in the market to prop up the value of their national currency vis-a-vis the dollar.

The BRICS fund was proposed at a meeting of the group in Durban earlier this year, and bringing it to life has become more urgent as global funds exit emerging markets for a resurgent United States, battering the currencies of developing countries.

7. **Options:** An option gives the buyer the right to buy or sell a given sum of foreign currency at a predetermined rate on a future date. On the due date, the buyer of the option may or may not exercise his right. The main features of currency options are as under:

   (*a*) **Two parties:** There are two parties to an option contract—the option buyer and the option seller. An exporter/importer or a corporate treasurer is usually the buyer. Option seller or writer of the option is usually the bank.

   (*b*) **Call and put options:** Call option is the right to buy whereas put option is the right to sell. The foreign currency to be bought or sold is generally in terms of the US dollar which serves as the base currency.

   (*c*) **Premium:** It means the fee or consideration which buyer pays to the seller at the time of the contract. The premium paid is not refundable whether the buyer exercises his right or not.

   (*d*) **Strike price:** The exchange rate at which the two parties agree to exchange the two currencies is called strike price. Different rates may be quoted for option, each at a different premium. The amount of premium depends upon market expectation about future exchange rate.

   (*e*) **Execution:** Under **Amercian option,** the buyer can exercise his right on or before maturity. In case of **European option,** the right can be exercised only on maturity date. Premium charged is higher in case of the former.

   In a forward contract, the benefit of any favourable change in exchange rate is not available to the hedger. Option contract gives an opportunity to the hedger to gain from favourable changes in the exchange rate. But option contract is costly due to the upfront premium and interest on it till the execution of the contract.

   When there is a definite exposure and the movement in exchange rate can be anticipated, forward contract is better than option for hedging because no cost is involved in a forward contract. But currency option contract is preferable in the following situations:

   (*a*) When the exposure is uncertain—for example, if a company bids in a foreign currency denominated tender, the exposure will arise only when the bid is accepted and the company is offered the contract. At the time of bidding, the company can make an option contract. In case the contract is not accepted, the company can allow the option to expire. On the other hand, option can be exercised if the contract is awarded and there is an adverse movement in exchange rate.

(*b*) When the exposure is certain but movement in exchange is uncertain.

India Moves to Make Currency Future(s) Secure

India is preparing a plan to allow greater overseas participation in the domestic currency futures market to protect the rupee from the kind of attack by speculators that saw it crash to a record low recently.

Much of the speculative trade that led to the slide in the Indian currency took place in the offshore non-deliverable forwards (NDF) market, largely focused on currencies such as the rupee belonging to countries with capital controls. The rupee plunged to 68.85 to the dollar in August-end before recovering to around 61.5 following a series of measures by the central bank and government.

The government wants to kill the rupee NDF market–where contracts in the currency worth billions of dollars are traded every day—by persuading those active in it to shift to the onshore currency futures market in India by easing restrictions. The move is part of the next generation of financial sector reforms on the government's agenda.

Foreign investors are currently not allowed to hedge their rupee exposure in the Indian over-the-counter (OTC) or exchange-traded markets and must go through category-I banks. This has forced them to use the NDF market, where there are no restrictions and transaction costs are lower as are barriers to trade.

RBI naturally has no jurisdiction over the NDF market.

SUMMARY

Concept and Features: Foreign exchange market is a market in which foreign currencies are bought and sold. Informal location, round-the-clock operation, participants, currencies traded, efficiency are its main features.

Functions: Transfer of purchasing power, hedging, provision of credit.

Dealings: Spot transactions, forward contracts, futures, options, swaps, arbitrage

Concept of Exchange Risk: Risk caused by changes in exchange rate

Types of Exchange Risk: (*i*) Transactions or conversion, (*ii*) Translation or accounting, and (*iii*) Economic or operating

Methods of Handling Risks: (1) Internal methods—exposure netting, denomination in local currency, foreign currency accounts, leads and lags. **(2) External methods:** hedging (forward contract hedge, and money market hedge), currency futures (standard size, specified delivery dates, trading through members, price movements, settlement through clearing house, margins, marking to market, liquidity), currency options (two parties, call and put options, premium, strike price, execution).

TEST QUESTIONS

1. What is meant by a foreign exchange market? Explain its features.
2. Discuss the functions of a foreign exchange market.
3. Explain various types of transactions that can be made in a foreign exchange market.
4. Explain at par, at premium and at discount forward exchange rates.
5. What is exchange risk? Is it the same as exchange exposure?
6. Explain different types of exchange risks.
7. Describe internal methods of managing exchange risks.
8. Explain external methods of handling exchange risks.
9. Distinguish between:
   (*a*) Spot transactions and forward transactions
   (*b*) Currency futures and currency options.
   (*c*) Call option and put option
   (*d*) Forward contract hedge and money market hedge
10. Write short notes on:
    (*a*) Swap
    (*b*) Arbitrage
    (*c*) Hedging
    (*d*) Exposure netting
    (*e*) Leads and lags
11. What are currency futures? Explain their features.
12. Explain the meaning and features of currency options.
13. "Economic exposure is insidious and difficult to measure". Elucidate.
14. Explain forward, futures and options as methods of managing currency risks.

CHAPTER

12 Foreign Investments

LEARNING OBJECTIVES

After studying this chapter, you should understand:

- 12.1 Concept of Foreign Investments
- 12.2 Types of Foreign Investments
- 12.3 Forms of Foreign Direct Investment
- 12.4 Advantages of Foreign Investments
- 12.5 Limitations of Foreign Investments
- 12.6 Factors Influencing Foreign Investments
- 12.7 Theories of Foreign Investment
- 12.8 Flows of Foreign Investments in India.
- 12.9 Foreign Investment from Developing Countries.
- Summary
- Test Questions

International business includes international trade and international investment.

12.1 Concept of Foreign Investments

Foreign investment simply means the investment made by a firm in a foreign country. For example, investments made by American companies (Coca-Cola Corporation, Pepsi Corporation, IBM, etc.), Japanese companies (Honda Motors, Toyota, Mitsubishi, etc), Korean firms (LG, Hundayi, Samsung) and other foreign companies in India are foreign investments. Similarly, acquisition of Corus Steel by Tata Steel, Novelis by Hindalco and other investments made by Indian companies abroad are all foreign investments.

12.2 Types of Foreign Investments

There are two broad categories of foreign investments — (*i*) Foreign Direct Investment, and (*ii*) Foreign Portfolio Investment.

1. **Foreign Direct Investment (FDI):** It refers to investment in a foreign country with the purpose of retaining control over the investment. It is investment in the real or physical

assets abroad either by floating a new enterprise abroad or by acquiring shares in an existing firm in a foreign country. An investment is considered foreign direct investment when the intention of the investor is to take active part in the management of the firm in which the investment is made.

According to the International Monetary Fund (IMF), FDI is "the category of international investment that reflects the objective of obtaining a lasting interest by a resident entity in one economy in an enterprise resident in another country. The lasting interest implies the existence of long-term relationship between the direct investor and the enterprise and a significant degree of influence by the investor on the management of the enterprise."

The Committee on Compilation of FDI in India, in its report submitted in October 2002, defines FDI as "the process whereby residents of one country (the home country) acquire ownership of assets for the purpose of controlling the production, distribution and other activities of a firm in another country (the host country)."

According to the UNCTAD World Investment Report, FDI is an investment involving a long-term relationship and reflects a lasting interest and control by a resident entity in one economy in an enterprise resident in another economy. Such investment includes both the initial transaction and all subsequent transactions between the two entities.

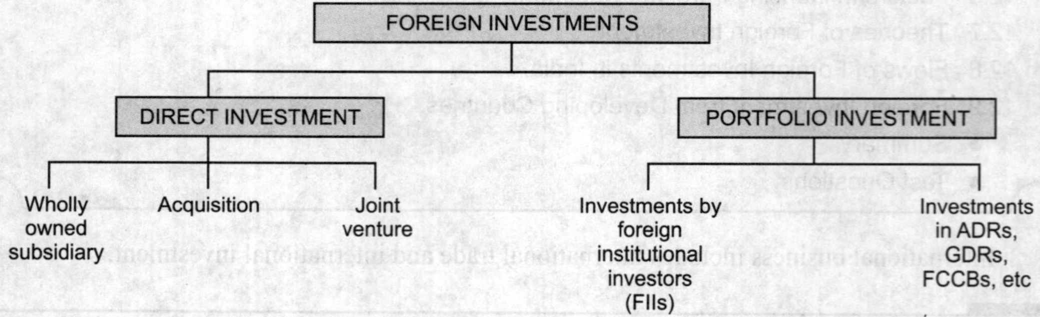

Fig. 12.1 : Types of Foreign Investment.

Foreign direct investments cannot be liquidated easily. Therefore, long-term considerations like political stability, government policy, industrial situation, economic prospects, etc. influence such investments.

2. **Foreign Portfolio Investment (FPI):** It refers to investing capital in buying equities, bonds and other securities abroad. The investment is made to earn a return in the form of dividend, interest, etc. The investor does not exercise control over the investment. Foreign Institutional Investors (FIIs) like mutual funds invest in capital markets abroad. Residents of a country may invest in American Depository Receipts (ADRs), Global Depository Receipts (GDRs) and Foreign Currency Convertible Bonds (FCCBs).

Portfolio investment is a method of diversifying risks involved in foreign investments. Such investment is held relatively for a short term. The investor holds the securities so long as his perception of risk and return is favourable. Whenever the perception turns unfavourable investment is liquidated and shifted to better securities. A typical foreign investment involves investing in a number of ventures.

Table 12.1. Distinction Between FDI and FPI

Basis of Distinction	FDI	FPI
1. Purpose	To manage and control the investment – business interest in the venture	To earn return and to diversify risk, no intention to manage and control
2. Nature of assets	Real or physical assets	Financial assets–equity and debt instruments
3. Time-period	Long term	Short term
4. Investors	Mainly business firms	Mainly FIIs and individuals
5. Size of investment	Usually large investment in one or two ventures	Usually small investment in several entities
6. Forms	Floating a new firm or acquiring shares in an existing firm	Shares, debentures and bonds
7. Main considerations influencing the decision	Political stability, Government policy, market size and other long-term factors	Risk and return equation

12.3 Forms of Foreign Direct Investment

Foreign direct investment is classified on several bases. On the basis of the form of investment, it is classified into: greenfield investment, and acquisitions. On the basis of product line, FDI may be: horizontal, vertical and conglomerate. On the basis of the motive behind investment, FDI can be: market seeking, resource seeking, efficiency seeking, and creative asset seeking.

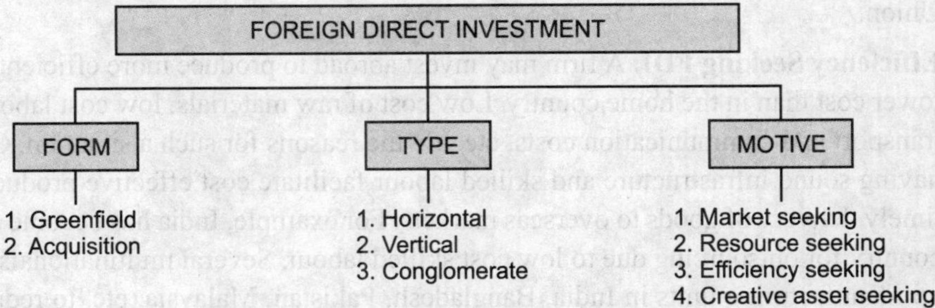

Fig. 12.2 : Forms of Foreign Direct Investment.

1. **Greenfield Investment:** Setting up of new enterprise is known as greenfield investment. Investment in the form of a new facility adds to wealth in the host country. It provides full control to the investing company. But greenfield investment involves time, costs and risks.

2. **Acquisition:** In this form, investment is made in an existing enterprise abroad. This involves transfer of ownership and no addition to the real assets in the host country. But there may be increase in efficiency if the investing firm has better technology or systems. Many countries regulate acquisitions and mergers by foreign investors. Acquisition involves less delays, costs and risks as compared to greenfield investment. The acquiring firm may get the benefit of established brand equity, intellectual property and distribution system.

3. **Horizontal FDI:** When a firm invests abroad in the same industry in which it is engaged in the home country, the investment is known as horizontal FDI. It represents geographical diversification for the investing firm. A company may set up production facilities abroad to expand the market for its product. But it is more costly and more risky than exporting and licensing. Yet a firm may prefer FDI if it can effectively utilise its knowledge and resources to gain entry in foreign countries.
4. **Vertical FDI:** Backward FDI and forward FDI are two forms of vertical FDI. Backward vertical FDI refers to setting up or acquiring a firm abroad to manufacture intermediaries which can be used in the domestic firm or by other units. For example, a readymade garment manufacturer may set up a cloth manufacturing firm abroad. In forward vertical FDI, a firm sets up a firm abroad to distribute its products. It may also establish a firm abroad to manufacture final products using intermediaries supplied from the domestic firm.
5. **Conglomerate FDI:** When a firm invests abroad to manufacture a product unrelated to its product line, it is called conglomerate FDI. The motive behind such FDI may be to make use of capital or managerial resources.
6. **Market Seeking FDI:** Such FDI is made to take advantage of foreign markets. Countries with huge market size, high per capita income, growing market and low competition attract such FDI. The investing firm gets access to regional and global markets. It reaps the benefits of economies of scale. Customers in different countries may have different preferences and a firm may invest abroad to produce the product suitable to host country. In the service sector, FDI is needed because services are not tradable and have to be delivered only through firms abroad. A firm which sets up a unit in a foreign country can gain access to all other countries in that regional economic group, *e.g.,* European Union.
7. **Efficiency Seeking FDI:** A firm may invest abroad to produce more efficiently or at a lower cost than in the home country. Low cost of raw materials, low cost labour, lower transport and communication costs, etc. are the reasons for such a situation. Countries having sound infrastructure and skilled labour facilitate cost effective production and timely delivery of goods to overseas markets. For example, India has become a leading country for outsourcing due to low cost skilled labour. Several multinationals have set up manufacturing units in India, Bangladesh, Pakistan, Malaysia, etc. to reduce costs of production.
8. **Resource Seeking FDI:** Countries with ample natural resources attract such FDI. These nations lack the capital, technology and infrastructural facilities required to exploit their abundant natural resources. Many developing countries have attracted FDI due to availability of raw material, low cost unskilled labour, physical infrastructure in the form of ports, power, telecommunications, etc.
9. **Created Assets Seeking FDI:** Created or strategic assets are made and these may be tangible or intangible. Physical and financial assets such as communication or marketing network are tangible assets. Intangible assets such as technological innovation, managerial expertise, organising competencies, information, trade marks, goodwill etc. are knowledge-based.

12.4 Advantages of FDI

Foreign investment is playing a vital rale in the economic development of several countries in the following ways:

1. **Higher Investment:** Developing countries suffer from shortage of capital. Foreign investment supplements domestic investment. As a result, total investment increases leading to higher Gross Domestic Product (GDP).
2. **Advanced Technology:** Foreign direct investment from developed nations bring with it advanced technology needed by developing countries for high-tech industries such as telecommunications, power, steel, petrochemicals, etc.
3. **Employment Generation:** Higher investment creates millions of jobs. Employment opportunities in India, for example, have increased significantly due to foreign direct investment by multinational corporations.
4. **Exports:** Foreign investment and advanced technology help to reduce costs and improve quality. As a result developing countries can compete successfully in global markets and their exports grow significantly. For example, Maruti Udyog and Hero Corp could export in large numbers due to their joint ventures with Suzuki and Honda Motors respectively.
5. **Improved Balance of Payments:** Increase in exports and reduction in imports due to FDI help to reduce deficit in the balance of payments of a country. FDI helps to increase international trade.
6. **Reduced Risk:** Due to FDI, the risk of an investment is shifted from domestic investors to foreign investors.
7. **Linkages:** FDI has backward, forward and horizontal linkages. Backward linkages occur when foreign affiliates acquire goods and services from domestic firms. Forward linkages take place when foreign affiliates sell goods and services to domestic firms. Horizontal linkages arise due to interactions with domestic competitors. These linkages can have several beneficial influences for the domestic economy.

   The role of foreign investment has increased due to economic reforms and political change. International flows of capital have increased. Therefore, FDI now contributes a significant share of the domestic investment, GDP, employment generation, exports, tax revenue, foreign exchange reserves, etc. FDI helps to fill gaps in capital, technology, foreign exchange, managerial knowhow of developing countries. China, for example, has been able to maintain a high growth rate due to huge inflow of FDI.

12.5 Limitations of Foreign Investment

Foreign investment involves certain limitations and dangers for host countries. Some of the costs and risks of foreign investment are given below:

(*i*) The recipient country may not be able to effectively utilise foreign capital. Poor infrastructure, lack of technical knowhow, limited market, inefficient administration and unskilled labour can restrict the absorptive capacity.

(*ii*) Several 'strings' are attached to foreign capital. The recipient country may be under pressure to follow the ideology of the investor.

(*iii*) FDI tends to flow into high profit sectors rather than into sectors that are of high priority to the host country.

(*iv*) The technology which the foreign investor brings may not be appropriate to the market size, consumption needs and resources of the domestic economy.

(*v*) When outflow of foreign exchange in the form of dividend, royalty, etc exceeds the inflow, foreign investment can have adverse impact on the host country's balance of payments.

(*vi*) Multinational corporations may misuse their power to undermine the interests and autonomy of a nation's economy. They sometimes interfere in the nation's politics. In some cases these corporations indulge in unfair and unethical trade practices.

(*vii*) Foreign investment may destroy small enterprises. It may create monopolies by eliminating competition and displacing domestic firms.

(*viii*) Foreign portfolio investment flows are temporary and speculative. These may destabilise capital markets in emerging economies.

(*ix*) Adverse impact on domestic savings, deterioration in the terms of trade, etc. are other dangers of foreign investment.

12.6 Factors Influencing Foreign Investment

The main determinants of foreign investment are as follows[1]:

1. **Stable, predictable macroeconomic policy:** Companies must have the confidence that the economy in which they make an investment will be managed in a competent and predictable way. Simply stated, investors must believe that the rules of the game will not change in the middle of a contract.
2. **An effective and honest government:** An investor must be able to rely upon the integrity of the host government and its ability to maintain law and order.
3. **A large and growing market:** The size and potential for growth of a country's domestic market, especially the purchasing power of its customers, are key. Companies do not seek to invest in a market where there is little potential to make a profit.
4. **Freedom of activity in the market:** The strength of the competition, as well as the degree of government (theirs and ours) interference to entering a country's market, are important factors. The freer the market, the more attractive it becomes as an investment site for international investors.
5. **Minimal government regulation:** The cost of government regulation and intervention in the affairs—and profits—of private companies must be kept to a minimum.
6. **Property rights and protection.** Private property must be protected. The likelihood that a company's real or intangible (patents, copyrights, etc.) property will be stolen must be avoided.

1. John D. Sullivan, "Prospering in the Global Economy", *Economic Reforms* Today, 2000 (1).

7. **Reliable 'infrastructure':** The ability to consummate transactions and get products and services to market is also critical. Whether it be reliable transportation, power generation, insurance and accounting services, a competent financial system or other basic factors, investments cannot yield a sufficient or reliable financial return without them.
8. **Availability of high-quality factors of production:** While the investor brings capital, technology and management to the table, the quality of the indigenous workforce and the availability of local raw materials are also key ingredients in the recipe for success.
9. **A strong local currency:** The local currency must retain its value. If you make an investment in dollars and then the local assets (valued in the local currency) are devalued, you have lost part—or possibly all—of your original dollar-based investment.
10. **The ability to remit profits, dividends and interest:** If you cannot get your money out of the country, why invest?

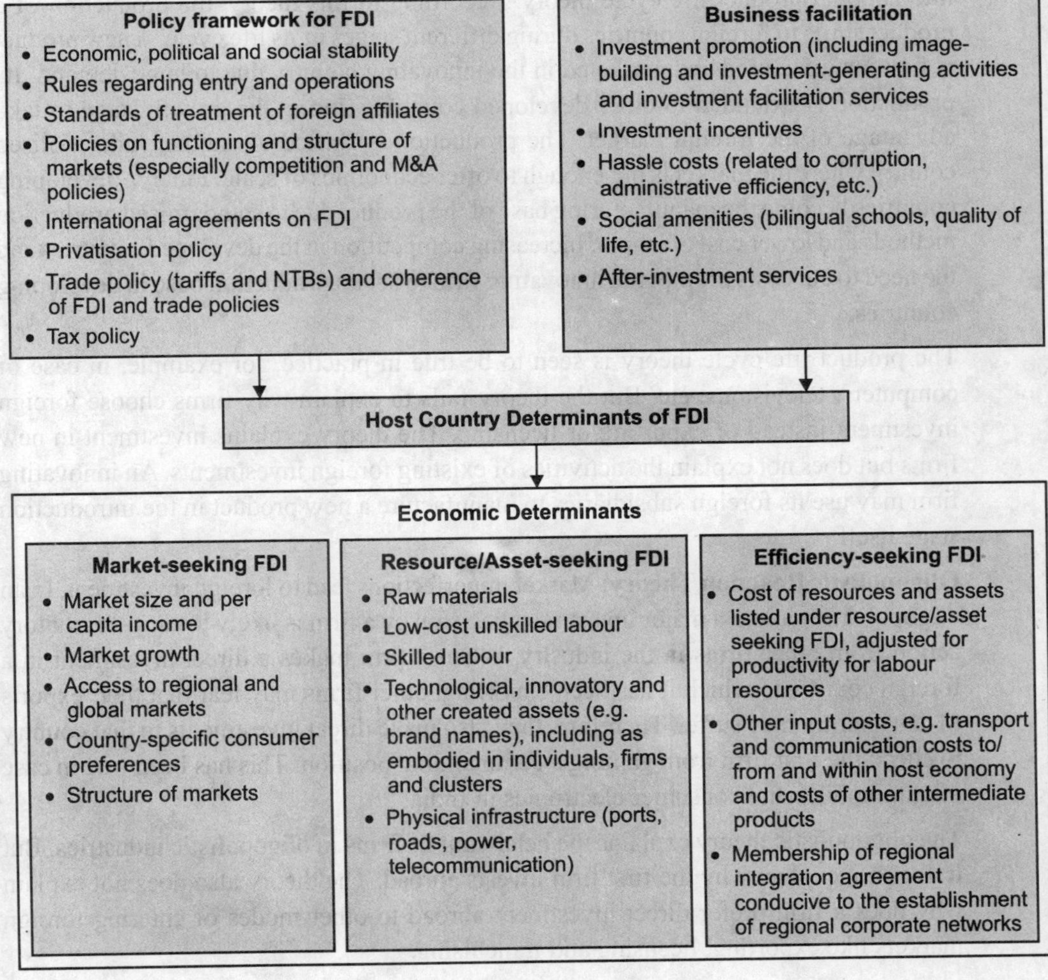

Fig. 12.3 : Host Country Determinants of FDI
(Reproduced from UNCTAD, *World Investment Report,* 2002).

11. **A favourable tax climate:** Although tax incentives geared to attract initial investments are important, a company's final investment decision is usually based on how a country's taxation will affect the normal operating environment once the venture is off the ground.
12. **Freedom to operate between markets:** A company must be able to source goods and services from its operating unit in one market in order to serve other markets or to maximize its global efficiency by trading among its operating entities in different countries to 'round out' its product lines.

12.7 Theories of Foreign Investment

Several theories have been formulated to explain why foreign investments take place. Some of these theories are summarised below:

1. **Product Life Cycle Theory:** Raymond Vernon and Lewis T. Wells developed the international product life cycle theory. According to this theory, the production of a product shifts to foreign countries during different stages of its life cycle. A new product is first manufactured and marketed in the innovating country due to huge demand. Its production is extended to other developed countries during the growth stage to take advantage of the foreign market. The production is shifted to another industrialised country where the market is big enough to offer economies of scale. Finally, developing countries become the manufacturing base of the product due to standardised production methods and lower cost of labour. Increasing competition in the developed countries and the need to cut costs prompt the innovating firm to set up production base in developing countries.

   The product life cycle theory is seen to be true in practice, for example, in case of computers, televisions, etc. But the theory fails to explain why firms choose foreign investment instead of exporting or licensing. The theory explains investment in new firms but does not explain the activities of existing foreign investments. An innovating firm may use its foreign subsidiaries to manufacture a new product in the introduction stage itself.
2. **Oligopolistic Reaction Theory:** Market imperfections lead to foreign investment. In an oligopolistic market, a major investment decision by a firm is likely to cause retaliatory action from other firms in the industry. When a firm makes a direct investment in a foreign country to which it has been exporting, other firms may fear that their exports to that country may suffer. Therefore, they also make direct investments in that country to check the first firm from gaining a commanding position. This has been true in case of automobiles and consumer electronics in India.

   The oligopolistic theory explains the behaviour of firms in oligopolistic industries. But it does not explain why the first firm invests abroad. The theory also does not explain why does a firm prefer direct investment abroad to other modes of entering foreign markets like exporting, licensing and franchising.
3. **Internalisation Theory:** According to this theory, a multinational corporation internalises its operations by setting up units in different countries. These units are bound by a unified governance structure and common ownership. In a vertical FDI, the

corporation avails of economies of scale, secures reliable sources of factors of production and obtains outlets for its final products. In case of horizontal FDI, the firm overcomes import quotas and restrictions that impede its exports.

The firm can also retain control over its specific advantages arising from knowledge and technology. These advantages may also be exploited through licensing and franchising. But internalisation enables the firm to retain direct control over the assets abroad and to avoid the risk of adoption by competitors. The firm can maintain flexibility by shifting its operations between different centres.

A firm will adopt internalisation so long as the transportation cost in the external market exceeds the cost of transactions within the intra-organisational market.

4. **Firm Specific Advantage Theory:** According to Stephen H. Hymer, FDI takes place due to certain specific advantages which the foreign investing firm has over domestic firms. These advantages are known as firm specific advantages because these are related to the firm rather than to the location of its production facilities. A foreign firm is at a disadvantage due to lack of knowledge about local market conditions; legal, cultural and language differences; higher cost of communicating and operating from a distance. In such a situation, it can invest and compete successfully with domestic firms only if it has superior knowledge, economies of scale and such other advantages. Superior knowledge may relate to technology, product knowledge, managerial expertise and economies of scale due to large size.

5. **Eclectic Theory:** John Dunning believes that no single theory can explain all forms of foreign investment. Therefore, he has attempted to formulate a general theory by combining the postulates of other theories. According to Dunning, foreign investment occurs due to three types of factors which are as follows:

   (*a*) **Ownership factors:** Exclusive ownership of tangible and intangible resources can enable a foreign firm to compete successfully with domestic firms. Technology, superior knowledge, economies of scale, access to financial markets, monopolistic power in input and output markets, patents and trade marks are examples of ownership advantages.

   (*b*) **Location factors:** These are country specific advantages available to a firm. These influence the decision as to in which country to invest. These can be economic, social and political advantages existing in a country. Economic factors relate to inputs, market and infrastructure. Social factors include attitudes towards foreigners, language and culture. Political advantages comprise favourable government policy towards FDI, political stability, etc.

   (*c*) **Internalisation factors:** Internalisation means a firm's capability to produce and market through its own network of subsidiaries. An international firm can overcome imperfections of external markets and reduce costs through internalisation. When the costs of internalisation (administrative cost and cost of raising huge funds) are lower than the costs of market imperfection, FDI can take place. Ownership (or firm specific) advantages would lead to foreign investment only when the firm internalises. In order to internalise, there must exist locational advantages.

Eclectic theory provides a more comprehensive explanation of FDI than any other theory. However, this theory fails to explain foreign acquisitions which have become a significant method of internalisation.

12.8 Flows of Foreign Investment in India

There has been a significant increase in the flows of foreign investment particularly since economic liberalisation and globalisation. During 1980–2010 there was sevenfold increase in FDI inflows as a percentage of gross domestic capital formation. In 2002 the inward FDI stock in developing countries accounted for almost one-third of their gross domestic product. In case of India, FDI inflows increased from 379 million dollars in 1990 to 5,518 million dollars in 2002.

India's policy towards foreign investment has restricted FDI inflows. Since 1991, India's policy became liberal. As a result both FDI and FPI have increased. Foreign institutional investors (FIIs) are now playing a vital role in India's capital markets. The major share of the FDI inflows in India has gone to priority sectors.

12.9 Foreign Investment from Developing countries

Foreign direct investment from developing countries has been increasing steadily. Malaysia, Korea, Singapure, Mexico, South Africa, Brazil, China and India have made investments in different countries, sectors and industries. During 1988–2003, annual FDI outflows from developing countries grew faster than those from developed countries. In 2009, outward FDI from developing countries accounted for more than 15 per cent of the world's total FDI stock.

FDI flows between developing countries is growing faster than FDI from developing countries to developed countries. Therefore, developing countries are now more financially integrated with one another. Several Indian companies have made acquisitions in Europe, USA, Africa, Latin America and other parts of the world.

SUMMARY

Concept: Foreign investment is investment in foreign countries.

Types: (*i*) FDI – Wholly owned subsidiary, acquisition, joint venture (*ii*) FPI – FIIs, GDRs, ADRs, FCCBs.

Forms of FDI: (*i*) Form – greenfield, acquisition (*ii*) Type – horizontal, vertical, conglomerate (*iii*) Motive – market seeking, resource seeking, efficiency seeking, created asset seeking.

Advantages of FDI: (*i*) Higher investment (*ii*) sophisticated technology (*iii*) employment (*iv*) exports (*v*) balance of payments (*vi*) less risk (*vii*) backward and forward linkages.

Limitations of FDI: (*i*) ineffective use (*ii*) strings (*iii*) low priority sectors (*iv*) inappropriate technology (*v*) excessive outflows (*vi*) misuse of power (*vii*) demise of small scale sector (*viii*) speculation (*ix*) adverse terms of trade.

Theories of FDI: (1) Product life cycle theory (2) oligopolistic reaction theory (3) internationalisation theory (4) firm specific advantage theory (5) eclectic theory.

Flows of FDI in India: Low but increasing since 1991.

FDI from Developing Countries: Increasing rapidly. Indian companies making acquisitions in USA, Europe, Africa, Latin America, etc.

TEST QUESTIONS

1. What is meant by foreign investment? Distinguish between Foreign Direct Investment (FDI) and Foreign Portfolio Investment (FPI).
2. Define FDI and explain its different types.
3. Explain market seeking, efficiency seeking and resource seeking FDI with suitable examples.
4. Discuss the advantages and limitations of foreign direct investment.
5. Explain the determinants of FDI.
6. Describe different theories of FDI, stating their merits and demerits.
7. Write notes on:
   (*a*) Foreign Portfolio Investment (FPI).
   (*b*) Greenfield investment.
   (*c*) Horizontal and vertical FDI.
   (*d*) FDI from developing countries.
8. Explain the advantages and disadvantages of Foreign Direct Investment. Critically evaluate the various steps taken by the Government and Industry to attract more foreign direct investment. What are various obstacles to foreign direct investment which are still to be removed?

UNIT – IV

UNIT – IV

13. Organisational Structure for International Business

14. International Production Management

15. International Marketing Management

16. International Financial Management

17. International Human Resource Management

18. International Business Negotiations

CHAPTER

13 Organisational Structure for International Business

LEARNING OBJECTIVES

After studying this chapter, you should understand:

This unit of the book is concerned with the internal management of international firms. The management of an international firm involves effective coordination between different functional areas like production, marketing, finance, personnel etc. To achieve the overall corporate objectives, a sound organisational structure is required to ensure such coordination. In this chapter various types of organisational structures that can be used in international business are described. The choice of a specific organisational structure depends on several factors such as the mode of entry into foreign markets, the nature of international orientation, the size of international business, expansion plans, the number and consistency of the firm's product lines, nature of foreign markets, the degree of control desired over the overseas operations, the market needs, the demands of the people working in the overseas unit(s), etc. For example, when a domestic firm extends its activities abroad, it may adopt domestic structure. Later on, the firm may choose international structure to take care of its overseas business. Ultimately, the firm may adopt a global structure to manage its global operations.

Thus, the oranisational structure keeps on changing during different stages of a domestic firm into a transnational corporation. Various stages in the process of evolution and corresponding organisational structures are given in Table 13.1

Table 13.1 : Evolution of International Firm and Organisational Structures

Stage of evolution	Organisation Structure	Characteristics
1. Domestic	Export within marketing department	Minimum product/market diversification, no specialisation
2. Export	Export department or export subsidiary (Low)	Early product/market diversification, specialisation
3. International	International division (Low)	Export bias, strategy to eliminate barrier to foreign market entry, mature stages of a few products
4. Multinational	Product/area/functional structure (Medium)	Growth through diversification
5. Transnational	Matrix/network structure (High)	Global rationalisation

Source: S. Shiva Ramu, ***International Business–Governance Structure***, Wheeler Publishing, New Delhi, 1994, p 132.

13.1 Domestic Organisation Structure

To begin with, a domestic firm may start exporting its product. It may carry out its export function in an **ad hoc** manner or through an export department or export sales subsidiary.

13.1.1 Corollary Model

In this model, exports are handled by the firm's marketing department. This built-in arrangement is the simplest and the most economical form of export organisation. But this arrangement is suitable only when the export business is shall, the firm's resources are limited, its orientation is domestic and it is new to international business.

The corollary model suffers from several limitations. The marketing department has to carry out advertising, credit, shipping and other activities for both domestic and foreign business. Therefore, it may consider export business as subsidiary to domestic business. The people in various departments of the firm may not have adequate knowledge and experience to deal with issues concerning foreign markets. The export manager may not receive the necessary support from the personnel in other departments as they are not under his control. Thus, the built-in export model is an **ad hoc** and temporary structure.

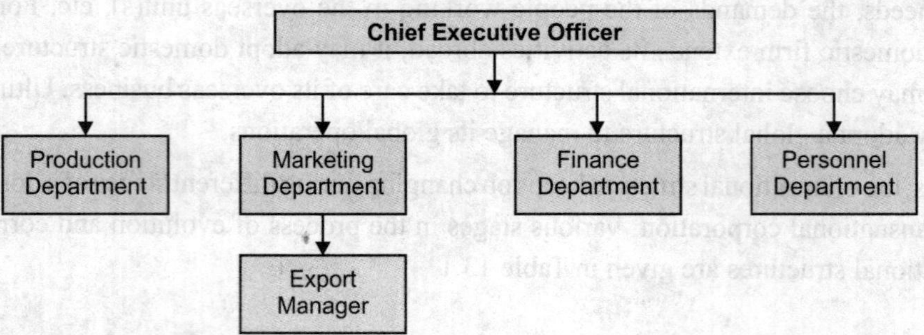

Fig. 13.1 : Built-in Export Structure

13.1.2. Separate Export Department

In this type of structure, a separate full-fledged export department is created to handle the firm's overseas business. This department is usually established at the firm's head office and is responsible for overseas business. This arrangement is suitable when export business is large and regular but its volume is small in comparison with the domestic business. Moreover, a company which plans to expand its export business substantially would set up a separate export department in place of the built-in system. The export department is well-equipped to handle all the activities relating to overseas business.

Export department structure is simple to create and operate. It avoids the problems of lack of expertise, clash with domestic operations, lack of export orientation. But when the international business of the firm expands fast and it faces greater competition, this arrangement may be unable to meet the challenge.

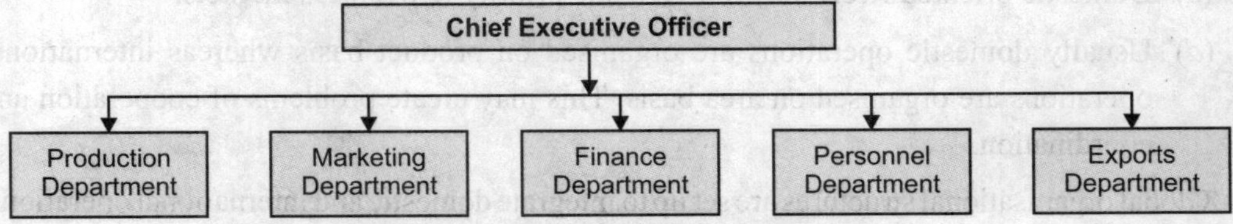

Fig. 13.2 : Export Department Structure

Some firms which have large export business may establish export subsidiary rather than a separate export department. The export sales subsidiary is a separate company, but is wholly owned and controlled by the parent company. The subsidiary buys goods from the parent firm and other sources and markets them abroad. An export subsidiary is more independent than an export department. It can more easily develop export marketing facilities and organise overseas operations more effectively due to greater autonomy, expertise and flexibility. The subsidiary may be assigned the job of exploring developing and expanding export markets for the firm. For example, HMT Ltd. established its subsidiary HMT (International) Ltd. for handling its export business.

13.2 International Division Structure

With growth in exports, the firm may be under pressure to establish manufacturing facilities abroad. The host country government may restrict imports through tariffs and quotas and may ask government agencies to buy locally made goods. In order to face these constraints, the firm may create an International Division in the head office. The creation of the international division leads to vertical separation of the firm's operation into two parts—domestic and international. This division has its own team of experts. The head of the division reports directly to the chief executive.

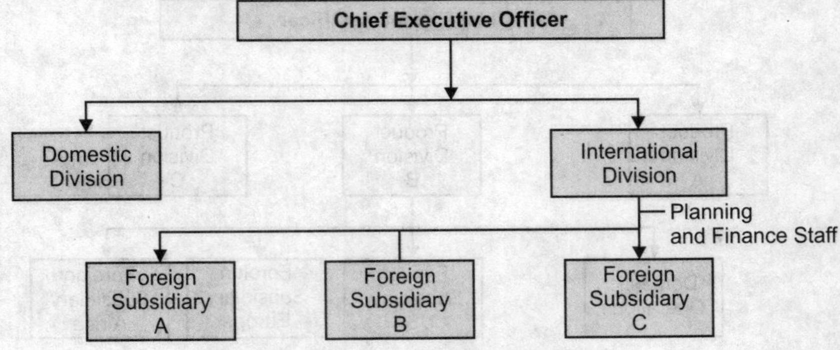

Fig. 13.3 : International Division Structure

International division facilitates concentrated attention on overseas business. It can be treated as a profit centre and helps in a unified approach to the firm's operations in different countries. The centralised coordination of foreign business activities enables the firm to make cost-efficient decisions concerning procurement-production and marketing. If necessary, the international division may be located abroad and staffed with host country managers.

International division structure suffers from some drawbacks:

(*a*) Domestic and international division may pursue conflicting objectives.

(*b*) The international division may find it difficult to get due share in the firm's resources for growth of overseas business.

(*c*) Domestic oriented R&D may not give due priority to overseas markets.

(*d*) Usually domestic operations are organised on product basis whereas international operations are organised on area basis. This may create problems of cooperation and coordination.

Global organisational structures are set up to integrate domestic and international operations.

13.3 Global Organisational Structure

As the firm becomes a multinational, an integrated global orientation is adopted thereby eliminating the distinction between domestic and foreign operations. The corporate office makes strategic decisions without differentiating between domestic and foreign business. Global opportunities and threats are considered while acquiring and allocating the firm's resources. These changes in strategy and functioning require a global organisational structure which may be based on products, geographical areas or functions.

13.3.1 Global Product Structure

Under global product division structure separate operating divisions are created and each is given worldwide responsibility for production, marketing, finance, etc. for a specific product line. Different foreign subsidiaries of the firm dealing with different product lines report to the headquarters. Each division enjoys considerable autonomy to operate as a profit centre. But it has to function within the corporate strategy of the firm.

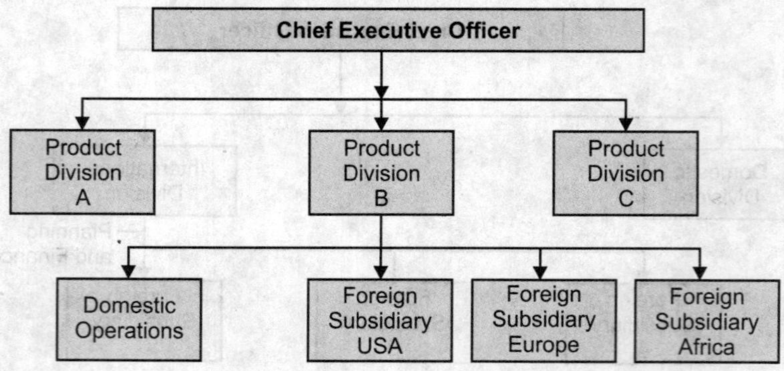

Mertis: Global product structure offers the following advantages:

(*i*) The firm can effectively manage diverse product lines.

(*ii*) The firm is able to meet the diverse needs of customers in different markets due to free flow of product knowledge and technology between the divisions and subsidiaries.

(*iii*) The firm can produce at low cost by properly locating and coordinating production facilities.

(*iv*) Research and development on specific products is possible.

Demerits: Global product structure suffers from the following drawbacks:

(*i*) Duplication of facilities and staff increases administrative costs.

(*ii*) Divisions may concentrate on more familiar domestic markets neglecting the overseas markets.

(*iii*) Divisions may focus on geographical areas with immediate return overlooking those with potential in future.

(*iv*) Cooperation and coordination between product divisions may become difficult. Product division structure is suitable for large conglomerates having multiple and unrelated product lines. Such a firm has diverse product lines which require different technologies and have different end uses. Close coordination on production and marketing between domestic and foreign affiliates is possible. But coordination between different product lines is difficult.

13.3.2. Global Geographic Area Structure

Under the global area structure, the world market is divided into geographical regions. Regional headquarters are set up in different parts of the world each being responsible for all products sold and distributed in the region. Countries are grouped into specific regions on the basis of location of affiliates, volume of business, sources of materials, etc. Each regional head exercises supervision and control over all affiliates in that region. The regional heads participate in the formulation of corporate strategies and plans. They report directly to the chief executive officer.

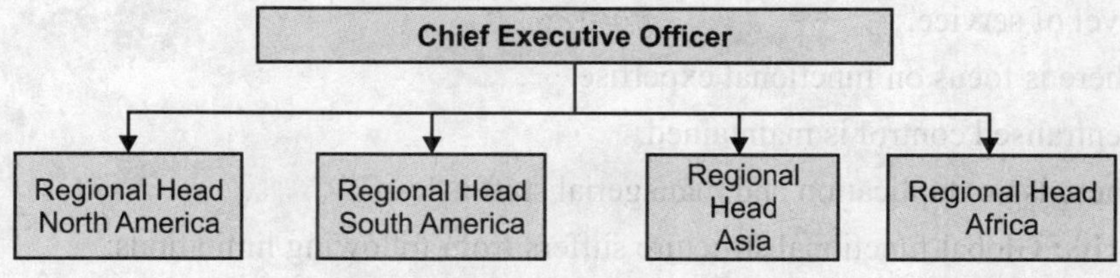

Fig. 13.4 : Global Area Structure

Merits: The main advantages of global geographic structure are as under.

(*i*) The firm can effectively cater to local customer needs and make quick decisions to meet the challenges.

(*ii*) Knowledge and technology can be easily transferred from one region to another.

(*iii*) Cooperation and coordination between subsidiaries within a region can be maintained.

Demerits: The drawbacks of global area structure are given below.

(*i*) There is duplication of facilities and staff increasing costs.

(*ii*) Lack of centralised management and control may create problems.

(*iii*) Regional heads may focus on proven products ignoring research and development on new products.

The global area structure is suitable for multinationals with narrow product lines. Coordination of all product lines within a zone becomes easy but coordination between regions for any one product line is difficult.

Global area structure is suitable when.

(*a*) the firm has a narrow product line; (*b*) well differentiated geographical preferences exist for a product line; (*c*) economies of scale can be achieved through integration of procurement, production and marketing within a region. Multinationals operating in food, beverages, pharma are characterised by these features. For example, Ranbaxy Laboratories divided the world market into four regions after abolishing its export division.

13.3.3 Global Functional Structure

Under global functional structure, the head of each functional area like production, marketing, finance, personnel, etc. is responsible for the firm's worldwide operations in that area. Each functional division or department may be subdivided into regions.

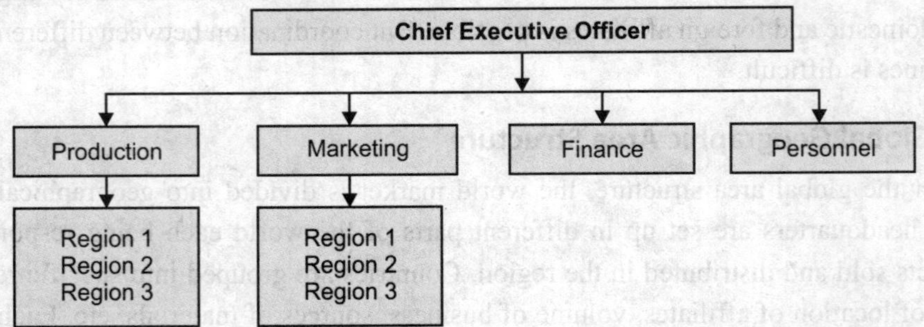

Fig. 13.5 : Global Functional Structure

Merits: The advantages of global functional structure are as under:

(*i*) The key functional areas are coordinated creating one global brand image and a uniform level of service.

(*ii*) There is focus on functional expertise.

(*iii*) Centralised control is maintained.

(*iv*) There is no duplication and managerial staff is lean.

Demerits: Global functional structure suffers from following limitations:

(*i*) Coordination between functional areas becomes difficult.

(*ii*) It is difficult to manage multiple products.

(*iii*) There is lack of accountability for profits as no single function can be held responsible for overall results.

Global functional structure is suitable for firms with narrow product lines which are easily transferable around the world. Extractive industries like oil and mining and airlines adopt this organisation structure.

13.3.4. Global Matrix Structure

Global matrix structure represents an attempt to combine the merits of other structures given above. It is a combined or hybrid structure. For example, global product structure may be combined either with global area structure or global functional structure. Foreign subsidiaries of the firm report simultaneously to several divisions at the headquarters. For instance, the head of a foreign subsidiary may report to a product division head as well as to a regional head.

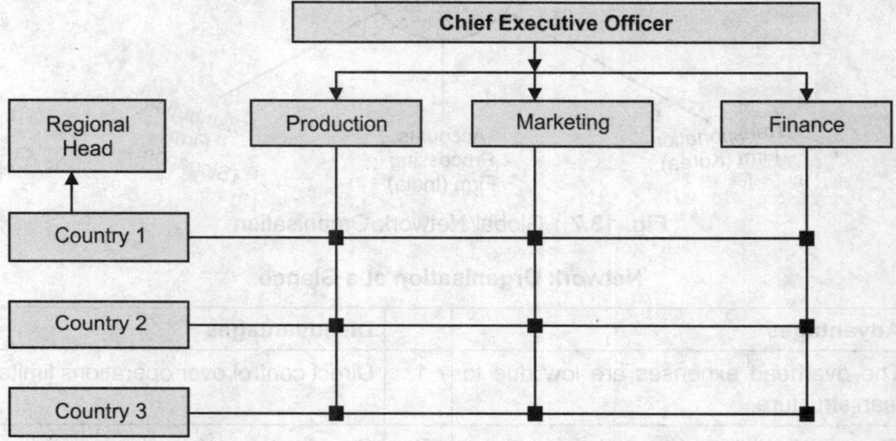

Fig. 13.6 : Global Matrix Structure

Merits: Global matrix structure offers the following advantages:

(*i*) The firm can respond simultaneously to all the critical factors in the environment.

(*ii*) Knowledge creation, communication and information sharing are improved.

(*iii*) Better information flow improves planning and implementation.

(*iv*) The flexibility of the firm increases.

Demerits: Global matrix structure suffers from following shortcomings :

(*i*) It is difficult to design and implement on a global scale.

(*ii*) There is lack of unity of command. Dual reporting often leads to confusion and conflict.

(*iii*) There is lack of accountability due to overlapping responsibilities.

(*iv*) Disputes and problems occur in the absence of cooperation among managers.

Global matrix structure helps to overcome the disadvantage of focus on a single aspect e.g. product, function or geographic area. It is suitable for firm's highly diversified products and markets which require equal attention. Limited resources may have to be shared by two or more functions, products or geographic divisions.

13.4 Transnational Network Structure

Under transnational network structure various subsidiaries around the world are linked by a network arrangement. At the centre of the network are nodes to coordinate product, functional and geographic information. Different product line units or geographic units adopt different structures depending on their operations. The units specialise in different areas such as manufacturing, marketing and so on. Different subsidiaries are given different degrees of autonomy as per requirements.

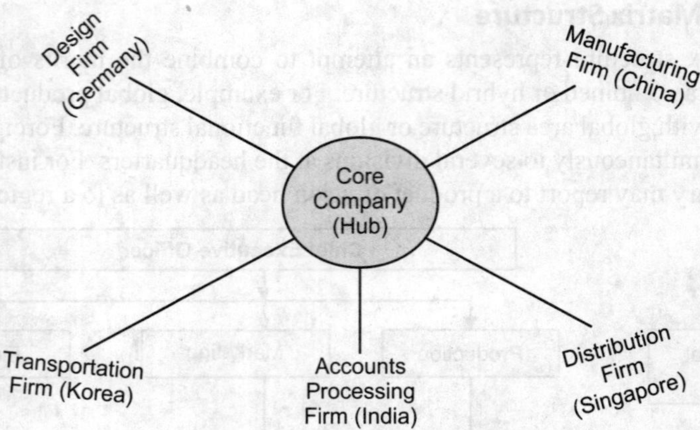

Fig. 13.7 : Global Network Organisation

Network Organisation at a Glance

	Advantages		**Disadvantages**
1.	The overhead expenses are low due to lean structure.	1.	Direct control over operations limited.
2.	There is flexibility of control due to very few employees at headquarters.	2.	Coordination of various activities and subcontractors becomes difficult.
3.	There is choice of subcontractors on the basis of quality and control.	3.	With change in subcontractors new relationships need to be developed.
4.	Subcontractors all over the world can be located.	4.	Employees may get demotivated and frustrated due to poor performance of subcontractors.

Like many old multinational (MNC) organizations in India, Otis had become one large bureaucracy. The company's sparkling headquarters in suburban Mumbai was structured into verticals like new equipment sales, field operations, and service, headed mostly by expatriate suits. But at construction sites across the country, where its elevators were being installed, things had become messy — delays were a rule and service levels had slipped to an all time low. People in the field had to approach the head office for everything. A sale would be stalled because the service guys hadn't serviced one of the customers' older lifts. The local sales guy would call the sales director at HQ for help and the sales director would talk to the service director at HQ, who would then, hopefully, tell the local service manager to get on with the job. It created a lot of customer dissatisfaction this way.

Decentralisation is improving response times, since decisions are now taken at the local level with all employees reporting to their regional bosses, with the directors at headquarters playing an advisory role. The new structure has created a churn, with senior expatriate staff being replaced by local managers, many drawn from the parent company. There has been 8% improvement in employee engagement scores. Employees feel more empowered.

Network structure is a complex structure that offers economies of scale as well as flexibility needed to respond to local customer needs. Multinationals like N.V. Philips have adopted this structure.

SUMMARY

Domestic Structure: (*i*) corollary model – one marketing department for both domestic and export sales (*ii*) export department for foreign business.

International Division: It caters to all foreign affiliates of the firm.

Global Structures: (1) Product – a separate division for each product line (2) Geographic – a separate division for each region (3) Functional – a separate department for each functional area (4) Matrix – hybrid structure with dual command.

Network Structure: All foreign affiliates linked by node or hub.

TEST QUESTIONS

1. Explain how do organisation structure change with evolution of international firm?
2. Describe corollary and export department forms of domestic organisation structure in international business.
3. Discuss international division structure pointing out its merits and demerits.
4. Explain various types of global organisation structures stating their merits and demerits and suitability.
5. Explain transnational network structure.

CHAPTER

14 International Production Management

LEARNING OBJECTIVES

After studying this chapter, you should understand:

14.1 Plant Location Decision

14.1.1 Centralised *Vs.* Decentralised Location

14.1.2 Factors Affecting Location

14.1.3 Role of Foreign Plants

14.2 Make or Buy Decision

14.3 Global Outsourcing

14.4 International Logistics

14.5 Global Networking of Operations

- Summary
- Test Questions

Production or operations management is concerned with systems, processes and decisions involved in the production of goods and services. It manages the transformation process which converts inputs (material, energy, information, etc) into outputs. International production management involves decision concerning the following:

1. Location of production facilities
2. Make or buy decision.
3. Global sourcing of inputs
4. International logistics and materials management
5. Global networking of operations

14.1 Plant Location Decision

The location of production facilities is a crucial decision because it influences the operational efficiency and cost of production. Moreover, location is a strategic or long term decision which cannot be reversed easily. The basic objective in the selection of plant site is to achieve economy in production and distribution. In international business, plant location is a complex decision because production can be carried on globally and inputs can be sourced from all over the world.

14.1.1 Centralised Vs. Decentralised Location

Two alternative location strategies are available to an international firm. First is to concentrate manufacturing at one place and serve the world market from there. The alternative strategy is to disperse manufacturing in different countries which are close to the main markets. Each of the two strategies is suitable under different conditions which are summarised in Table 14.1.

Table 14.1: Conditions Influencing Location Strategy

Centralised Location	Decentralised Location
1. Customer tastes and preferences in different markets are similar.	Customer tastes and preferences differ widely in different markets.
2. A standardised global product is to be produced.	Different varieties of the product are to be produced.
3. Cost of manufacturing differs widely between countries.	Cost of manufacturing does not differ significantly between countries.
4. There are very low trade barriers.	Trade barriers are high
5. Historically similar enterprises are concentrated at the place.	There is no such concentration.
6. Exchange rates between major currencies are stable.	Exchange rates between major currencies fluctuate widely.
7. Break-even point in relation to global demand is high.	Break-even point in relation to global demand is low.
8. The ratio between value and weight of the product is high.	The ratio between value and weight of the product is low.
9. Sources of inputs and markets are concentrated at few places.	Increasing competition and customisation.

Table 14.2: Centralised Vs. Decentralised Location

Centralised Location	
Merits	**Demerits**
1. Maximisation of efficiency is possible.	High transportation costs
2. Products can be standardised.	Delay in delivery of products.
3. Economies of large scale.	Complex process due to large size.
4. Reduction in cost of production per unit.	Political uncertainty in host country is great risk.
5. Uniform procedures help to simplify administration.	

Decentralised Location

Merits	Demerits
1. Easy to adapt to local conditions.	High cost of production per unit due to small scale production at each location.
2. Flexibility of operations.	High cost of administration due to multiple locations.
3. Customisation in production and marketing.	
4. Less political, natural and commercial risks.	

According to Dicken[1], production strategies adopted by international firms are of four types:

(*i*) **Globally Concentrated Production:** In this strategy, the firm produces the entire output at a single place and the output is exported to different markets.

(*ii*) **Host Market Production:** The production facilities are dispersed. Each production unit produces a range of products for the country in which it is located. No sales are made across nations. This multi-domestic strategy is essential for local production and local market.

(*iii*) **Product Specialisation:** Under this strategy each production unit produces only one product for sale throughout a regional market consisting of several countries. This strategy is appropriate for regionally integrated market such as European Union.

(*iv*) **Transnational Vertical Integration:** The international firm specialises by process semi-finished product. There are two variants of this strategy:

(*a*) Each production unit performs one part of the production process. Production units located in different countries are linked in a chain-like sequence

(*b*) Each production unit performs a different part of the production process and ships its output to a final assembly plant in another country.

The choice of the final strategy depends upon economies of scale through product specialisation and extra cost of moving the product from plant to plant/market.

14.1.2 Factors Affecting Location

Once a firm decides to locate its manufacturing unit abroad, the next decision is to choose the exact location. Several factors need to be considered in making the location decision. These factors may be classified and discussed into four groups as follows:

1. **Production-Related Factors:** These are as follows:

(*a*) **Nature of Product:** The weight, size and perishability of the product and whether or not weight is lost during the production process are important. For example, a weight losing product like sugar is likely to be produced near the source of raw material. Products with low value-to-weight ratio like cement, steel, etc can be produced in dispersed locations while products with high value-to-weight ratio like diamonds, microprocessors, etc. are produced in centralised location.

(*b*) **Availability of Raw Material:** Access to raw materials is a major determinant in industries in which product has low weight ratio. Availability of skilled labour at low cost is another factor. Productivity of labour is also significant. Infrastructural facilities like power and transportation influence location.

(*c*) **Technology:** The firm's technology will determine whether production should be centralised at one place or spread out at several places. A plant using technology that involves huge investment and fixed costs tends to be centralised at a single or very few places.

(*d*) **Product Life Cycle:** The product's stage in its life cycle may influence location. When the product is in the declining stage or becomes standardised, its production

1. P. Dicken, *A Global Shift – Transforming the World Economy,* Paul Chapman, London, 1998.

base tends to shift to developing countries. For example, some Japanese multinationals which market VCRs/VCPs now outsource them from developing countries.

2. **Market-Related Factors:** These are given below:

   (*a*) **Demand Pattern:** Products which have declined in demand or become obsolete are often produced in developing countries. When some version of a product has a large demand in a particular country but small demand in other countries it is manufactured in that country and exported to other countries. For example, Suzuki produced its Maruti 800 car in India and exported it to other countries.

   (*b*) **Market Size and Potential:** The current size of the market and its future potential are important considerations in location. Countries with huge demand and high growth rate in demand pull production units to them. Several American and Japanese car firms have set up production facilities in India to manufacture compact models. Similar is the case in FMCG industry.

   (*c*) **Customer Feedback:** When customer feedback is vital for the success of business, manufacturing may be located near the market so as to respond quickly to changes in customer needs and preferences.

   Type of products demanded in the market and the degree of competition are other important market related considerations.

3. **Country-Related Factors:** The main country-related factors are as under:

   (*a*) **Availability of Inputs:** Availability of raw materials, labour and infrastructure affect location decision. India attracted several IT firms due to low cost software professionals. Singapore has become a production centre for international firms due to sound infrastructure.

   (*b*) **Country of Origin:** Advanced countries like USA and Japan are known for quality Italy is known for style and Germany is known for durability of products.

   (*c*) **Social and Cultural Factors:** Countries with favourable attitudes towards foreign business and cultural and linguistic affinities attract production units. An international firm can adopt similar business practices and communicate easily with host country customers.

   (*d*) **Logistics:** Some locations are preferred due to the ease and cost of moving products to various markets. Singapore, China and Malaysia, for example, have become the hub of international operations.

   (*e*) **Political Factors:** Government policies and regulations such as foreign investment policy, local content requirements, taxes, labour laws, environmental regulations, repatriation rules, procedural formalities, incentives, etc. influence location.

   The import duty structure also influences the location. When the import duty on components is low but high on the finished product, a firm is likely to manufacture components in the home country and do assembly operations in the foreign country. Similar is the outcome when assembly operations are labour intensive.

(*f*) **Exchange Rate Fluctuations:** Changes in exchange rate may influence import vs. manufacturing decision. When the value of the home currency appreciates, imports into the foreign country become costly. It may encourage production in the foreign country.

(4) **Organisational Factors:** Nature of the firm is a major determinant of plant location. In case of a multinational corporation, subsidiaries produce most of the products for their respective markets. On the other hand, in a global corporation, core production activities are often centralised in the home country. There exists a globally integrated network of production facilities in case of a transnational corporation. International firms with cost leadership strategy select the location where the cost of production is the lowest. For example, Intel located its production in Ireland, Puerto Rico, Malaysia and Philippines due to low labour cost. In order to minimise inventory levels, Compaq Computers set up its primary assembly plants in Houston (USA), Scotland and Singapore.

No single location has all the advantages. Every location has its own merits and demerits. Therefore, all the main factors influencing location may be listed in order of their significance. Then weights are assigned to each factor depending on its significance. Each location is given a score in respect of each of the factors. The location with the highest aggregate score is ultimately chosen.

14.1.3 Role of Foreign Plants

Initially, foreign plants are set up to produce labour intensive products at a low cost. Over a period of time, some of these plants acquire strategic importance due to pressure for cost reduction or technological advancement in the foreign country. These plants become centres of excellence for design and final assembly of products for global markets.

On the basis of their strategic roles, foreign plants have been classified into six categories as follows[2]:

(*i*) An **offshore** factory is set up to gain access to low wages or other factors integral to low-cost production. Its role is limited to low cost production of specific items which are exported for further work or for sale. Such a factory is not expected to be innovative. It follows the plans, methods and instructions given by the head office. It depends on others for expertise in new products, processes and technologies.

(*ii*) A **source** factory is also set up to gain access to low cost production. But it has the resources and expertise needed to develop and produce a component or a product for the company's global markets.

(*iii*) A **server** factory is a production site that supplies to specific national or regional markets.

(*iv*) A **contributor** factory both serves a local market and assumes responsibility for customisation, process improvements, product modifications or product development.

(*v*) An **outpost** factory is set up primarily to gain access to the knowledge or skills required by the company

(*vi*) A **lead** factory has the ability and knowledge to innovate and create new processes, products, and technologies for the company.

Some factories may perform two or more of these roles. For example, a factory may be a server for a particular region and an offshore site for the production of some components.

2. Kasara Fedrows, "Making the Most of Foreign Factories," ***Harvard Business Review***, March-April, 1997, pp. 76-77.

14.2 Make or Buy Decision

A major decision involved in production management is whether to manufacture in-house at the firm's plants or to procure from third party suppliers. Domestic firms also need to make such a decision. But it is more complex in case of an international firm due to political risks, exchange rate changes, changes in relative factor costs, etc. The make or buy decision has become more relevant because globalisation has increased the scope of sourcing. Both the alternatives of making and buying have advantages and disadvantages. The choice is made keeping in view the trade-off involved. The aim is to get the product of right quality at the least cost.

Advantages of Making

Manufacture in-house offers the following benefits:

1. **Cost Control:** A firm can maximise efficiency in production by continuously manufacturing the product in-house. It may result in better utilisation of the firm's facilities and cost effective production.
2. **Quality Control:** In-house manufacturing enables the firm to maintain strict control over the product quality. It can make adjustments/improvements in product design, production process, etc. Therefore, when quality is of prime importance, making is preferable to buying.
3. **Control Over Supply:** When the product is manufactured in-house, the quantity and timing of production can be easily adjusted to suit the firm's requirements. In case of outsourcing, the vendor may not agree for change in the supply schedule at a short notice. In international business, time and distance between the firm and its suppliers aggravate the problem of scheduling. Higher bargaining power of suppliers, under-developed vendor base, labour problems of the suppliers, etc. do not create uncertainty of supply.
4. **Protection of Technology:** A firm may command competitive technology due to its proprietary or unique technology. In case of buying the firm runs the risk of losing its competitive edge. The vendor expropriates the firm's technology. By manufacturing in-house, the firm can maintain the secrecy of its technology.
5. **Specialised Investment:** When the product is of special variety used only by a single buyer, there is mutual dependence between the supplier and the buyer. Each party fears that the other may misuse the situation to extract more favourable terms. In order to avoid such a risk, the firm would prefer to create its own manufacturing facility. Substantial investment in specialised assets is required in such a situation to manufacture the product in-house. The firm can take initiatives for research and development.
6. **Transfer Pricing:** The question of transfer pricing arises when an item is manufactured at one plant and supplied to others. Transfer price is the price at which the item is supplied by the manufacturing plant to the user plant. This price may be cost-based or market- based. A firm can use transfer-price to generate more profits at a low tax country and reduce the profits at high tax country. Thus, transfer pricing can be used to save tax through in-house manufacturing.

When it is decided to manufacture inhouse, the firm has to choose between: (*a*) manufacture at one plant and distribute to others; (*b*) manufacture in industrial plants for their own needs; and (*c*) manufacture at selected plants to meet the needs of specific regions. Generally, in-house manufacturing is preferred in case of specialised items of strategic importance.

Advantages of Buying

Outsourcing or buying offers the following benefits:

1. **Lower Cost:** The firm may be able to procure the component at lower cost than incurred-under in-house manufacturing. The supplier may specialise in the manufacture of the component. He may be able to produce at lower cost due to operational efficiency and economies of scale. There is scope for bargaining to secure a price advantage. Benefits of technological innovations and product improvements by the vendor become available to the buying firm.
2. **Wide Choice:** Trade barriers, exchange rate fluctuations and other external changes may alter the relative attractiveness of suppliers. The firm can change its suppliers whenever necessary to minimise cost and to ensure steady supply. Thus, outsourcing offers a wide choice concerning the source of supply.
3. **No Investment:** In case of outsourcing the firm need not make capital investment needed in case of in-house manufacturing. This is a great advantage where the technology involved is subject to rapid obsolescence. Managerial and other resources involved in in-house manufacturing are also free for use.
4. **Concentration on Core Activities:** Outsourcing enables the firm to concentrate its resources, time and efforts on key activities.
5. **No Labour Problems:** By outsourcing components from suppliers, a firm can avoid industrial relations and other problems associated with large workforce.
6. **Low Impact of Recession:** In case of recession, demand for the firm's final product declines. Accordingly the firm can outsource lesser quantity of components. Therefore, recession has a lower adverse impact on its profitability.
7. **Ease of Exit:** Whenever it becomes essential to exit a product line/industry, the firm can more easily exit in case of outsourcing than in-house manufacturing.
8. **Other Advantages:** When a firm manufactures solely for internal use, there is little incentive to maximise efficiency or reduce costs. Transfer pricing passes on the total cost to the user plant also. These hidden inefficiencies are avoided in case of outsourcing. Offsets are possible in case of outsourcing. For example, the USA insisted that Japan should import components from it as an offset for imports of cars from Japan.

When the firm decides to buy rather than make, it has to choose between the following alternatives:

(*a*) procure components domestically or import them from abroad;

(*b*) procure from a single supplier or from several suppliers;

(*c*) centralise buying at one plant or allow plants to buy independently;

(*d*) import directly or through intermediaries;

(*e*) set up international procurement offices run by professionals;

(*f*) enter into strategic alliance with suppliers to ensure steady supply at the right time so as to minimise inventory.

Thus, both make and buy options have their own advantages and disadvantages. Some international firms partly make and partly buy. This option is known as make-and-buy option. Under this option, an international firm makes those inputs which it can produce at lower cost as compared to suppliers. It buys the inputs which suppliers can supply at a comparatively lower cost.

Table 14.3: Advantages and Disadvantages of Make and Buy Options

	Make Option	Buy Option
Advantages	1. Control over costs	• Wide variety and choice
	2. Control over quality	• No investment
	3. Control over delivery	• Less business risk
	4. Control over technology	• No need for expertise
	5. R and D initiatives	• No problems of large labour force
		• Low impact of recession
		• Ease of exit
		• Concentration on core activities
Disadvantages	1. Higher investment	• No control on cost
	2. Need for expertise	• Less control on quality
	3. May be inefficient	• Less control on delivery
	4. Problems due to large labours force	• Less control on technology
	5. High impact of recession 6. Difficulty of exit	• High bargaining power of supplies

14.3 Global Outsourcing

Globalisation provides the opportunity to source inputs, components and finished products from the best sources anywhere in the world. Even a firm which markets the products only within the domestic market may be outsourcing inputs or finished products from abroad. A dynamic firm will take advantage of low cost and superior quality existing anywhere in the world. Several Japanese and American companies ship the components to assembly plants abroad where the labour is cheap. These companies bring the finished product back home or ship it to other foreign markets. China, India, Malaysia, etc. have become a global manufacturing hubs for some products of multinational companies. General Motors, Toyota, Nissan are some examples of such multinationals. Several companies have adopted global sourcing as a major competitive strategy.

The main reasons for increasing offshore purchases are as follows:

1. Lower price
2. Better quality
3. More advanced technology
4. Only available source
5. More cooperative delivery

6. More consistent attitude
7. Less capital and manpower requirements
8. More flexibility to adjust to recession
9. Counter trade requirements

It is estimated that global sourcing accounts for about one-third of the world trade.

Production Sharing: According to Peter Drunker, production sharing means the practice of carrying out different stages of manufacturing of a product in different countries. Production sharing is a natural corollary of global sourcing. It has become quite popular in high technology and sophisticated products. A product is designed and developed in one country, its components are manufactured in different countries and final assembling is done in another country. For example, most of the components of an American car or computer are manufactured abroad.

Product sharing is a win-win situation for both developed countries and developing countries. The technology, managerial skills, purchasing power and other resources of developed countries are combined with low cost labour and materials of developing countries. Production sharing creates jobs for millions and leads to better utilisation of natural resources in developing countries. Developed nations gain in terms of low cost. Thus, production sharing is the form of economic integration most needed by both developing and developed countries.

Partnering: Due to the need for offshore sourcing and production sharing, buyer supplier partnership is emerging as a strategic issue in international operations. Competition is replacing competition. For example, when Microsoft develops more powerful software, demand for Intel chips increases. Similarly, the value of Microsoft increases when Intel produces faster chips. Japanese industry has gained considerably from collaboration relationship with suppliers. Anderson and Narus define partnering as "a process where a customer firm and supplier firm form strong and extensive social, economic, service and technical ties over time, with the intent of lowering total costs and/or increasing value, thereby achieving mutual benefit"[3].

Partnering is a collaborative rather than an adversial approach. It is based on mutual trust.

$200-mn Pune facility will make India a manufacturing hub: GE

GE, which pioneered the outsourcing of services from India in the 1990s and turned this country into one of the world's leading business process outsourcing destinations, is now looking to replicate the model in the manufacturing sector.

US multinational's first-of-its-kind multi-modal manufacturing facility coming up in Pune will feed the company's supply chains across the globe.

"We have an opportunity on our hands to transform India into a great destination for manufacturing and sourcing. We will build the entire ecosystem to make India a globally competitive manufacturing centre," president and CEO of GE said.

The Pune facility, being set up at a cost of $200 million (₹1,250 crore) will become operational in 2014. It will be GE's largest manufacturing facility outside the US. With $100 billion (₹6.2 lakh crore) in revenues, GE is the largest and most profitable infrastructure company in the world, and the sixth-most valuable brand globally.

3. James C. Anderson and James A. Narus "Partnering as a Focused Market Strategy," *California Management Review*, 33(3)

Multi-modal factories have the flexibility to manufacture multiple and often diverse products that cater to different businesses and is a relatively new concept in India.

The Pune facility will feed the production lines of GE's power generation, transmission and distribution units in India and abroad as well as its oil and gas and transportation factories and its healthcare business.

GE's strategy assumes significance as it comes at a time when India is trying to emerge as an attractive manufacturing destination to provide jobs to millions. GE's experience will be closely watched by multinationals that are holding back from investing in India because of the difficulties of doing business here.

14.4 International Logistics

Logistics or supply chain is the process of planning, implementing and controlling the efficient, cost effective flow and storage of raw materials, in-process inventory, finished goods, and related information from point of origin to the point of consumption, for meeting customer requirements.

Logistics system can be simple or complex. It is simple when manufacturing facilities are located near the source of inputs and markets. Logistics consists of two main parts – (*i*) inbound logistics or materials management, and (*ii*) outbound logistics or physical distribution. Inbound part involves procurement, handling, storage and movement of materials from suppliers to plants. Outbound component includes packaging, storage and movement of finished products from plants to customers.

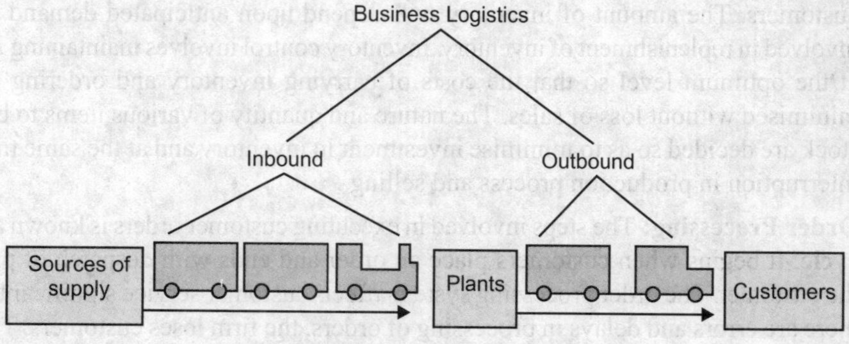

Fig. 14.1 : Logistics System

Source: *Ronald H. Ballou, Business Logistics Management: Planning and Control.*

Management of logistics requires **decisions** concerning the following:

1. **Network Design:** First of all, it is necessary to decide the number and location of facilities needed for logistics operations. Proper design of network and infrastructure improves efficiency of logistics. The facilities in this network are manufacturing plants, materials handling system, distribution system, order processing system, after-sale service, etc.
2. **Information System:** In logistics, information is needed to forecast sales and to process customer orders. Sales forecasting helps in inventory management. Correct information is necessary to avoid errors and delays in order processing.
3. **Transportation:** A cost effective and speedy transportation system improves efficiency of logistics. Roadways, railways, airways and waterways are the different modes of

transport. Road transport is suitable for carrying goods of medium bulk and weight over short distances and for point to point service. Rail transport is suitable for carrying heavy goods over long distance. Air transport is suitable for carrying light and valuable goods at a fast speed. Water transport is appropriate for carrying bulky goods of low value.

4. **Warehousing:** Proper storage of goods is necessary to serve customers efficiently. Warehousing decisions are as follows:
   (*a*) How many warehouses
   (*b*) What type of warehouses
   (*c*) Where to locate warehouses
   (*d*) What size of warehouses
5. **Procurement:** Acquiring raw materials, semifinished items and finished products is an important part of logistics. It consists of several activities, *e.g.,* requirement planning, sourcing suppliers, negotiation, order placement, receipt and inspection, quality assurance, handling, etc. It provides support to manufacturing and resale operations.
6. **Packaging and Labelling:** 'Packaging' involves designing and producing appropriate packages for various products. Effective packaging protects the product, makes product handling convenient, and serves as a silent salesman. 'Labelling' refers to putting identification marks on packages. A label provides information about the brand, grade, price, manufacturing date, expiry date, etc. It may be a part of the package or may be attached to the product.
7. **Inventory Management:** A business firm maintains inventory to fulfil orders of customers. The amount of inventory will depend upon anticipated demand and time involved in replenishment of inventory. Inventory control involves maintaining inventory at the optimum level so that the costs of carrying inventory and ordering costs are minimised without loss of sales. The nature and quantity of various items to be kept in stock are decided so as to minimise investment in inventory and at the same time avoid interruption in production process and selling.
8. **Order Processing:** The steps involved in executing customer orders is known as **orders cycle**. It begins when customers place an order and ends with despatch of product to the customer. The order processing system affects customer service significantly. When there are errors and delays in processing of orders, the firm loses customers. Therefore, an accurate, quick and efficient system is essential for success.

Logistics plays a vital **role** in international production and marketing in the following ways.

(*i*) Significant cost savings can be achieved in the area of logistics.

(*ii*) Logistics influences customer satisfaction through the time and cost involved in meeting customer needs:

(*iii*) Sound logistics management can provide a sustainable competitive advantage to an international firm.

Logistics is important as it creates time, place and possession utilities. Time utility is the value added to the product by making it available to the customer at the **right time**. Place utility is created by making the product available at the **right place.** Logistics creates possession utility by transferring ownership of the product. Logistics is also important because it helps in providing the **right product** in the **right condition** and at the **right cost**.

14.5 Global Networking of Operations

In order to optimise its efficiency and increase competitiveness, an international firm opts for global networking of its operations in different countries. Economic liberalisation and globalisation have facilitated the movement of inputs and production activities across nations. Therefore, international firms can now more easily set up linkages with suppliers and buyers. According to the World Investment Report 2002, governance, value chains and geographic configuration are the three core elements that are critical to the international production systems:

1. **Governance:** The governance structure of an international production system may be in various forms such as subsidiary, licensing, subcontracting, franchising, etc. Governance determines the linkages with suppliers, producers, marketers, etc. It also helps to exercise control over business activities spread over several countries and to maintain coordination between them.
2. **Global Value Chain:** The organisation and dispersion of production activities is known as value chain. Value chains are becoming fragmented due to specialisation and differentiation of business functions. An international firm can have its core competitive advantages anywhere along the value chain.
3. **Geographic Configuration:** There is now a trend towards integration of production facilities spread across the globe. Service and support functions are being increasingly internationalised. The technology, innovation and manufacturing activities are now more widely distributed geographically.

Global networking of operations have important implications for firms in developing countries. These firms can establish links with global production systems. They can emerge as global suppliers. For example, in the automobile industry several Indian firms are major suppliers of components to leading multinational auto companies in the world. Global networking and integration of operations will gain momentum due to cross-border mergers and acquisitions. For instance, more than 50 per cent of the total revenue of some Indian conglomerates such as Aditya Birla Group and Tata Group comes from overseas operations.

SUMMARY

Plant Location: Centralised Vs. decentralised location, each has its own merits and demerits (2) Production strategies are of four types – global concentration, host market, product specialisation, and transnational vertical integration. (3) Factors affecting location are classified into – (*a*) product related (*b*) market related (*c*) country related, and (*d*) organisation related. (4) Role of foreign plants – offshore, source, contributor, outpost, and lead factories.

Make Vs. Buy Decision: Making offers the advantages of cost control, quality control, supply control, protection of technology, specialised investment, transfer pricing, **Buying** offers the advantages of lower cost, wide choice, no investment, concentration on core activities, no labour problems, low impact of recession, and easy exit.

Global Outsourcing: (1) Advantages in terms of lower price, better quality, advanced technology, cooperative delivery, less capital and labour needs, flexibility, counter trade. (2) Production sharing – beneficial to both developed and developing nations, (3) Partnering with suppliers.

International Logistics: Network design, information system, transportation, storage, procurement, packing, inventory management, order processing.

Global Networking of Operations: Governance, global value chain, geographic configuration.

TEST QUESTIONS

1. International production can be centralised or decentralised. Give the merits and demerits of each option.
2. Describe the conditions which favour (*a*) Centralised production, (*b*) decentralised production
3. Explain Dicken's four types of production strategies.
4. Discuss the factors affecting international plant location.
5. What is make or buy decision? Discuss the merits of both making and buying.
6. What is global outsourcing? State its reasons.
7. Explain the concept, elements and importance of international logistics.
8. What is global networking of operations? Why is it growing?
9. Explain the core elements that are critical to international production system.
10. Write short notes on:

    (*a*) Role of foreign plants

    (*b*) Production sharing

    (*c*) Partnering.

CHAPTER

15 International Marketing Management

LEARNING OBJECTIVES

After studying this chapter, you should understand:

The objective of both domestic and international marketing is to satisfy the needs of customers at a profit to the firm. The basic concepts and principles of marketing are also the same for both domestic and international marketing. The difference lies mainly in the context. A domestic marketing firm operates in a single set of economic, social, cultural, political and legal environment. On the other hand, an international marketing firm has to face many different types of environment in different countries. Therefore, marketing decision-making becomes much more complex and riskier in case of international marketing.

International marketing may be defined as the process of planning and executing the conception, pricing, promotion and distribution of ideas, goods and services globally to achieve the individual, organisational and societal objectives.

International marketing management involves decisions concerning the following:

1. International market segmentation
2. Target market selection
3. International product decisions
4. International pricing decisions
5. International distribution decisions
6. International promotion decisions

First of all, a firm that intends to go international has to decide which country or region to enter. The firm must select the specific foreign markets that it intends to serve. This decision is made in two stages. First, the firm identifies the countries and consumer segments that have similar characteristics and are suited to the firm's product and Philosophy. This is called international market segmentation. Second stage involves choosing the specific foreign market that the firm can profitably serve. This is known as target market selection.

15.1 International Market Segmentation

International market segmentation is the process of identifying countries and customer groups that have similar needs and wants, and are likely to show similar buying behaviour. Market segmentation in an international firm is done at two levels – (*i*) macro or country level, and (*ii*) micro or customer level.

1. **Macro Segmentation (Country Level) Analysis:** Market segmentation at the macro level involves grouping of countries on the basis of similar environment and market potential. Countries with severe environmental problems are deleted from consideration. The remaining countries are grouped on the basis of market size and growth potential.

   The purpose of macro segmentation is to judge (*i*) the market potential for the industry, and (*ii*) sales potential for the firm.

   (*i*) **Assessing Market Potential:** The total market potential for an industry means the size of existing and future markets. The techniques used to assess market potential are as follows:

   (*a*) **Income Elasticity of Demand:** Change in the level of demand due to changes in consumers' income is known as income elasticity of demand. At low income levels, the elasticity of demand for most products is high. It means a small increase in income will result in more than proportionate increase in demand. At higher income levels, the rate of increase in demand tends to be low. Therefore, countries with low per capita income have high income elasticity. In other words, emerging markets are attractive due to high income elasticity of demand.

(*b*) **Market Audit:** In this technique, the total consumption for a specific product in a country is computed as follows:

Domestic output + Imports – Exports

It is however difficult to obtain current and reliable data for such computation.

(*c*) **Multiple Factor Indices:** A multiple factor index is computed taking into account the variables which have close correlation with the market potential for the product. For example, a luxury car manufacturer may consider factors like individuals with income levels above say ₹ 1 crore per annum, population in the age group of 20–35 and road infrastructure. Correlation between past sales figures and these variables may provide an estimate of market potential.

(*d*) **Analogy:** In case of countries with inadequate data, market potential can be estimated by using the data of another country having similar demand pattern. Suppose countries *X* and *Y* have similar demand pattern with a time lag of two years. Market potential of country *X* for white goods may be estimated by using income levels and sales data of such goods in country *Y* allowing for the time lag.

(*e*) **Cluster Analysis:** Under this mathematical technique, similar countries are grouped into a cluster. Similar marketing strategies can be adopted for all countries within a cluster. However, there may be some time lag in demand pattern among countries within a cluster. For example, suppose a new product is accepted in Bangla Desh two years later than in India. Then the information about India's market may be used to estimate the market potential in Bangla Desh. Time lags between countries are however vanishing fast due to modern means of communication and liberalization.

(*ii*) **Estimating Sales Potential for the Firm:** Gap analysis is used to judge the firm's sales potential in an overseas market. Gap is the excess of total market potential over the firm's sales. The gap can arise due to four reasons:

(*a*) **Usage gap:** It indicates underutilisation of the product and can be bridged through promotion of the product. Usage gap occurs when total industry sales are less than the total market potential.

(*b*) **Competition gap:** It refers to the difference between the expected market share and the actual market share of the firm. It can be bridged through strategies to overcome competition.

(*c*) **Product line gap:** It occurs when a firm loses sales due to an incomplete product line.

(*d*) **Distribution gap:** Inadequate distribution facilities create distribution gap. It can be bridged by expanding the distribution network so as to make the product available to all market segments.

Once the gap is identified the firm has to decide how far the potential can be converted into actual sales. This will depend on the following factors:

(*i*) Level of competition in the market and the expected response to the firm's entry (*ii*) Availability and reliability of distribution and logistics

(*iii*) Availability of competent local partners

(*iv*) The firm's brand equity

(*v*) Fit between the firm's goals, policies and resources and the market

(*vi*) Trade barriers to entry of foreign firms

(*vii*) Ability and willingness of consumers to buy

(*viii*) Product's suitability to the market

2. **Micro Segmentation:** Segmentation of the market within a country or region is known as micro segmentation. A market segment consists of relatively homogeneous groups of consumers with similar consumption patterns. Consumers within a segment usually respond in a similar manner to the firm's marketing strategies. The purpose of market segmentation is to design a marketing mix that can properly meet the needs of the consumers in a particular segment. Market can be segmented on several bases:

(*a*) **Demographic segmentation:** Age, gender, race, income, education, occupation, size of household and other characteristics of the population are used as the basis.

(*b*) **Psychographic segmentation:** Attitudes, interests, values, opinions, life styles and other such traits are used to group consumers.

(*c*) **Benefit segmentation:** Motives behind buying serve as the basis. For example, dishwashers are bought as necessary kitchen equipment in the USA but more as a status symbol in India.

(*d*) **Usage segmentation:** In this basis, consumers are classified according to the rate of usage of the product, *e.g.,* heavy users, medium users, occasional users, and non-users.

(*e*) **User status segmentation:** The status of the consumers as potential users serves as the basis. Non-users, first time users, regular users and users of competitive brands are the main categories of potential buyers.

15.2 Target Market Selection

Market segmentation helps to identify countries as markets with similar customer needs, wants and preferences. The next step is to identify the specific markets with highest potential for the firm's products/services. The process of screening different overseas markets and selecting the markets that best suits their objectives and capabilities of the firm is known as target market selection or market targeting.

Selection of target market becomes necessary because a firm cannot serve all the markets. There is a large number of markets in the world and there are wide differences in their attractiveness. The main steps involved in the process of market selection are given in Fig. 15.1.

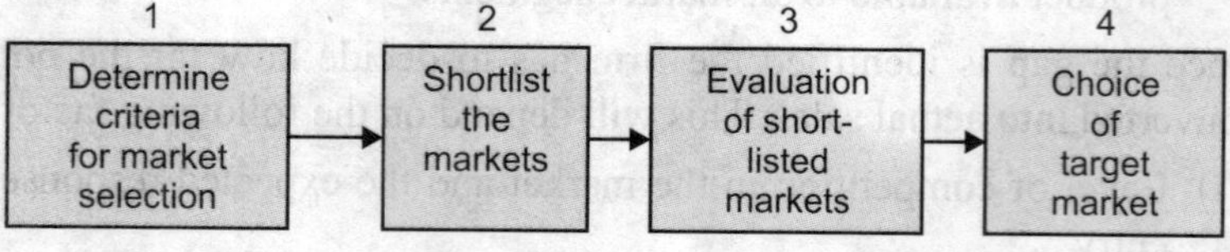

Fig. 15.1. Market Selection Process

1. **Criteria for Selection:** Several criteria are used to identify the markets/countries with good potential and low risk. Some of these criteria are as follows:
   (*a*) Current size of the market and its potential for growth;
   (*b*) Existing and potential competition;
   (*c*) Market's compatibility with the firm's goals, policies, strategies and resources;
   (*d*) Degree of political, exchange rate and financial stability;
   (*e*) Marketing infrastructure in the country;
   (*f*) Sources of competitive advantage for the firm, *e.g.,* brand equity; and
   (*g*) The country's policies and regulations and procedures. A score may be assigned to each of these criteria. The market/ country with the highest score may be selected as the target market.
2. **Shortlist the Markets:** Markets which do not deserve consideration may be identified through preliminary screening. Small population, very low per capita income, lack of infrastructure, political instability, etc, may be the reasons for deleting certain markets. For example, there exists no market for TV sets in a country where there is no telecasting.
3. **Target Marketing Strategy:** Once the target market is selected, the international firm has to decide the strategy for its coverage. Two decisions have to be taken: (*a*) Whether to concentrate on a single market or to diversify into several segments, and (*b*) Whether to adopt differentiated or undifferentiated strategy for the chosen segment. Marketing strategies are prepared keeping in view the profiles of selected markets. The profile consists of the demographic, economic, political and cultural characteristics of the market. It describes the relevant characteristics of the market such as competition, trends in domestic production, demand, imports and exports; customer tastes and preferences, buying habits and attitudes, etc.

   (*i*) **Concentrated Vs. Diversified Marketing:** Concentrated marketing involves focusing on a part of the market. A firm with limited resources is likely to opt for concentrated marketing. Firms dealing in specialised products meant for specific markets may also adopt this strategy. Even in one market the firm may focus on a small niche segment. Firms in the cosmetics industry often adopt this strategy.

   An international firm with huge resources can meet the needs of several segments and many markets. Therefore, they adopt diversification strategy. For example, multinationals like Proctor and Gamble and Unilever target all consumers with all their products. Diversified marketing can help to spread the firm's risks but it is difficult to manage.

   An international firm may enter into a **niche market** which has a gap to be filled. In such a market, the firm may face little competition. After establishing a strong position in the niche, the firm may enter other segments. For example, Toyota of Japan entered India with its multi-utility vehicle (MUV) **Qualis** because except Tata's Sumo there was no MUV brand. Once it became a well established brand, Toyota introduced its **Corolla, Camry** and other cars in the Indian market.

Table 15.1: Merits and Demerits of Marketing Strategies

	Merits	Demerits
Concentrated Marketing	• Concentration of resources and capabilities enables the firm to attain a strong position in the market • Enables a small firm to compete successfully • The firm can design products that match market demand	• The risk of keeping all eggs in one basket.
Niche Marketing	• Avoids direct competition with major firms • Provides experience and resources for entry into other segments • High margin	• Difficult to identify niche markets
Diversified Marketing	• Better utilisation of resources and capabilities • High total sales volume	• Requires huge resources and capabilities • Not suitable for small firms

(*ii*) **Differentiated Vs. Undifferentiated Strategy:** An international firm operating in several overseas markets may adopt differentiation or non-differentiation strategy. Under differentiation strategy, the firm uses different marketing mixes for different segments. This strategy helps the firm to achieve wider coverage of its markets. Large firms like Proctor and Gamble and Unilever adopt differentiation strategy by offering brands for both mass market and luxury market.

Under undifferentiated marketing the firm uses the single marketing mix in all segments. The whole market is treated as a single unit. It is similar to mass marketing in a single country. International firms are able to do mass marketing due to the existence of similar consumer needs in several countries. Undifferentiated strategy helps to reduce costs of production, promotion and distribution due to standardisation of the product. But this strategy requires extensive distribution of the product. In actual practice, even global brands such as Coke, Colgate. and Nokia are offered with slight modifications in taste, design, colour, size, etc so as to meet local preferences and cultures in different countries.

Many Indian companies have also adopted niche marketing. For example, Balsara identified a niche for a herbal dental product and Vicco spotted a niche for a sugar free toothpaste in foreign markets dominated by multinationals. While selecting a niche, the firm must ensure that the niche is: (*a*) adequate in size to be profitable, (*b*) is free from competition by large firms, (*c*) the firm can serve so well that it will have a competitive edge, and (*d*) the firm can defend it.

15.3 International Product Decisions

Once the market is segmented and the target market is selected, the firm has to design and develop an appropriate marketing mix for each/all markets. The marketing mix consists of four Ps — product, price, place (distribution), and promotion.

In international marketing, the main decisions concerning the product are as follows:

1. Product standardisation or customization
2. Branding
3. Packaging and Labelling
4. Warranty and after-sale service

15.3.1 Product Standardisation Vs. Customization

An international firm can either market the same product in every market or adapt (customize) the product for each market. Standardisation or globalisation means offering the same product in all markets whereas product adaptation involves changes in design, size, brand, package-label and other features of the product to suit different markets. Both product standardisation and product adaptation (localisation) have their advantages.

Advantages of Product Standardisation

1. **Reduction in Cost:** Standardisation offers economies of scale which help to reduce cost of production per unit. Marketing costs can also be reduced through product standardisation due to savings in inventory, promotion, and after-sale services.
2. **Centralised Marketing:** Standardisation of product facilitates centralised control over marketing activities of the firm.
3. **Better R&D:** When the product is standardised, research and development activities can be more concerted and efficient. Product development in short time and at lower cost becomes possible.
4. **Uniform Image:** Uniformity of product helps to build a consistent image of the firm and the product world over. For example, McDonald has a worldwide reputation due to consistent product quality and services.
5. **Similar Needs:** Needs and preferences of consumers in different markets are becoming similar. Therefore, identical products can be marketed successfully in different markets. Diamonds for prestige and watches for time keeping are examples. As the economies develop and income levels become similar, consumption patterns tend to converge. Now firms can sell standardised products in European countries due to the creation of the European Union.
6. **High-Tech Products:** In case of industrial and high technology products, industry specifications are prescribed which facilitate standardisation. Therefore, industrial products are more standardised than consumer products.
7. **Urban Markets:** Products targeted at developed and urban markets require less adaptation. The need for product customization is more in rural and suburban markets.
8. **Resource Constraints:** A firm with limited resources may opt for standardised products to be marketed in countries which accept such products.
9. **Country of Origin Effect:** Some products enjoy reputation due to their country of origin. For example, France is known for perfumes, Switzerland for watches, Japan for electronics, Germany for machines, etc. Firms from these countries can sell their home products in overseas markets without modifying them.

Product standardisation, however, overlooks differences in consumer tastes and preferences and other differences between markets. It also inhibits local marketing initiatives.

Advantages of Product Adaptation

1. **Local use Conditions:** The conditions under which a product is used may differ from one market to another. Habits, customs, space constraints, climate and physique of consumers are different in different countries. For example, automobiles meant for countries with rough roads need changes to make them more sturdy. Philips downsized its shaver to fit the smaller hands of Japanese. Similarly, word processors are adapted to local languages. McDonald developed Aloo Tikki Burger to suit the taste of Indians.
2. **Income Level Differences:** The per capita income varies widely among countries. As a result buying ability of consumers differs. Expensive products having good demand in high income countries need modification for selling in low income countries. For example, American publishers bring out low priced editions of their books for South Asian countries.
3. **Cultural Differences:** Product features such as size, colour, design, brand name, etc, are perceived differently in different cultures. These attributes may have to be changed to create a positive impact and increase sales in some markets. For example, Coca-Cola had to change the name of its Diet Cola to Cola Light in Japan because diet implies sickness or medicine in Japan.
4. **Government Regulations:** The laws in a country may specify some standards or ban certain ingredients in products. The product offered in a particular country must comply with these regulations. For example, added vitamins in margarine are compulsory in U.K. and Holland but forbidden in Italy. Package size, safety standards and quality requiremente may also be different in different countries.
5. **Technical Standards:** Standards relating to the product, electric current, measurement, etc, may differ among countries. The product must be adapted to suit local standards in each market. For example, different pollution control standards for automobiles in different countries require product adaptation.
6. **Non-Tariff Barriers:** Testing or approval procedures, subsidies for local products, bureaucratic red tape and other non-tariff barriers can be overcome through product adaptation. For example, compulsion to use local language in advertising, instructions for use, guarantees, etc., require changes in packaging, labelling, etc.
7. **Local Initiatives:** Foreign subsidiaries of some multinational corporations are given autonomy due to the strategy of decentralisation. These subsidiaries design and develop products for each host market.

Globalisation and increasing competition have led to the product strategy of globalisation with localisation. International firms try to develop a global product and then make minor changes in it to meet the needs of different markets.

15.3.2 Branding

A brand means a name, word, sign, symbol, design, or any combination of these used by a manufacturer or merchant to identify his product and to distinguish it from those of competitors.

An international firm has to make the following decisions about branding:

1. **Brand or No Brand:** The first decision concerning branding is whether to brand the product or not. Branding provides the following benefits to exporters:

   (*a*) better identification and awareness of the product among the consumers;

   (*b*) better brand loyalty;

   (*c*) scope for higher pricing and better profit margins;

   (*d*) protection against price competition;

   (*e*) improvement in corporate image;

   (*f*) facility of market segmentation.

   Branding, however, increases costs of production and marketing. Branding may not be needed in cases where the consumers do not identify the product with a particular supplier. For example, in case of agricultural products grading is more important than branding.

   There is an increasing trend throughout the world towards non-branding. This is so because prices of non-branded products are lower and such products are available in several sizes and models.

2. **Own Brand Vs. Private Brand:** Most exporters use the dealer's brand or **private brand**. Private branding offers several advantages: (*a*) the firm can concentrate on its core activity of manufacturing leaving the difficult task of marketing to retailers, (*b*) the firm can use the credit of the retailer to expand its market share, (*c*) dealers easily accept such products, (*d*) promotional expenses are reduced. But the firm may not get right price for its product. Private branding is appropriate for small firms who have limited resources but export to several countries. Indian exporters of textiles and sports goods use private brands.

   The manufacturing firm may export the products under its **own brand**. It enables the firm to exercise better control of product features, to charge higher price, to retain brand loyalty and to exercise better bargaining power. Large firms with adequate resources prefer own brand.

3. **Global Brand Vs. Local Brands:** Exporters usually adopt a global brand. Advantages of global brand are: better image of the firm, reduction in advertising and marketing costs, no brand confusion, better marketing focus, ease in getting shelf space with retailers, etc. However, it is difficult to promote a global brand. It is essential to deliver consistent quality and global brand may face resistance in low income countries. Global brand is appropriate in case of a global product which means a standardised product recognised and used around the world.

   Local brands provide the following advantages: no difficulty in pronunciation, no negative impression, no taxation of international brand, greater acceptability in low income countries, flexibility to modify the quality and size to suit local markets. However, local brands increase advertising and inventory costs, and poor image of the manufacturing firm.

4. **Single Brand Vs. Multiple Brands:** An international firm may promote a single brand in a market or promote several brands simultaneously in the same market. The advantages of a single brand include: marketing focus, better impact on the market, reduction in

cost of promotion, brand gets full attention of consumers, no brand confusion. But the firm may fail to exploit full market potential due to heterogeneity of the market.

Multiple brands are used when tastes and preferences of consumers differ widely from one segment of the market to another segment. Multiple branding enables the firm to meet the needs of all segments and thereby maximise sales. Other advantages of multiple branding are: no negative impression of one brand, access to more shelf space, excitement among employees and generation of competitive spirit. But multiple branding increases marketing and inventory costs.

Branding Strategies

(*i*) It is advisable to adopt branding when the product quality is consistent and its attributes can be differentiated, otherwise no brand is better.

(*ii*) A large firm with abundant resources can adopt own brand, otherwise a private brand is preferable.

(*iii*) Local brands are better when significant inter-market differences exist otherwise adopt a global brand.

(*iv*) Multiple brands are preferable in case of inter-market differences, otherwise adopt a single brand.

15.3.3 Packaging and Labelling

Packaging serves two main functions —

(*a*) protection of the product till it reaches the consumer; and

(*b*) promotion of the product

Special packaging may be needed for goods meant for exports due to several reasons:

(*i*) Extra protection is required due to distance and time involved in transportation.

(*ii*) Changes in climate across countries require protection against extreme cold and heat.

(*iii*) Ability to buy large packs differs across countries, so packages of different sizes are needed.

(*iv*) Legal requirements of a country may require modifications in packaging.

(*v*) Consumers in some countries may prefer glass bottles or metal boxes due to their reuse value.

The promotional function of packaging is closely related to labelling. Adaptation in labelling may be needed to provide information in a language understood by local people and to meet host country regulations. Regulations in several countries require printing the details of ingredients and nutritional, values precautions in use on the package. Some countries require use of two languages in the label. For example, India requires the information to be in Hindi and English. Colours and symbols used in packaging and labelling must conform to local culture.

15.3.4 Warranty and After sales Service

An international firm has to decide whether to offer the same standardised warranty worldwide or to change it to suit different markets. Standardised uniform warranty creates the impression of high quality and is suitable in case of global products. In case of food products and medicines, the warranty accepted in developed nations is considered as evidence of high quality in developing countries.

Dilution of warranty terms reduces cost and may be adopted in price-conscious markets. It may also be used in markets where the firm has monopoly. In countries having stringent regulations a stringer warranty may be required. In a highly competitive market, a stringer warranty may help to gain market share. A stringer warranty may be offered in new markets to gain consumer acceptance of the product.

A strong after-sale service network is required for proper execution of the warranty terms. Such a network can be created through proper planning, investment in physical facilities, logistics and infirmation system, recruitment and training of staff. The firm has to choose between its own after-sale service network or through authorised service centres.

15.4 International Pricing Decisions

International pricing is more difficult than domestic pricing due to two reasons. **First,** several players with different characteristics are involved. It is very difficult to assess the tastes and preferences of consumers and the moves of competitors. **Second,** a large number of unique factors affect export pricing. Product differences, additional costs of transportation and communication, availability of export incentives, differences in terms of contract are some of these factors.

15.4.1 Factors Affecting Export Pricing

The main factors that determine international pricing are given below:

1. **Pricing Objectives:** Price is a strategic tool to achieve certain objectives. When the objective is market penetration or to increase market share, the firm may charge a low price. A high initial price may be charged in case of innovative products to skim the cream of the market or to recover investment quickly. A price cut may be offered to fight competition or to dispose of surplus stock. A company may adopt a pricing policy to achieve stable and increasing exports in the long run. Price may be set at a competitive level or even below competition to achieve a specified share of the country's exports.

Pricing Objectives	Price Level
1. Market penetration 2. Increase in market share 3. Fighting competition 4. Preventing entry of new firms 5. Meeting export obligation 6. Disposal of surplus stock 7. Optimum capacity utilisation	Low
8. Skimming the market 9. Reducing the pay back period 10. Target return on investment 11. Profit maximisation 12. Early recovery of cash	High

2. **Nature of the Market:** Usually, the international market is highly competitive with several suppliers chasing select customers. Even then a few leading brands may dominate the market. A small exporter may price below the established brands due to lack of influence over market prices. Alternatively, the firm may create a niche market and price its product high. High degree of competition in the market leaves little freedom in pricing except for exporters of well known brands and patented products.

3. **Nature of the Product:** In case of low value products, demand may decline with increase in income. Consumers may switch over to higher priced products. When the demand for the product is highly price elastic, a low price would help to maximise sales volume. On the other hand, if price elasticity of demand is very low (as in case of agricultural products) prices may be kept high. Similarly, if the product is highly differentiated from competitive products or has strong unique features, the firm can charge a high price. Income levels of consumers and importance of the product to consumers are also important.

4. **Costs:** The fixed and variable costs of production and marketing are a major determinant of price. In the short run the export price may even be lower than the full cost. But in the long run, a firm has to recover full costs and a profit margin. A firm whose costs are lower than those of competitors has greater freedom in pricing.

5. **Image of the Firm and the Country:** A well-reputed firm can more easily charge a higher price than less reputed firms. Similarly, firms from countries with a high quality image are able to charge comparatively high prices. India has a poor quality image abroad which restricts the freedom to charge a better price.

6. **Exchange Rate:** The exchange rate of the currency may also influence pricing. For example, when the rupee is depreciating, Indian exporters have the freedom to quote low dollar prices because they realise more rupees for every dollar earned by exports.

7. **Domestic Production and Market Conditions:** When the domestic market cannot absorb full production, the plant remains under utilised. Exports may be used to fully utilise the plant. In such a situation the firm may fix price to cover variable cost and some margin. On the other hand, if additional production capacity has to be put up for exports, price should cover full costs.

8. **Statutory Requirements:** Government policies and regulations also influence export pricing. Government may specify margins/mark up, price ceilings (Minimum Export Price), etc. In order to improve export competitiveness of domestic firms, Government may offer subsidies (*e.g.,* cash compensatory support), tax concessions or exemptions (duty drawback scheme) and other incentives (cheap export credit, supply of raw materials at regulated prices, etc.) to exporters. Government may even directly compete in the market to control prices. Import duty and other taxes in the importing country also influence export pricing. Anti-dumping regulations (*e.g.,* countervailing import duties) in the importing country act as a deterrent in fixing prices below the cost of production. International prices of some commodities are controlled through international agreements such as quota agreements, buffer stock agreements, bialateral/multilateral contracts, etc.

15.4.2 Methods of Export Pricing

The major methods of export pricing are as under:

1. **Cost-Based Pricing:** Under this method price includes cost and profit margin. Therefore, it is also known as cost plus pricing. While computing costs, costs of production and marketing are included. In addition, costs incurred on the following are also considered:

   (*a*) special inputs specified by the importer.

   (*b*) special packaging.

   (*c*) freight, insurance and handling charges.

   (*d*) agency commission.

   (*e*) export duties and exchange rate changes.

   Cost-based pricing may be **total cost pricing** or **marginal cost pricing.** Usually an exporter attempts to recover all costs. However, in the short run, only variable costs may be included in export pricing due to the following reasons:

   (*i*) when the international market is highly competitive;

   (*ii*) fixed costs have already been recovered through domestic sales;

   (*iii*) exports at marginal cost pricing will boost employment in the home country;

   (*iv*) when the firm wants to enter new markets, marginal cost pricing may help in market penetration;

   (*v*) the product has no brand reputation;

   (*vi*) export is insignificant and domestic sales are quite large;

   (*vii*) fixed costs constitute insignificant proportion of total cost; and

   (*viii*) export pricing does not affect domestic demand for the product.

2. **Market Oriented Pricing:** In this method, exports are priced at the level acceptable to the overseas markets. The product may be priced high when the demand is high and low when the demand is sluggish. This method is also known as **charging what the traffic will bear,** *i.e.,* charging the maximum possible price in the given market conditions.

3. **Competition Oriented Pricing:** Some firms follow the dominant competitor (price leader) in setting export prices. The price leader is the international firm that initiates the price trends. A firm may set the price at par, below or above the competitor's price. The choice will depend on comparative quality of the product, the firm's reputation, etc.

Table 15.2; Advantages and Disadvantages of Major Pricing Methods

Advantages	Disadvantages
TOTAL COST PRICING	
• Recovery of all the costs	• The price may be uncompetitive
• Provides target margin	• Opportunity to charge a high price may be lost
• Widely accepted method	• Overlooks elasticity of demand
• Simple and easy to understand	• The method is inflexible

MARGINAL COST PRICING	
• Helps in utilisation of idle plant capacity • Chance of increasing profits when fixed costs are recovered from domestic sales • Makes the firm more competitive • Helps in market penetration • Helps in entry into new markets	• Not possible in the long run • Difficulty in raising the price later • Not advisable when no idle capacity exists
MARKET ORIENTED PRICING	
• Very flexible approach • Suitable for products with short life cycles • Takes care of market conditions	• Difficulty in estimating what the market will bear • Elasticity of demand may be ignored • Risk of grey market
COMPETITION ORIENTED PRICING	
• Very simple method • Relevant to competitive position of the firm	• Competitor's price may be unrealistic • Costs ignored • Firm's pricing objective may be different

4. **Negotiated Pricing:** The price may be decided through bargaining between the exporter and the importer. This method is flexible and takes into account the viewpoints of both the buyer and the seller. But the seller may not get a good price due to weak bargaining power. This method is common in institutional and government purchases.

   In most cases, the buyer specifies the price at which he is prepared to buy the goods. Whether the seller will accept this price depends on his cost structure, objectives, business conditions, etc.

5. **Retrograde Pricing:** When the importer specifies the price, the exporter estimates whether this price will be profitable to him or not. This is known as retrograde pricing. Direct costs, overheads, export overheads (if any); agent's commission; forwarding, packing and freight costs; documentation charges, duties payable, etc. are taken into account in retrograde pricing.

15.4.3 Price Discrimination

One major decision which an international firm has to take is whether to charge a uniform price worldwide or to charge different prices in different markets. A uniform price is advisable. When significant price differences in different markets are likely to give rise to grey markets. **Grey marketing** means unauthorised import and sale of goods meant for one market in another higher priced market. A grey marketer may buy through an intermediary in the low price market and divert the goods to the high price markets. Gey markets exist in products like cars, watches and cameras. Such a market causes financial loss to the manufacturer and loss of reputation. A manufacturer may have to charge different prices when the cost and conditions differ between different markets.

15.4.4 Export Pricing Process

The main steps involved in the process of export pricing are given below:

1. **Defining Pricing Objectives:** First of all, the firm has to define the objective of pricing policy. Market penetration (building market share) objective requires setting a low price while high profile positioning objective results in high price. When the objective is to utilise excess capacity through exports, the firm may even adopt marginal cost pricing.

2. **Analysing Nature of the Market:** After defining the pricing objectives, a firm analyses the characteristics of the market. Prevailing price ranges, trade customs and practices (such as discounts, credit and payment terms, etc.) are examples of market characteristics. But the degree of competition is the most important feature. In case competition is not intense, the firm has flexibility in pricing.
3. **Estimating Costs:** Export costs include (*a*) direct production costs (materials, labour and other direct expenses), (*b*) production overheads, and (*c*) costs of marketing and distribution (*e.g.,* agency commission, packing charges, transportation expenses, etc.).
4. **Calculating Export Incentives:** The incentives available to an exporter help in reducing the price. Cash compensatory support, duty drawback, income tax benefits are examples of export incentives.

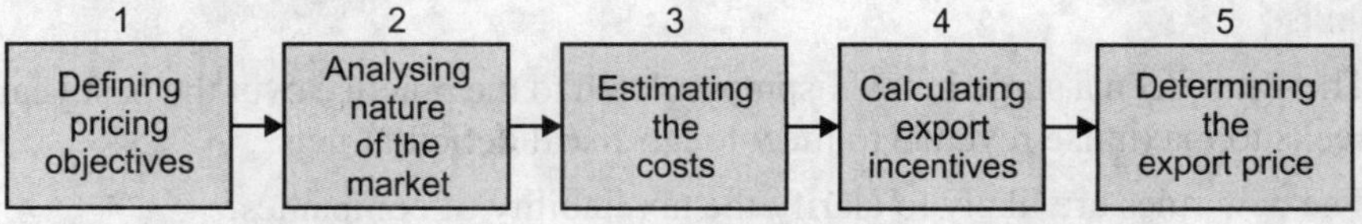

Fig. 15.2. Steps in the Process of Export Pricing

5. **Determining the Export Price:** The last step is to fix the export price. Costs and export incentives help in deciding the minimum price the firm must realise. In case exports are not feasible at this price, the firm will have to decide whether it is possible to quote a lower price.

15.4.5 Transfer Pricing

The pricing of goods transferred from the company's production or sales unit in one country to another unit in another country is known as transfer pricing or intra-company pricing. In most cases, the parent company decides the transfer prices irrespective of the company's nationality. The basis used for transfer pricing depends on several factors such as market conditions, nature of the affiliates, government policies and regulations, etc. The main bases of transfer pricing are as follows:

(*i*) Local manufacturing cost plus a standard mark-up.
(*ii*) Cost of the most efficient manufacturing unit plus a standard mark-up.
(*iii*) Negotiated price.
(*iv*) Charging the price as quoted to outside buyers.

The main objectives of transfer pricing are given below:

1. To maximise the company's total profits.
2. To facilitate control by the parent company.
3. To provide all levels of management a sufficient opportunity to maintain, develop and receive credit for the profitability of their divisions.

Transfer pricing has become a controversial issue. Multinational corporations are accused of manipulating transfer pricing system to avoid taxes and dividend regulations. In order to mitigate the impact of taxes on profits, these corporations charge a low transfer price in countries where taxes are high and charge a high price in nations where tax rates are low.

Therefore, governments in different countries have become more concerned about transfer pricing. Multinationals adopt the following strategies relating to transfer pricing to maximise profits:

(*a*) Quoting minimum transfer prices on goods shipped to high-tariff countries.

(*b*) Overpricing the goods shipped to units in high-tax countries.

(*c*) Charging high prices on goods shipped to units in countries which restrict repatriation of dividend.

Clearing the Air to Help Taxation

- Transfer pricing is a practice used by multinational companies around the world to reduce their tax burden by paying for services across borders between their different units.
- There has been a surge in tax disputes related to the practice over the past year as India seeks to maximise revenue to meet tough fiscal deficit targets.
- The new rules are likely to clarify the tax liability of companies.
- Applicable to six sectors including IT and ITeS (information technology-enabled services), auto ancillary and pharma, companies can take refuge under the norms for five years to avoid getting into long tax disputes.
- Transaction up to ₹500 crore would have a safe-harbour margin of 20% and those above ₹500 crore would have margin of 22%.
- The new rules are based on the recommendations made by a committee headed by former Central Board of Direct Taxes (CBDT) chairman N Rangachary.

15.4.6 Dumping

Dumping means selling goods and services in the foreign market at a price below the domestic price or cost of production. Most countries·take steps such as anti-dumping import duties to prevent dumping. Dumping is of the following types:

(*a*) **Sporadic dumping:** It is adopted mainly to dispose of the excess stock of goods that may occur occasionally.

(*b*) **Intermittent dumping:** Periodic sale of goods abroad at below the domestic price is called intermittent dumping. It may be adopted to establish a foothold in the foreign market (called predatory dumping) to eliminate competitors, and to prevent emergence of new competitors.

(*c*) **Long-term or persistent dumping:** Such dumping is adopted to make full utilisation of plant capacity. Such utilisation helps reduce cost per unit and to increase profits in the domestic market. For example, Japanese firms continuously sell electronic goods at lower prices in USA and India.

Thus, dumping is a form of price discrimination. It is harmful to the local manufacturers in host countries. For example, producers of cooking oil in India suffered when Malaysia dumped. Therefore, Government of India took steps to protect the domestic firms. Dumping also affects economic activity and public revenue.

(*d*) **Reverse dumping:** In this type of dumping, the product is sold at a high price in foreign markets and at a low price in the domestic market.

15.5 International Distribution Decisions

In international business, distribution channels differ widely between markets and regions. Success in international marketing depends on making the products available at the right time, at the right place and at the minimum distribution cost. The main decisions involved in international distribution are given below:

15.5.1 Channel Design

Channel design involves determining the length and width of the distribution channel.

1. **Channel Length:** The length of channel refers to the number of intermediaries between the manufacturer and the consumer. When there are several intermediaries, the channel is long. It is short when few intermediaries are involved. When the manufacturer sells directly to consumer, the channel is the shortest.
2. **Channel Width:** The width of channel means the number of intermediaries employed at a particular level, *e.g.,* the number of retailers employed. The channel is wide when more intermediaries are employed and it is narrow if there are few intermediaries at a specific level.

15.5.2 Factors Influencing Channel Design

The main determinants of international distribution channel are as follows[1]:

1. **Customer Characteristics:** The demographic (the number and geographical dispersal of customers, size and frequency of purchase) and psychographic (buying habits and preferences, etc) of customers differ from country to country. Therefore, different channels may be needed for different countries. In case of a large number of widely dispersed customers a longer channel is required. What, how, why and when customers buy are significant. For customers who make low volume purchases frequently, indirect distribution is economical. But if the customers are large volume retailers or institutional buyers, direct selling may be cheaper.
2. **Culture of Market:** A market's distribution culture means the existing channel structure which may be a statutory requirement or a historical practice. For example, foreign firms find it difficult to penetrate the Japanese market due to the country's complex distribution system. Foreign country's laws may prohibit the use of a particular channel. Door-to-door selling is not allowed in France. A foreign firm may have to employ a local distributor adding to the channel length. In a particular country exclusive distribution may be prohibited as a restraint of trade. Thus, foreign laws affect both length and width of distribution channel.
3. **Competitors' Strategies:** A firm may have to use the channel of competitors when it is the only distribution system acceptable to the trade and customers. Alternatively, the firm may design a totally new distribution system to gain a competitive advantage. But the new channel must be consistent with the foreign country's political, legal, social and cultural environments.

---

1. Michael R. Czinkota, Ilkka A. Ron Kainen and Michael H. Moffet, ***International Business***, South-Western Pub. Co; 2002, pp. 349–57.

4. **Company Objectives:** A company which aims at capturing a large market share through low cost products needs to employ intensive distribution. On the other hand, if the company seeks to develop a prestige image for its high cost product, it will choose exclusive distribution through speciality stores.
5. **Character of the Product:** Distribution channel also depends on the nature and type of the product. Low priced, high turnover products need intensive distribution while high priced low turnover speciality products are distributed through a short and narrow channel. The distribution channel changes with change in product positioning. For example, initially personal computers were considered a speciality product and were available only at exclusive outlets. But now they have become a consumer durable and require a longer and more intensive distribution channel.
6. **Capital:** Financial resources of the firm will determine the type of distribution channel. A financially strong firm can establish its own distribution network. But a small firm has to depend on wholesalers and retailers.
7. **Cost:** Once a channel is established, expenses have to be incurred to maintain it. Costs differ over the product's life cycle. Distributor's promotional expenses, and subsidies given to distributors to face adverse market conditions are these costs.
8. **Coverage:** The geographical areas in which the product is represented and the quality of such representation represent coverage. It relates to both the length and the width of distribution channel. To begin with, a firm may appoint one distributor and gradually increase the number of distributors.
9. **Control Over Marketing:** A firm that wants full control over marketing may not depend on intermediaries. As the length of the distribution channel increases, control over price, promotion and types of outlets in which the product is available becomes more difficult.
10. **Continuity:** In order to maintain relationship with foreign distributors, the firm has to offer proper incentives to them and continuously improve the product.
11. **Communication:** Effective functioning of the distribution channel requires two-way communication between the manufacturer and the intermediaries. The manufacturer should keep the intermediaries informed about marketing objectives, assist in marketing and help resolve conflicts. The distributor should provide timely feedback about changing market conditions.

15.5.3 Direct and Indirect Exporting

There are two broad ways of exporting – direct and indirect. In **direct exporting,** the manufacturer directly sells the product in foreign markets. The goods may be sold directly to foreign customers or to a dealer located abroad. Direct exporting provides the opportunity to increase profits and to control marketing. But investment and risk involved in direct exporting are high.

Various channels of direct exporting are as follows:

(*i*) export division or department at the head office.

(*ii*) overseas sales branch or subsidiary.

(*iii*) travelling salespersons for foreign markets.

(*iv*) foreign-based distributors.

Indirect exporting involves employment of middlemen or intermediaries. The manufacturer transfers the selling responsibilities to independent organisations. Firms which are entering foreign markets for the first time and those whose export business is insignificant prefer indirect exporting. Investment and risk involved in case of indirect exporting are low. But the firm loses control and development of overseas market to intermediaries.

Middlemen employed in case of indirect exporting are given below:

(*i*) **Export Merchants:** The home-based merchant buys the product from the manufacturer and sells it abroad. In India, these merchants are known as **export trading houses.** Other types of export merchants are.

Trading Companies: A trading company is engaged in both exports and imports. Mitsubishi, Mitsui, Itochu are some of the largest trading companies in Japan.

Export drop shipper is a special type of export merchant. Upon receipt of a foreign order, he places an order with a manufacturer and directs the manufacturer to deliver the product directly to the importer. The drop shipper makes payment to the manufacturer and receives payment from the importer. Export drop shippers are employed in coal, construction materials and other bulky products of low unit value.

(*ii*) **Agents/Brokers:** Unlike the export merchant, the agent does not take ownership of the goods. He merely seeks foreign buyers for a commission. Therefore, the manufacturer assumes all the risks of exports. There are several types of agent middlemen in international marketing. **Export buying agents** or **export commission houses** are representatives of importers. They are located in the exporter's country. Brokers bring buyers and sellers together for a commission. **Manufacturer's export agents** represent several exporters. An **export management company** manages the entire export activities of a manufacturer under a contract.

(*iii*) **Cooperative International Marketing Cooperatives:** These undertake export activities on behalf of several manufacturers. These are of two types: (*a*) pigyback marketing or allied company management — one producer uses its overseas distribution facilities to export his own products as well as those of other manufacturers; (*b*) exporting combination — a formal association of independent and competitive business firms for the purpose of export marketing.

15.5.4 Selection of Channel Members

Once the channel is designed, an international firm has to locate and select the specific intermediaries. The criteria used to evaluate and select channel members includes: (*a*) volume of business handled, (*b*) financial position, (*c*) managerial capability, (*d*) reputation in the market.

15.5.5 Managing Relationship With Channel Members

After entering into an agreement with each channel member, the international firm must develop and maintain a cordial relationship for mutual benefit. Differences and conflicts may arise due to differences in interests, cultures, etc. It is, therefore, necessary to anticipate and resolve such differences and conflicts. A proactive approach consisting of good incentives, marketing support, regular interaction, personal visits, inviting channel members to headquarters, and honours to outstanding performers will help in effective management of relationships with channel partners.

15.6 International Promotion Decisions

Promotion or marketing communication play as, if not more, important role in international business as in domestic business. It seeks to achieve the following objectives:

(*i*) To make potential customers aware of the product;

(*ii*) To explain unique features of the product to them;

(*iii*) To persuade them to buy the product: and

(*iv*) To improve the image of the product, the company and the country.

Promotion in foreign markets is a much more difficult task than promotion in the domestic market. Each country has its own socio-cultural environment and laws governing promotion. The customs, traditions, business practices regarding trade promotion differ from country to country. For example, Japanese practices relating to rebates, entertainment, and gift giving are quite different from those of western countries. Therefore, it is necessary to modify promotion schemes to suit each foreign market, otherwise business suffers. A foreign company advertised in Japan that making cake with its cake mix was as easy as cooking rice. Housewives in Japan got offended because they felt that cooking rice was a skilled task.

In addition to socio-cultural differences, government regulations concerning promotion may be different in different countries. For example, television advertising and direct marketing are very important media of promotion in some countries. But in many other countries, telecast is a government monopoly and direct marketing has limited appeal. In the words of Angela Mills, "In the U.K. all advertising is allowed if not specifically forbidden. In Germany, everything is forbidden if not specially allowed. In Italy, everything is allowed even if forbidden, and in Belgium, nobody knows what is forbidden".[1]

15.6.1 International Promotion Mix

The promotion mix consists of four major elements — advertising, personal selling, sales promotion, and public relations. Differences in marketing environment may require variation in the promotion mix because a mix that is very effective in one foreign market may not be effective in another foreign market.

1. **Advertising:** The main decisions involved in international advertising relate to market, message, media and management.

   (*i*) **Market:** The first decision to be made is whether to standardise or localise the advertisement. Standardised or global advertising means using the same copy, theme and illustration internationally. On the other hand, localised or national advertisement involves a separate advertisement for each market. Both the alternatives have their own merits.

1. Quoted in Warren J. Keegan, *Global Marketing Management,* Prentice Hall Inc., 1995, p. 553

Table 15.3: Standardisation Vs. Localisation of Advertising

Factors in Favour of Standardisrtion	Factors in Favour of Localisation
• Cost reduction due to economies of scale	• Differences in socio-cultural and economic environment
• Uniform image of the company and the brand	• Protection against competitive advertisements who use local themes
• Use of global media	• Statutory restrictions on certain advertisements in some countries
• Centralised management	• Non-availability of certain media in some markets
• Better use of creative skills	• Operational autonomy to foreign subsidiaries
• Maximum utilisation of good ideas	
• Greater control over foreign subsidiaries	

Standardised advertising is possible in case of global products and global markets. In other cases, localised advertising becomes necessary.

(*ii*) **Message:** The words, pictures and other information contained in the advertisement must be appropriate to the target audience. The message must be in tune with the cultural, social, economic and other conditions in the market. What is considered ingenious and funny in one culture may be viewed as indecent in another culture. While translating the message from one language to another the subtleties and nuances of both the languages must be clearly undershood. Otherwise, unintentional blunders and misunderstandings can occur.

(*iii*) **Media:** Selection of media and the frequency of advertisement depend on the advertising budget. Generally, per capita advertising expenditure in developed nations is higher than in developing nations. Consumer goods industries spend more on advertising than industrial goods industries. How much an international firm spends on advertising depends on several internal and external factors. Internal factors include the firm's financial position, advertising objectives, nature of the product, executive judgment, etc. Level of competition, number and location of customers, availability of media, etc., are the external factors.

Choice of media depends on its cost, reach, availability and restrictions. **Costs of media** vary widely between different media and countries. **Media reach** means the number of potential customers who take notice of the advertisement within the time frame. **Media availability** is the extent to which the needed media exists locally. For example, television telecast may not exist in some countries or may not allow certain types of advertisements. In some Islamic countries, there are **restrictions** on the portrayal of women in advertisements. The availability, reach and effectiveness of different media may be different in different countries. Small exporters may prefer direct advertising while big exporters depend on mass media. As far as possible, an international firm would prefer international media to achieve economies of scale and to maintain high image.

(*iv*) **Management:** Advertising management involves control over the activities relating to advertising. An international firm can opt either for centralised or for decentralised set-up. In case of centralised set-up, all advertising decisions are taken at the head office, whereas in decentralised set-up these decisions are taken by local units in foreign markets.

Global firms with global brands prefer the centralised set-up. When socio-cultural, economic and competitive differences are significant, decentralised set-up is more appropriate. Some firms adopt a mixed set-up. Under it, the head office develops the core objectives, policy and themes for advertising, and provides advice and expertise to foreign affiliates. Detailed preparation and execution are done by local affiliates.

2. **Personal Selling:** Generally, personal selling is a more effective method of promotion, particularly in case of technical products of high unit value in concentrated markets. Such products require demonstration and explanation. Personal selling is cheaper or necessary when: (*a*) media availability is restricted, (*b*) markets value personal relations, (*c*) sales force is available at low cost. For example Supermax shaving blades became successful in London due to door-to-door selling. Personal selling efforts may be standardised in case of standardised or global products. But salespersons are recruited mostly from local population in each foreign market.

Salespersons can contact the foreign prospects in three broad ways:

(*i*) **Meeting prospects in foreign markets:**

(*a*) Company's travelling salespersons attached to the head office travel in foreign markets, when the company does not have foreign offices;

(*b*) Company's salespersons attached to its foreign office; these salespersons are local people and can better deal with foreign prospects.

(*c*) Local salespersons hired for a temporary period for market entry, product launch or special marketing campaign.

(*ii*) **Meeting prospects at trade fairs and exhibitions:** International fairs and exhibitions may be held in India (*e.g.,* World Book Fair held every year at New Delhi) or in foreign countries (*e.g.,* Frankfurt Book Fair held in Germany)

(*iii*) **Visiting foreign buyers:** They may visit on the initiative of the importer or exporter. Export promotion councils in India arrange buyer-seller meets.

Trade fairs and exhibitions bring together potential importers and exporters from all over the world. They provide an opportunity for direct interaction, product demonstration, booking orders, exchanging trade information, etc. They play a vital role in countries where there are restrictions on media advertising.

3. **Sales Promotion:** Samples, free gifts, prize contests, coupons, price-offs, premiums, money refund offers, trading stamps are the main forms of sales promotion. These are effective for introduction of a new product. Sales promotion is also effective in increasing the sales volume of low unit value products in the face of competition. But it is a temporary measure used to supplement advertising and personal selling. Sales promotion activities targeted at intermediaries are trade discounts, point of purchase materials, demonstrations, etc.

There are several psychological, cultural and legal restrictions on the use of sales promotion. Foreign customers may view rebates, money back guarantees and freebies as efforts to push a low quality product. The sales promotion schemes must be attractive enough to local customers. Foreign laws may prohibit or restrict sales promotion activities.

4. **Public Relations:** Sustained and concerted efforts made to develop, maintain and improve company and product image are known as public relations. International firms often face negative publicity about their dominance. Therefore, they have to portray them selves as good citizens in host countries. These firms attempt to get positive news and reports in local media. They contribute to the host country's public health, education, wildlife, environmental protection, etc. For example, Microsoft sponsors computer education in schools in India.

   An international firm has to counter negative publicity due to a misunderstanding or mistakes of its staff. Press release may be used to counter a false statement. A voluntary and quick action is necessary in case of a genuine mistake. For example, when there were reports in the press about harmful elements in chocolates, Cadbury got its chocolates tested in laboratories and published the test reports in newspapers. These efforts helped the company to retain customer goodwill and confidence.

Splitting the check when dining with colleagues is directly linked to how a culture perceives business relationships. Monochronic cultures being pro-transactional, businesspersons don't mix their professional and personal relationships. In these cultures you are not expected to pay for your colleagues when dining out *e.g.* North Europe, USA, Canada and Australia. On the other hand, Polychronic cultures being pro-partnership, they view business relationships as life-long. In these cultures, business meals are seen as occasions to build better bonds. Usually, the senior most person pays for the group and 'going Dutch' is considered rude, even taboo, *e.g.,* Indian sub continent, Italy, Greece, Middle East, China and Latin America.

SUMMARY

International Market Segmentation: (*i*) Macro segmentation or country analysis — assessing market potential, estimating firm's sales potential, (*ii*) micro segmentation — demographic, psychographic, benefit, usage, user status.

Target Market Selection: (*i*) Criteria for selection, (*ii*) Shortlisting the markets, (*iii*) Target marketing strategy — concentrated vs. diversified marketing, differentiated vs. undifferentiated strategy.

International Product Decisions: (*i*) Product standardisation vs. customization, (*ii*) Branding — brand or no brand, own brand vs. private brand, global vs. local brand, single vs. multiple brands, (*iii*) Packaging and labelling—protection and promotion functions of packaging, (*iv*) Warranty and after-sale service.

International Pricing Decisions: (*i*) Factors influencing pricing, (*ii*) Methods of pricing—cost plus, marginal cost, market oriented, negotiated, retrograde, (*iii*) Price discrimination, (*iv*) Export pricing process, (*v*) Transfer pricing, (*vi*) Dumping.

International Distribution Decisions: (*i*) Channel design – length and width, (*ii*) Factors influencing channel design, (*iii*) Direct and indirect exporting, (*iv*) Selection of channel members, (*v*) Managing channel relationships.

International Promotion Decisions: (*i*) Promotion mix — (*a*) advertising – market, message, media, management, (*b*) personal selling – meeting in foreign markets, meeting at trade fairs and exhibitions, visiting foreign buyers, (*c*) sales promotion, (*d*) public relations.

TEST QUESTIONS

1. Explain macro segmentation and micro segmentation in international business.
2. Discuss the process of target market selection.
3. Explain the following marketing strategies:
   (*a*) Concentrated Vs. Diversified marketing.
   (*b*) Differentiated Vs. Undifferentiated strategy.
   (*c*) Niche marketing.
4. Explain globalisation (product standardisation) and localisation (product adaptation) pointing out the advantages of each.
5. Discuss branding decisions involved in international business.
6. Why special packaging may be needed for exports?
7. Explain the factors affecting export pricing.
8. Describe the methods used in export pricing.
9. Explain the steps involved in the process of export pricing.
10. What is transfer pricing? Explain its objectives and strategies.
11. What is dumping? Explain different types of dumping.
12. What is channel design? Explain the factors influencing channel design.
13. Discuss direct and indirect exporting, pointing the channels of both.
14. Explain the objectives of promotion in international business. Why promotion decisions are more difficult in international business?
15. Explain different elements of international promotion mix.
16. Write short notes on:
    (*a*) Role of warranty and after-sale service in export marketing.
    (*b*) Retrograde pricing.
    (*c*) Price discrimination.
    (*d*) Standardised Vs. Localised advertising.
17. Discuss various issues faced by an international firm in designing its international advertising strategy.
18. What do you mean by transfer pricing? Discuss its role in the international business.
19. "It is always desirable for an exporter to quote export price in importer country's currency." Comment.
20. Why is pricing in international markets an issue? Discuss.
21. Discuss various issues involved in designing an overseas distribution system.
22. Describe various factors that make it feasible to offer a standardised product across world markets.
23. Discuss various strategies available to a firm to deal with adverse 'country of origin' effect.

CHAPTER 16

International Financial Management

LEARNING OBJECTIVES

After studying this chapter, you should understand:

16.1 International Capital Budgeting

16.2 Capital Structure of International Projects

16.3 International Working Capital Management

16.4 Sourcing International Financial Markets

- Summary
- Test Questions

International business involves some unique financial issues such as currency to be used, assessment of importer's creditworthiness and acceptable methods of payment. Risk involved in exports is high and both importers and exporters want to play safe. Exporters prefer payment in hard currencies like $ or £. That is why most exports of developing countries are invoiced in US dollar. Once the importer's creditworthiness is ascertained and currency to be used is decided, the method of payment acceptable to both the exporter and the importer is selected.

16.1 International Capital Budgeting

An international firm may have several capital expenditure proposals on hand. The nature and types of these proposals differ from one foreign country to another. Capital expenditure analysis or capital budgeting is required to select the most profitable project. International capital budgeting involves decisions on setting up projects abroad. The objective is to identify the project(s) that can maximise the wealth of shareholders. A project that has the highest net present value adds the maximum value to shareholder's wealth. The net present value is estimated by discounting the net cash flows of the project over its economic lifetime. In case of international projects, this may be the period up to which the parent company wants to retain the ownership of the subsidiary formed to set up and run the overseas project. The discount rate may be the company's average cost of capital or the expected rate of return on projects with similar risk.

16.1.1 Estimating Cash Flows

Preparation of the capital budget for a project involves three types of cash flows:

1. **Initial Investment:** This includes the money spent on creating the infrastructure and setting up the project, and other incidental expenses until the production begins. These cash outflows are substantial and have a major impact on the project's present value.
2. **Operating Cash Flows:** The project creates cash inflows through sales and cash outflows in the form of costs of production, administration and selling. Both the inflows and outflows are estimated for each year of the project's economic life. The difference between the inflows and outflows are the net cash flows or operating cash flows of the project. The success or failure of the project depends on these cash flows.
3. **Terminal Cash Flows:** These refer to the salvage value of the capital and recovery of working capital in the final year of the project.

   The net present value of the project can be estimated by deducting the present value of cash inflows from operations and the terminal value from the initial investment. The project is acceptable only when the net present value is positive.

16.1.2 Evaluation of International Projects

Both domestic and international projects involve the same basic principles. But some special problems are involved in evaluating international projects. Some of these problems are given below:

1. **Currency of Evaluation:** Initial investment is reckoned in the home currency whereas operating and terminal cash flows are in the foreign currency. The final assessment of net present value is reported in the home currency. For example, if an Indian from sets up a subsidiary in Germany, the initial investment will be in Indian rupees. Once the project starts production, all income, expenses, profits and taxes are computed in German Mark. However, the net cash flows received by the Indian firm will be reported to the shareholders in Indian rupee. In case the parent company wants to hold the investment in Germany for ten years, the rupee value of the remittances from the German subsidiary will depend upon the exchange rate between Indian rupee and German Mark. Therefore, it is necessary to estimate this exchange rate during the next ten years. This will depend on the relative inflation rates prevailing in the two countries in future.
2. **Incremental Cash Flows:** The parent firm's general cash flows are influenced by the setting up of the German subsidiary. For example, the project's sales may partly affect the sales of the parent firm which was exporting to Germany before the project was set up. Therefore, incremental cash flows rather than the total cash flows must be considered while judging the viability of the project.

   Establishment of the foreign project may affect the parent firm's cash flows in the following ways:

   (*a*) **Cannibalisation:** Setting up of a foreign project reduces the parent firm's sales because the foreign production substitutes the exports made prior to the project. This situation is known as cannibalisation. This loss of sales and profits must be taken into account while estimating the incremental cash flows.

(*b*) **Sales Creation:** The foreign project creates additional sales for the parent firm. The overseas project may also improve the firm's image and demand for its products.

(*c*) **Transfer Pricing:** The transfer price at which goods and services are moved between the subsidiaries can significantly distort the project's profitability. Therefore, market rates should be used as transfer prices.

(*d*) **Royalties and Fees:** Royalties and fees paid by the subsidiary to the parent firm is a cost to the project but an income to the parent firm. They do not create net cash flows and should, therefore, be ignored while calculating incremental cash flows.

3. **Economic and Political Risks:** International projects involve additional economic and political risks. These risks arise due to differences in economic, socio-cultural and political environments. The foreign country government may restrict free movement of capital and goods among the parent firms, the project and other countries on which the project depends for inputs or sales. Foreign tax laws may restrict the amount and time of transfer of profits to the parent firm. In order to provide for the higher economic and political risks of a foreign project, the net cash flows may be estimated conservatively or the discount rate used to calculate the present value may be increased.

16.2 Capital Structure of International Projects

Capital structure means the ratio between equity and debt in financing the project. This decision influences the objective of maximising the wealth of shareholders. Equity and debt are treated differently under tax laws. Dividend on equity can be paid only out of post-tax profits while interest paid on debt is allowed as a deduction in calculating the net profits. Therefore, the real cost of debt is lower than the rate of interest. A firm with reasonable rate of return can use a high proportion of debt (leverage) to increase earnings per share. But leveraging will increase the cost of equity and subsequent borrowings. Therefore, it is necessary to strike a proper balance between equity and debt as sources of investment in the project. However, in case of international projects, the host country's regulations may prescribe the degree of leverage that can be used.

Secondly problem arises because the project's capital structure may affect the parent firm's risk profile. The financial position of subsidiaries affects the firm's financial position. The shareholders look at the consolidated financial statements of the parent firm.

Thirdly, what is debt for the parent firm may be equity for the foreign project or *vice versa*. For example, the parent firm may raise debt and invest the funds as equity in the project. When the parent firm lends to the project the foreign subsidiary can save taxes on the interest. However, for the firm as a whole the capital structure does not change.

When the parent firm extends loans to the subsidiary, the former's financial risk may be reduced. Interest payable on such debt provides a definite cash inflow for the parent firm. On the other hand, dividend on equity may be restricted by the foreign country. The parent firm may initially make equity investment in the overseas project. The subsidiary may be asked to manage its finances itself so as to minimise the cost of funds and to meet the local legal requirements. However, subsidiaries functioning in countries with underdeveloped capital markets may face difficulty in implementing this strategy. In case of such subsidiaries the parent firm will have to provide both equity and debt to its foreign subsidiaries.

16.3 International Working Capital Management

Management of short-term sources and uses of funds is known as working capital management or management of current assets and current liabilities. The objective of working capital management is to maintain a proper balance between liquidity and profitability. But in case of international firm currency fluctuations, foreign exchange regulations and multiple taxation authorities make working capital management very complex and difficult.

Cash management in an international firm may involve some additional dimensions which are given below:

(*i*) **Centralised Vs. Decentralised Set-up:** In a centralised cash management system, the parent company collects and manages all the cash resources including those of subsidiaries. This system enables the firm to manage with lower level of cash leading to higher profitability. The firm can take better decisions relating to inter-firm payments, foreign currency exposures of subsidiaries, etc. It can negotiate with banks for better rates for foreign currency transactions and other financial services. The firm acquires expertise in the management of cash and portfolio.

Centralised cash management system, however, does not provide adequate operational freedom to subsidiaries. Such autonomy is required to meet contingencies and local regulations. Moreover, foreign exchange regulations may not permit complete concentration of cash management at the corporate office.

(*ii*) **Netting:** The parent firm has both operational (buying/selling) and financial (lending/borrowing) transactions with its foreign subsidiaries. Such transactions also take place among the subsidiaries. Settlement of these transactions involves costs because the services of a bank and exchange of currencies are required. The transaction costs and the cash balances needed at both the corporate office and at the subsidiaries can be reduced through netting.

Suppose that an Indian parent firm has a subsidiary in the USA. It has to pay to its subsidiary $6 million for the finished goods supplied to it by the subsidiary. It has also to receive $4 million for raw materials and components supplied to the subsidiary. In the normal course, the parent firm will remit $6 million to its subsidiary and receive $4 million from the subsidiary. Instead of these two transactions involving cash of $10 million, the mutual liabilities can be settled by the parent firm remitting $2 million to the subsidiary. This is known as **bilateral netting**. In case of more than one foreign subsidiary or affiliate, the process in called **multilateral netting**.

When the Indian parent company has three subsidiaries, one each in USA, UK and Germany, the steps involved in multilateral netting will be as follows:

(*a*) The net amount payable to or receivable from another unit is calculated as was done under bilateral netting.

(*b*) The net balance is converted into a common currency at the agreed exchange rate. The common currency may be the parent firm's currency or any other major currency on which exchange controls are minimum. Let us assume the currency chosen is in US dollar. The inter-firm payments matrix may be as follows:

Table 16.1 Inter-Firm Liabilities

Payable By	Payable to				(USD million)
	India	USA	UK	Germany	Total
India	...	20	...	...	20
USA	...	...	10	12	22
UK	8	6	...	...	14
Germany	6	...	16	...	22
Total	14	26	26	12	78

Through bialateral netting, the inter-unit dues can be settled by exchange of USA 78 million. When multilateral netting is used, only US$ 16 milliion will be needed for settlement

Table 16.2 Settlement Under Multilateral Netting (USD million)

Unit	Total Receivable	Total Payable	Net Receivable	Net Payable
India	14	20	...	6
USA	26	22	4	...
UK	26	14	12	...
Germany	12	22	...	10
Total	78	78	16	16

The netting centre decides which unit should pay to which other unit. In the above case, Germany will pay to UK $10 million, Indian parent firm will pay $2 million to UK and $4 million to USA.

3. **Transfer Pricing:** As stated earlier, transfer pricing influences the taxes payable and net profit of the firm. An international firm keeps the transfer price low in case a buying unit is located in a low tax country. As a result the supply unit pays less tax and its profit remains high. On the other hand, the transfer price is kept high when the buying unit is located in a high tax country. The import duty paid by the purchasing unit should also be considered. Adjustments in transfer pricing should also be made keeping in view exchange controls which facilitate repatriation of profits to the parent firm.

4. **Reinvoicing:** In order to avoid government scrutiny, to disguise profitability and to coordinate transfer pricing policy invoicing may be centralised in a low tax country with little foreign exchange restrictions. Each supplying unit raises invoice on the reinvoicing centre which reinvoices the sale to the buying unit. The buying unit pays to the reinvoicing centre which in turn pays to the selling unit. After taking ownership of goods, the reinvoicing centre decides the common currency, nets payments, hedges against currency exposures or reprice keeping in view the tax benefits.

5. **Leading and Lagging:** Timing of payments between various units in order to manage liquidity risk and currency risk is known as leading and lagging. Leading involves expediting payments while lagging involves delaying payments in comparison with the contracted/normal dates. Leading and lagging helps to ensure that the cash remains at the unit which is most needy. Dues from the unit whose currency is likely to depreciate may be expedited whereas dues from the units whose currency is likely to appreciate may be delayed to manage currency risk.

6. **Inter Firm Loans:** An international firm can resort to inter-firm loans to help its subsidiaries operating in countries where credit is scarce and interest rates are high. For example, an Indian firm may have a subsidiary in Bangladesh. It may lend to the subsidiary in three forms. In case of **direct loans,** the parent firm lends directly to the subsidiary. In **back-to-back** loans, the parent firm deposits with State Bank of India's Kolkata branch. The Dacca branch of the SBI lends in the currency of Bangladesh to the subsidiary keeping the deposit in India as security. In **parallel loans**, Indian parent firm lends to a branch of the Bangladesh firm in India. The firm in Bangladesh lends equal amount to the Indian firm's branch in Bangladesh.
7. **Internal Banks:** The money market in several countries where the international firm has subsidiaries may not be developed. Therefore, the firm sets up internal banks to meet the financial needs of its subsidiaries. The internal bank buys the receivables of its subsidiaries and provides them working capital. As a result, the subsidiaries can concentrate on their core business operations.

16.4 Sourcing International Financial Markets

In order to augment its financial resources an international firm may tap international capital and money market for both equity and debt. While deciding to approach these markets, the firm takes into account factors like availability of funds, costs of funds, etc. Key issues concerning international financial markets are described below:

1. **Euro Currency Markets:** Euro currency is a currency held outside the issuing country. For example, deposits in dollars with a bank in London are Euro dollars. Similarly, pound sterling held by banks in the USA is Euro sterling. Euro currency market means an international capital market which specialises in borrowing and lending of currencies outside the country of issue. London, Singapore, Hong Kong are some of the main euro currency countries.

   Several factors which affect the demand and supply of a currency determine the interest rates in euro currency markets. Volume of world trade in the currency, domestic monetary policy and reserve requirements, domestic interest rate, domestic government regulations, relative strength of the currency in the foreign exchange market are some of these factors. In practice, domestic interest rates act as a floor to euro currency rates because the funds seeking higher interest flow into euro currency market.

   Some of the interest rates in euro currency markets are given below:

   (i) **London Inter-Bank Offered Rate (LIBOR):** It is the rate at which banks in London will lend a currency to other banks for a specific period. LIBOR is used as the basis for most euro-currency transactions because London is a major euro currency market. LIBOR differs from one maturity period (say 3 months) to another maturity period (6 months). Different banks may offer different rates, with bigger banks offering lower rates. The nominating reference banks fix the rates for a LIBOR based contract (e.g. a euro bond issue). The reference banks may be from among those syndicating the issue.

   (ii) **London Inter Bank Bid (LIBID):** It is the rate at which banks accept euro curency deposits. Bid rates are usually 0.125 to 0.25 per cent lower than offered rates. The average of LIBOR and LIBID is known as the LIMEAN.

(*iii*) **Euro Libor:** LIBOR is applicable in case of transactions in dollars. Euro Libor is used for transactions in euro. Rates quoted by 16 banks in London serve as the basis of euro libor.

(*iv*) **Euro Inter Bank Offered Rate (EURIBOR):** It is the benchmark rate of the large euro money market. One prime bank offers euro term deposits at this rate. Rates quoted by 57 banks in the Eurozone serve its basis.

(*v*) **Prime Rate:** The rate of interest which first class banks in the USA charge on advances to their first class borrowers is known as the prime rate. For example it may relate to an advance made to an international firm with a very high credit rating. Prime rate depends on discount and Federal funds rate and money marketes rate. Every bank in the USA independently announces its prime rate. This rate influences and is influenced by the Euro dollar rate.

(*vi*) **Singapore Inter-Bank Offered Rate (SIBOR):** It is the rate at which principal banks in Singapore lend dollars and other currencies to Asian banks. SIBOR serves as the basis for interest rate on syndicated loans.

2. Euro Credits: Medium and long term loans which international banks provide to borrowers are known as euro credits. These involve large amounts and relate to wholesale sector of the international capital market. Most of the lending in euro currency markets takes place in the form of euro credits.

The main features of euro credits are as under:

(*a*) **Type of Credit:** Euro credits are provided in the forms of term credit and revolving credit. **Term credit** is a medium term loan which is utilised in full and then the repayment begins. The repayment schedule is fixed in advance taking into consideration the expected flow of revenues from the investment. The loan agreement may allow pre-payment of the loan. **Revolving credit** is a standby facility to meet temporary but recurring financial needs of the borrower. Interest is charged on the amount actually utilised rather than on the sanctioned amount.

Repayment can be made in instalments.

(*b*) **Period of Credit:** Euro credits are usually for periods of five to eight years. In some cases the period may extend up to fifteen years.

(*c*) **Security:** In most cases the borrower is not required to offer collateral security. Focus is on the borrower's credit rating rather than on tangible security. Euro credits are thus unsecured and avoid the complications of taking charge of the security.

(*d*) **Interest Rate:** The inter-bank rate for euro currency deposits is generally used as the basic to fix interest. LIBOR is the reference rate for dollar loans and EURIBOR is for Euro loans. The Paris Inter-Bank Offered Rate (PIOR) is used in case of loans in pound sterling.

The interest rate is revised every six months keeping in view the changes in LIBOR. Thus, the credit is renewed or rolled over every six months. The lending margin (the excess of interest charged on LIBOR) depends on the borrower's credit rating and bargaining capacity.

(*e*) **Currency:** Most of the euro credits are raised in dollars. In some cases the borrower is given the option to roll over the loan in some other currency as per his needs. The multi-currency option enables the borrower and the bank to avoid exchange risk.

(*f*) **Loan Syndication:** A euro credit involves a huge amount (e.g. 500 million dollars). It is not safe or possible for a single bank to lend the entire amount. Therefore, a few banks form a syndicate to provide funds to the borrower. Laws in the USA also limit the amount which any single bank can lend to any single borrower. The syndicate consists of (*i*) the managing bank appointed by the borrower to arrange the credit, (*ii*) the lead bank which provides most of the money and (*iii*) the agent bank which takes care of the lender's interest after the loan agreement is signed.

3. **Eurobonds:** The international bonds sold by international banks in several international capital markets simultaneously are known as Eurobonds. These bonds are a major source of borrowing in Euro markets. These are issued on behalf of multinational corporations, international agencies and governments. In case of governments, most of these bonds are issued to meet directly or indirectly balance of payments problems.

Most eurobonds are unsecured and bearer securities. Therefore, borrowers with high credit rating only are able to issue these bonds. Eurobonds are usually denominated in US $ 10,000. The average maturity period is 5-6 years though it may extend to 15 years. Bank syndicates sell eurobonds.

Eurobonds are different from foreign bonds though both are issued on behalf of non-resident borrowers. Foreign bonds are sold only in the domestic capital markets of issuing countries. These are subject to the regulations of the issuing countries. For example, a foreign bond may be issued on behalf of an Indian firm exclusively in the USA. On the other hand, eurobonds are outside a single country's regulations as their investors are spread over the world.

Various types of eurobonds are as follows:

(*a*) **Fixed Rate or Straight Bonds:** These bonds carry a fixed rate of interest payable at yearly (360 days) intervals. Maturity periods range from 3 to 25 years. But borrowers can exercise their right of redemption before maturity. There is no deduction of tax at source but the investor is expected to declare his interest income to the tax authorities. Market prices of these bonds, depend on short term interest rates and liquidity in the money market.

(*b*) **Convertible Bonds:** In case of these bonds, investors are given the option to convert them into equity shares of the borrowing company. The conversion is done during a stipulated period and at a stipulated price which is normally higher than the market price. The interest rate on convertible bonds is lower than that offered on non-convertible bonds. Investors can gain from rise in market price of shares (capital gain) in addition to interest income. When the bonds are issued in a currency other than the currency in which the company's shares are denominated, currency risk can be diversified. There is a fixed exchange rate clause which specifies the rate at which the conversion into shares will be accounted.

(*c*) **Currency Option Bonds:** These bonds are issued in one currency with the option to take payment of interest and principal in a second currency. Usually, the bonds are issued in pound sterling with option for payment in dollar or Euro. The rate of conversion is fixed at the time of issue itself. It case floating rates for conversion are allowed, the spot rate quoted in the market three business days before each payment is due is used.

(*d*) **Floating Rate Notes (FRNs):** The maturity and denomination of these notes is the same as in case of straight bonds. But interest payable on these notes varies with the market conditions. Interest on FRNs is normally to 1.5 perent higher than LIBOR and is adjusted half-yearly. In many cases a provision for minimum interest is made in case the LIBOR and the margin fall below a certain level. A 'drop lock' clause may also be included for payment of the minimum rate for the remaining period of the notes. FRNs provide the investors the benefits of long term investment and gains from charges in short term rates.

4. **Euro Notes:** Corporates directly issue euro notes in the euro currency markets to borrow funds. Banks may or may not underwrite these notes. Euro notes are of the following types:

(*a*) **Commercial Paper (C/P):** It is a promissory note with maturity for less than a year (90-180 days) issued by companies. It is issued by companies with high credit standing in high denominations like $ 1,00,000. It is an unsecured instrument and is normally issued on a discount to yield basis. Mutual funds, insurance companies, banks and corporates buy commercial paper.

Commercial paper is a cheap source of short term finance because the interest rate is lower than on bank borrowings. It also provides flexibility as the size of issue can be changed according to the borrower's needs. Investors get a higher yield than that on bank deposits. Commercial paper is negotiable and, therefore, offers liquidity.

All About Commercial Papers

- Commercial papers are financial instruments used for raising short-term money.
- They are mostly used by companies and banks.
- However, individuals and financial institutions can also invest in these instruments.
- Commercial papers can be issued for maturities between a minimum of seven days and a maximum of one year.

(*b*) **Medium Term Notes (MTNs):** These are a fixed interest rate and non-underwritten source of raising funds. These notes are meant to bridge the maturity gap between Euro bonds and commercial paper. MTNs are issued for maturity periods ranging between one and ten years. These notes have become quite popular due to their flexibility, liquidity and simple documentation procedures.

5. **Euro Issues:** Depository receipts are issued to raise capital in international capital markets. A Global Depository Receipt (GDR) is a negotiable instrument dominated in US dollars and represents shares issued in a local currency. The shares of the issuing company are issued in the name of an international bank (known as the depository bank) located in a foreign country. A 'custodian' in the issuing country has physical possession of the shares which are issued to the depository in the local currency. On the basis of these shares, the depository issues the GDRs in US dollars. The issuing company pays dividend to the depository in the local currency. The depository converts the dividend into US dollars and distributes it among holders of GDRs.

GDRs are bearer instruments and are traded in international financial markets. The issuing company is saved from the exchange risk because dividend is paid in local currency. Voting right is vested only with the depository and is regulated. The issuing company can broaden its equity base by tapping large equity markets abroad. However, a company with poor credit rating may not be able to issue GDRs except at a high cost. The value of GDRs depends upon the share prices of the issuing company. When the share prices fall in the domestic market, the company may not be able to issue GDRs in future.

Investors get the benefit of diversifying their portfolio in a freely traded instrument. But they have to bear both exchange risk and risk of erosion in capital.

American Depository Receipts (ADRs) are similar to GDRs but are issued in the USA. A bank or a depository issues ADRs in the USA against underlying shares of a company incorporated outside USA.

SUMMARY

International Capital Budgeting: (*i*) Estimating cash flows — initial investment, operating flows, terminal flows, (*ii*) International project evaluation — currency of evaluation, incremental flows (cannibalisation, sales creation), (*iii*) Transfer pricing, (*iv*) Royalties and fees, (*v*) economic and political risks.

Capital Structure for International Projects: (*i*) equity, (*ii*) debt

International Working Capital Management: (*i*) Centralised Vs. Decentralised cash management, (*ii*) Netting — bialateral and multilateral, (*iii*) Transfer pricing, (*iv*) Reinvoicing, (*v*) leading and lagging, (*vi*) International loans, (*vii*) Internal banks

Sourcing International Financial Markets: (*i*) Eurocurrency markets — LIBOR, LIBID, EURO LIBOR, EURIBOR, Prime Rate, SIBOR, (*ii*) Euro credits — term credit, revolving credit, (*iii*) Eurobonds — fixed rate, convertible currency option, FRNs, (*iv*) Euronotes CP, MTN, (*v*)Euro issues — GDRs, ADRs.

TEST QUESTIONS

1. Explain various steps involved in estimating cash flows of foreign projects.
2. Discuss the issues involved in the evaluation of international projects.
3. Explain the capital structure for foreign projects.
4. Discuss the issues involved in international working capital management.
5. Explain the following:
   (*a*) Euro currency markets
   (*b*) Euro credits
   (*c*) Euro bonds
   (*d*) Euro notes
   (*e*) Euro issues

CHAPTER

17 International Human Resource Management

LEARNING OBJECTIVES

After studying this chapter, you should understand:

17.1 Sources of Global Recruitment

17.2 Staffing Policies or Models for Global Firms

17.3 Selection Criteria for Overseas Assignment—Expatriates

17.4 Cultural Shock and Repatriation

17.5 Cross-Cultural Training

17.6 Performance Appraisal in Global Firms

17.7 International Compensation

17.8 International Industrial Relations

- Summary
- Test Questions

The basic functions involved in international human resource management are the same as in domestic human resource management. But human resource management in an international firm is much more complex and challenging than in a domestic firm due to the following reasons:

(i) **Cultural Differences:** Human resources in an international firm hails from different countries with varied cultures, languages and social conditions. Their values, beliefs, attitudes and outlook differ which affect their productivity, loyalty and mobility. For example, in countries like India people value hierarchy and designations making organisational restructuring difficult. In some countries employees address the boss by his/her name but this practice is unwelcome in India. Therefore, it is necessary that the recruited staff fit into the culture of the company and the country in which they work.

(ii) **Differences in Regulations:** An international firm operates in several countries. Government policies and regulations relating to labour differ from country to country. Labour practices (e.g. child labour, contract labour, etc.) common in one country may not be allowed in another country.

(iii) **Differences in Labour Markets:** Demand and supply of labour, skill levels, etc., differ widely between countries. Some countries face shortage of talent in certain industries while others have abundant talent. These differences cause shift of production activities

across countries. For example, availability of low cost skilled labour is leading to location of both manufacturing and service units in India, China, Malaysia, etc. India has emerged as a global hub for information technology and R&D. Such global shifts in industries and business processes is a great challenge to human resource management in global firms.

(*iv*) **Differences in Employment Conditions:** Systems régarding promotion, incentives, labour welfare, social security, etc., vary significantly between countries. These differences pose a great challenge for international human resource management.

(*v*) **Differences in Employer-Employee Relations:** Attitudes of employers and employees towards employment differ among countries. In some countries lifelong employment is common while hire and fire policy is followed in other countries. The expectations of employer and employees from each other are not the same in all countries.

17.1 Sources of Global Recruitment

An international firm may tap the following sources of recruitment:

1. **Home Country Nationals:** Also known as parent country nationals, they are citizens of the country in which the firm's head office is located. For example, Indians working in foreign affiliates of TCS are home country nationals. These managers, technicians and software professionals are called **expatriates** as they live and work outside their home country.

   Home country nationals are sent to manage foreign operations due to several reasons:

   (*a*) To start up operations.

   (*b*) To transfer technical or managerial expertise.

   (*c*) To motivate competent staff to remain in the company.

   (*d*) To groom managers for senior positions by providing them international exposure.

   (*e*) To maintain financial control over foreign operations.

   (*f*) To improve the parent company's image in the foreign country.

   Sending parent country nationals abroad, however, involves cost and cultural problems.

2. **Host Country Nationals:** They are the citizens of the host (foreign) country where the firm's subsidiary/branch is located. In other words, they are the local managers/technicians hired by the firm. For example, Indians employed by Microsoft to manage its subsidiary in Bengaluaru are host country nationals.

   Host country nationals are employed due to the following reasons:

   (*a*) They are familiar with local culture, language, business norms and practices, local bureaucrats, market intermediaries and suppliers of inputs.

   (*b*) They know the tastes and preferences of the local customers.

   (*c*) They can better motivate and control the local workers.

   (*d*) They are less costly than home country nationals.

   (*e*) They can maintain better ties with local government and local business community.

   (*f*) They meet the host country government's requirement of 'nativisation'.

   (*g*) They can develop critical skills locally to improve operational efficiency.

Host country nationals, however, are unfamiliar with the goals, needs and strategies of the parent firm. They may lack the global perspective and work ethics needed by the firm.

3. **Third Country Nationals:** They are the citizens of a country other than the country where the firm's head office is located and the country where they are assigned to work. For example, an Indian manager recruited by an American company to manage its subsidiary in Germany is a third country national. Several Indians are working as software professionals in the subsidiaries of IBM, Microsoft, Apple, etc., located in European countries.

   Third country nationals are employed due to many reasons:

   (*a*) They are less costly than home country nationals.

   (*b*) They may possess the required knowledge and skills.

   (*c*) They may know the local language and culture due to their work experience in multicultural environment.

   (*d*) They can have an impartial and global perspective.

   The local government may, however, regulate employment of third country nationals.

4. **Impatriates:** Impatriates are host country nationals or third country nationals who are assigned to work in the firm's home country. They are appointed to help them gain critical work experience and become multilingual and multicultural global managers. Impatriates help an international firm in meeting challenges of globalisation.

5. **Offshore Outsourcing:** This has emerged as an important source of global recruitment, especially in the service sector. Several firms in developed countries are now outsourcing medical, legal, accounting and other services from units located in India, China, Philippines, etc. Offshore outsourcing provides opportunities for cost saving and lower overheads. Extensive outsourcing may, however, create political controversy and quality control problems. For example, there are public protests in some parts of the USA due to the perception that offshore outsourcing is reducing employment opportunities for US citizens.

17.2 Staffing Policies or Models

The source of recruitment adopted by an international firm depends on its staffing policy or model. The main types of staffing models are given below:

1. **The Ethnocentric Model:** Under this approach, home country nationals are selected for all the key management positions. For example, Philips filled the key jobs by Dutch nationals. Ethnocentric staffing model is used when the firm believes that (*a*) parent firm's perspectives should override local issues, (*b*) host countries do not have suitable persons for senior management positions, (*c*) this is necessary to maintain unified corporate culture, and (*d*) it is the best way to transfer core competencies to a foreign affiliate.

The ethnocentric model offers the following **advantages**:

(*i*) It facilitates centralised decision making.

(*ii*) It is simple to recruit and monitor home country nationals.

(*iii*) It helps to motivate home country managers through long-term career progression.

(*iv*) Home country nationals can transfer their tacit knowledge to foreign subsidiaries.

The ethnocentric model suffers from some **disadvantages**:

(*i*) Local managers feel frustrated when all key positions are filled with home country nationals.

(*ii*) Home country nationals may not understand local culture (cultural myopia).

(*iii*) Local managers do not get promotion beyond a certain level.

(*iv*) Cost of operations increases as home country managers are paid higher compensation than host country managers.

(*v*) Home country managers deputed abroad may lose chances of promotion at the head office.

The ethnocentric approach is suitable for multinational firms operating in countries having similar culture, laws and political systems. Firms with international strategy prefer the ethnocentric model.

2. **The Polycentric Model:** Under this approach, host country nationals are selected for senior management positions in foreign subsidiaries while home country nationals occupy key positions at the corporate office.

The **advantages** of polycentric model are as under:

(*i*) Local managers better understand the local culture and business practices.

(*ii*) Host country nationals can better deal with the local laws and political system.

(*iii*) Operating and training costs are reduced as there are little adjustment problems.

(*iv*) Host country nationals have greater opportunities for promotion and career progression. Therefore, their motivation and morale is high.

(*v*) Compensation paid to host country nationals is generally lower than that of expatriates.

The **disadvantages** of the polycentric model are as follows:

(*i*) Differences in culture, language and working styles of managers may create problems in coordination.

(*ii*) Home country nationals may lose opportunities to gain overseas experience.

(*iii*) Career progression of host country managers is limited to a certain level and within the same country.

(*iv*) The mobility of managers and cultural exchange between head office and subsidiaries are restricted.

The polycentric approach is suitable for transnational corporations operating in countries with different cultures, laws and political conditions. Firms with multidomestic strategy prefer polycentric or regiocentric model.

3. **The Regiocentric Model:** Under this approach the staffing policy is based on geographic regions rather than on countries. For example, all subsidiaries in Europe are staffed with European managers. Thus, regiocentric model is a variation of the polycentric model. The advantages and disadvantages of the regiocentric model are similar to those of the polycentric model. An additional advantage is that it provides greater flexibility to a firm having strong regional markets and operations. But subsidiaries/customers may feel neglected when the region comprises competing nations.

4. **The Geocentric Model:** Under this approach, the most suitable persons are selected for key jobs irrespective of their nationality. Home country nationals, host country nationals and third country nationals are all treated alike.

   The geocentric model offers the following **advantages:**

   (*i*) It creates a large pool of candidates for selection of key executive. A wide choice is possible.

   (*ii*) It helps to develop a cadre of global managers capable of working in diverse cultures.

   (*iii*) It builds a strong unifying corporate culture which facilitates adoption of a global strategy.

   (*iv*) It facilitates multidirectional transfer of core competencies.

   (*v*) It reduces cultural myopia and enhances responsiveness to local environment.

   The geocentric model suffers from many **disadvantages:**

   (*i*) In most countries, immigration laws restrict employment of expatriates.

   (*ii*) Time and cost are involved in training and developing people in multicultures.

   (*iii*) Compensation levels tend to be high because the firm has to follow a standardised international package.

   (*iv*) Problems of relocation arise when managers are transferred from one country to another.

The geocentric model is suitable for firms with global strategies. This model is becoming increasingly popular due to growing competition, workforce diversity, unification of national economies, etc.

The choice of staffing policy or model depends upon the following factors:

(***a***) **Parent firm:** The characteristics of the parent company (e.g., strategic orientation) is the main determinant of staffing policy.

(***b***) **Overseas subsidiary:** In a new subsidiary, someone familiar with the parent firm's culture is appointed as the head. As host country nationals learn the company's culture they take over from home country nationals.

(***c***) **The cultural dimension:** Firms from countries like Japan and South Korea depend heavily upon home country nationals because few foreigners are fluent in the mother tongue of the home country. On the other hand, firms having English as mother tongue, find it easier to adopt ethnocentric policy.

(***d***) **Host country:** Government policies, social environment and nature of human resources in the host country influence the staffing policy.

(***e***) **Costs:** Cost becomes an important consideration when there are significant differences between the salary levels in different countries.

17.3 Selection Criteria for Overseas Assignment–expatriates

Persons working in a foreign country are known as **expatriates**. The parent country nationals (e.g., Indians) working in foreign subsidiaries (e.g., Canada, Germany, USA, etc.) and third country nationals (e.g., Chinese working in a Korean subsidiary of an Indian company) are examples of expatriates.

An expatriate should not only possess knowledge and skills for the job. In addition he and his family must have the capability to adjust in a new culture and environment. Expatriates or their families who fail to adjust to the host country's culture have to return back before completing their overseas assignments. This causes loss both to the company and to the expatriates. Thus, the major problem with the expatriates is adjustment in the foreign environment. Therefore due care is needed in the selection of a person for an overseas assignment. The steps in selection process of expatriates are shown in Fig. 17.1.

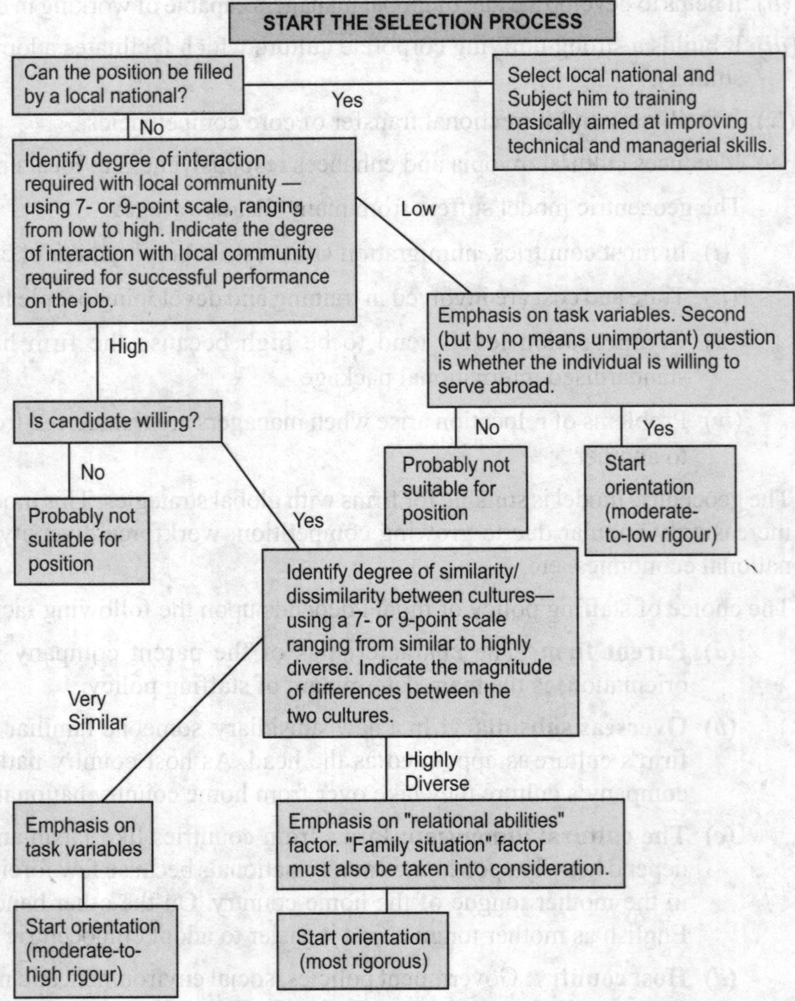

"Emphasis does not mean ignoring the other factors. It only means that it should be the dominant factor.

Fig.17.1 Steps in the International Selection-Decision Process

Source: R.L. Tung, 1981, *"Selection and Training of Personnel for Overseas Assignments"*, Columbia Journal of World Business, Vol. 16, No. 1, pp. 68-78.

The criteria used by international firms to select expatriates for overseas assignments consists of the following:

1. **Technical Competence:** The expatriate must have superior technical competence. Otherwise it would be less costly for the firm to employ a local candidate. The expatriate must understand clearly his new role and foreign culture.
2. **Age and Experience:** Young persons are eager to work abroad and can more easily adjust to foreign environment. On the other hand, old persons have better work experience. A firm may strive for a balance between age and experience.
3. **Education:** Most firms insist on an academic degree for an international manager or engineer.
4. **Past Performance:** A good track record of performance is necessary for a foreign assignment.
5. **Physical and Emotional Health:** An overseas assignment can be exhausting and stressful. Therefore, the expatriate must enjoy a good health. Moreover, the expatriate requires emotional stability and maturity to cope with the stress.
6. **Language and Communication Skills:** Language is the most effective method of learning the values, customs, etc., of a country. Most expatriates are conversant with English. But they must know the local language to develop close personal and business relationships in a foreign country.
7. **Motivation:** The expatriate must have a genuine interest and zeal in the foreign assignment. He must not consider such assignment as an escape from the boredom with the current situation at work or home. He requires a keen desire to learn the foreign culture and to work abroad. Self-confidence, self-esteem and desire for career progression are important.
8. **Leadership:** The capacity to work independently, to accept setbacks, to influence and guide others exhibit leadership.
9. **Adaptability:** Expatriates must be able to adapt to change and adjust in an alien environment easily. Previous exposure to different culture can be helpful. Desire and ability to interact and develop relationships with host country nationals enhance adaptability.
10. **Family:** Adaptation involves not only business relations but the entire aspect of living in a foreign country. The spouse and children of the expatriate must be able to adjust to the life in a foreign country. In case the spouse is also working, she/he may have to sacrifice the job or attempt to find a job in the host country

Table 17.1 Rank of Criteria in Expatriate Selection

	Australian managers *n* = 47	Expatriate managers *n* = 52	Asian managers *n* = 15
1. Ability to adapt	1	1	2
2. Technical competence	2	3	1
3. Spouse and family adaptability	3	2	4

4. Human relations skill	4	4	3
5. Desire to serve overseas	5	5	5
6. Previous overseas experience	6	7	7
7. Understanding of host country culture	7	6	5
8. Academic qualifications	8	8	8
9. Knowledge of language of country	9	9	9
10. Understanding of home country culture	10	10	10

Note: "U.S., British, Canadian, French, New Zealand, or Australian managers working for an MNC outside their home countries.

Source: Raymond J. Stone, "Expatriate Selection and Failure", *Human Resource Planning,* Vol. 14, no. 1, 1991, p. 10.

17.4 Cultural Shock and Repatriation

Managers posted abroad face a new environment quite different from the ones they are used to. They have to adjust to the new climate, culture, life styles, socio-political conditions, etc. While working and living in a new environment, some executives experience psychological uncertainty and mental tension. They are unable to cope with the new environment. This is known as **cultural shock.** It manifests in various forms ranging from a sense of frustration and anxiety to full-fledged depression or hypertension. In extreme cases, the expatriate may develop hostility towards anything in the host country environment.

According to Nancy Adler, "Cultural shock is the frustration and confusion that result from being bombarded by uninterpretable cues". For example, students in the USA drink beverages in the classroom which may cause a cultural shock to an Indian. Cultural shock needs to be managed as otherwise, it will spoil the individual's health and job performance. The individual should become familiar with the culture and environment of the host country in advance. The global firm may arrange for a brief visit by the expatriate and his family to acclimatize them with the new environment.

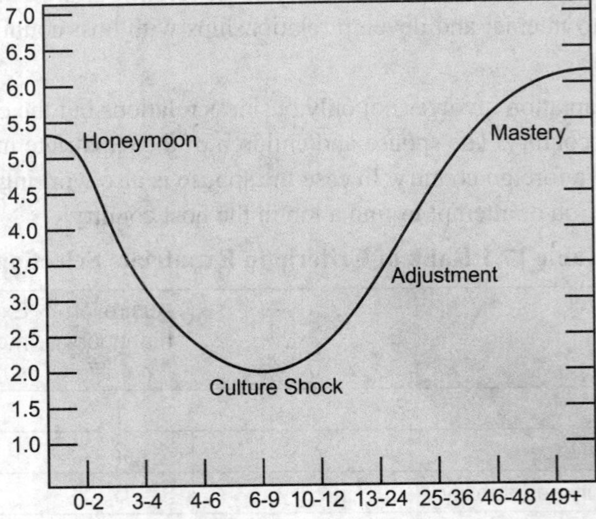

Fig. 17.2. The U-Curve of Cross-Cultural Adjustment

Research reveals that cultural shock largely follows the general pattern of U-shaped curve (Fig 17.2). The curve is divided into four stages which are as follows:

(*i*) **Honemoon Stage:** First of all, the expatriate and his family are fascinated by the host country's culture, accommodation, transportation system and educational facilities. This stage usually lasts for a period of two to three months.

(*ii*) **Cultural Shock Stage:** An international firm may neglect the previously arrived employees and their families to take due care of the new arrivals. Therefore, the employee has to take care of himself and his family. The expatriate may feel confused, frustrated and disillusioned. He gets the shock of the new culture.

(*iii*) **Adjustment Stage:** The expatriate gradually learns the norms, values and behaviour of people in the new culture. He slowly adjusts himself to the culture of the foreign country.

(*iv*) **Mastery Stage:** After adjusting with the foreign culture, the expatriate starts concentrating on the job. He completely learns and adapts to the new environment. At this stage, the expatriate behaves and functions like a citizen of the foreign country.

2. **Repatriation:** Repatriation means returning of expatriates to their home countries. An expatriate may return back to his home country after successfully completing the foreign assignment. Alternatively, he may return back before completing the assignment due to failure to adjust or family reasons. On returning back the expatriate may feel discomfortable with the new situation in his home country. This is known as reverse cultural shock. Such a shock may be caused by several factors. During his stay abroad, the individual may have enjoyed certain privileges and status. These are lost when he return back home. If he is placed on the job he occupied prior to overseas assignment he may feel demoted. Some of his peers might have got promoted. They may not value his overseas experience or new values and life style. In an extreme case, he may resign in desperation and take a job elsewhere.

Special care is needed in the selection of expatriates to avoid 'expatriate failure' which means premature return of an expatriate from a foreign assignment. Expatriate failure has both direct costs (salary, airfare, relocation expenses, training expenses, etc.) and indirect costs.

The main causes of expatriate failures are as follows:

(*i*) Selection based on head office criteria rather than needs of the overseas assignment.

(*ii*) Inadequate preparation, orientation and training prior to joining the assignment.

(*iii*) Alienation or lack of support from the local office.

(*iv*) Inability to adapt to local culture and work environment.

(*v*) Problems with spouse and children—poor adaptation and family unhappiness.

(*vi*) Inadequate compensation and poor financial support.

(*vii*) Weak program for career support and repatriation

17.5 Cross-cultural Training

In order to be effective, the expatriate employees must adapt to the culture of the host country. Without an understanding of the host country's culture, the expatriate may fail to behave properly and face difficulty in the international environment. Research studies reveal that expatriates with cross-cultural training proved to be more efficient. Cross-cultural training enables the expatriate to learn the cultural norms, values, attitudes, beliefs and behaviour patterns of the host country. However, some companies do not provide cross-cultural training to their expatriate employees due to lack of adequate time between selection and departure, failure of training programmes in the past and high cost of training. Cross-Cultural training is best provided before the departure of the employee. But it may also be provided in the host country.

Need for Training and Development for Global Firms

1. To match employee qualifications with job requirements and organizational needs.
2. To facilitate visibility and transformation of the enterprise.
3. To meet the challenges of technological advances.
4. To improve motivation and morale of the employees.
5. To improve superior-subordinate relations.
6. To help the employee and his family members to understand and adapt to the language, customs and traditions of various countries.

Contents of Cross-Cultural Training: Cross-cultural training programmes usually consist of the following:

(1) Information and facts about the economy, resources, currency, climate, eating and dressing habits, housing, banking, insurance, medical facilities, etc., of the host country.

(2) Reasons or causes for the behaviour of the people of the host country. For example, Japanese do not say "No" because they do not want to hurt the feelings of others. On the other hand, Americans do not hesitate to say "No" because they want to make things clear. The purpose of such training (called **attribution training**) is to understand the values, norms and perceptions in the host country. The expatriates can more easily adapt to the host country's culture once they understand the reasons. Indian expatriates in USA and Europe are given brief training regarding punctuality and work perfection.

(3) **Cultural awareness training** is given to explain the common values, attitudes and behaviour patterns in the host country. The purpose is to make the expatriate understand how culture affects the behaviour of people in the host country

(4) **Behaviour modification training** provides information about the desirable behavioural practices in the host country. For example, Indian expatriates are informed that commitment, hard work, sincerity and efficiency are rewarded in the culture of USA. With the help of such training they can modify their behaviour to maximize rewards and avoid penalties.

(5) **Experimental training** exposes the expatriates to real life situations through field visits, preliminary visit to the host country, complex role plays and cros-cultural simulations.

Techniques of cross-cultural training: Most commonly used training techniques are given below:

(*i*) Lectures
(*ii*) Video Films
(*iii*) Case Studies
(*iv*) Reading Material
(*v*) Role Plays
(*vi*) Area Briefings
(*vii*) Field Trips
(*viii*) Simulation
(*ix*) Cultural Assimilation
(*x*) Sensitivity Training

Human resource managers in global firms have to decide how rigorous the training of expatriates should be. This decision depends on the following factors:

1. **Job Novelty:** When the job in the host country is more novel, more rigorous training and assistance is needed. The novel job poses a great challenge. Therefore, the expatriates need to be given cross-cultural training to perform the job successfully.
2. **Degree of Interaction:** Rigorous training becomes necessary if the degree of interaction of the expatriate with the host country's customers, workers, government officials, bankers and the like will be high.
3. **Culture Novelty:** If the host country's culture is very different from the home country's culture, rigorous training becomes necessary. Adjusting to the host country's culture is more difficult than adjusting to the international assignment. If the expatriate is familiar with the host country's culture less rigorous training may be needed.

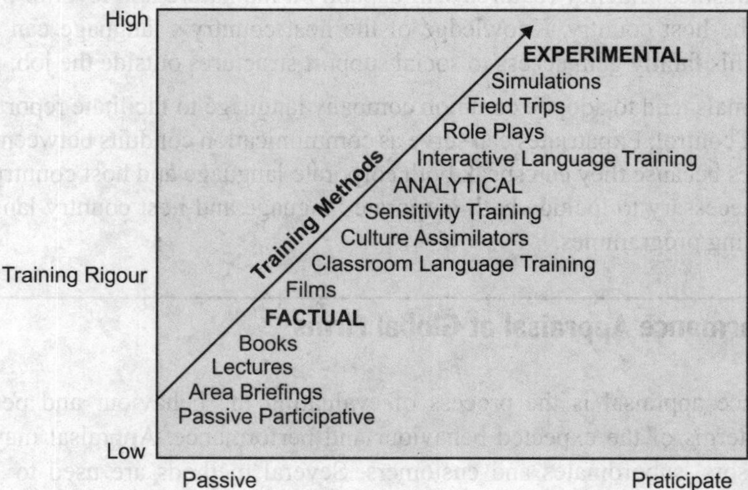

Fig. 17.4. Techniques of Cross-Cultural Training

Source: Black, J.S. & Mendenhall, 1989, "A Practical but Theory-based Framework for Selecting Cross-Cultural Training Programs", *Human Resource Management*, 28 (4), pp. 511-539.

Other situational factors such as cultural toughness, length of overseas assignment and nature of the job may influence cultural training.

In a multinational firm, employees require orientation and training in technical, business, social and method and process of cross-cultural content, aspects.

One expert[1] suggests that overseas employees need four-tier training.

Level I training focuses on the impact of cultural differences, and on raising trainees' awareness of such differences and their impact on business outcomes.

Level II focuses on attitudes and aims at getting participants to understand how attitudes (both positive and negative) are formed and how they influence behaviour.

Level III training provides factual knowledge about the target country.

Level IV provides skill building in areas like language, adjustment and adaptation skills.

In addition to these special training practices, traditional training is necessary for developing overseas employees. At IBM, such training is imparted by rotating the assignments of employees for their professional growth. IBM and other major multinational corporations have also established their management development centres around the world where executives can come to hone their skills. In addition to honing functional skills, international executive development often seeks to foster improved control of global operations by building a unifying corporate culture. The firm brings together managers from its far-flung subsidiaries and steeps them for a week or two in the firm's cherished values and current strategy and policies.

Language Training: English is generally accepted as the language of world business. Multinationals from USA, UK and other English speaking countries do not put much emphasis on language training as a part of the pre-departure programme. But lack of language skill restricts the multinational's ability to monitor competitors and collaborations. For example, in an international joint venture, one partner may fail to detect theft of technology due to inability to understand the language of the other partner.

The ability to speak the foreign language can help the expatriate in negotiation. However, the degree of business fluency required will depend on the nature and level of position of the expatriate in the host country. Knowledge of the host country's language can also help the expatriate and his family gain access to social support structures outside the job.

Multinationals tend to adopt a common company language to facilitate reporting and other mechanisms of control. Expatriates can serve as communication conduits between headquarters and subsidiaries because they can speak both corporate language and host country language. It is, therefore, necessary to include both corporate language and host country language in pre-departure training programmes.

17.6 Performance Appraisal at Global Firms

Performance appraisal is the process of evaluating the behaviour and performance of employees in terms of the expected behaviour and performance. Appraisal may be done by peers, supervisors, subordinates and customers. Several methods are used to evaluate job performance of employees. The objectives of performance appraisal are to create and maintain a satisfactory level of performance, to facilitate employee development and to guide job changes.

1. Daniel Fieldman: "Repatriate Moves as Career Transition", *Human Resource Management Review,* Vol. II No. 3, 1991, pp. 163-78.

Appraising job performance of expatriates is very difficult because of the multifarious experience of a multinational. Moreover, work practices, job dimensions and organisational culture differ from one country to another. Therefore, a global firm must take due care in appraising the performance of its employees.

Both host country managers and home country managers appraise the performance of expatriate employees. The home country managers may rate the employees biasedly due to lack of face-to-face interaction. Host country managers may be biased due to their cultural frame and expectations. For example, a US expatriate manager in India may be appraised somewhat negatively by his host country bosses who find his use of participative decision-making inappropriate in their culture. The expatriate may be appraised by objective criteria such as profits and market share, but local events such as political instability may undermine the manager's performance.

Two experts[1] have suggested the following measures to improve performance appraisal of expatriates:

(*i*) Stipulate the difficulty level involved in assignment at the expatriate's workplace. For example, working as expatriate in China is generally considered more difficult than working in England.

(*ii*) Give more weight in evaluation towards the on-site manager's appraisal than towards the home-site manager's appraisal which is based mainly on distant perceptions the employee's performance.

(*iii*) In case the home-site manager appraises the expatriate, background advice from a former expatriate from the same overseas location should be taken to ensure that unique local issues are considered in appraisal.

(*iv*) The performance criteria used for a particular job should be modified to fit the overseas position and characteristics of that particular locale. For example, maintaining and improving labour relations might be more important in India than in the United States.

(*v*) Appraise the expatriate not only in terms of quantitative criteria like profits or market share but also qualitative criteria like insights of the expatriate into the functioning of overseas operations.

(*vi*) Host country managers should give weightage to the culture of the expatriate employee.

(*vii*) Due weight should also be given to self-appraisal.

17.7 International Compensation of Global Staff

Compensation means the remuneration which an employer pays to the employees in return for their services and contributions to the company. It includes salary, allowances, fringe benefits, bonus, profit sharing, stock options and employee benefits. Several factors influence the compensation policy of a multinational. These are the company's ability to pay, cost of living in different countries, employee productivity, compensation levels in comparable multinationals, and the like.

1. Garry Addou and Mark Mendenhall, "Expatriate Performance Appraisal—Problems and Solution", in *International Human Resource Management* (ed.), PWS Kent Pub. Co., Boston, 1991, pp. 364-74.

Objectives

While formulating compensation policies, global companies seek to achieve the following objectives:

(*i*) to ensure consistency with the overall strategy and business needs of the company
(*ii*) to attract qualified and competent employees
(*iii*) to retain the present employees
(*iv*) to facilitate transfer of international employees in the most cost effective manner
(*v*) to give due consideration to equity and ease of administration
(*vi*) to motivate employees for desired behaviour and performance
(*vii*) to provide incentive for foreign service and to equalize tax burden
(*viii*) to promote growth of the organisation

Global employees expect financial protection (in terms of benefits, living costs and social security) in the host country. They also want opportunities for financial advancement and benefits such as housing, education of children and recreation.

Importance

Compensation plays a vital role in international human resource management. Most of the expatriates leave their home country, relatives and friends to earn money. Some even sacrifice their family life for better prospects. Global firms have to keep in mind that:

(*a*) Compensation has significant impact on employee performance and job satisfaction.
(*b*) Employees compare their pay with that of similar employees in other companies.
(*c*) Inequalities in compensation affect motivation and morale of staff.
(*d*) A sound compensation policy can be a source of competitive advantage

17.7.1 Components of International Compensation

1. **Base Salary:** In a domestic context, base salary is the amount of money that provides a bench mark for other elements of the compensation package. But for expatriates it is the primary component. It may be paid in home or local country currency. Base salary may be an international rate. Alternatively it may be linked to host country, parent country or third country.

2. **Allowances:** These include the cost of living allowance (COLA), housing allowance (HA), home leave allowance, education allowance and relocation allowance. Cost of living allowance is paid to compensate for differences in the cost of living between the home country and the host country. Housing allowance is meant to maintain the employee's home country living standards in the foreign country. Other alternative can be company accommodations. Housing issue is often addressed on a case-by-case basis. Some multinationals, particularly in banking and finance sectors, offer financial assistance and/or protection in connection with the sale or leasing of an expatriate's former residence. As regards home leave allowance, any multinationals cover the expenses of one or more trips back to the home country each year. The purpose of paying for such trips is to give the expatriate an opportunity to renew family and business

ties. This will help to avoid adjustment problems when the employee is repatriated. Allowance for education of children covers tuition enrolment fees, books, uniforms and transportation. Relocation allowance usually covers moving, shipping and storage charges, temporary living expenses, subsidy on durables. At senior positions allowances for car, club membership and servants are given. Some multinationals offer spouse assistance to offset income lost by an expatriate's spouse due to relocating abroad. All these allowances are dependent upon tax equalization policies and practices in both the home and the host countries.

Thus, multinationals pay various types of allowances to encourage employees to take up international assignments and to keep employees living relative to home standards. A hardship allowance is given in case of expatriates posted in hardship locations.

3. **Fringe Benefits:** Gratuity, pension, medical coverage and other social security benefits are paid to international employees. But pension plans create problems because practices vary considerably from country to country. International firms have to deal with the question:

   Whether to maintain expatriates in home country scheme or host country scheme. In many cases, host country laws provide no option and the multinational firm makes up for the difference in coverage.
4. **Incentives:** Bonus, employee stock option plans (ESOP) and other financial incentives are offered to retain and motivate employees.
5. **Taxation:** Multinationals adopt one of the two approaches to handle tax burden on expatriates. Under *tax equalization approach*, an amount equal to the home country tax obligation is held and all taxes in the host country are paid. In the *tax protection approach*, the employee pays up to the amount of taxes payable in the home country. The employee is entitled to any windfall received if total taxes are less in the foreign country.

MNCs SEND EXPATS HOME AS COSTS RISE

Leading multinational companies including Procter & Gamble, Hyatt and Marriott have started cutting down on expensive expat assignments to slash costs in the face of deepening global slowdown. Several multinationals, across industries, have asked their subsidiaries to get local nationals to do the job as pay and perks for overseas employees have shot up considerably, say sources.

Industry reports suggest that even Unilever and Pepsi Co have been looking at the issue closely. In a marked change from its culture of actively posting senior executives around the world, Procter & Gamble (P & G) has officially stated plans to cut long-term assignments outside home countries. Already, P & G's expat assignments have fallen by over 40% in recent years, say company watchers. "One of the ways we have to continue to change is to get more from what we have. The challenge for the company is to now offer suitable growth opportunities roles for senior-level expats," P & G's chief operating officer Robert A McDonald is reported to have said.

"P & G's India operation predominantly employees indigenous talent, recruited and grown in India and this will not have an impact on the India business," P & G India HR head Sonali Roychowdhury said.

The strengthening US dollar and the deep recessionary trends have made expatriate lifestyle, the pays and perks hugely expensive. "Expat costs are three or five times the cost of a hiring a local employee. This is especially true of expats sent to countries where the dollar impact is high," said a top official of a Mumbai-based multinational FMCG company. Expat assignments involve huge relocation costs including housing, social perks and education.

American companies have been more concerned over the issue as US citizens working abroad have to pay taxes both in the US and the country where they reside. This is because US tax is on the basis of citizenship and not residency. HR experts say corporates are trying to figure out ways to balance the need for competent managers in emerging regions with an eye on productivity at lower costs.

Hotel companies have also clamped down on top level expat assignments. Many premium hotels now prefer nationals in key positions like CEO's but they continue to employ expats with technical expertise like chefs.

"There is a shortage of talent in specialised areas. This is a specific need and difficult to replace," said Gurmeet Singh, area director, HR, India, Maldives, Pakistan, Marrott International. This means increased job opportunities for Indians in the hotel industry.

"The huge rise in pay roll costs fuelled by the skewed manpower demand-supply ratio is now expected to attract a lot of Indian employees back to the hotel industry," said HVS International MD Manav Thadani.

Source: The Economic Times

17.7.2 Approaches to International Compensation:

There are two main approaches to international compensation. These are as follows:

1. **The Going Rate Approach:** Under this approach, the base salary of an expatriate is linked to the salary structure in the host country. Compensation surveys are conducted to find out the local market rates for the specific job position. If the location is in a low-pay country, the multinational usually supplements base pay with additional benefits and payments.

   The going rate approach offers the following **advantages**:

   (*i*) There is equality in pay with local nationals.

   (*ii*) It is very effective in attracting talent to a location that pays higher salaries than those received in the home country.

   (*iii*) The approach is simple and easy for expatriates to understand

   (*iv*) Expatriates are able to identify with the host country.

   (*v*) Equity in pay amongst expatriates of different nationalities is maintained.

   The **disadvantages** of the going rate approach are as follows:

   (*i*) There can be variations in pay between assignment for the same employee due to differences in salary levels and tax burden. Employees are very sensitive to this issue.

   (*ii*) There can be variations between expatriates of the same nationality in different locations. It may lead to rivalry for assignments to financially attractive locations and little interest in financially unattractive locations.

(*iii*) There may be problems upon repatriation when the employee's salary reverts to a home country level that is below that of the host country.

2. **The Balance Sheet Approach:** Under this approach the base salary is linked to the salary structure of the relevant home country. For example, a US executive taking up an international position in India would be paid US base salary level rather than the salary level of India. The basic assumption of this approach is that foreign assignees should not suffer a material loss due to their transfer. The objective is to maintain home country living standard. Financial incentives (expatriate or hardship allowance) are added to make the package attractive. The following outlays incurred by expatriates are incorporated in the balance sheet approach:

   (*a*) expenses on goods and services such as food, personal care, clothing, household furnishings, transportation, medical care and recreation.

   (*b*) costs of housing

   (*c*) income taxes

   (*d*) contributions to pension, education, servings, etc.

   The balance sheet approach offers the following **advantages**:

   (*i*) The approach provides equity between foreign assignments and between expatriates of the same nationality.

   (*ii*) Repatriation of expatriates becomes smoother as the pay remains linked to the parent country levels.

   (*iii*) This approach is easy to communicate to employees.

   The balance sheet approach suffers from the following **disadvantages**:

   (*i*) This approach can result in considerable disparities between expatriates of different nationalities, and between expatriates and local nationals.

   (*ii*) Problems occur when international staff are paid different amounts for performing the same job in the host locations according to their different home base salaries.

   (*iii*) The administration of this approach is complex. Difficulties arise due to differences in taxation and pension laws of different countries.

In spite of these drawbacks, the balance sheet approach is more popular than the going rate approach.

Table 17.1: Comparison Between Balance Sheet Approach and Market Rate Approach

	Balance Sheet Approach	Market Rate Approach
Advantages	1. Equity	1. Simplicity
	2. Ease in repatriation	2. Equality with locals
		3. Identification with the host country
Disadvantages	1. Complexity in administration	1. Rivalry for overseas assignments in a particular country
	2. Disparity between expatriates of different countries	2. Difficulty in repatriation
		3. Variation between assignments for the same employee

Whatever approach is adopted, the compensation structure should fulfil the following main objectives:

(*i*) The compensation policy should be consistent with the overall strategy and business requirements of the enterprise.

(*ii*) It should help in attracting and retaining the needed talent.

(*iii*) It should enhance employee satisfaction and motivation.

(*iv*) It should be fair and equitable.

(*v*) It should be convenient to administer.

17.8 International Industrial Relations

Labour relations are an important part of human resource management in global firms. Labour relations refer to the relations between employers and employees. An international firm has to deal with employees of several countries having different cultural, social, political and economic conditions. Therefore, it cannot apply the home country practices in all its affiliates abroad. There is no global approach to industrial relations. Major issues in international labour relations are as follows:

1. **Labour Participation in Management:** The form and degree of workers' participation in management differ from one country to another. However, employees at all levels of an organisation have the right to participate in decisions affecting their welfare. Employee compensation, appraisal, working conditions, etc., are some of these areas. At the plant level **works councils** are formed. A work council consisting of workers and managers takes decisions on working conditions, training, work allocation, transfers, etc. At the unit level, **joint management councils** are constituted for joint consultation and collective bargaining between trade union officials and departmental heads. At the **top level**, a representative of workers may be appointed as a member of the board of directors. The **worker director** attempts to protect and promote the interests of labour by participating in strategic decisions.

2. **Role of Labour Unions:** Labour unions attempt to influence decisions relating to location, expansion, etc., in international firms. They seek the help of local governments and international organisations like the International Labour Office (ILO) for this purpose. The extent of power exercised by labour unions differs across countries.

   Labour unions perceive **threat concerns** to their bargaining power from the following actions of multinational corporations:

   (*i*) The company may move production to another country to secure better terms of employment. For example, Ford Motors threatened British unions to move production to continental Europe.

   (*ii*) The company may retain highly skilled jobs in the home country and shift only low skilled jobs to foreign plants.

   (*iii*) The company may adopt employment practices and contractual agreements of home country in host countries.

   (*iv*) The company may focus on global optimisation overlooking local issues.

(*v*) Unions are not provided sufficient data

(*vi*) Unions find it difficult to meet the decision makers at higher levels of the firm.

Labour unions adopt the following **strategies** to counter the bargaining power of international firms:

(*a*) Trying to secure international labour standards — freedom of association, right to bargain collectively, etc., are obtained as basic human rights through United Nations.

(*b*) Lobbying with the local government for legislation that restrict freedom of multinational corporations.

(*c*) Seeking support of ILO and other international bodies. ILO and OECD have framed codes of conduct for multinational corporations.

In 1960s, labour unions established International Trade Secretariat (ITSs) to develop worldwide links for national unions in particular industries. They believed that through ITS labour unions could counter the power of international firms by threatening to disrupt production on an international scale. However, ITS, were not a success because national unions compete with each other to attract foreign investment and hence jobs for their members.

3. **Organising Labour Relations:** The main issue in organising labour relations is the degree of centralisation or decentralisation of labour relations activities. Generally, international firms decentralise these activities at the subsidiary level due to differences in labour laws, union power, and collective bargaining practices in different countries. Local managers can better handle such divergent conditions than the corporate headquarters. However, nationality of the parent firm influences the decision. For example, the US firms tend to centralise authority at corporate office while British firms allow local units to deal with day-to-day issues concerning industrial relations. The parent firm only provides guidance and assistance to the subsidiaries.

These days, there is a trend towards centralisation of labour relations as a result of the attempts of global firms to rationalise their operations. These firms are under pressure to control costs due to intense competition. Labour costs constitute a major part of total cost and international firms attempt to increase their bargaining power while negotiating with labour unions. Centralised decision making and threats to shift production to some other country are used when unions refuse to agree for changes in work rules and limiting increase in wages.

The manner in which work is organised within a plant can be a major source of competitive advantage. For example, Japanese auto makers have gained competitive advantage through self-managing teams, cross-cultural training, job rotation, etc., Japanese firms attempt, to replicate their work practices abroad. But these attempts create conflicts in countries which have traditional work practices. Therefore, the headquarters of Japanese firms directly bargain with local unions to make them agree to radical changes in work practices, before making foreign investments. For example, Nissan decided to invest in England after British unions agreed to Japanese work practices. Centralised control over labour relations becomes necessary in order to pursue such a strategy.

SUMMARY

Problems in International HRM: Differences in culture, laws, labour markets, employment conditions, labour relations

Sources of Global Recruitment: (*i*) Home country nationals (*ii*) host country nationals (*iii*) third country nationals (*iv*) impatriates (*v*) off shore outsourcing

Staffing Policies/Models: (*i*) Ethnocentric model (*ii*) polycentric (*iii*) regiocentric (*vi*) geocentric

Selection Criteria for Expatriates: (*i*) Technical competence (*ii*) age and experience (*iii*) education (*iv*) health (*v*) language and communication skills (*vi*) motivation (*vii*) adaptability (*viii*) family

Cultural Shock: Anxiety and frustration due to inability to adjust in foreign environment (*i*) Honeymoon stage (*ii*) cultural shock (*iii*) adjustment stage (*iv*) mastery stage

Repatriation: Coming back of expatriate to the home country after or before completion of the overseas assignment

Training and Development: (*i*) Job training (*ii*) cross-cultural training – information sharing, attribution, awareness, behaviour modification-experimental training (*iii*) Job novelty, degree of interaction and cultural novelty determine rigorous training (*iv*) Language training

Performance Appraisal: Difficulty level, onsite appraisal, local issue, job performance, qualitative criteria, cultural adaptation, self-appraisal

Compensation: Base salary, allowances, fringe benefits, incentives, taxation are the components (*i*) going rate approach (*ii*) balance sheet approach

Labour Relations: (*i*) Labour participation—works council, joint management council, worker director (*ii*) Role of labour unions — concerns of labour due to high bargaining power of MNCs, strategies adopted by unions are international labour standards, lobbying with local government, international bodies (e.g., (LO), ITSs (*iii*) Centralisation vs. decentralisation—trend towards centralisation

TEST QUESTIONS

1. Explain the reasons due to which HRM in international firms becomes complex and challenging.
2. Discuss the sources of global recruitment, pointing out their merits and demerits.
3. Explain staffing policies/models which international firms follow, stating the advantages and disadvantages of each strategy.
4. Explain the selection criteria for expatriates
5. What is cultural shock? Describe the stages involved in it.
6. Why does cultural shock arise and how can it be prevented?
7. What is repatriation? What are the causes of expatriate failures?
8. Explain the factors that influence the staffing policy of an international firm.

9. Why is training of expatriates necessary?
10 What is cross-cultural training? Discuss its contents and techniques.
11. How would you appraise the performance of expatriates.
12. Explain the objectives and significance of compensation in international HRM.
13. What are the components of compensation paid to expatriates?
14. Discuss various approaches to international compensation, stating their advantages and disadvantages.
15. Explain the main issues in labour relations at the international level.

CHAPTER 18

International Business Negotiations

LEARNING OBJECTIVES

After studying this chapter, you should understand:

18.1 Steps in the Negotiation Process

18.2 Behaviour and Tactics in Negotiation

18.3 Approaches to International Negotiation

- Summary
- Test Questions

Negotiation refers to bargaining between two or more parties to arrive at a mutually acceptable agreement. It involves a formal discussion and is-the process of give and take. In business, negotiations take place between buyers and sellers regarding the price, terms of payment, etc. International business negotiations also relate to quantity and quality of product, price, terms of payment, delivery schedule, mode of transportation, insurance, exchange rate, etc. But international negotiations are complicated because the two parties belong to different countries. The mode of negotiation and expectations of parties differ from country to country.

In case of large orders and long term contracts, international negotiations may be less complicated. But negotiations between international firms and governments are more complex.

Such negotiations are made to get approval for starting, expanding and closing operations in a foreign country. An international firm may enter into negotiations to acquire ownership interest in or to sell technology to a foreign firm. Such negotiations involve large and long term financial commitments.

Therefore, a more thorough preparation and involvement of top management in the negotiation process become necessary.

18.1 Steps in the Negotiation Process

The process of international business negotiations typically involves the following steps.

1. **Planning:** Thorough preparation and advance planning are essential for success in international business negotiations. Both the parties have to do considerable preliminary work before the actual negotiation starts. Each side must decide its objectives and

the options available to reach these objectives. The identification of options enables the negotiator to change his strategy during negotiations so as to meet the cultural requirements. Once the objectives and options are determined, each side collects information and thinks out the probable decisions on key issues such as:

(*a*) deciding limits on goals

(*b*) short term and long term considerations

(*c*) key issues to be taken up during negotiations

(*d*) objectives and limitations of the opposite side

(*e*) strengths and weaknesses of the other party

(*f*) sequence of discussions

(*g*) action plan and back up plans

2. **Building Relationship:** In several cultures, it is necessary to build personal relationship between the parties before starting negotiations. This is considered a 'warm up' phase before the parties begin serious negotiations. Each side attempts to know the other side, to ascertain its reasonableness, and to establish personal bond if found trust worthy. In countries like Japan, Saudi Arabia, etc. People do business with partners they know and can trust. Starting business discussion before establishing personal relationship may be considered an insult.

   In countries like the USA, on the other hand, negotiators want to start negotiations quickly and draw up precise legal contracts. Therefore, a US firm may be frustrated by the longtime taken in beginning negotiation in Japan. For the US negotiation, attending diners and ceremonies are unnecessary formalities. Therefore, most successful global executives invest considerable time and effort to understand the prospective business partners and business culture of the host country.

3. **Exchange of Information:** The negotiation process actually begins when each side makes known to the other side its position on the key issues and makes the first offer At-this stage, the negotiators try to understand what the other side wants.

   The nature and extent of information given out and sought from the other side depends upon the cultural background of the negotiators. In some cultures, negotiators seek in-depth technical details while in other cultures negotiators overlook such details and focus on relationships. Chaney and Martin state the typical information which negotiators from five different cultures like to exchange with the other party.

   (***a***) **Americans:** Provide information directly and briefly often through multi-media presentation. They believe that once the parties agree in principle, details can be worked out later. They keep a margin of 5 to 10 per cent in the first offer.

   (*b*) **Japanese and Russians:** Seek extensive details and technical information. They believe that all details of the proposal should be discussed before reaching an agreement. Japanese keep a margin of 10 to 20 percent in the first offer, While Russians keep a margin of 50 to 60 per cent.

(c) **Latin Americans and Arabs:** Focus more on information about the relationship and less on technical details of the proposal. During initial discussions, the parties focus on why business should be done together rather than on how to do it. Latin Americans keep a first offer margin of 20 to 40 per cent while Arabs keep a 20 to 50 per cent margin.

The negotiation process initiated by the first offer may undergo changes through persuasion, concessions, etc. before the final agreement is made.

4. **Persuasion:** At-this stage, each party attempts to convince the other party that the later should improve its offer. Each party tries to extract the maximum benefits from the other party and wants to give away the least. Therefore, this is the most important step in the negotiation process. This stage can be successful provided:

   (a) each party understands the other's position

   (b) the two parties are able to create new options, and

   (c) they are willing to work towards a mutually acceptable solution.

   During persuasion, the parties may use certain desirable, and undersirable behaviour and tactics which are described later in this chapter.

5. **Concessions:** In their attempt to find a mutually acceptable agreement each party offers some concession from the first offer. These concessions are ceded in two ways — sequential, and holistic.

   (a) **Sequential Approach:** Under this approach, the two parties work through the contract item by item. The concessions are made in a piecemeal manner. As one issue is resolved, the parties shift their focus on the next issue. The sequential approach to concession making is followed in North America.

   (b) **Holistic Approach:** Under this approach, the parties first work their way through the entire proposed agreement. Thereafter, they discuss the total agreement and make proposals and counter proposals. The holistic approach is followed in most Asian countries. A negotiator used to sequential approach may be confused under the holistic approach thinking that issues are unnecessarily cropping up again and again.

6. **Agreement:** The last step in negotiation process is the signing of the mutually acceptable and legally binding contract. In different cultures the contract is viewed differently. In America, the contract is considered a legal document that spells out the mutual obligations of the parties. In China and Japan the contract is viewed as a written recognition of personal commitments by the two sides. It is considered as the beginning rather than the end to working together. The contract is written in general terms to permit changes in future required by changes in the circumstances.

Table 18.1: Variables in the Negotiation Process

1. **Basic conception of negotiation process:** Is it a competitive process or a problem-solving approach?
2. **Negotiator selection criteria:** Is selection based on experience, status, expertise, personal attributes, or some other characteristic?
3. **Significance of type of issue:** Is it specific, such as price, or is the focus on relationships or the format of talks?

4. **Concern with protocol:** What is the importance of procedures, social behaviours, and so forth in the negotiation process?
5. **Complexity of communicative context:** What degree of reliance is placed on nonverbal cues to interpret information?
6. **Nature of persuasive arguments:** How do the parties attempt to influence each other? Do they rely on rational arguments, on accepted tradition, or on emotion?
7. **Role of individuals' aspirations:** Are motivations based on individual, company, or community goals?
8. **Bases of trust:** It trust based on past experience, intuition, or rules?
9. **Risk-taking propensity:** How much do the parties try to avoid uncertainty in trading information or making a contract?
10. **Value of time:** What is each party's attitude toward time? How fast should negotiations proceed, and what degree of flexibility is there?
11. **Decision-making system:** How does each team reach decision – by individual determination, by majority opinion, or by group consensus?
12. **Form of satisfactory agreement:** is agreement based on trust (perhaps just a handshake), the credibility of the parties, commitment, or a legally binding contract?

Source: Adapted from S.E. Weiss and W. Stripp, Negotiation with foreign Business persons: An Introduction for Americans with Propositions on Six Cultures (New York University Faculty of Business Administration, February 1985).

18.2 Behaviour and Tactics in Negotiation

In order to achieve their objectives, negotiators adopt different verbal and nonverbal behaviour during the negotiation process. They may even adopt undesirable posturers and tactics to gain advantage over each other. A good negotiator should clearly understand the nature and purpose of these postures and tactics and develop appropriate strategies to counter them.

(*i*) **Verbal Behaviour:** Promises, threats, rewards, etc. used to influence the other side in negotiations is known as verbal behaviour. Graham has listed the verbal behaviours of negotiators as follows:

(*a*) **Promise:** One party offers something pleasant, positive or rewarding to the other party in return.

(*b*) **Recommendation:** The party foresees a beneficial environmental outcome, but its occurrence is beyond the party's control.

(*c*) **Threat:** One party indicates to the other party that the first party will react with something noxious, unpleasant or punishing to the latter.

(*d*) **Warning:** The party foresees an unpleasant environmental outcome, the occurrence of which is beyond the party's control.

(*e*) **Reward:** A statement by one party that is thought to create a pleasant consequence to the other party.

(*f*) **Punishment:** A statement by one party that is thought to create unpleasant consequence to the other party.

1. John L. Grasham, "The Influence of Culture on the Process of Business Negotiation," **Journal of International Business Studies**, Spring 1983, p.88

(*g*) **Positive Normative Appeal:** One party appreciates that the other party's past, present or future behaviour is or will be in conformity with social norms.

(*h*) **Negative Normative Appeal:** One party deprecates that the other party's behaviour violates social norms.

(*i*) **Commitment:** One party affirms that its future bids will not go above or below a certain level.

(*j*) **Self-disclosure:** A statement in which a party reveals information itself.

(*k*) **Question:** A statement in which a party seeks information about the other party.

(*l*) **Command:** One party suggests that the other party perform certain behaviour.

(*m*) **Rejection:** The word 'no' is used during bargaining.

Graham found during his research that the frequency of the type of verbal behaviour used differed widely among Americans, Japanese and Brazilian negotiators.

2. **Nonverbal Behaviour:** What people do rather than what they say is called nonverbal behaviour. Such behaviour mainly includes the followings:

(*a*) **Silence:** the negotiator remains silent during conversations.

(*b*) **Facial Glazing:** one party stares at the other party's face or at the roof.

(*c*) touching the other party during conversation.

(*d*) **Conversational ones lap:** where in two or more persons talk at the some time.

3. **Dirty Tactics:** These mean the unfair, deceitful or unethical tactics used by negotiators to win a situation. Michael Kublin' has listed the following questionable tactics used by negotiators:

(*a*) **Deliberate Deception:** deliberately misrepresenting the facts on offer to make it look better – than it is.

(*b*) **Stalling:** delaying negotiations and pushing for concessions to close a deal prior to the opponents's departure.

(*c*) **Escalating Authority:** agreeing to a deal but-then claiming it must be aproved by superiors, hoping to extract further concessions.

4. **Extreme Behaviour:** Another tactic used by negotiators is to make extreme offers or requests. For example, a party may make an initial demand of $ 80 million though the contract is expected to yield $ 20 million. Contrary to the popular impression such extreme behaviour does not obstruct the negotiation process. The party showing extreme behaviour may secure better results due to the psychological pressure created on the other party. The other party may perceive the aggressive position as an indication of the first party's strength. Moreover, the party using extreme behaviour is able to gain time and deliberate on the other party's moves until the other party responds.

1. Michael Kublin, **International Negotiating.** International Business press, 1995.

18.3 Approaches to International Negotiation

There are two basic approaches to international business negotiation. These are – (*i*) competitive approach, and (*ii*) problem solving approach.

1. **The Competitive Negotiation Approach:** Under this approach, the parties view negotiations as a win – lose situation. Each party believes in extracting maximum possible gain from the deal irrespective of its impact on the other party. Therefore, negotiations begin with very high of initial demands. Each side looks for weaknesses in the position of the other side but reveals as little as possible about itself. They use pressure tactics and dirty tactics to secure a win. They adopt a rigid attitude by making their position explicit and sticking to it. Each party makes an initial offer which is the most favourable to it. It makes concessions only when it is unavoidable and that too grudgingly and slowly. No attempt is made to build a long term relationship between the parties. At the end of the negotiation process one party feels victorious and the other party feels defeated. As a result, each party develops negative attitude towards the other party. The losing side keeps waiting for a chance in its favour and take revenge at a later date. The competitive approach may yield short term gains but is not suitable for long term relationship between the parties.
2. **The Problem solving Negotiation Approach:** Under this approach, the negotiation process is considered a win-win situation. The negotiators seek an agreement that is beneficial to both. They are open minded and are ready to overcome cross-cultural barriers to a mutually satisfying outcome. Each side gives to and seeks, from the other party objective information. They show patience and tolerance for cultural difference in the nature of information sought and the speed of response. They make reasonable and firm offers and identity creative options beneficial to both. In order to develop cordial long term relationship no dirty tricks are used. The agreement is signed when it is mutually beneficial. In case an agreement cannot be reached, they depart without any ill will. Therefore, it is possible to renegotiate in future whenever the opportunity arises.

   The problem soling approach is better as it helps in developing long term relationships. However, Americans prefer the competitive approach while Japanese believe in the problems solving approach.

Table 18.2: Comparison of Negotiation Styles – Japanese, North American, and Latin American

Japanese	North American	Latin American
Emotional sensitivity highly valued, Hiding of emotions.	Emotional sensitivity not highly valued Dealing straight forwardly or impersonally.	Emotional sensitivity valued Emotionally passionate.
Subtle power plays; conciliation.	Litigation not so much as conciliation.	Great power plays; use of weakness.
Loyalty to employer; employer takes care of employees.	Lack of commitment to employer; breaking of ties by either if necessary.	Loyalty to employer (who is often family).

Face-saving crucial in decision often made on basis of saving someone from embarrassment.	Decisions made on a cost benefit basis; face saving does not always matter.	Face-saving crucial in decision making to preserve honor, dignity.
Decision makers openly influenced by special interests.	Decision makers influenced by special interests but not considered ethical.	Execution of special interests of decision maker expected, condoned.
Not argumentative; quiet when right.	Argumentative when right or wrong, but impersonal.	Argumentative when right or wrong; passionate.
What is down in writing must be accurate, valid.	Great importance given to documentation as evidential proof.	Impatient with documentation as obstacle to understanding general principles.
Step-by-step approach to decision making. Good of group is the ultimate aim.	Methodically organised decision making profit motive or good of individual ultimate aim.	Impulsive, spontaneous decision making. What is good for group is good for the individual.
Cultivate a good emotional social setting for decision making; get to know decision makers.	Decision making impersonal; avoid involvements, conflict of interest.	Personalism necessary for good decision making.

SOURCE: From Pierre Casse, Training for the Multicultural Manager: A Practical and Cross-Cultural Approach to the Management of People (Washington D.C.: Society for Intercultural Education, Training, and Research, 1982).

Negotiations That Led to Jet – Etihad Deal

"Are you out of your Mind?" James Hogan thundered. It was late – 2012, about four months into the talks between Jet Airways and Etihad Airways for a seminal deal, and the investment banker representing the Indian airline had just stated how much his side throught their asset was worth: $3.5 billion. And Hogan, president and CEO of Etihad, lost it.

An industry veteran, Hogan has steered 10-year- old Etihad's flight from the wish of a sultanate in the Persian Gulf to an airline that could fly with the best, the biggest and the profitable. Since taking charge in 2006, he had scaled it up from 22 aircraft to 70 aircraft, from 2.8 million passengers flown to 10.2 million passengers. He had cut equity deals with four international airlines.

Yet, the investment bank, which represented Hogan's side in one of those four deals, was asking $3.5 billion for a loss-making airline, one the stock market valued at $400 million and which came with $2.1 billion of debt. Blunt and remonstrative, the Australian digressed, and told the investment bankers they had just lost a client for the future in Etihad. Sitting across from Hogan, Naresh Goyal, the man who built Jet, kept a studied silence. That side-show over, talks resumed.

It was just another moment in a long, complicated, bitter-sweet courtship that was sanctified by the high priests of the Indian government last week. After 15 months of yes and no, ifs and buts. After, as one Jet executive counted for himself, 46 trips to Abu Dhabi, Etihad' headquarters in the sands of the middle-east.

The deal was aptly christened, by Jet, as 'Project Sand Dunes'. And the exchanges above typified the layered corporate drama the deal, the first of its kind in Indian aviation, was: grandstanding and brinkmanship, old associations and new relationships, boardroom negotiations and back-channel talks, breakups and makeups. Thrice, it collapsed, only to be revived.

The web of relationships on the table were as intricate as the route map of a well-travelled airline.

This inside account of the deal that valued Jet at $1.5 billion is pieced together by speaking to many people involved, directly or indirectly, including executives, bankers, aides and consultants. None wanted to be on record given the secrecy of those talks and to guard relationships.

That day, on the table, there was a web of relationships on the table as intricate as the route map of a well-travelled airline. The gulf in valuations was as wide as on ocean. A meeting point could not be seen. Yet, if the two sides kept talking, it was because they stood to lose more, none more so than Goyal—a tough-as-nails businessman and a one-man networking army for whom creating from chaos is almost second nature.

4 Negotiators...

The airline Goyal formed in 1993 was number two in India, but it was ailing from the years of profitless growth that is characteristic of this industry. He needed a rich airline to add ballast to Jet with its cash and global network.

In June 2012, three months before the government would change its rules to allow foreign airlines to buy 49% in Indian carriers, three Jet officials landed in London. They were taken to the office of an Etihad associate. Here, they met Etihad officials, and blueprint for talks was drawn. Talks began in August, mostly at Etihad's headquarters in Abu Dhabi, adjoining the front, sometimes from the air port and the Yas Marina Formula 1 circuit. Goyal, 62, led the Jet side—sometimes from the rear. When Hogan, his Etihad counterpart, was absent, Goyal stayed away too. It they were talking valuations, he let his investment bankers make the pitch.

On occasions, Goyal would bide his time in a luxury hotel room, either at the Radisson or The park Hotel in Abu Dhabi. His team would meet him in his room early morning to chalk outstrategy and debrief him after the meeting.

In the interregnum, Goyal would make courtesy calls to old, influential contacts in Abu Dhabi.

In the seventies, he was general sales agent for several airlines, including middle-eastern carriers Gulf Air and Kuwait Airways. He helped sell their tickets, and negotiate with Indian authorities for airport and landing rights.

Goyal's networking traits are legendary. He always stays in touch. Even if he does not have an agenda, he makes calles or visits people, if just for five minutes. " He is shrewd, pushy but soft-spoken," says Jitendra Bhargava, former executive director of Air India. " He knows how to go about getting his things done. He knows Indian politicians well and knows how to use his money."

But here, he had to contend with Hogan, a man the first family of Abu Dhabi, which owned Etihad, trusted implicitly. His lieutenant was Etihad CFO James Rigney, a fellow Aussie. While Rigney was the numbers man, Hogan was the execution specialist with lines that lingered. One time, when he felt the Jet team was exaggerating their airline's true worth, he growled: " You don't teach your father how to such eggs."

Hogan had an old Jet connection, through Hameed Ali, Goyal's right-hand man and firefighter. In the late-90s and early-2000s when Hogan was the CEO of Gulf Air, Ali was chief pilot for the Bahrain-headquartered airline.

Jet and Etihad, too, had shared history. In 2003, the royal family of Abu Dhabi had asked Goyal to help create a blueprint for a new airline that would be Etihad. Some Jet executives from that team, like KG Vishwanath, were involved in the current negotiations. That gesture was typical of Goyal, who is known to dish out favours to earn goodwill later.

3 Walkouts...

For the hard-nosed Australians, such niceties mattered little. Hogan and Rigney were combative and regularly punctured many Jet arguments. Once, Hogan posed a question to a senior Jet official, who turned to Goyal in askance. "Look at me," hollered Hogan, " I asked you the question." They knew Jet was desperate for cash and they tried to capitalise one that weakness.

One at least three occasions, the talks froze when one of the two walked out—Jet twice and Etihad once. The first was in December 2012, when Jet quoted a $3.5 billion valuation—and Etihad responded with $450-500 million. With neither side budging, Jet walked out. In January, Etihad walked out, over the same issue. And, in February, Jet left on news that Etihad was looking at Kingfisher Airlines, reportedly at the behest of the Abu Dhabi royal family.

Kingfisher, Vijay Mallya's airline that had been grounded since October 2012, was Etihad's lever age. Jet found its own leverage in Etihad's neighbourhood: it sent feelers to Kuwait Airways and a few other middle-eastern carriers.

Whatever was happening on—and off—the negotiating table, Goyal kept open a line of communication. He assigned that job to Hameed Ali—an outcome of bargaining realities, personal temperament and a shared connection.

More than any other executive in Jet, the unflappable Ali enjoys Goyal's respect and space. While Goyal often loses his temper with other executives, he always defers to Ali. The COO comes from a business family in Bahrain. One a typical week, Ali leaves Mumbai for Bahrain on a Thursday evening for the weekend, which starts on a Friday there; and returns on a Monday. But during the deal, he was continuously talking to Hogan and Rigney.

On February 17, Sheikh Hamed bin Zayed alNahyan, chairman of the Etihad board, told Reuters on the sidelines of a defence exhibition in the UAE capital that the Jet deal needs to be revised. It was back-handed way of bringing the two sides back on the table. Again.

This time, on a parallel track, the governments too would be involved. The sheikh, in that same conversation alluded to a meeting Abu Dhabi officials were to have with Anand Sharma, the Indian commerce minister. In the recent past, the Indian commerce minister. In the recent past, the emirate had seen the Indian business of one of its companies, telecom operator Etisalat, evaporate following a regulatory ruling by a court, and it wanted to avoid a repeat. And India wanted to make amends for Etisalat.

Meanwhile, Goyal was working the back-channels furiously. One of those trips was to Kerala, to meet MA Yousuf Ali, who was ranked by *Forbes* magazine as the top Indian business leader in the United Arab Emirates—the federation of seven emirates, one of which is Abu Dhabi. Ali is the chairman of the $4.5 billion Lulu Group and has built India's largest mall in Kochi, Kerala. He would do his bit with Abu Dhabi to revive the Jet-Etihad deal.

Goyal led from the front. But on valuations, he let his bankers make the pitch – and feel the backlash

On April 24, a day after the Inidan government announced a three-fold increase in the seat allotment for Abu Dhabi, the deal was announced. "Both gain. Jet gets a much-needed infusion of funds, global network and synergy benefits, procurement of oil, aircrafts, spares, facilities, manpower etc," says Amber Dubey, partner and head-aerospace and defense at consultancy KPMG. "Etihad gets a four-fold access to the large Indian market, which will help it compete better with its rivals in the Gulf."

Since then, the two have been dealing with the Indian bureaucracy and regulators. For Etihad, Goyal was a good man to help navigate the regulatory maze the Indian airline industry is. And it helped that the first family of Abu Dhabi knew him personally. Last week, the cabinet cleared the deal, the last of the big government nods. It's not all over as BJP leader Subramanian Swamy has challenged the deal in the Supreme Court.

Its's a new flight for Jet, born from a new flying stance. All these years, Goyal opposed foreign airlines investing in Indian ones, and is now the first beneficiary of a policy change. Just when he needed it. "He has in the past, had policies reframed to harm rivals," say Bhargava. " But now private airlines have voice. They can lobby too, unlike an Air India chairman who could not muster courage to confront his minister."

A superstitious man, Goyal has things for the digit five. So, Jet takes all aircraft deliveries and launches new routes on the 5th, 14th or 23rd. The deal with Etihad does not have the number five, but it is stamped with another Goyal trait: creating from chaos.

2 Imperatives...

Both Goyal and Hogan wanted the deal revived. Both were desperate, in their own ways. Jet needed cash to avoid going the Kingfisher way. Etihad could give it cash, as well as feed Goyal's ambition of becoming a global airline. Its other option was to join a multi-airline alliance. But jet joining, say, the Star Alliance would have meant dealing with 28 partners, most of them larger and more influential than it. And it would have fetched no cash. With Etihad, it would have only one partner to deal with. It could use Abu Dhabi as a hub for its flights to Africa, Europe and North America. And receive Cash.

Etihad, the by-product of an oil economy, had plenty of cash. It was hungry for growth. It wanted to challenge the hegemony of global airlines and keep pace in the radical realignment being forged by a trio of middle-east carriers—besides Etihad, Emirates (from fellow emirate, Diubai) and Qatar Airways (from Qatar). Emirates was setting the pace. Using Dubai as its hub, it was servicing 6,800 routes, just about everywhere and especially in growth markets of India, Europe and Africa. By comparison Etihad had 1,800 routes.

By Etihad's estimate, control over India—a battleground in that larger war—could give it 5,000 routes in five years. Emirates has 9-12 points of call in India. By comparison, Jet could fly 23 flights from India to Abu Dhabi, and feed Etihad for onward travel to Europe, Africa and North America.

Hogan and Rigney were combative. They regularly punctured Jet arguments with bluntness and numbers.

Jet and Etihad spent almost seven months focused on just network partnership—who would fly where, which meant carving new routes for both and letting go of some existing routes. So, for example, into New York area, Jet would fly to Newark Airport, while Etihad would continue to use its base at John F Kennedy Airport.

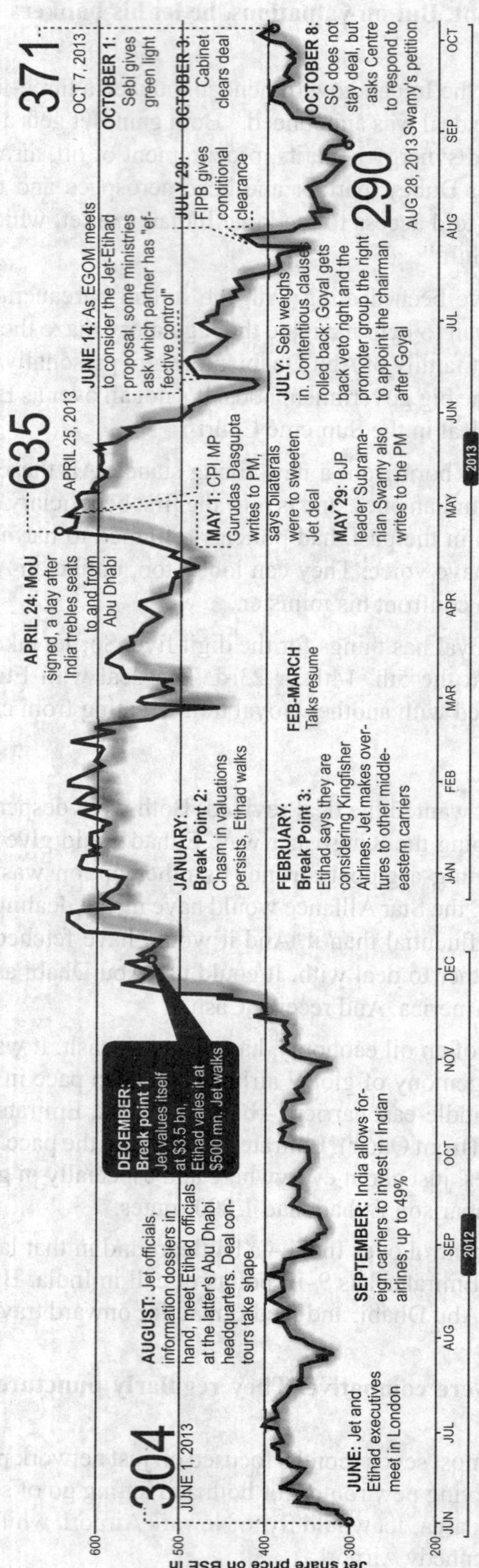

Fig.18.1. The Long Crawl to a Deal

It helped that Eithad and Jet both had about the same number of aircraft, which meant they could order replacements simultaneously to derive better value form aircraft manufactures—a saving of $200-300 million on an order of 100 planes. Jet and Etihad made sense for the other.

1 Deal

But they differed over valuation—$3.5 billion versus $500 million. Eventually, they found middle ground for a 24% stake sale in jet to Etihad: $1.5 billion, which was the amount the Jet management had, at the start of the talks, realistically calculated would be theirs.

The Jet Crew...

Naresh Goyal, Founder and Chairman: He sat on the deal table only when James Hogan was on the side. Off it, he was everywhere–in government corridors, in offices of airport operators, meeting people of influence in Abu Dhabi...

Hameed Ali Chief Operating Officer: A pilot by training, the unflappable Bahrain national has Goyal's ear, and he ensured that telephone lines were crackling even when talks broke down.

Raj Sivkumar Senior Vice-President, Alliances and Planning: Provided inputs on two key facets–route network and revenues. Before joining jet in 2007, he spent 15 years at United Airlines.

KG Vishwanath Head of Commercial Strategy: Joined Jet in 1998 as a trainee and rose to handle MIS, treasury, financ, strategy and investor relations. Left Jet last month.

Investment Bankers: Credit Suisse team, led India head Mickey Doshi; Bank of America Merrill Lynch team, led by India head Kaku Nakhate.

And the Etihad Crew

James Hogan President and CEO: The aggressive Aussie has shepherded Etihad since 2006. Jet is his fifth equity alliance with an international airline, and Hogan led from the front straight-talking, challenging, rebuking...

James Rigney Chief Financial Officer: Hogan's right-hand man played a critical role in valuing the deal to the satisfaction of Etihad's promoters, its partners and jet.

Sheikh Hamed Bin Zayed Al-Nahyan Chairman of the Board: A member of the ruling family of Abu Dhabi, he stayed in the shadows, but let the cat among the pigeons in February when he hinted at a revision in deal terms.

Investment Bankers: PricewaterhouseCoopers team from UK, led by Ken Walsh partner-Pwc (UK) airlines M and A.

SUMMARY

Negotiation Process: (*i*) Planning (*ii*) Relationship building (*iii*) Exchange of information (*iv*) Persuasion (*v*) Concessions (*vi*) Agreement

Behaviour and Tactics of Negotiation: (*i*) Verbal behaviour (*ii*) Non-verbal behaviour (*iii*) Dirty taction (*iv*) Extreme behaviour

Approaches to Negotiations: (*i*) competitive approach (*ii*) Problem solving approach.

TEST QUESTIONS

1. Explain the steps involved in the process of international business negotiation.
2. Discuss the verbal and nonverbal behaviour of international negotiators.
3. Describe the dirty ticks and extreme tactics used in international negotiations. How will you counter such tactics and tricks.
4. Explain the alternative approaches to international business negotiations. Which approach is better and why?
5. How does culture influence international business negotiations? Explain giving suitable examples.

UNIT – V

19. Strategic Alliances, Mergers and Acquisitions
20. Foreign Trade Promotion
21. Indian Joint Ventures Abroad
22. Financing of Foreign Trade and Payment Terms
23. Recent Developments and Issues in International Business

CHAPTER

19 Strategic Alliances, Mergers and Acquisitions

LEARNING OBJECTIVES

After studying this chapter, you should understand:

19.1 Meaning of Global Strategic Alliance
19.2 Types of Strategic Alliances
19.3 Advantages of Strategic Alliances
19.4 Disadvantages of Strategic Alliances
19.5 Making Strategic Alliances Successful
19.6 Concepts of Cross-Border Mergers and Acquisitions
19.7 Advantages/Motives of Mergers and Acquisitions
19.8 Disadvantages of Mergers and Acquisitions

- Summary
- Test Questions

As stated earlier, there are several modes of entry into international business. Global strategic alliances, cross-border mergers and acquisitions are some of these modes.

19.1 Meaning of Global Strategic Alliance

Strategic alliance refers to a cooperative agreement between two or more firms for achieving some specific objective. It is a collaboration or coalition wherein two or more firms share their capabilities to enhance their competitive strength without losing their respective autonomy. The collaborative arrangement may be between

(*a*) a manufacturer and its supplier to minimise inventory (JIT)

(*b*) between competing firms as a strategy to reinforce their strengths

(*c*) between non-competitors with complementary strengths, e.g., between a clinic and a testing laboratory.

A global or international strategic alliance is an alliance between two or more firms of different countries to either develop a global market presence (global reach alliance) or to enhance their global competitive strength (global leverage alliance). For example, Tata Tea had entered into an alliance with Tetley to take advantage of Tetley's expertise in marketing tea abroad. Later on, Tata Tea acquired Tetley.

Thus, a global strategic alliance is both an entry strategy as well as a competitive strategy.

In international business, strategic alliance is becoming increasingly popular. As competition is increasing, competing firms form alliances to enhance their long term competitive advantage. Leveraging critical capabilities, increasing flexibility in responding to technological and market changes, increasing the flow of innovation, avoiding unnecessary fragmentation of resources and duplication of investment, increasing productivity and profitability, etc. are other objectives of strategic alliances.

Sometimes, global strategic alliance is used as a strategy to enter foreign markets. For instance, an Indian firm may form a strategic alliance with a US firm to use its sales promotion and distribution network to sell its products in the USA.

Strategic alliances are common in pharmaceuticals, computers, telematics and such other industries characterised by high fixed costs in R & D and fast changing technology. Firms in mature and slow-growth industries form strategic alliances for their survival. Global strategic alliances are also seen in the service sector such as between airlines and hotels, tour operators and airlines, accounting and consulting firms, investment banks, construction firms, etc. Globalisation has given a boost to global strategic alliances.

Strategic alliances are not a recent phenomenon. However, the variety and number of strategic alliances have increased rapidly. In a global alliance two or more firms from different countries share their capabilities with a view to enhance their competitive advantages and/or creating new business while retaining their respective strategic autonomies. It is called a strategic alliance because the sharing of capabilities improves long term competitiveness and involves long term commitment of resources. A global strategic alliance may be formed to gain entry into a foreign market or to gain access to resources in a foreign country.

19.2 Types of Strategic Alliances

Strategic alliances differ both according to their purpose and structure.

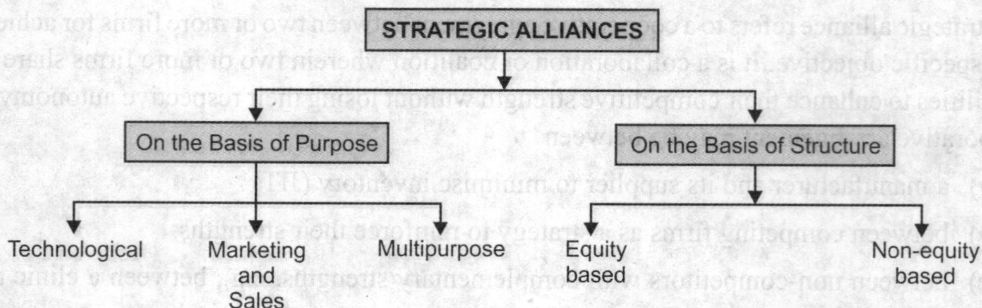

1. **Technological Alliances:** These alliances include R & D consortium, simultaneous engineering agreements, licensing and joint development programmes. For example Ranbaxy Laboratories has a strategic alliance with Glaxo Smithkline (GSK) for R & D.
2. **Marketing and Sales Alliances:** Under such an alliance a company makes use of the marketing infrastructure of another company abroad for selling its products in the foreign market. This may enable the firm to easily penetrate the foreign market and to

preempt its potential competitors. For example, Xerox of the USA and Fuji of Japan joined hands to explore new markets in Europe and in Pacific Rim countries.

3. **Multipurpose Alliances:** A multipurpose alliance is a combination of technological and marketing alliances. A marketing alliance is often a single country alliance because a global firm takes on different allies in each country. But technological and operational alliances are usually multicountry alliances because such activities can be employed over several countries.

4. **Equity Alliances:** In an equity alliance, two or more firms share ownership of a venture by contributing to its equity capital. The alliance may result in the setting up of a joint venture or a merger/acquisition.

   (*a*) An **international joint venture** is a new firm established jointly by two or more firms belonging to different countries. It is a separate legal entity with its own board of directors. It is formed when the firms contributing to its equity want a long term business relationship. For example, Maruti of India and Suzuki of Japan formed a joint venture Maruti Udyog which lasted for about 25 years.

   (*b*) An **international merger** is an amalgamation of two or more firms belonging to different countries. None of the old firms exists after the merger.

   (*c*) In **international** acquisition, one firm buys out another firm in a foreign country. The acquired firm no longer exists and the acquiring firm continues with larger resources. For example, Tata Steel of India acquired Corus Group of UK/Netherlands for $9.5 billion.

   Fig. 19.1 illustrates joint venture, merger and acquisition.

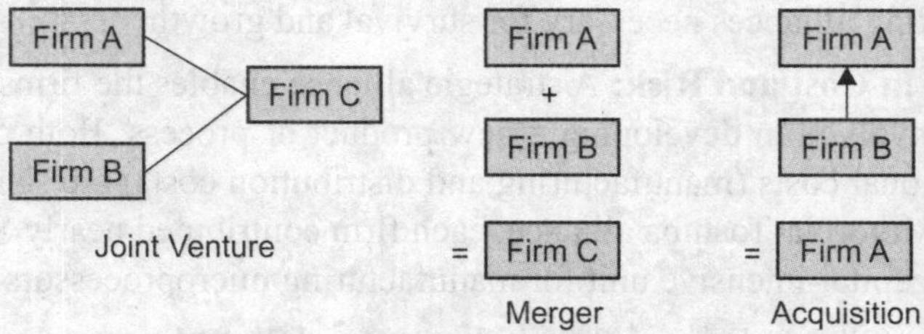

Fig. 19.1: Joint Venture, Merger and Acquisition

5. **Non-Equity Alliances:** A non-equity alliance is an arrangement which is of mutual convenience to both the parties. No new firm is formed and no new equity investment is made by either party. The two parties share the responsibility and profits of the alliance as per the contract. There are several forms of non-equity alliances such as co-production agreement, co-service agreement, co-marketing agreement, co-management agreement, technology transfer agreement, resources renting agreement, cooperative bidding agreement, long term support agreement, etc. Doz and Hamel[1] describe three broad types of strategic alliances as under:

   1. **Cooptions or Coalitions:** These are alliances of competitors, suppliers and distributors in the same industry. The alliance partners pool together their capabilities with a view to span world markets or to establish a common standard. STAR in the airlines industry is an example of coalitions.

1. Yves L. Doz and Gary Hamel, *Alliance Advantage,* Harvard Business School Press, Boston-MA, 1998

2. **Co-Specialisations:** These are alliances of firms which combine their unique but complementary capabilities to create a business or to develop a new product or technology. Each partner contributes a unique resource, competency or asset. Airbus in the aero-space industry is an example of co-specialisations.
3. **Learning Alliances:** These alliances are formed for transfer of know-how between the partners. For example, Toyota of Japan and Gernal Motors of USA formed alliance called the NUMMI project. In this alliance the basic purpose of GM was to learn 'lean manufacturing' and that of Toyota was to learn how to operate in a highly unionised environment in North America.

19.3 Advantages of Strategic Alliances

The main advantages/motives of strategic alliances are as follows:

1. **Easy Market Entry:** Strategic alliance with a local firm facilitates market entry in those countries where entry of foreign firms is difficult due to government regulations or other conditions. For example, Motorola faced difficulty in entering the cellular phone market in Japan, allegedly due to formal and informal trade barriers. Then Motorola made an alliance with Toshiba to build microprocessors. Toshiba provided marketing assistance and Motorola could enter the Japanese market.
2. **Competitive Advantage:** Alliances are not only an entry strategy but also offer a competitive advantage. Productivity and profitability of resources can be increased through strategic alliances. Globalisation and increasing competition in global markets, etc are making alliances necessary for survival and growth.
3. **Reduction in Cost and Risk:** A strategic alliance enables the firms to share the costs and risks involved in developing a new product or process. Both development costs and operational costs (manufacturing and distribution costs) are shared. For example, in case of Motorola-Toshiba alliance, each firm contributed nearly $1 billion to set up the highly capital-intensive unit for manufacturing microprocessors.
4. **Sharing Knowledge:** Firms with complementary skills and resources can form a strategic alliance to develop something which none of them alone could develop. For example, in the alliance between Microsoft and Toshiba, Microsoft contributed system skills and Toshiba provided manufacturing skills. As a result, they could develop embedded microprocessors which perform entertainment functions in an automobile.
5. **Synergy:** A strategic alliance offers benefits of synergy. Hugh-tech firms can form alliances to set the industry standards. These standards help to reduce R & D costs benefiting all the firms in an industry.

19.4 Disadvantages of Strategic Alliances

Strategic alliances suffer from some drawbacks:

1. **Goal Conflict:** The goals and working style of partners in an alliance may be incompatible. For example, one firm may focus on engineering while the other firm emphasises finances. Such incompatibility may arise due to differences in national cultures, corporate goals, personal values of partners.

2. **Loss of Control:** After entering into a strategic alliance, a firm may realise that it has lost control over its core competency. It may have given its competitor a low-cost route to new technology or market. As a result, the firm may lose its competitive advantage in the global marketplace.
3. **Lack of Trust:** In case there is lack of trust and openness between the partners, an alliance is likely to fail. A firm may refuse to share key information relating to its operations. This will cause misunderstanding among the partners and the alliance may not be successful.
4. **Change in Conditions:** The alliance may no longer serve the interests of partners due to changes in business environment. For example, an alliance formed to overcome trade barriers may be of no advantage when the barriers are removed.

19.5 Making Strategic Alliances Successful

Most strategic alliances fail due to various reasons. Success in a strategic alliance requires care and caution on the following aspects:

1. **Strategic Context and Value:** First of all, it is necessary to understand thoroughly the industry drivers and competitive forces that shape the current position and challenges of alliance partners. The scope and strategic objectives of the alliance and the potential benefits to the partners need to be defined clearly.
2. **Selection of Partners:** There should be a fit between partners in terms of strategy, structure, capabilities and culture. **Strategic fit** means the degree of compatibility among the partners. Answers to questions such as: how important is the alliance for the partners? Do they need an alliance to achieve their objectives? can indicate the degree of strategic fit between the partners. **Structural fit** means compatibility – in terms of organisational structures, systems and procedures. It can be judged in terms of the degree of decentralisation of decision-making, degree of documentation of polices and rules, accounting and reporting systems and methods, degree of formalisation of decision-making, the type of incentives used to motivate staff. **Capabilities fit** refers to the capabilities which the partners can contribute to the alliance. It is necessary to determine the competencies and resources needed in the alliance. Then the specific contribution needed from each partner is decided. Any potential gap needs to be filled to make the alliance effective. **Cultural fit** requires assessment of differences in national and corporate cultures of partners, anticipating possible consequences of these differences and taking steps to prevent any negative effects.

   According to Hamal et. al[1] an alliance will be beneficial when:

   (*a*) The strategic goals of partners converge while their competitive goals diverge;

   (*b*) The size and market power of both the partners is modest compared with industry leaders.

   (*c*) Each partner believes it can learn from the other and at the same time limit access to proprietary skills.

   There must exist mutual understanding and trust between the partners.

1. Gary Hamel, Yves L. Doz and C.K. Prahalad, "Collaborate with Your Competitors and Win," *Havard business Review*, Jan-Feb. 1989, pp. 133-35

3. **Negotiation and Design:** The organisational design and the operating system of the alliance are decided by the partners. The alliance should be so structured that the interests of both the firms are taken care. The agreement should provide for swap of knowledge, technology and resources to the extent acceptable to the firms. No opportunism should be allowed to any partner and there must be safeguards for proprietary information. It is necessary for the partners to agree on the legal structure, decision-making mechanisms, degree of task integration, reporting and communication process, sharing of gains and conflict resolution mechanisms.

4. **Implementation:** The final stage in the management of an alliance is implementation which involves integration, cooperation, and learning. Integration and cooperation refer to constitution of teams and working together to perform the tasks. Learning can be **co-learning** (partners learn within the alliance) and **captured learning** (partners learn from each other). Partners in an alliance can learn about the business—the tasks, expectations and capabilities of each other.

Table 19.1: Criteria For Successful Alliances

• Individual excellence	Both partners are strong; have something to contribute; have positive intent
• Importance	Fits strategy of both partners; long term view
• Interdependence	Partners need each other; complementary capabilities; no-body can go it alone
• Investment	Partner shows commitment; Investment/ re-investment
• Information	Reasonable open communication; sharing of operational information
• Integration	Shared operating procedures; numerous connections; teachers/ learners
• Institutionalisation	Clear responsibilities; clear decision processes
• Integrity	No abuse; willingness to enhance trust

Source: Moss Kanter Rosabeth, "Collaborative Advantage," *Havard Business Review*, July-August 1994, pp. 96-108.

19.6 Cross-border Mergers and Acquisitions

Mergers and Acquisitions (M & A) may be domestic or global. In a domestic merger or acquisition both the firms belong to the same country while in a global one they belong to different countries.

In a cross-border **merger**, a domestic firm and a foreign firm combine together to establish a new firm. The combining firms no longer exist after the merger. On the other hand, in a cross-border **acquisition,** a domestic firm buys a foreign firm and becomes bigger. The bought out firm no longer exists as a separate legal entity but the acquiring firm exists with a larger size. For example, Coca-cola entered the Indian market by acquiring Parle.

Quite often the terms 'merger', 'acquisition' and 'takeover' are used interchangeably.

M & As: Will 2013 be Different?

Among the 18 cross-border M & A deals with an investment value of above $1 billion undertaken by Indian companies during 2005-11, 13 were in developed countries. A look at some of the largest deals...

Largest Cross-Border M & As by Indian TNCs, 2005-12

Year	Acquiring co	Target company	Value ($ billion)
2007	Tata Steel UK	Corus Group PLC	11.791
2010	Bharti Airtel	Zain Africa BV	10.700
2007	LV Aluminium	Novelis	5.789
2010	Investor Group	Venezuela-Carabobo	4.848
2010	Adani Mining	Linc Energy (Australia)	2.740
2008	Investor Group	Sabiha Gokcen International	2.656
2008	Jerpeno (OVL arm)	Imperial Energy Corp PLC (UK)	2.608
2008	Tata Motors	Jaguar Cars (US)	2.300
2011	Mundra Port & SEZ	Abbot Point Coal Terminal	1.951
2005	Ratnagiri G&P	Dabhol Power Co	1.939

Source: World Investment Report 2013, Unctad

However, the impact of the financial crisis became evident after 2011, when the total value of cross-border M&As undertaken by Indian companies dropped by nearly three-fifths in 2012 to about $2.6 billion.

Cross-border M&As, have been a very important market entry strategy as well as expansion strategy. A major part of the recent foreign direct investment has been cross-border M&As. During 1980-2000, the value of cross-border M&As grew at an average annual rate of more them 40 per cent. M&As continue to be a power driver of globalisation and foreign investment. Several industries such as automobiles, pharmaceuticals, banking, telecom, etc. have undergone global restructuring due to cross-border M&As. Economic liberalisation and deregulation have given a fillip to cross-border M&As. both in developed and developing countries.

Indian companies are increasingly acquiring foreign firms. Tata Group acquired Tetley and Corus and Birla Group acquired Novelis and Madura Coats. There have been several other acquisitions by Indian firms in Europe, USA, Africa and other parts of the world.

19.7 Motives/advantages of Cross-border M & As

1. **Entry into Foreign Markets:** A common strategy used to enter foreign markets involves M & As. For example, the L.N. Mittal group became a global firm by acquiring steel mills in several countries. Acquisitions help to overcome regulatory hassles abroad.
2. **Economies of Scale:** M & As have been used as an expansion strategy. Expansion offers economies of large size.
3. **Competitive Advantage:** Cross-border M & As help a firm to increase its market share and consolidate its competitive strength in the global marketplace. M & As have also been used to pre-empt competition.

4. **Marketing Network:** Marketing infrastructure is one of the most difficult areas in international business. M & As enable a firm to obtain a distribution network abroad. For example, the acquisition of Wiltshire Brewery enabled the United Breweries to gain access to a readymade chain of pubs throughout England. Asian Paints gained access to eleven markets in China, South East Asia, Middle East and Africa by acquiring Berger International based in Singapore.
5. **Diversification:** Through M & As a company can enter new businesses and thereby diversify. Backward and forward integration can also be achieved through M & As.
6. **Access to Technology:** M & A can provide access to foreign technology and R & D facilities. Essar Steel gained access to downstream steel technology by acquiring Ilva Laminati Piarri of Italy.
7. **Optimum Utilisation of Resources:** The desire to make use of surplus funds, plant capacity, managerial expertise and other facilities also leads to M & As. The merger of Brooke Bond and Lipton eliminated unhealthy competition and duplication of resources. In the pharmaceutical industry, the need to fill gaps in the product mix has resulted in M & As.
8. **Brand Power:** It is very difficult for a new company to build global brands. Acquisition of foreign firms is an easy way to building such brands. For example, Coca-Cola acquired the popular Thumps Up brand of soft brink by taking over Parle Drinks.
9. **Risk Reduction:** Acquisitions are less risky than greenfield ventures because revenue flows and assets are known.
10. **Logistics:** M & As can help a firm to improve its logistical strength. For example, Tata Steel got logistical advantage by acquiring Singapore based Natsteel.

19.8 Disadvantages of cross-border M & As

Cross-border M & As suffer from some drawbacks.

1. When a foreign firm is taken over, its problems and weaknesses are also taken over.
2. Indiscriminate acquisitions can lead to financial and other problems for the acquiring company.
3. Too high a price may be paid in case acquisition was hasty and adequate assessment was not done.
4. Acquired firm may suffer from old plant, obsolete technology, demoralised labour, militant unions.
5. The acquiring company may lack the expertise and experience required for successful management of the acquired firm.
6. Acquiring a foreign firm is a difficult and complex task involving bankers, lawyers, regulations, etc. Sometimes, the host country may impose restrictions on such acquisitions.

SUMMARY

Meaning of Strategic Alliance: A global strategic alliance is a cooperative agreement between firms of different countries to achieve mutually beneficial goals.

Types of Strategic Alliances: (*i*) Technological (*ii*) Marketing, sales and service (*iii*) Multipurpose (*iv*) Equity based (*v*) Non-equity based (*vi*) Cooption or coalition (*vii*) Specialisation (*viii*) Learning

Advantages of Strategic Alliances: (*i*) Easy market entry (*ii*) Competitive advantage (*iii*) Cost and risk reduction (*iv*) Knowledge sharing (*v*) Synergy

Disadvantages of Strategic Alliances: (*i*) Goal conflict (*ii*) Loss of control (*iii*) Lack of trust (*iv*) Change in conditions

Making Alliances Successful: (*i*) Strategic context and value (*ii*) Selection of partners – strategic, structural, capabilities and cultural fit (*iii*) Negotiation and design (*iv*) Implementation

Cross-Border Mergers and Acquisitions: In a cross-border merger firms of different countries combine together. In an acquisition a domestic firm takes over a foreign firm.

Advantages of M & As: (*i*) Foreign market entry (*ii*) Competitive advantage (*iii*) Marketing network (*iv*) Diversification (*v*) Economies of Scale (*vi*) Foreign technology (*vii*) Optimum use of resources (*viii*) Brand building (*ix*) Risk reduction (*x*) Logistics.

Disadvantages of M & As: (*i*) Problems of acquired firm (*ii*) Foreign technology (*iii*) Heavy cost (*iv*) Obsolete technology (*v*) Problem in management and control (*vi*) Acquisition a complex task.

TEST QUESTIONS

1. What do you understand by global strategic alliances? State their advantages and disadvantages.
2. Explain different types of strategic alliances.
3. "The rate of failure of strategic alliances is quite high". How will you ensure success in a strategic alliance?
4. What is meant by cross-border mergers and acquisitions (M & As)? Describe their advantages and disadvantages.
5. "Mergers and acquisitions have become a major form of foreign direct investment". Explain.
6. "Mergers and acquisitions have been used as a market entry strategy as well as an expansion strategy by international firms". Elucidate.
7. Distinguish between
   (*a*) Equity and Non-equity alliances
   (*b*) Coalitions and Co-specialisations
8. Write notes on:
   (*a*) Criteria for successful alliances
   (*b*) Selection of partner for a strategic alliance
9. Write a brief essay on the unique features of Japanese management and culture and also identify the factors to be kept in view while conducting business negotiations with Japanese partners. Illustrate your answer with suitable examples.
10. "Strategic Alliances should be strictly seen as a means to an end and not the end in itself." Comment on the above statement and explain the different types of strategic alliances. Also discuss the various challenges to be faced for successfully implementing such alliances.

CHAPTER

20 Foreign Trade Promotion

LEARNING OBJECTIVES

After studying this chapter, you should understand:

20.1 Measures for Export Promotion
20.2 Organisations for Export Promotion
20.3 Special Economic Zones (SEZs)
20.4 Export-Oriented Units (EOUs)

- Summary
- Test Questions

Export promotion occupies a significant place in India's economic policy because exports provide several benefits such as foreign exchange earning, more employment, increase in GDP, better utilisation of the country's resources, etc. Government of India has, therefore, offered several facilities and incentives to exporters.

20.1 Measures for export promotion

Export promotion measures can be classified into the following categories:

1. Import Facilitation Schemes
2. Export Incentives
3. Export Houses
4. Production Assistance
5. Marketing Assistance.

20.1.1 Import Facilitation Schemes

The purpose of these schemes is to improve export competitiveness of Indian firms by assisting in the imports of inputs and capital equipments at low cost. There are two separate schemes for imports of capital goods and imports of inputs.

1. **Exports Promotion of Capital Goods (EPCG) Scheme:** This scheme allows import of capital goods, including computer software, at 5 per cent customs duty. The importer is required to export eight times the duty saved over a period of eight years. In case the duty saved is ₹ 100 crore or more, the export obligation can be completed in twelve

years. The aim of the EPCG scheme is to enable exporters create and upgrade their production facilities at lower cost.

2. **Advance Authorisation:** An advance authorisation is issued to allow duty-free import of inputs which form part of the product to be exported. It is issued on the basis of inputs and export items given under standard input-output norms. Advance authorisations are of three types:

   (*a*) Advance authorisation for physical exports is issued for the import of inputs needed for manufacturing exports.

   (*b*) Advance authorisation for intermediate supplies is granted to a manufacturer for the import of inputs needed for manufacture of goods to be supplied to the ultimate exporter holding an advance licence. In order to ensure that total advance authorisations do not exceed the eligible limit, the ultimate exporter is required to surrender his advance licence for physical exports to the extent of this authorisation.

   (*c*) Advance authorisation for deemed exports is granted to the manufacturer-exporter for import of inputs needed for manufacture of goods for deemed exports.

   Licences issued under this scheme can be used only by the licence holder. The authorisation or the materials/supplies imported cannot be transferred to a third party.

20.1.2 Export Incentives

1. **Duty Drawback:** A manufacturer of exported goods might have paid two types of duties: (*a*) import duties on imported raw materials and components; and (*b*) excise duty on the goods manufactured in India.

   These duties are refunded to the exporter on the completion of exports. There are two rates for duty drawback – all-industry rate, and brand rate. All-industry rate is applied to all exporters alike. The brand rate is applicable only to particular manufacturers. The brand rate is fixed when the exporter submits the required information to the authorities. The brand rate is fixed in the absence of all-industry rate or when the rate of drawback is less than 80 per cent of the duty paid.

   In order to claim the drawbuck, the exporter must file three copies of the shipping bill within 60 days of receiving the 'Let Export' order. The drawback is remitted to the exporter's bank account on a fortnightly basis.

2. **Excise Rebate:** Under this scheme, finished goods meant for home consumption are exempt from the excise duty when they are exported. The exporter can avail of this facility in either of the following ways:

   ***(a)* Export under Bond:** In this method, the exporter has to execute a bond in favour of the Central Excise authorities.

   The amount of the bond will be equal to the estimated duty. The exporter need not pay excise duty.

   ***(b)* Refund of Duty:** In case the exporter has already paid the duty, he can file a claim for refund after making exports. The excise duty is refunded after verification of the claim.

3. **Duty Entitlement Pass Book (DEPB):** The aim of this scheme is to neutralise the customs duty paid on the import content of the export product by way of grant of credit to the exporter. The exporter can claim credit as a specified percentage of FOB value of exports of specified commodities made in freely convertible currency. The exporter can use the credit so earned to import any freely importable commodity without payment of customs duty. DEPB is granted against exports already made and is valid for two years. The DEPB and/or the items imported against it are freely transferable.
4. **Duty-Free Replenishment Certificate (DFRC):** Under this scheme, an exporter is allowed to import inputs without payment of customs duty. The certificate is issued against exports already made. It is valid for two years. DFRC and the materials imported against it are freely transferable. This scheme has been withdrawn from May 2006.
5. **Duty-Free Import Authorisation:** This scheme was introduced in May 2006 and it combines the features of advance authorisation and DFRC schemes. The scheme permits duty-free imports of required inputs before the exports. The exporter can transfer the scrip after completing the export obligations. The authorisation is issued on the basis of inputs and export items given under standard input-output norms. It is issued for physical exports, intermediary supplies and deemed exports. The export obligation is to be completed within two years with a minimum value addition of twenty per cent.
6. **Served from India Scheme:** This scheme seeks to accelerate the exports of services and to create a unique and powerful 'Served From India' brand which is recognised and respected throughout the world. All service providers with a total foreign exchange earnings of ₹10 lac or more (₹5 lac in case of an individual) in the current or preceding financial year are eligible for a duty credit as a percentage of foreign exchange earnings. The exporter can use duty credit entitlement for import of any capital goods which are a part of his main line of business.
7. **Vishesh Krishi and Gram Udyog Yojana:** The objective of this scheme is to promote exports of agricultural items and village industry products. Exporters of these products are entitled for duty credit-scrip equal to 5 per cent of the FOB value of exports. The scrip and the items imported against it are freely transferable. The duty credit can be used for import of inputs and capital goods which are freely importable.
8. **Focus Product Scheme:** Under this scheme, incentives are given to exporters of products having high employment potential in rural and semi-arban areas. A duty credit facility at 2.5 per cent of the FOB value of 50 per cent exports on notified products is allowed. The scrip and the items imported under it are freely transferable.
9. **Focus Market Scheme:** The objective of this scheme is to facilitate penetration of strategic markets in which Indian exports are comparatively low. In order to enhance Indian's export competitiveness in such markets, the high freight cost and other constraints are offset. The scheme allows duty credit facility at 2.5 per cent of the FOB value of all exports to the notified countries. The duty credit may be used for imports of inputs and capital goods. The scrip and the items imported under it are freely transferable.

An exporter has the choice of availing any one of the schemes given at 7 to 9.

10. **High-tech Product Export Promotion Scheme:** Under this scheme export of notified high-tech products through EDI enabled ports to all countries are entitled for duty credit scrip equal to 10 per cent of incremental growth in exports of notified products. The total scrip for an exporter shall not exceed ₹ 15 crore.

    The enttlement excludes the following:

    (*a*) exports of imported goods;

    (*b*) exports originating in third country but transhipped through India;

    (*c*) exports of SEZ units or SEZ products exported through DTA units; and

    (*d*) deemed exports.

11. **Cash Compensatory Support (CCS):** It is a cash subsidy scheme to compensate exporters for indirect taxes and to provide funds for product/market development. The scheme enabled exporters to reduce price or to increase profits. The scheme was withdrawn with the devaluation of the rupee in July 1991.

12. **Export Awards:** Several awards have been instituted to recognise excellence in exports and to encourage exporters. There are separate awards for different categories of exporters. These awards are given on the basis of specified criteria such as development of new markets, introduction of new products, substantial increase in exports, etc.

20.1.3 Export Houses

An export house is a registered exporter who fulfills the prescribed criteria. It is entitled to certain facilities and incentives. Established exporters are recognised as export houses of different grades. An exporter is categorised on the basis of total FOB exports during current year plus previous three years. On the basis of the export performance, there are five categories of export houses.

Status Category	Export Performance (₹ crore)
Export House (EH)	15
Star Export House (SEH)	100
Trading House (TH)	500
Stat Trading House (STH)	1500
Premier Trading House (PTH)	5000

A status holder is eligible for the following facilities:

(*i*) authorisation and customs clearances for both imports and exports on self-declaration basis.

(*ii*) fixation of input-output norms on priority within 60 days.

(*iii*) exemption from compulsory negotiation of documents through banks.

(*iv*) 100 per cent retention of foreign exchange in EEFC account

(*v*) extension of normal repatriation period from 180 days to 360 days

(*vi*) exemption from providing bank guarantee.

(*vii*) permission to establish export warehouses.

20.1.4 Production Assistance

The Government of India has taken several measures to enlarge and strengthen the production base, to improve quality of products and make products price competitive in the international markets. Some of these measures and facilities are given below:

(*i*) Export Processing Zones have been set up to provide a duty-free environment for production at low cost.

(*ii*) The Export Oriented Units (EOUs) are eligible for several incentives.

(*iii*) Making raw materials and other inputs of good quality at reasonable prices.

(*iv*) Facilities to set up, modernise and expand production capacity for exports.

(*v*) Provision of infrastructure for the growth of export-oriented industries.

(*vi*) Duty-free imports of capital goods and raw materials for export production.

(*vii*) Establishment of Software Technology Parks to promote IT related exports.

(*viii*) Electronic Hardware Technology Parks were set up to encourage exports of electronics.

(*ix*) Setting up of Agriculture Economic Zones to promote exports of agro and agro-based products.

(*x*) Quality control and pre-shipment inspection to improve the quality of exports.

20.1.5 Marketing Assistance

1. **Market Development Assistance:** Under this scheme assistance is provided for market research, trade delegations, participation in trade fairs and exhibitions, setting up offices and branches abroad.
2. **Market Access Initiative:** This scheme is for undertaking promotion abroad on country product basis. The scheme has been widened to include activities considered necessary for focused market promotion efforts.
3. **Foreign Exchange:** Foreign exchange is provided for undertaking approved market development activities such as foreign travel for export promotion, advertising abroad, procuring samples and technical information from abroad, etc.
4. **Export Credit:** Steps have been taken to enhance adequate and timely credit for export at low interest rates. Commercial banks provide pre-shipment and post-shipment credit. The Reserve Bank of India refinances such credit.
5. **India Brand Equity Fund:** Government of India established this fund to promote the made-in-India image abroad.
6. **Brand Acquisition Fund:** This fund was set up to help exporters to acquire global brands and build them as Indian brands in international markets.
7. **Export Credit Insurance:** The Export Credit Guarantee Corporation (ECGC) covers political and commercial risks of exporters.

20.2 Organisations for Export Promotion

Government of India has established or sponsored several organisations to assist exporters. These organisations may be classified as follows:

1. Advisory Bodies
2. Promotional Organisations
3. Service Institutions

20.2.1 Advisory Bodies

Advisory bodies have been set up to advise government in formulating foreign trade policy and matters relating thereto. The main advisory bodies are as under:

1. **Board of Trade:** This is a consultative and deliberative body set up to provide recommendations on:
   (*a*) policy measures for increasing exports;
   (*b*) industry-specific measures to improve exports;
   (*c*) streamlining the institutional framework for imports and exports;
   (*d*) rationalisation of policy measures and procedures for imports and exports; and
   (*e*) improving the international competitiveness of Indian goods and services.
2. **Export Promotion Board:** This board was set up in the Ministry of Commerce. Its main function is to coordinate the activities of different authorities for the effective execution of export related matters.
3. **Director General of Anti-Dumping and Allied Duties (DGAD):** This Directorate was constituted in April 1988 for carrying out investigations and to recommend the amount of anti-dumping duty/countervailing duty on the identified articles which would be adequate to check injury to the domestic industry.
4. **Director General of Foreign Trade (DGFT):** The **DGFT** is responsible for the execution of the export-import policy of the Government.
5. **Central Advisory Council on Trade:** This council advises the Government on matters relating to:
   (*a*) export and import policies
   (*b*) operation of import and export controls
   (*c*) organisation and development of commercial services.

20.2.2 Promotional Organisations

1. **Export Promotion Councils:** These are non-profit organisations set up under the Companies Act with a view to prevent exports of specific commodities. Their main function is to promote the interests of member exporters and serve as a link between the Government and the exporters. Export incentives are available to only those

exporters who are members of these councils. These councils provide a platform where exporters can discuss their problems. They assist exporters through publicity, trade fairs and exhibitions. They also convey the problems and suggestions of exporters to the Government.

Export promotion councils may also take up the following functions:

(*a*) arranging supplies of raw materials;

(*b*) compiling and disseminating information;

(*c*) securing assistance under Marketing Development Assistance Scheme;

(*d*) advising members;

(*e*) locating suppliers for imports; and

(*f*) arranging exploration tours in India for foreign suppliers.

2. **Commodity Boards:** These boards have been set up for important commodities (e.g., coffee, jute, tea, rubber, coir, spices, etc.) to guide their production and exports. Unlike export promotion councils, commodity boards are statutory bodies established under Acts of Parliament. Commodity boards deal with all problems relating to the commodities. They conduct market surveys, sponsor trade delegations, provide information and participate in trade fairs and exhibitions.

3. **Development Authorities:** Marine Products Export Development Authority (MPEDA) and Agricultural and Processed Food Products Development Authority (APEDA) have been set up to function as export promotion councils. These authorities work for the production, development and export promotion of the commodities concerned.

20.2.3 Service Institutions

Specialised institutions have been set up to provide services like market research, publicity, quality control, packaging, etc to exporters. These service institutions are as follows:

1. **Indian Institute of Foreign Trade (IIFT):** This institute was established in 1963 at New Delhi under the Societies Registration Act. The institute is now a deemed university.

   The main functions of IIFT are as follows:

   (*a*) Training of personnel in modern techniques of international trade.

   (*b*) Sponsoring suitable personnel for training abroad in export management.

   (*c*) Organising and sponsoring marketing research in india and abroad.

   (*d*) Undertaking commodity studies to identify their export potential and for development

   (*e*) Providing consultancy in foreign trade.

   (*f*) Dissemination of information through its publications.

2. **Indian Institute of Packaging (IIP):** This institute was set up under the Societies Registration Act. Its main function is to create consciousness among exporters about packaging. It undertakes research on raw materials used in packaging so as to improve packaging standards. It keeps track of the international developments in packaging and informs exporters. It also organises training programmes on packaging and provides consultancy to exporters.

3. **India Trade Promotion Organisation (ITPO):** The ITPO was formed by merging together the erstwhile Trade Development Authority of India (TDAI) and Trade Fair Authority of India (TFAI) in 1992. It is the nodal agency for promoting India's foreign trade. Its main functions are as under:
   (*a*) develop and promote exports, imports and technology through trade fairs in India and abroad;
   (*b*) organise visit of foreign buyers and trade delegations to promote trade contracts;
   (*c*) undertake publicity through print and electronic media;
   (*d*) compile and disseminate trade related information; and
   (*e*) organize export development programmes, buyer-seller meets and assist in trade development.
4. **Federation of Indian Export Organisations (FIEO):** The FIEO was established in 1965 at New Delhi. It is an apex body and serves as a common coordinating forum for export promotion councils, commodity boards, service institutions, etc. It also acts as the primary servicing agency for providing integrated assistance to recognised export houses.
5. **Export Inspection Council (EIC):** The Export (Quality Control) Inspection Act 1963 provides for compulsory pre-shipment inspection of specified goods exported from India. The EIC was established to coordinate inspection and certification of export products. It has set up laboratories and test houses for this purpose. The council is empowered to constitute specialised committees to investigate and advise on matters relating to quality control and pre-shipment inspection.
6. **Export Credit Guarantee Corporation (ECGC) of India:** The ECGC provides credit guarantee to exporters and their banks. It issues policies to cover commercial and political risks of exporters. The commercial risks arise out of the failure of foreign buyers to accept the exported goods or to pay for them. The political risks refer to the loss due to restrictions, imposed by the importing country's government or the Government of India, war, revolution civil disturbance, etc. Now ECGC also provides factoring services. To the banks ECGC provides guarantees against the failure of exporters to repay the export advances made to them.
7. **Indian Council of Arbitration (ICA):** The ICA was set up under the societies, Registration Act to promote arbitration as a means of settling commercial disputes and to popularise arbitration among importers and exporters.

20.3 Special Economic Zones (SEZs)

A special economic zone is a specifically delineated duty-free enclave which is deemed to be a foreign territory for the purposes of trade operations and duties and tariffs. Units in a SEZ may be set up for manufacture of goods or for rendering of services. Goods and services going into the SEZ area from the Domestic Tariff Area (DTA) are treated as deemed exports and goods coming from the DTA are treated as imports. Units located in a SEZ are allowed to import/procure from the DTA without payment of duty all types of goods and services, including capital goods, whether new or second-hand required by it for its activities or in connection therewith.

A SEZ can be established by a private party or a State Government or the Central Government or jointly by two or more of them. The main objectives of the SEZ scheme are to increase exports, encourage foreign investment and transfer of technology, generate employment, and promote economic development.

Benefits of SEZs: Units in a SEZ enjoy the following concessions and exemptions:

(*i*) They are exempted from **customs duty on imports.**

(*ii*) They are exempted from **customs duty on exports.**

(*iii*) Goods brought from DTA to SEZ are exempt from **central excise duty**.

(*iv*) **Duty drawback and** other benefits are admissible on goods or services from DTA to SEZ or services provided in a SEZ.

(*v*) Units in a SEZ are exempt from **income tax** on export income as under:

(*a*) **First five years:** 100% exemption

(*b*) **Next five years:** 50% exemption

(*c*) **Next five years:** 50% of the ploughed back export profit

(*vi*) Exemption from **service tax** on taxable services

(*vii*) Transactions made by a non-resident through the International Financial Services Centre are exempt from **Securities Transaction Tax.**

(*viii*) Goods meant to carry on the authorised operations are exempt from **Central Sales Tax.**

(*ix*) Apart from the fiscal benefits given above, units in a SEZ enjoy benefits of

(*a*) simplified procedures for development, operation and maintenance for setting up units and conducting business

(*b*) single window clearance for setting up of a SEZ and for setting up units in a SEZ

(*c*) single window clearance on matters relating to Central and State Governments.

(*d*) simplified compliance procedures and documentation with an emphasis on self certification.

Criticism of SEZs: The SEZ scheme has been criticised for several reasons:

(*i*) Public has protested against acquisition of agricultural land for SEZs and connection of separate islands within the country giving wide powers to private developers

(*ii*) SEZs violate the guiding principles of the Indian Constitution as these are exempt from Central and State regulations

(*iii*) Private developers who are not accountable to the public control a wide range of public services from water supply to disease control.

(*iv*) People in SEZs are denied the right to elect a local government.

(*v*) Labour employed in SEZs are denied several of their rights.

(*vi*) Industries in SEZs are exempt from environmental public hearing.

(*vii*) Electricity generating firms in SEZs may bypass the State Electricity Authorities.

(*viii*) There exists no mechanism for denotifying unsuccessful SEZs which leaves units located is these zones in a limbo and large areas of land locked in.

SUMMARY

Measures for Export Promotion: (*i*) Import facilitation schemes: EPCG scheme, Advance Authorisation, (*ii*) Export incentives: Duty drawback, Excise rebate, DEPB, DFRC, Duty-free import authorisation, Served from India scheme, Vishesh Krishi and Gram Udyog Yojana, Focus product scheme, Focus market scheme, High-tech product export promotion scheme, CCS, export awards (*iii*) Export houses – EH, SEH, TH, STH, PTH (*iv*) Production assistance (*v*) Marketing assistance: Market development assistance, Market access initiative, foreign exchange, export credit, India Based Equity Fund, Brand Acquisition Fund, Export Credit Insurance

Organisations for Export Promotion: (*i*) Advisory bodies – Board of Trade, Export Promotion Board, DGAD (2) Promotional organisations–EPCs, Commodity Boards, Development authorities (MPEDA, APEDA) (3) Service institutions — IIFT, IIP, ITPO, FIEO, EIC, ECGC, ICA

Special Economic Zones (SEZs): Specifically delineated duty-free enclaves deemed to be foreign territories for purposes of trade operations, duties and tariffs, Exemptions and concessions in duties and taxes, simplified procedures and single window clearance.

Criticised for acquisition of agricultural land, exploitation of labour and other people, too many powers to private developers, etc.

TEST QUESTIONS

1. Why export promotion is necessary? Explain the incentives available to exporters in India.
2. What are Expert Houses? Describe the facilities available to them.
3. Discuss the production assistance and marketing assistance provided to exporters.
4. Explain in brief the organisations which work for export promotion in India.
5. What are Special Economic Zones? Explain their benefits and criticism.
6. Write short notes on:
   (*a*) Duty Drawback
   (*b*) Cash Compensatory Support
   (*c*) Export Houses
   (*d*) Export Promotion Councils
   (*e*) Export Credit Guarantee Corporation
   (*f*) Special Economic Zones

CHAPTER

21

Indian Joint Ventures Abroad

LEARNING OBJECTIVES

After studying this Chapter, you should understand:

Joint ventures are one of important strategies of entering international markets.

21.1 Meaning of A Joint Venture

A joint venture is a firm jointly owned by two or more otherwise independent firms. Each participating firm shares ownership, control, profits and risk of the new venture. The contribution to the equity of the new venture may be in the form of cash or machinery or technology.

Joint venture is a long term arrangement and it is established in accordance with the host country's laws. The partners in a joint venture may be from the same country or from different countries. When the participating firms are from different countries, it is called an international or foreign joint venture. For example, Maruti Suzuki was a joint venture between Suzuki of Japan and Maruti Udyog of India. Similarly, Hero Honda Motors was a joint venture between Hero Motors of India and Honda Motors of Japan.

21.2 Advantages of Joint Ventures

As a mode of doing international business, joint ventures offer several benefits:

1. **Pooling of Resources:** A joint venture facilitates combination of local partner's knowledge of the host country's political system, culture, market conditions, etc. and the technical know-how, manufacturing expertise and capital of the foreign partner. Pooling of resources provides strength to the joint venture.

New Market	To take existing products to foreign markets	To diversify into a new business
Existing Market	To strengthen the existing business	To bring foreign products to local markets
	Existing products	**New products**

Fig 21.1: Motives for International Joint Venture Formation

Source: Paul W. Beamish *et. al.*, *International Management*, Irwin McGraw Hill, New York, 2000, p.116

2. **Risk Sharing:** A joint venture enables the participating firms to share the risks involved in setting up business in a foreign country. It also allows sharing of costs. In case the local partner has more influence on the host government's policies, the risk of government interference or nationalisation is reduced.
3. **Good Entry Strategy:** When the host country's government does not perimit complete ownership of a firm by foreign investors, joint venture is only feasible alternative.
4. **Foreign Support:** Where the local partner is the Government or a political influencial business house, the joint venture may obtain tax concessions, grants and othe types of government support.

21.3 Disadvantages of Joint Ventures

Joint ventures suffer from some drawbacks:

1. **Potential Competition:** After gaining experience of political system, market conditions and culture of the host country, the foreign partner may divorce the local partner and start its independent competing firm. Similarly, the local partner after getting foreign technology and manufacturing know-how may divorce the foreign partner and emerge as a competitor.
2. **Problem in Policy Execution:** The foreign firm may not be able to implement its global marketing and manufacturing policies in the joint venture due to opposition from the local firm or other reasons.
3. **Conflicts:** In a joint venture, conflicts among the participating firms may arise on issues of objectives, strategies and control. Prolonged conflicts ultimately lead to dissolution of the joint venture.
4. **Decline:** The participating firms may not sustain the initial interest and enthusiasm shown in the joint venture. For example, the foreign partner may depute incompetent managers to the joint venture leading to its ultimate decay.

Table 21.1: Joint Venture Checklist

1. Test the strategic logic.
   - Do you really need a partner? For how long? Does your partner?
   - How big is the payoff for both parties? How likely is success?
   - Is a joint venture the best option?
   - Do congruent performance measures exist?
2. Partnership and fit.
   - Does the partner share your objectives for the venture?
   - Does the partner have the necessary skills and resources? Will you get access to them?
   - Will you be compatible?
   - Can you arrange an "engagement period"?
   - Is there a comfort *versus* competence trade-off?
3. Shape and design.
   - Define the venture's scope of activity and its strategic freedom *vis-a-vis* its parents.
   - Lay out each parent's duties and payoffs to create a win-win situation. Ensure that there are comparable contributions over-time.
   - Establish the managerial role of each partner.
4. Doing the deal.
   - How much paperwork is enough? Trust *versus* legal considerations?
   - Agree on an endgame.
5. Making the venture work.
   - Give the venture continuing top management attention.
   - Manage cultural differences.
   - Watch out for inequities.
   - Be flexible.

Source: Paul W. Beamish, *et. al*, *International Management*, Irwin McGraw Hill, New York, 2000, p. 122.

Thus, joint ventures are useful for political, social, economic and technological reasons. These enable an international firm with limited resources to enter foreign markets than might be possible through wholly owned subsidiaries. The firm may retain control despite a minor shareholding. Equity ownership by local firm and public helps the joint venture get public support.

According to a model developed by Dr. S. Raghunath of IIM, Bangalore, there are three distinct stages in the life cycle of a joint venture. During the exploratory phase, the partners explore their options. In the first stage both the partners normally reap significant gains. During the second stage the gains stabilise. By the end of this transitionary stage the joint venture is on an even keel but unable to leverage the competitive edge that it had acquired by pooling the competencies of its partners. As a result the partners reassess the situation and decide on the future course of action.

The main reason for the failure of joint ventures in India has been the unequal resources and bargaining powers of the partners. The Indian partner may sell its shares to the foreign partner due to shortage of funds. The foreign partner may buy out the Indian partner as the liberalised environment allows fully owned foreign subsidiaries.

Indian MNCs Continue Global March: ISB Study

Charging Ahead

***India's Top 15 Transnational Companies in FY12**

Company	TNI (%)
ONGC Videsh	77
Tata Steel	63
Tata Global Beverages	60
Motherson Sumi Systems	60
HCL Technologies	57
Tata Communications	56
Hindalco Industries	55
Suzlon Energy	55
Tata Motors	53
Dr.Reddy's Laboratories	49
Jubilant Life Sciences	47
Tata Consultancy Services	44
Infosys	44
Punj Lloyd	43
Tata Chemicals	40

*with International Asset Base greater than or equal to $500 million
SOURCE: ISBINSIGHT, THE FLAGSHIP RESEARCH QUARTERLY OF THE INDIAN SCHOOL OF BUSINESS

Today, there are some 8,000 large companies worldwide — with revenues of $1 billion or more — according to new research from the Mckinsey Global Institute. Almost three-quarters of these are based in developed economies. Another 7,000 companies will grow to this size by 2025, and seven out of 10 of these newcomers are likely to be based in emerging regions.

SUMMARY

Meaning: A joint venture is an enterprise set up jointly by two or more independent firms which may belong to the same country or to different countries.

Advantages: (*i*) Pooling of resources (*ii*) Risk sharing (*iii*) Entry strategy (*iv*) Government support

Disadvantages: (*i*) Potential competition (*ii*) Problems in Policy implementation (*iii*) conflicts (*iv*) Decline.

TEST QUESTION

1. What is an international joint venture? Discuss its advantages and disadvantages.

CHAPTER

22 Financing of Foreign Trade and Payment Terms

LEARNING OBJECTIVES

After studying this chapter, you should understand:

22.1 Methods of Payment in International Trade

22.2 Sources of Finance for Exporters

22.3 Export-Import (EXIM) Bank of India

22.4 Export Credit Guarantee Corporation (ECGC) of India

- Summary
- Test Questions

International markets are highly competitive and the success of exports depends to some extent on the credit facilities provided to foreign buyers. The extent of credit depends on the buyer's creditworthiness, exporter's financial position, terms of sale, etc. There are several, methods of payment and terms of payment used in foreign trade. The sale credit usually specifies when, where and how the payment will be made.

22.1 Methods of Payment in International Trade

Various methods of payment used in international trade are described below:

1. **Payment in Advance:** Exporters generally prefer advance payment before shipment of goods because it involves no risk for them. But advance payment is most risky for importers. Advance payment may be in cash or by draft, cheque or telegraphic transfer. The exporter may insist on advance payment when the importer is unknown or when goods are as per the importer's specifications and the exporter enjoys monopoly in the industry.
2. **Cash on Delivery (COD):** In case of small products sent through post or courier, the importer may be asked to make payment on delivery of the item. This is not a popular method of payment in foreign trade.
3. **Open Account:** Under this method, the importer makes payment after receiving the goods. Therefore, importers prefer this method. But this method is most risky and undesirable for exporters. Open account method is suitable when the importer has well-established long-term business relations with the exporter or when an authorised agency has certified the importer's creditworthiness. Indian exporters require the Reserve Bank of India's permission to export on open account. Normally foreign companies operating in India are given such permission.

4. **Documentary Collection:** Under this method, the exporter draws a bill of exchange on the importer. Documents of title to the goods such as bill of lading, etc. are attached with the bill. Therefore, it is known as documentary bill of exchange. It is of two types:

   (*a*) **Documents Against Acceptance (D/A):** Documents of title to the goods are handed over to the importer when he accepts or signs the bill of exchange which may be for 30, 60 or 90 days. Thus, the exporter extends credit to the importer and assumes risk. Therefore, D/A method is used in case of importers having proven integrity and creditworthiness. The exporter may obtain finances from banks by selling the D/A bills with **recourse**. D/A bill is also known as **time bill of exchange.**

   (*b*) **Documents Against Payment (D/P):** The documents of title to the goods are given to the importer after he makes payment of the bill of exchange. Therefore, such a bill is called **sight bill of exchange**.

   This method is safe and risk free for the exporter. Transactions involved in D/P bill are shown in Fig. 22.1

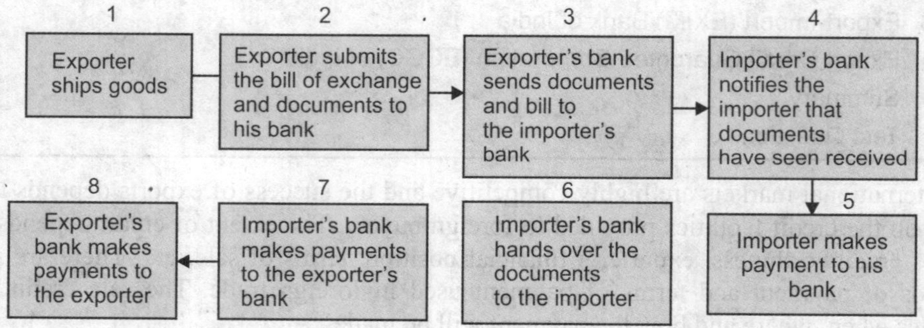

Fig. 22.1:. Transactions under D/P Bill of Exchange

5. **Documentary Letter of Credit:** A letter of credit (L/C) is a document issued by the importer's bank. In this document the bank gives a guarantee to pay the exporter up to the specified amount upon completion of all the necessary formalities. A letter of credit eliminates risk for both exporter and the importer. It also serves as a proof of export and enables the exporter to avail packing credit from his bank. Therefore, this is the most widely used method of payment. But the importer has to pay some fee and security to his bank for obtaining a letter of credit. Steps involved in a letter of credit are given in Fig. 22.2

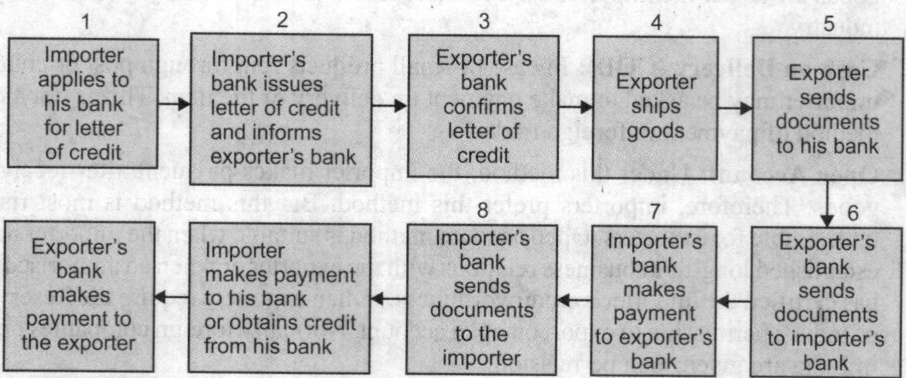

Fig. 22.2: Transactions under Letter of Credit

Table 22.1: Payment Methods for International Trade

Method	Timing of Payment	Timing of Delivery of Goods	Risk(s) for Exporter	Risk(s) for Importer	Availability of Financing for Exporter	Condition(s) Favouring Use
Payment in advance	Prior to delivery of goods	After payment when goods arrive in importer's country	None	Exporter may fail to deliver goods	N/A	Exporter has strong bargaining power; importer unknown to exporter
Open account	According to credit terms offered by exporter	When goods arrive in importer's country	Importer may fail to pay	None	Yes, by factoring of exporter accounts and account receivable	Exporter has complete trust in importer; importer is part of the same corporate family
Documentary collection	At delivery if sight draft is used; at specified later time if time draft is used	Upon payment if sight draft is used; upon acceptance if time draft is used	Importer may default or fail to accept draft	None	Yes, by discounting draft from its face value	Exporter trusts importer to pay as specified; when risk of default is low
Letter of credit	After terms of letter are fulfilled	According to terms of sales contract and letter of credit	Issuing bank may default; document may not be prepared correctly	Exporter may honour terms of letter of credit but not terms of sales contract	Yes, by discounting letter from its face value	Exporter lacks knowledge of importer; has good credit with local bank
Credit card	According to normal credit card company procedures	When goods arrive in importer's country	None	Exporter fails to deliver goods	N/A	Transaction size is small
Counter trade	When exporter sells counter-traded goods	When goods arrive in importer's country	Exporter may not be able to sell counter-traded goods	None	No	Importer lacks convertible currency; importer or exporter wants access to foreign distribution network

Source: Ricky W. Griffin and Michael W. Pustay, *International Business*, p. 665.

6. **Credit Cards:** Retailers and customers use credit cards for small international transactions. Visa, Mastercard, American Express, etc. are various types of credit cards.
7. **Countertrade:** Payment for imports with something other than cash is known as counter trade. In other words, imports are paid for by exports instead of money payments. Several companies use countertrade as an entry strategy. For instance, Pepsico gained entry into the USSR through countertrade. Developing countries use countertrade as a strategy to increase exports.

   The method of payment used in a particular transaction depends on several factors such as the nature of the product, the profit margin, customs of trade, firm's organisation, cost and availability of credit, legal requirements, etc.

   The main **advantages of counter trade** are as under:

   (*i*) Firms can finance their imports through counter trade when other means of finance are not available.

   (*ii*) Developing countries suffer from shortage of foreign exchange. They can use counter trade to pay for imports

   (*iii*) Many countries prefer counter trade to cash deals

   (*iv*) Firms which are unwilling to make a counter trade agreement may lose an export opportunity to a competitor who is willing to make such an agreement.

   (*v*) The government of an importing country may require payment through exports. For example, Boeing often has to make counter trade agreements in order to sell its commercial jet aircraft in foreign markets.

   (*vi*) International liquidity and debt problems may require counter trade.

   (*vii*) Multinationals can gain access to markets in developing countries through counter trade. Japanese firms have used counter trade to boost their exports to China and former USSR who did not have enough hard currency.

   (*viii*) Counter trade facilitates bilateral agreements between governments. Counter trade accounts for a significant share of world trade:

   Counter trade suffers from the following **disadvantages**:

   (*i*) Counter trade has an adverse impact on development of export market.

   (*ii*) It discourages multilateralism by encouraging bilateralism.

   (*iii*) Developing countries lose in terms of price in counter trade.

   (*iv*) Counter trade discourages competition.

Types or Forms of Counter Trade

1. **Barter:** This type of counter trade involves simultaneous exchange of goods/services of equal value. For instance, MMTC of India exported iron ore and pallets valued at $38 million and imported rails of the same value from a company in Yogoslavia, with no money involved.

2. **Counter Purchase:** Under this form two separate cash transactions of equal value take place in books of accounts without exchange of money. The exporter agrees to spend an equal amount to purchase from the importing firm/country. For example, Pepsico purchased vodka and wine against sale of its concentrates in the USSR. Similarly, Boeing purchased 34 million barrels of oil from Saudi Arabia against sale of its ten 747 aircrafts.

3. **Switch Trade:** When the importer is unable to offer in exchange goods which the exporter needs, a third party enters the agreement by buying those goods and paying in hard currency. For instance, India exports software to USA and needs oil which USA does not have. Therefore, USA pays dollars to United Arab Emirates (UAE) so that India can import oil from UAE without paying cash. Thus, switch trading is a triangular trade agreement.

4. **Compensation Deal:** Under this deal, a country exports plant and machinery and technology and agrees to import goods manufactured with that plant and machinery and technology. For instance, the former Soviet Union exported 200 sophisticated looms to the National Textiles Corporation and purchased the textiles manufactured with the help of these looms. Under the deal, the full payment may be made in kind or a part in kind and the balance in cash.

5. **Offset:** In this form of counter trade, a company is permitted to sell its goods in a foreign country with the condition to buy foreign goods. For example, USA exported defence equipment to Middle East and imported oil in exchange.

22.2 Sources of Finance for Exporters

Exporters need finance both before and after the shipment of goods.

1. **Pre-Shipment Finance:** An exporter requires finance before shipment to meet his working capital needs for raw materials, labour, packing, warehousing, transportation, etc. Pre-shipment finance or *packing credit* is short-term finance. It is meant for financing the purchase, processing, manufacturing and packing of goods for export. Commercial banks provide pre-shipment finance on receipt of an export order or letter of credit and against export incentives. Such loans must be repaid from export proceeds. Reserve Bank of India has created the Packing Credit Scheme to govern the pre-shipment credit advanced by commercial banks.

   Packing credit is normally extended in the form of a loan account, a separate account being maintained for each export order. But banks may also extend in the form of a running account provided the following conditions are satisfied:

   (*a*) The exporter has established the need for 'running account' facility to the bank's satisfaction;

   (*b*) The exporter has a good track record.

   (*c*) The exporter produces the letter of credit or firm order within a reasonable time.

   (*d*) The packing credit account is not mixed with the current account or cash credit account of the exporter.

The period of packing credit depends on the time needed for processing, manufacturing or processing, packing and shipping of goods. The maximum period of packing credit is normally 180 days.

The amount of pre-shipment credit is FOB price or domestic cost of production whichever is lower. The packing credit should be repaid out of export proceeds or export incentives. The exporter can also avail of the pre-shipment finance in foreign currency. The currency may be either the currency in which raw materials are imported or the currency in which exports are made. While sanctioning pre-shipment credit, the bank will verify that:

(*i*) The applicant has the import-export code number.

(*ii*) The applicant's name is not in the exporters' caution list of the RBI.

(*iii*) The goods to be exported are not banned for export.

(*iv*) The letter of credit/firm order contains all essential details and does not violate any of the exchange control regulations relating to the terms and methods of payment.

(*v*) The letter of credit/firm order allows adequate time to the exporter to manufacture and export.

2. **Post-Shipment Finance:** In order to boost exports, it is necessary to extend credit to foreign buyers. But most exporters are not in a position to provide such credit. Therefore, financial institutions, directly or indirectly, provide credit to exporters. Post-shipment finance is provided in several forms such as the following.

(*a*) **Buyer's Credit:** Financial institutions located in the exporter's country extend credit to overseas buyers to enable them to import. Such credit is generally provided for imports of capital goods. The loan does not involve transfer of funds to the importer's country. Rather the exporter obtains the payment directly from the financial institution by presenting the relevant export documents.

(*b*) **Line of Credit:** The financial institution in the exporter's country extends a line of credit to a financial institution in the importer's country which in turn disburses the funds to the importer. This method avoids the problem of dealing with several individuals. Moreover, the responsibility for assessing the importer's creditworthiness is shifted to financial institution in the importer's country.

(*c*) **Other Forms:** Commercial banks provide short-term credit by purchasing D/A and D/P bills, lending against export bills, advances against export incentives, etc. In case of a bill drawn under a letter of credit, the process is called negotiation of export bill. When a bill is negotiated or purchased the bank pays the bill's amount less charges. If the exporter does not need the money immediately, he may ask the bank to collect the bill on the due date.

Post-shipment credit is also given in foreign currency.

(*d*) **Advance Against Duty Drawback:** Under the duty drawback scheme, the import duty or excise duty paid by the exporter is repaid on completion of the export. There may be delay in the scrutiny of the applications and disbursal of drawback. Therefore, advance against duty drawback is granted to exporters either at the pre-shipment stage or at the post-shipment stage. Such advance is available for a maximum period of 90 days. The advance is credited to the exporter's bank account and is adjusted out of the duty drawback amount.

The Export-Import Bank (Exim Bank) of India provides refinance facilities to commercial banks against long term credit extended by them. It also operates a Buyer's Credit Scheme for promoting exports of capital goods from India. It extends lines of credit to overseas financial institutions enabling them to provide loans for imports from India. Exim Bank also provides supplier's credit, project export credit, pre-shipment credit, guarantees, underwriting, forfaiting, etc.

Forfaiting: Forfaiting means a financing mechanism that enables an exporter, to convert credit sale into cash sale on 'without recourse' basis. The forfaiter buys the exporter's claim for payment with no recourse to the exporter or his bank. The Reserve Bank of India has authorised the Exim Bank to facilitate export financing through forfaiting. The Exim Bank charges a service fee payable in Indian rupees.

All exports of capital goods and other goods made on medium to long term credit are eligible for financing through forfaiting. Export receivables evidenced by bills of exchange or promissory notes can be forfaited. The time duration of receivables is normally one to five years. The export contract must be executed in any of the major convertible currencies like US dollar, Pound sterling, Deutsche Mark, or Japanese Yen. The minimum value of the contract should be equivalent to $1 lac.

The exporter surrenders, without recourse to him, his right to claim for payment of exports, in return for immediate payment from the forfaiter. Forfaiting enables an exporter to extend supplier's credit to the importer and recoup his financial position immediately.

Hunting for More Funds

What are offshore Rupee bonds?

- **These are bonds** denominated in rupees but issued in international markets
- **Investor has to** convert its currency into rupees before investing
- **The returns and** final redemption is also in rupees

Why are such Offshore Bonds important?

They are an important way of internationalising the Indian currency

It will improve acceptance of the Indian currency in settling trade

A deep market for local currency will help reduce dollar needs of the economy

They diversify fund raising options for Indian borrowers

IFC's offshore bond programme will pave the way for an alternative source of funding for Indian companies

---

Forfaiting offers several **advantages**:

(*i*) Forfaiting improves cash flow and liquidity by converting a deferred payment transaction into a cash transaction.

(*ii*) It saves the exporter from crossborder commercial and political risks involved in export receivables.

(*iii*) Forfaiting offers finance upto the full value of exports wheeveras conventional export credit schemes provide only 80–85 per cent financing.

(*iv*) Exporter's borrowing limits are not affected as forfaiting offers finance without recourse.

(*v*) Finance is available at fixed rate of interest thererby avoiding the interest and exchange risks involved in deferred export credit.

(*vi*) A forfaiting transaction does not require a long-term relationship with the bank.

(*vii*) There are no credit administration and collection problems for the exporter.

(*viii*) Forfaiting arrangement can be made quickly due to simple documentation.

(*ix*) Forfaiting avoids the need for export credit insurance, thus saving insurance cost for the exporter.

22.2 Export-Import (Exim) Bank of India

Two major institutions which provide finance to exporters are the Export-Import Bank of India, and the Export Credit Guarantee Corporation.

The Export-Import Bank of India was established on January 1, 1982 under an Act of Parliament for the purpose of financing, facilitating and promoting India's foreign trade. It is the principal financial institution for coordinating the working of institutions engaged in financing exports and imports.

Mission: The mission of Exim Bank is "to develop commercially viable relationships with externally oriented companies by offering them a comprehensive range of products and services to enhance their internationalisation efforts".

Objectives: The main objectives of the Exim Bank are as follows:

(*i*) To translate India's foreign trade policies into concrete action plans.

(*ii*) To assist exporters to become internationally competitive by providing them alternate financing solutions.

(*iii*) To develop mutually beneficial relationships with international financial community.

(*vi*) To forge close working relationships with other export financing agencies, multilateral funding agencies and investment promotion agencies.

(*v*) To initiate and participate in debates on issues central to India's international trade.

(*vi*) To anticipate and absorb new developments in banking, export financing and information technology.

(*vii*) To be responsive to export problems of Indian exporters and pursue policy resolutions.

Exim Bank concentrates on medium and long-term financing, leaving the short-term financing to commercial banks. The Bank has developed a global network through strategic linkages with World Bank, Asian Development Bank and other agencies.

Functions

The Exim Bank provides a wide range of financial facilities and services. Some of these are summarised below:

(*i*) **Pre-Shipment Credit:** This credit is provided to buy raw materials and other inputs required to produce capital goods meant for exports. It meets temporary funding requirement of export contracts. Exim Bank offers pre-shipment credit for periods, exceeding 180 days. Exporters can also avail of pre-shipment credit in foreign currency for imports of inputs needed for manufacture of export products.

(*ii*) **Supplier's Credit:** Exim Bank offers supplier's credit in rupees or foreign currency at post-shipment stage to finance exports of eligible goods and services on deferred payment terms. Supplier's credit's available both for supply contracts and project exports which includes construction, turnkey or consultancy contracts undertaken overseas.

(*iii*) **Finance for Exports of Consultancy and Technology Services:** A special credit facility is available to exporters of consultancy and technology services on deferred payment terms. The services include transfer of technology/know-how, preparation of project feasibility reports, providing personnel for rendering technical services, maintenance and management contracts, etc.

(*iv*) **Finance for Project Export Contracts:** This scheme is meant to finance rupee expenditure for execution of overseas project export contracts such as for acquisition of materials and equipment, mobilisation of personnel, payments to be made to staff, subcontractors, and to meet project related overheads. The amount involved is usually in excess of ₹50 lacs and the maximum period of loan is four years.

(*v*) **Credit to Overseas Entities:** Overseas buyers can avail of *Buyer's Credit* for importing eligible goods from India on deferred payment basis, Exim Bank also extends *Lines of credit* to overseas financial institutions, foreign governments and their agencies for enabling them to provide term loans for importing eligible goods from India.

(*vi*) **Finance for Export-Oriented Units:** Exim Bank offers several facilities to export-oriented units (EOUs)[1]. Some of these are:

(*a*) **Project Finance:** Exim Bank offers term loans for setting up new units and for modernization/expansion of existing units. The Bank also extends 100 per cent refinance to commercial banks for term loans sanctioned to an EOU.

(*b*) **Equipment Finance:** Exim Bank offers a line of credit for Indian/foreign production equipment, including equipment for packaging, pollution control, etc. It also provides term loans to vendors of EOUs to enable them to acquire plant and machinery and other assets required for increasing export capability. Such finance is given for non-project related capital expenditure of EOUs.

(*c*) **Working Capital Finance:** Exim Bank provides term loans both in rupees and foreign currency to help EOUs meet their working capital requirements. Short-term working capital finance is provided for imports of eligible inputs.

1. An EOU is any company with a minimum exports of 10 per cent of net sales or annual exports of ₹5 crore, whichever is lower

(*d*) **R & D Finance:** Exim Bank offers term loans to EOUs for development of new technology as well as to develop and/or commercialise new product/process applications.

(*e*) **Import Finance:** Term loans in Indian rupees/foreign currency are available to Indian manufacturing companies for import of consumable inputs, canalised items, capital goods, plant and machinery, technology and knowhow.

(*f*) **Export Facilitation:** Exim Bank offers term finance and non-funded facilities to Indian companies to create infrastructure facilities for developing Indian's foreign trade and thereby enhance their export capability. Software exporters can get term loans to set up/expand software training institutes and software technology parks. This facility is also available to Indian companies involved in development of ports and port related services.

(*g*) **Export Marketing Finance:** Term loans are offered to assist the firms in export marketing and development efforts. Desk/field research, overseas travel, quality certification, product launch are the typical activities eligible for finance under this schemes. Finance is also given to support export product development plans with focus on industrialised market.

(*h*) **Underwriting:** Exim Bank extends underwriting facility to help the firms raise finance from capital markets. It also issues guarantees to facilitate export contracts and import transactions.

(*vii*) Finance for Joint Ventures Abroad

(*a*) **Overseas Investment Finance:** Any Indian promoter making equity investment abroad in an existing company or in a new project is eligible for finance under the scheme. Assistance is provided both in terms of loans and guarantees

(*b*) **Asian Countries Investment Partners Programme:** This programme seeks to promote joint ventures in India between Indian companies and companies from other Asian countries. Finance is provided at various stages of project cycle, *viz.*, sector study, project identification, feasibility study, proto-type development, setting up project, and technical and managerial assistance.

Exim Bank also offers a wide range of information, advisory and support services which help exporters to evaluate international risks, exploit export opportunities and improve competitiveness.

22.4 Export Credit Guarantee Corporation (ECGC) of India

The ECGC of India is a company wholly owned by the Government of India.

Objectives: The ECGC seeks to achieve the following objectives:

(*i*) To provide insurance cover to exporters against political and commercial risks.

(*ii*) To provide insurance cover to exporters against the risk of exchange rate fluctuations in respect of deferred payments.

(*iii*) To provide insurance cover to banks against export credit and guarantees extended by them.

(*iv*)To provide insurance cover to Indian investors abroad against political risks.

The ECGC plays a vital role in developing India's exports by providing a range of insurance policies to exporters, and by offering guarantees to banks and financial institutions who provide financial assistance to exporters.

SUMMARY

Payment Methods: (*i*) Advance payment, (*ii*) Open account, (*iii*) D/A and D/P (*iv*) Letter of credit (v) Cash on delivery (vi) Counter trade — Barter, counter purchase, switch trade, compensation deal, offset

Sources of Finance for Exporters: (*i*) Pre shipment finance (*ii*) Post-shipment Finance —Buyer's credit, Line of credit, Advance against duty drawback.

Forfaiting: Conversion of credit sale into cash sale without recourse.

Exim Bank of India: (*i*) Pre-shipment credit (*ii*) Supplier's credit (*iii*) Finance for exports of services (*iv*) Finance for Project Export (*v*) Credit to overseas entities (*vi*) Finance for export oriented units (EOUs)—Project finance, equipment finance, working capital finance R & D finance, import finance, export facilitation, export marketing finance, underwriting (*vii*) Finance for joint ventures—overseas investment finance, Asian Countries Investment Partners Programme.

Export Credit Guarantee Corporation (ECGC) of India: (*i*) Insurance cover to exporters against various types of risks (*ii*) Guarantees for banks and financial institutions for providing assistance to exporters.

TEST QUESTIONS

1. Explain various methods of payment in international trade.
2. What is counter trade? Describe its advantages.
3. Explain different types of counter trade.
4. Give a comparative study of different methods of payment used in international trade.
5. Explain the sources of pre-shipment and post-shipment finance available to exporters in India.
6. What is meant by Forfaiting?
7. Discuss the mission and objectives of the Export-Import Bank of India.
8. Explain in brief the functions of the Export Import Bank of India.
9. What are Export-oriented Units? Describe the facilities available to them in India.
10. Explain the objectives and role of the Export Credit Guarantee Corporation of India.
11. Write notes on:
    (*a*) Documentary Bill of Exchange
    (*b*) Documentary Letter of Credit
    (*c*) Counter trade
    (*d*) Forfaiting

CHAPTER

23 Recent Developments and Issues in International Business

LEARNING OBJECTIVES

After studying this chapter, you should understand:

23.1 Role of Information Technology in International Business

23.2 Ecological Considerations in International Business

23.3 Global Outsourcing

23.4 Ethical Issues in International Business

23.5 Future of International Business

- Summary
- Test Questions

There have been dramatic advancements in Information Technology (IT) over the past few decades. These developments include cellular phones, electronic mail, video conference, computer networks, neural networks, etc. These advances in IT are considered a major force behind globalisation. IT has redefined the competencies of firms and has led to a sea-change in the way business is conducted around the world.

The integration of computers and telecommunications into a unified system of collecting, processing and interchanging business information has been a major advancement in IT. The business application software packages have become more user-friendly, more customised and more capable of handling huge data. The size and costs of laptops, iPhone, iPad, tablet, etc have decreased while their computing power has increased. Spreadsheets, databases and word processors have made it easy for managers to process and present data. Similarly, decision support systems, expert systems, intelligent data bases, artificial intelligence, neural networks, etc. have facilitated analysis of huge and complex data worldwide for international firms. Inter-connectivity has augmented the capabilities of individual systems. Local area networks, wide area networks, satellite, and cable links have dramatically improved intra-firm and inter-firm communications

Business firms have used developments in the IT on a very wide scale. Some of the business applications of IT are as follows:

(*i*) Firms can create new products, services, work flows, work processes, work groups and knowledge base.

(*ii*) Decision-making can be decentralised. Decision centres can be placed at local units due to linkage through networks. Corporate headquarters can exercise real time control.

(*iii*) IT facilitates wider spans of control, new reporting relationships and virtual organisations.

(*iv*) New customer-supplier relations, alliances and partnerships can be developed.

(*v*) IT can be used to gain competitive advantage through cost reduction and better customer service.

(*vi*) Firms use IT to improve quality, reduce labour and improve product and process design.

(*vii*) A company can expand its geographic scope without opening branch offices.

IT helps to save time, cost and space due to high speed, huge storing capacity and accuracy of technological devices. It helps to overcome barriers of distance and time. Round-the-clock working has become possible from any part of the globe.

23.1 Role of IT in International Business

IT plays a vital role in international firms. These firms can coordinate and control the activities of their branches and subsidiaries spread across national boundaries in remote places with the help of networking and connectivity. At the same time, they can respond quickly to local needs and maintain flexibility of operations. Due to satellite television needs and wants of customers converge enabling firms to develop global products and strategies.

Organisational learning and knowledge management have become major sources of competitive advantage in international business. It facilitates organisational learning and knowledge management. It has become essential for speedy, low cost and accurate processing, storage and transmission of information. It is an important tool for generation of organisational knowledge.

IT helps in building cooperative business networks in which participants pool their core competencies leading to synergy. Integration of network activities in an efficient and effective manner through IT has given rise to virtual organization. A virtual corporation is composed of several business partners, each with a special advantage. They share their resources and cost to produce a product or render a service.

IT has led to the growth of electronic commerce (e-commerce). Such commerce is carried out through internet, telephone, fax, television, electronic payment systems, electronic data interchange and other electronic channels.

IT not only facilitates international business. Rather IT products themselves are an important part of international trade. At the first WTO Ministerial Conference held in December 1996 in Singapore, 23 economies signed the Informational Technology Agreement (ITA). The objectives of the ITA are: (*a*) to encourage the continued technological development of the IT industry on a worldwide business; (*b*) to achieve maximum freedom of world trade in IT products; and (*c*) to spread the positive contribution of IT to global economic growth and welfare. During 1997-2007, 33 more economies joined the ITA. Now the information and communication industry is seen as a major engine of the globalisation process. Users of internet exceed 5 billion and mobile subscribers are more than 10 billion.

IT products now account for about 25 per cent of world merchandise exports. World exports of IT products grew about 10 per cent during 1996-2006. Asian countries account for more than half of world exports of IT products. Computers, semiconductors and telecom equipment are the major IT products in world trade.

India Among Least Connected

India fares poorly when it comes to internet access for its citizens. The country, ranked 121st out of 157 economies, falls in the category of least connected countries, according to a UN report.

ICT Development Index, 2012: Select Country Rankings

SOUTH KOREA	1		**Key Findings**	
SWEDEN	2		**2.7b** people will connected to the internet by 2013-end	
FINLAND	5		**4.4b** will remain unconnected	
NETHERLANDS	7		**250m additional people cam online in 2012**	
UK	8			
QATAR	31			
RUSSIA	40	**Broadband is getting faster; 2Mbps now most popular basic package**	**6.8b** cell connections, almost equal to human population, by year-end	**30% of the global young population are "digital natives"**
BRAZIL	62			
CHINA	78			
GHANA	113			
KENYA	116			
INDIA	121			

Source: Measuring the Internet Society Report, 2013

23.2 Ecological Considerations in International Business

Globalisaiton is opposed on the ground that it is causing irreparable damage and speedy degradation of the environment. Increasing levels of industrialisation, urbanisation and intensification of agriculture are destroying ecological balance. Population explosion and modern technology are also adding to environmental pollution. Indiscriminate increase in the consumption of throwaway products such as napkins, towels, cans, plastic toys, etc. leads to the problems of solid waste.

Developing countries are at a disadvantage in this respect. Multinationals shift polluting industries to these countries. They dump nuclear and hazardous wastes in these countries. They exploit natural resources of developing nations. Multinationals transfer polluting and obsolete technologies to developing countries. Developed nations sometimes raise environmental issues as a trade barrier.

International trade can have adverse effects on the environment when property rights in environmental resources are ill-defined. Liberalisation of trade promotes environmental degradation due to low environment standards in developing countries.

Multinational corporations pollute the environment both directly and indirectly.

(*i*) **Direct Affect:** In order to avoid the cost of complying with higher environmental standards, in home countries, multinationals shift production to developing countries where environmental standards are less stringent.

(*ii*) **Indirect effect:** Shifting production leads to loss of investments and jobs in developed countries. As a result governments are under pressure to relax the laws and policies relating to environment.

International business also has adverse effects on environment in the following ways:

(*i*) Rapid and increased exploitation of natural resources due to globalisation causes environmental degradation. For example, international trade involves longer journeys thereby increasing fuel consumption and greenhouse gas problem.

(*ii*) In order to survive in a highly competitive environment, firms have to control costs. They compromise with environmental concerns.

(*iii*) Environmental costs, also known as externalities, are often overlooked in evaluating corporate performance.

Opponents argue that free and increased trade has favourable effects on environment.

(*a*) Free trade encourages specialisation so as to secure economies of scale. As a result labour-intensive industries tend to concentrate in developing countries. These industries are less polluting.

(*b*) In order to make better use of resources, international firms innovate and develop less polluting technology.

(*c*) Governments control pollution through strict laws and policies such as eco-labelling, emission norms, eco-taxation, etc.

(*d*) Free trade spreads environmental services and clean technology.

(*e*) Increase in trade leads to increase in incomes and living standards which in turn encourage demand for cleaner environment.

WTO has been concerned with adverse impact of international business on environment. The environmental issues have been addressed in different agreements of WTO. The Stockholm Conference on Human Environment suggested the following measures for protection of environment:

(*i*) The natural resources of the earth including the air, water, land, flora and fauna and especially representative samples of natural ecosystem must be safeguarded for the benefit of present and future generations through careful planning or management as appropriate.

(*ii*) The capacity of the earth to produce vital renewable resources must be maintained and wherever practicable restored or improved.

(*iii*) The non-renewable resources of the earth must be employed in such a way as to guard against the danger of their future exhaustion and to ensure that benefits from such employment are shared by all mankind.

(*iv*) States shall take all possible steps to prevent pollution of the sea by substances that are liable to create hazards to human health, to harm living resources and marine life, to damage amenities or interfere with other legitimate uses of the sea.

(*v*) For the developing countries, stability of prices and adequate earnings for primary commodities and raw materials are essential to the environment management since economic factors as well as ecological processes must be taken into account.

(*vi*) Resources should be made available to preserve and improve the environment, taking into account the circumstances and particular requirements of developing countries and any costs which may emanate from their incorporating environmental safeguards into their development planning and the need for making available to them upon their request, additional international technical and financial assistance for this purpose.

(*vii*) Rational planning constitutes an essential tool for reconciling any conflict between the needs of development and the needs to protect and improve the environment.

(*viii*) States have, in accordance with the Charter of the United Nations and principles of international law, the sovereign right to exploit their own resources pursuant to their own environmental policies, and the responsibility to ensure that activities within their jurisdiction or control do not cause damage to the environment of other states or of areas beyond the limits of national jurisdiction.

(*ix*) States shall cooperate to develop the international law regarding further liability and compensation for the victim of pollution and other environmental damage caused by the activities with the jurisdiction of such states to areas beyond their jurisdiction.

(*x*) International matters concerning the protection and improvement of the environment should be handled in a cooperative spirit by all countries, big or small, on an equal footing. Cooperation through multilateral or bilateral arrangements or other appropriate means is essential to prevent, eliminate or reduce and effectively control adverse environmental effects resulting from activities conducted in all spheres, in such a way that due account is taken of the sovereignty and interests of all states.

(*xi*) States shall ensure that international organisations play a coordinated, efficient and dynamic role for the protection and improvement of environment.

(*xii*) Man and his environment must be spared the effect of nuclear weapons and all other means of mass destruction. States must strive to reach prompt agreement, in the relevant international organs, on the elimination and complete destruction of such weapons.

23.3 Global Outsourcing

Rapid progress in IT and increasing communication networks have enabled global firms to get some of their activities performed by an outside service provider and concentrate on their core functions. Such an arrangement is known as Business Process Outsourcing (BPO). When the service provider is located in a foreign country, it is called offshore BPO and global outsourcing.

Global outsourcing may be defined as getting the repetitive and non-core business functions performed by a foreign service provider. The processes outsourced are non-core but essential for the smooth functioning of the firm. Customer relationship management, human resource activities (*e.g.* recruitment, selection, training, etc.), financial accounting, etc. are examples of these processes which are often outsourced.

Global outsourcing offers several **advantages:**

(*i*) cost savings due to economies of scale

(*ii*) better quality of service due to the expertise of the service provider

(*iii*) ability to focus on core competence which enhances international competitiveness.

(*iv*) freedom of resources from labour-intensive activities

(*v*) reduced capital and manpower required

(*vi*) greater flexibility of operations

The BPO industry has made rapid progress and is estimated to be $1000 billion. It has grown from task-oriented (transactional) to process-oriented (strategic). Table 23.1 summarises the evolution of the BPO industry.

Table 23.1: Evolution of BPO

Years	Process Outsourced
1960s	Time sharing
1970s	Date processing
1980s	All IT operations
1990s	Shared business activities
2000s	B2B partnership. via Internet, Process Outsourcing via Internet IT-enabled offshore services

International firms are increasingly outsourcing materials, components, after- sale service and other functions. Global outsourcing has created an ever-spreading web of global production and service networks that connect subsidiaries of a global firm to unrelated designers, producers and distributors. These networks provide the firm access to new technologies and markets. Advances in IT help to link firms of developing countries into global production networks. For example, firms all over the world participate in the global bid of General Electric.

Global sourcing offers tremendous opportunities for developing countries. India, China, Malaysia, etc. have become global hubs for outsourcing by firms of the USA, Europe and other developed areas. Some manufacturing industries in India have benefited greatly from global outsourcing. For example, auto components manufacturers in India have become major suppliers to General Motors, Fiat, Renault and other global firms. India is one of the major beneficiaries of global offshoring particularly in software development and other IT-enabled services.

International outsourcing now accounts for one-third of world trade. There has been a spurt in **offshoring of services**. Advances in information and communication technologies have made it possible to produce services in one country and consume them in another country. For example, information of all types can be stored by digitisation. Instantaneous exchange of information and voice communication between people anywhere around the globe have become possible. However, all services cannot be digitised and have to remain localised. Legal regulations (*e.g.* privacy) may also restrict tradeability of services.

There are two forms of offshoring:

(*i*) **Captive offshoring** through the establishment of foreign affiliates.

(*ii*) **Offshore outsourcing** through a third party service provider.

Captive offshoring is preferred when strict control is essential as in case of R & D, information is sensitive, internal interaction is necessary or when the firm wants savings. Back office and front office activities are more likely to be offshored as these can be easily standardised and separated from the core activities.

There is a wide range of services that can be outsourced. Some of these are given below:

1. **Administrative Support:** Data entry, document conversion, document scanning, form processing, indexing, secretarial support, etc.
2. **Customer Relationship Management:** Customer support, order taking, customer services, technical help desk, market research, etc.
3. **Finance and Accounting:** Internal auditing, time and expense management, credit and debit analysis, travel expenses, invoicing, accounts payable and receivable, billing dispute resolution, etc.
4. **Human Resources:** Recruitment, training, database management, contract labour.
5. **Legal Services:** Consulting, research transcription, documentation, regulatory compliance, translation, legal risk evaluation.
6. **Intellectual Property Research and Documentation:** Drafting and filing patent applications, licensing support, patent portfolio analysis.
7. **Medical Transcription:** Writing down patient history, lab reports, clinic notes therapeutic procedures, diagnosis, prognosis, discharge summaries, etc.
8. **Research and Analysis:** Data analytics, financial analytics, R & D, industry review, competitive intelligence, etc.
9. **Marketing and Sales:** Cold calling, e-mail pitches, telephone surveys, lead generation and qualifying, sales team management, stock trade processing, etc.
10. **Publishing:** Book design, book digitisation, e-publishing, graphics and drawings, indexing, etc.
11. **Payroll Maintenance:** Payroll accounting, credit and check, mortgage loans and insurance claims.
12. **Security:** Investigative services, physical security, electronic security, computer and network security, etc.
13. **Supply Chain Management:** Procurement, logistics, warehousing, supply chains relationship, etc.

Risks in Offshoring: International firms which outsource face several risks.

(*i*) over time, the firm may lose knowledge and expertise of carrying out the outsourced functions.

(*ii*) The firm may lose control over the outsourced processes.

(*iii*) The firm may not get the work done in time and quality of work may suffer when key personnel in the service provider leave the job.

(*iv*) The firm faces risk due to financial instability of the service provider.

(*v*) In case the service provider does not maintain strict security, data of the firm may not be secure.

(*vi*) Employees of the firm may resent outsourcing owing to the fear of loss of jobs and career.

Outsourcing firms may take the following steps to guard against the risks given above:

(*a*) Only non-core processes that are not critical or strategic to the firm are outsourced.

(*b*) Before deciding to outsource the firm consults its employees and shareholders.

(*c*) The firm takes advice of sourcing advisors before negotiating the deal with the service provider.

(*d*) The cost, quality, security, transparency, etc. of the service provider are thoroughly assessed before selection.

Potential of Outsourcing for India: India has emerged as one of the most preferred locations for outsourcing by global firms due to the following reasons:

1. **Abundant Talent:** India's young demographic profile is a unique and inherent advantage. More than half of the country's population is aged less than 30 years. We an have unmatched number of English-speaking young persons. Firms, industry and government have created a vast infrastructure for education and training.
2. **Cost Advantage:** India has a strong track record of delivering services at very low cost. Clients report savings of 25-50 per cent over the original cost. India has an absolute cost advantage due to low cost labour. Cost of infrastructure and overheads can be further reduced. There is scope for increasing efficiency through leveraging leading to further decline in costs.
3. **Focus on Quality and Security:** India has acquired reputation for quality and expertise in global service delivery. Over the years BPO firms have built robust processes and procedures to provide world class IT software and technology related services. They have aligned themselves with international standards. About 500 Indian companies have acquired global quality certifications with 90 of them certified at SEI CMM level which is 5 per cent higher than any other country in the world.

   In order to acquire unmatched reputation in information security, India's BPO industry is working on a four-phased programme. This programme consists of:

   (*a*) engaging key stakeholders to develop a common understanding on key issues concerning information security;

   (*b*) educating industry participants about developments in policies and practices relating to information security;

   (*c*) enactment of policy reforms needed to ensure compliance; and

   (*d*) assisting in the effective implementation of policies and practices through periodic security audits and certification, developing and maintaining an incident response database and facilitating better cooperation with enforcement agencies.

4. **Sound Infrastructure:** There has been rapid growth in high quality telecommunications connectivity thoughout India. Affordability has increased due to declining costs and increasing access has penetrated even remote rural areas. As a result there has been significant improvement in both international connectivity and service quality. Steady growth of world class office facilities, hotels, and other supporting infrastructure has supplemented strong telecoms links.

5. **Helpful Regulatory Environment:** Business-friendly government policies and regulations have driven rapid growth of IT-BPO sector in India. Our policymakers have recognised the significance of this sector as a source of foreign exchange and a mechanism for transfer of technology Therefore, IT-BPO firms face minimum regulations and enjoy fiscal incentives both at Central and State level. The Software Technology Parks of India (STPI) scheme has also catalysed the growth of IT-BPO sector. The tax-holiday scheme has boosted foreign investments in this sector.

   According to NASSCOM, India's IT-BPO sector has been growing more than 25 per cent per annum. The total revenue now exceeds $50 billion per year. India's share in global sourcing is estimated to exceed 65 per cent for IT and 45 per cent for BPO.

   BPO industry in India, however, faces several **challenges:**

   (*i*) **High Attrition:** IT-BPO firms face high rates of employee turnover. which is a matter of concern for both clients and service providers. High attrition increases recruitment and training costs and spoils both service quality and data security.

   (*ii*) **Inadequate Infrastructure:** India has no doubt made rapid progress in telecommunications. But inadequate roads, poor airport facilities and unreliable power supply are the major bottlenecks.

   (*iii*) **Mushrooming of Firms:** Desire to make quick money has led to rapid growth of firms. Several of them close down due to competition and lack of expertise. This situation is not conducive to the long term health of the BPO sector.

   (*iv*) **Unemployability:** A large number of graduates in IT are not employable. Therefore, IT firms have to provide inhouse training to new recruits. There is also a talent crisis in some firms.

Table 23.2: Key Factors for Sourcing from Abroad

Factor
Very Important
1. Better quality
2. Lower price
3. Unavailability of items in the U.S.
Important
4. More advanced technology abroad
5. Willingness to solve problems
6. More on-time delivery
7. Negotiability
8. Association with foreign subsidiary
Neutral
9. Geographical location
10. Counter trade requirements
11. Government assistance

Source: Adapted from Hokey Min and William P. Galle, "International Purchasing Strategies of Multinational U.S. Firms," *International Journal of purchasing and Materials Management*, Summer 1991, p.14

(*v*) **Keen Competition:** India's BPO industry is facing stiff competition from China and other developing countries.

(*vi*) **Rising Costs:** Labour and other costs are increasing rapidly. Rising costs of operations affect international competitiveness of Indian firms.

23.4 Ethical issues in International Business

Some key ethical issues in global business are:

1. **Bribes:** Business ethics requires that business firms must conduct their operations in accordance with certain moral standards. An international firm operates in several countries and ethical norms differ from country to country. In many countries, bribery, payoffs and kickbacks are common in business but their extent and intensity are different in different countries. In countries like Germany and France, bribes paid to secure business overseas is allowed as a tax write off. On the other hand, in the USA Foreign Corrupt Practices Act 1977 prohibits a firm from paying bribes for securing business. According to the World Bank estimates, more than $1 trillion are paid in bribes every year. Several initiatives have been taken to check corrupt practices. The UN General Assembly adopted a *Declaration against Corruption and Bribery* in 1996. The International Chamber of Commerce issued the *Rules of Conduct on Bribery* in 1977. In 1995 the World Bank issued *procurement guidelines in order to prevent corruption in projects financed* by the Bank

   Conflicts of interests, financial and accounting integrity, ethical advertising, employee privacy are other major ethical issues in international business.

2. **Selling Banned Products:** Another ethical issue is selling products which are banned in developed countries due to their harmful effects in developing countries. Some multinationals adopt double standards. For example, tests reveal that pesticide residues in many brands of soft drinks sold in India were 1.6 to 70 times the limit which EU norms permit.

3. **Social Responsibility:** Multinationals possess enormous power and influence over society. Therefore, they have greater obligations to society. Like individuals, they are citizens (corporate citizens) and their behaviour must be guided by social norms. An international firm must function as a responsible member of society like any other individual. Transnational corporations must show as much social responsibility in foreign countries as they do in the home country.

4. **Labour Issues:** People in the developed countries widely criticise the **child labour** used in the manufacture of exports from developing countries. Similarly, social activists in the developed nations demand ban on the imports of goods manufactured by labour working in inhuman working conditions and not paid fair wages (called **sweat labour**). **Trade union rights** is another issue concerning labour. Some countries enjoy a cost advantage due to the absence of trade union rights and multinationals take advantage of this situation. The International Labour Organization (ILO) issued a "Declaration of Fundamental Principles and Rights at Work" and member countries agreed to enforce them.

Ethical issues are not specific to international business. But differences in cultures and laws make the implementation of ethical behaviour an **ethical dilemma**. The moral conflict that occurs when making a morally right choice is known as ethical dilemma. For example, when an international firm terminates the contract to a supplier who employs children, it may lead to loss of income to poor families and to the firm itself.

The OECD has laid down guidelines for multinational enterprises. These guidelines contain ten chapters:

1. General principles for good corporate behaviour in the countries in which the enterprises operate.
2. Disclosure – public dissemination of essential information on the activities of the enterprises.
3. Employment and Industrial Relations covering issues such as rights and treatment of employees, and forced and child labour.
4. Environment – recommendations on preventing environmental damage.
5. Combating Bribery – recommendations to avoid bribery and other corrupt practices.
6. Consumer Interests – recommendations to ensure respect for all consumer rights.
7. Science and Technology – recommendations for contributing to local capacities through technology transfer.
8. Competition – consistent with all applicable competition laws
9. Taxation – fulfilment of tax liabilities and cooperation with the local tax authorities.

Source: http:/ www. oecd. org/dataoecd/56/36/1922428. pdf

The Work Visa Chronicle

What is the issue?

- Infosys will pay a fine of $34 million (₹ 207 crore) to the US Justice Department.
- The fine is to settle the alleged misuse of visa fraud allegations on the company
- Infosys was alleged to have sent its employees on B-1 visas rather than H-1B visas.

How Will It Affect Indian IT Firms?

- Indian IT companies will need to further brace up their local hiring
- Making people work on B1 visas is not "uncommon" in the industry
- Brand value of Infosys and other Indian IT firms may take a hit.

Each company needs to move its employees from one country to another to conduct its business, but then barriers (in the form of visas) are put up by governments that restrict these movements.

Even large multinational firms, when they send their executives to India, have often been found to violate visa norms. They get away lightly simply because India has a liberal visa policy.

"If India imposes restrictions on the workforce from multinational firms, then a lot of them can come under scanner for Indian visa violation rules," an industry analyst said.

Ankita Somani, an analyst at Angel Broking, said Infosys had already made a provision of $35 million in relation to the case in its accounts, so the actual payout should not make much of a difference operationally. "However, this case could have some impact on its brand image, especially since Infosys in the past was known for best corporate governance," she said.

The question that remains is whether India will take up with the US, the issue of work visas at the diplomatic level.

Dell suppliers accused of human rights violations

- Dell suppliers in China have been accused of human rights violations, as the company makes workers work for nearly 74 hours a week amid health risks, for as little as £0.66 an hour, a new report has revealed.
- The report also claims that thousands of underage workers are employed by Dell.
- It also says that most of the workers aged between 16 and 18 were hired though schools and recruiting agencies.

General Motors India faces an estimated penalty of at least ₹11 crore after a government panel said the company committed "corporate fraud". The subsidiary of the world's second-largest car maker had admitted in July to fudging data on Tavera utility vehicles manufactured and sold in the country during 2005-2012.

"The company's top management was in the knowledge of the critical development, including irregularities in exhaust emissions tests, which are not possible without their approval..."

SUMMARY

Role of IT: (*i*) Coordination and control of subsidiaries spread across the world (*ii*) competitive advantage through organisational learning (*iii*) building cooperative business networks (*iv*) synergy (*v*) e-commerce (*vi*) world trade in IT and IT enabled services

Ecological Considerations: (*i*) Environmental degradation due to increased production, consumption and transportation (*ii*) shifting polluting industries to developing nations (*iii*) ill- defined property rights in environmental issues (*iv*) rapid exploitation of natural resources (*v*)compromise with environment to gain competitive advantage Direct and indirect effects.

Global Outsourcing: (*i*) Cost savings (*ii*) better quality (*iii*) focus on core competence (*iv*) reduced resource requirements (*v*) flexibility of operations.

India has emerged as a major outsourcing destination due to talent, low costs, quality and security, sound telecommunications network, helpful regulatory environment. High attrition, inadequate power supply and poor roads, mushrooming of IT firms, unemployability, growing competition and rising costs are challenges before India's BPO sector.

Ethical Issues: (*i*) Corruption and bribery (*ii*) sale of banned products (*iii*) social responsibility (iv) Labour issues – child labour, sweat labour, trade union rights.

TEST QUESTIONS

1. Explain the role of IT in international business.
2. Discuss ecological considerations in international business.
3. How does international business cause damage to environment? Explain
4. What is global outsourcing/offshoring? Discuss its advantages.
5. Explain the services which international firms often outsource abroad.
6. Discuss the risks involved in offshoring. What steps can be taken to guard against these risks?
7. "India has emerged as a leading destination for global outsourcing." Explain the reasons. Also describe the challenges faced by BPO sector in India.